# Teaching African American Learners to Read

## Perspectives and Practices

Bill Hammond
DeKalb County Schools, Decatur, Georgia, USA

Mary Eleanor Rhodes Hoover
Howard University School of Education, Washington, DC, USA

Irving Pressley McPhail
The Community College of Baltimore County, Baltimore, Maryland, USA

EDITORS

INTERNATIONAL
**Reading Association**
800 BARKSDALE ROAD, PO BOX 8139
NEWARK, DE 19714-8139, USA
www.reading.org

IRA BOARD OF DIRECTORS
MaryEllen Vogt, California State University Long Beach, Long Beach, California, President • Richard Allington, University of Florida, Gainesville, Florida, President-elect • Timothy Shanahan, University of Illinois at Chicago, Chicago, Illinois, Vice President • Cathy Collins Block, Texas Christian University, Fort Worth, Texas • James Flood, San Diego State University, San Diego, California • Victoria J. Risko, Peabody College of Vanderbilt University, Nashville, Tennessee • Charline J. Barnes, Adelphi University, Garden City, New York • Rita M. Bean, University of Pittsburgh, Pittsburgh, Pennsylvania • Carrice L. Cummins, Louisiana Tech University, Ruston, Louisiana • David Hernandez, III, Washington DC Public Schools, Washington, DC • Susan Davis Lenski, Portland State University, Portland, Oregon • Jill Lewis, New Jersey City University, Jersey City, New Jersey • Alan E. Farstrup, Executive Director

The International Reading Association attempts, through its publications, to provide a forum for a wide spectrum of opinions on reading. This policy permits divergent viewpoints without implying the endorsement of the Association.

**Editorial Director**   Matthew W. Baker
**Managing Editor**   Shannon T. Fortner
**Permissions Editor**   Janet S. Parrack
**Acquisitions and Communications Coordinator**   Corinne M. Mooney
**Associate Editor**   Charlene M. Nichols
**Production Editor**   Amy Messick
**Books and Inventory Assistant**   Rebecca A. Zell
**Assistant Permissions Editor**   Tyanna L. Collins
**Production Department Manager**   Iona Muscella
**Supervisor, Electronic Publishing**   Anette Schütz
**Senior Electronic Publishing Specialist**   R. Lynn Harrison
**Electronic Publishing Specialist**   Lisa M. Kochel
**Proofreader**   Elizabeth C. Hunt

**Project Editor**   Shannon T. Fortner

**Cover**   Design, Linda Steere; Photographs (from top): Skjold, Image Productions, Skjold, Skjold, Image Productions, Image Productions

Copyright 2005 by the International Reading Association, Inc.
All rights reserved. No part of this publication may be reproduced or transmitted in any form or by any means, electronic or mechanical, including photocopy, or any information storage and retrieval system, without permission from the publisher.

Web addresses in this book were correct as of the publication date but may have become inactive or otherwise modified since that time. If you notice a deactivated or changed Web address, please e-mail books@reading.org with the words "Website Update" in the subject line. In your message, specify the Web link, the book title, and the page number on which the link appears.

**Library of Congress Cataloging-in-Publication Data**
Teaching African American learners to read : perspectives and practices / Bill Hammond, Mary Eleanor Rhodes Hoover, Irving Pressley McPhail, editors.
    p. cm.
Includes bibliographical references and index.
  ISBN 0-87207-540-0
  1. African American children--Education. 2. Reading--United States. I. Hammond, Bill, 1945- II. Hoover, Mary Rhodes. III. McPhail, Irving Pressley. IV. International Reading Association.
  LC2778.R4T39 2005
  372.4'089'96073--dc22
  Third Printing, December 2005                          2004024967

# Contents

## PART I

## Theoretical Foundations

## PART II

## Reading Methodologies

# PART III

# Cultural Considerations

# Contributors

Linda B. Akanbi
Professor of Reading Education
Kennesaw State University
Kennesaw, Georgia, USA

Rudine Sims Bishop
Professor Emerita, School
    of Teaching and Learning
The Ohio State University
Columbus, Ohio, USA

Wanda M. Brooks
Assistant Professor of Elementary
    Education
University of Maryland, Baltimore
    County
Baltimore, Maryland, USA

California Speech-Language-Hearing
    Association Task Force on the
    Assessment of the African
    American Child
Sacramento, California, USA

George O. Cureton
Former Professor of Education
Medgar Evans College
Brooklyn, New York, USA
(Deceased)

Charles E. DeBose
Professor of English
California State University, Hayward
Hayward, California, USA

Lisa Delpit
Executive Director for the Center for
    Urban Education & Innovation
Florida International University
Miami, Florida, USA

Ronald Edmonds
Former Assistant Superintendent
    of Instruction
New York City Schools
New York, New York, USA
(Deceased)

Bill Hammond
Literacy Coordinator
DeKalb County Schools
Decatur, Georgia, USA

Kelli Harris-Wright
Director, Department for Elementary
    Instruction
DeKalb County Schools
Decatur, Georgia, USA

Asa G. Hilliard III
Fuller E. Callaway Professor of Urban
    Education
Georgia State University
Atlanta, Georgia, USA

Sharroky Hollie
Assistant Professor of Teacher
    Education
California State University,
    Dominguez Hills
Carson, California, USA

Etta R. Hollins
Professor of Teacher Education
University of Southern California
Los Angeles, California, USA

Kimberly S. Hollins
Independent Research Associate
Los Angeles, California, USA

Mary Eleanor Rhodes Hoover
Professor of Reading
Howard University School
    of Education
Washington, DC, USA

Nancy Ichinaga
Former Principal
Bennett-Kew Elementary School
Inglewood, California, USA

Carol D. Lee
Associate Professor of Education,
    Social Policy, and African
    American Studies
Northwestern University
Evanston, Illinois, USA

E.R. Marnell Sr.
Instructional Assistant Principal
Southwest DeKalb High School
Decatur, Georgia, USA

Linda R. McIntyre
Assistant Professor
South Carolina State University
Orangeburg, South Carolina, USA

Irving Pressley McPhail
Chancellor
The Community College
    of Baltimore County
Baltimore, Maryland, USA

Robert L. Politzer
Former Professor of Romance
    Languages and Foreign Language
    Education
Stanford University
Stanford, California, USA
(Deceased)

Charlotte Rose Sadler
Assistant Principal
Margaret Winn Holt Elementary
Lawrenceville, Georgia, USA

Barbara J. Shade
Professor Emerita, School
    of Education
University of Wisconsin–Parkside
Kenosha, Wisconsin, USA

Dorothy S. Strickland
Samuel DeWitt Proctor Professor
    of Education
Rutgers, The State University
    of New Jersey
New Brunswick, New Jersey, USA

Orlando Taylor
Vice Provost for Research and Dean,
    Graduate School
Howard University
Washington, DC, USA

Arthurlene G. Towner
Dean, College of Education
    and Allied Studies
California State University, Hayward
Hayward, California, USA

# Introduction

*Bill Hammond, Mary Eleanor Rhodes Hoover,
and Irving Pressley McPhail*

> Black children are the proxy for what ails American education in general. And so as we fashion solutions which help Black children, we fashion solutions that help all children.
>
> —Augustus Hawkins, former Congressman and founder of the National Conference on Educating Black Children (cited in Jones-Wilson, 2003, p. 48)

Throughout the history of education in the United States, the treatment of people of color has not been kind. Aside from a pattern of historical neglect, underfunding and inequities in the distribution of resources at the state and local levels, and low expectations for academic achievement, a pattern of prejudice toward African American learners continues to exist in some circles of education and the larger community. Brady (2002) asserts,

> West Indian and other Negroes will never fit in, as multiracialists claim, to become equal and integrated members of a predominantly white society. This is because they are inherently unfitted to do so intellectually, and are thus condemned to exist in white society as permanent underclass, confined to the lower social strata and, not unnaturally, bitterly resentful of the alien society in which they are thus trapped. (p. 17)

A number of books and discussions have set forth to demonstrate the extent of racial differences in intellectual ability, including *The Testing of Negro Intelligence* (Shuey, 1966), *The Inequality of Man* (Eysenck, 1973), and the widely published book *The Bell Curve: Intelligence and Class Structure in American Life* (Herrnstein & Murray, 1994). As early as 1923, researchers set forth the argument based on "scientific research" that supported the view of the inferiority of people of color. Pintner, in his book *Intelligence Testing: Methods and Results* (1923), concludes,

> All results show the Negro decidedly inferior to the white on standardized intelligence tests. The difference is present among infants, elementary school children, high school pupils, university students and adult men. It occurs on Binet tests, on verbal group tests, on non-verbal group tests and on performance tests. (p. 434)

Today, many people dismiss these assertions as mere artifacts of days gone by and point to the achievements of large numbers of African American students in higher education and other high-performance areas. Although these achievements are welcomed and commendable, the struggle for recognition of the potential of these students is far from over. It is not sufficient to argue the absurdities of these views or to ignore them as being outdated, ignorant, and slanted. The fact that they still exist and have been shared and accepted by many people is sufficient cause to present counterviews for consideration. Thus, the editors of this book conclude that a critical need remains for literature that documents research-based practices and programs that successfully teach African American children to read.

This collection of thoughtful current and historical commentary, solid research-based practices, and culturally appropriate and relevant instruction has been assembled to demonstrate definitively two fundamental points: (1) African American children can be taught to read at levels of other students, and (2) examples of effective programs for children of color are numerous. This collection is a compilation of articles from members of the National Association of Black Reading and Language Arts Educators (NABRLE) and other distinguished educators who are concerned with the education of children of color. Several of the pieces have been published elsewhere, but this is the first time all of these hard-to-find works have been assembled in a single publication. In selecting them for inclusion, the editors hope to assist the reader in formulating a comprehensive view of the topic.

## Why Focus on African American Learners?

One reason we focus on African American learners in this book is because so many educators have low expectations about these students' ability to achieve, and thus accept excuses for failure. Rather than look at the research on successful approaches for teaching these students, many educators blame the victim and proffer pathological reasons for poor achievement. They want to design new, and often ineffective, remedies for children they view as exotic, primitive, and less educable than other students. Some educators advocate doing nothing because they have adopted the absurd notion that Black culture is adverse to academic success (McWhorter, 2000; Ogbu, 1995) or that Black students have genetic deficiencies (Herrnstein & Murray, 1994). Some scholars (Brown, 1933; Clarke, 1991; Dates & Barlow, 1990) have called for restructuring or reconstituting school administrations, whereas others (Hadderman, 2002; Hentschke, Oschman, & Snell, 2002; Snell, 2002) have suggested that private schooling, school-based management, and power sharing among teachers is the answer.

Another compelling reason for our focus on African American students is that they are arguably the most miseducated students in the United States. The editors of this book contend that much of this miseducation exists today as remnants of the deliberate resistance to providing children of African American descent with an equal education. Ineffective literacy and schooling practices—including low ability grouping, the overrepresentation of children of color in special education classes, the deliberate selection of instructional materials that are counter to the learning styles of many children of color, the high incidents of suspension and detention given to these students, the major discrepancies that exist in per pupil expenditures in poorer communities where many of these children live, and the poorly qualified teachers provided to these students—are so prevalent in schools with predominantly African American populations that these editors are reminded of the similar practices described over 70 years ago in Carter G. Woodson's landmark commentary, *The Mis-education of the Negro* (1933). Given the level of inequality that exists between the access to quality human and instructional resources in many communities where these children live and learn, there is little wonder that many African American learners at all grade levels today are performing at a level that is significantly behind other students. Or that the learning gap between African Americans and other learners that so many researchers are currently examining, discussing, and pondering is expanding.

## Organization of This Book

This book is divided into four parts. In Part I, Theoretical Foundations, the fundamental concepts and historical frameworks of teaching African American children are presented in Irving Pressley McPhail's chapter 1. This piece examines the critical place and role of education in the development of African Americans' liberation. Asa G. Hilliard III's chapter traces the beginnings of African Americans' connection to the importance of education from historic roots in Africa. Together these two pieces establish the background for the successful practices identified in Part II.

Part II, Reading Methodologies, presents a collection of new, adapted, and original articles on best practices at the elementary, middle, and high school levels for teaching African American children to read. Each of the authors discusses a specific aspect of this topic. The common thread throughout this section is the setting forth of the view that African American children can become successful readers. Programs have been developed in schools that have been meeting this challenge and making adequate yearly progress over the years.

Included in Part II is Ronald Edmonds's article, first published in 1979, which shows how little we have advanced since that time in our knowledge of what makes an effective school. George O. Cureton's landmark discussion of learning styles predates many of the discussions on this subject. Similarly, Mary Eleanor Rhodes Hoover revisits an article that dates back 20 years and is as timely in its discussion today as when it was first published. Nancy Ichinaga's invited article on her school's dramatic turnaround in academic performance is a practical, school-based example of how to teach African American children and improve their reading achievement scores. Irving Pressley McPhail's critique of a landmark study by George Weber again points to successful practices in four depressed urban schools housing primarily African American children. Linda B. Akanbi identifies methods of using multicultural literature to help guide African American children to become successful, independent readers. Rudine Sims Bishop presents a discussion of collaborative efforts to facilitate student learning in a specific program. A discussion of the dramatic results achieved by a duel-text approach to teaching high school students in a large, urban school system is presented by E.R. Marnell Sr. and Bill Hammond. Charlotte Rose Sadler presents specific strategies and techniques she uses to teach diverse student populations in a middle school setting. Part II concludes with a discussion by Dorothy S. Strickland on what the research says about improving the teaching of at-risk African American learners.

Part III, Cultural Considerations, considers the significance of culture in the teaching–learning process for African American learners. Lisa Delpit's chapter closely examines teacher knowledge and use of appropriate instructional approaches in the classroom and teachers' understanding of their students' language patterns. Kelli Harris-Wright explores the impact of oral language on the literacy development of African American children. Sharroky Hollie introduces effective language-sensitive instructional methods used in his school to teach African American learners. Barbara J. Shade presents her view of an African American cognitive learning style and the effect it may have on teaching and learning. Etta R. Hollins and colleagues discuss the importance of developing teachers who are aware of the importance of maintaining a high level of knowledge of appropriate methodology and pedagogy to teach primary-grade children of color. Wanda M. Brooks identifies linguistic features and a component of providing successful instruction for African American middle school learners. Carol D. Lee concludes Part III with her examination of techniques appropriate to teach African American high school students literary interpretation skills.

Part IV, Assessment Issues, addresses and examines these issues as they relate to African American learners. Because so much information has been written previously on this topic, the editors chose to limit what is included in this section. Two articles are featured: Hoover, Politzer, and Taylor's widely read review of bias issues related to reading assessments, and the practical and helpful Practice Guidelines for the Assessment of the African American Child, written by the California Speech-Language-Hearing Association Task Force on the Assessment of the African American Child.

Certainly, the discussions presented here have not begun to exhaust the body of research on the topic of teaching African American learners to read. The editors faced a difficult task in deciding which works to include. Many additional authors and articles on the topic exist in the literature. It is hoped that, in these selections, a representative sampling of the best of these discussions has been presented.

# Conclusion

Teachers of African American children have had an awesome responsibility to themselves, to their students and the students' parents, and to the community at large to leave no child behind, even before the advent of the current U.S. federal mandate. It is the responsibility of every person who teaches or who administers programs for children of color to seek practices and strategies that are well suited to their students. This book is offered to the reader as a celebration, not a rant—a methodical exposition of the best pedagogy, scholarship, and practical and effective approaches to the education of children who have been too long neglected, underappreciated, undervalued, and overlooked.

## REFERENCES

Barton, P.E. (2001). *Raising achievement and reducing gaps: Reporting progress toward goals for academic achievement: A report to the National Education Goals Panel.* Washington, DC: National Education Goals Panel. (ERIC No. ED453594)

Bennett, L., Jr. (1993). *Before the Mayflower: A history of Black America* (6th ed.). New York: Penguin.

Brady, S. (2002, May). Patterns of prejudice. *Vanguard, 36*(1), 15–27.

Brown, S. (1933). Negro character as seen by White authors. *Journal of Negro Education, 2,* 129–203.

Clarke, J.H. (1991). *Africans at the crossroads: Notes for an African world revolution.* Trenton, NJ: Africa World Press.

Dates, J.L., & Barlow, W. (Eds.). (1990). *Split image: African Americans in the mass media.* Washington, DC: Howard University Press.

Eysenck, H.J. (1973). *The inequality of man.* London: Temple Smith.

Fordham, S., & Ogbu, J.U. (1986). Black school success: Coping with the burden of acting White. *The Urban Review, 28,* 176–208.

Hadderman, M. (2002). Trends and issues: School choice. Educational Resources Information Center, Clearinghouse on Educational Policy and Management. Retrieved October 7, 2004, from http://eric.uoregon.edu/trends_issues/choice

Hentschke, G.C., Oschman, S., & Snell, L. (2002). Education management organizations: Growing a for-profit education industry with choice, competition, and innovation. Education Management Organizations Policy Brief 21, Reason Public Policy Institute. Retrieved September 27, 2004, from http://www.rppi.org/pb21.pdf

Herrnstein, R.J., & Murray, C. (1994). *The bell curve: Intelligence and class structure in American life.* New York: Free Press.

Jones-Wilson, L. (2003). *Elementary school age African American males: Factors promoting and inhibiting their academic success in a rural Mississippi school.* Unpublished doctoral dissertation, Jackson State University, Jackson, Mississippi.

Kirch, I.S. (1993). *Adult literacy in America: A first look at the National Adult Literacy Survey* (2nd ed.). Washington, DC: Office of Educational Research and Improvement.

Kozol, J. (1985). *Illiterate America.* Garden City, NY: Anchor/Doubleday.

Ludlow, L. (1988, March 16). Unorthodox "cure" for kids spawns lawsuits, outrage. *The San Francisco Examiner,* p. A20.

McWhorter, J. (2000). *Losing the race: Self-sabotage in Black America.* New York: Free Press.

Ogbu, J.U. (1978). *Minority education and caste: The American system in cross-cultural perspective.* New York: Academic Press.

Ogbu, J.U. (1995). *Black American students in an affluent suburb.* Mahwah, NJ: Erlbaum.

Pintner, R. (1923). *Intelligence testing; methods and results.* New York: Henry Holt.

Shuey, A.M. (1966). *The testing of Negro intelligence.* New York: Social Science Press.

Smith, T.M. (1994). *The condition of education.* Washington, DC: National Center for Educational Statistics.

Snell, L. (2002, September 4). Charter schools as school privatization. *Privatization Watch.* Retrieved September 27, 2004, from http://www.rppi.org/charterschools.html

Woodson, C.G. (1990). *The mis-education of the Negro.* Trenton, NJ: African World Press. (Original work published 1933)

# PART I

# Theoretical Foundations

Often, when curriculum-oriented educators are asked to write articles or books, they are expected to write only about pedagogical issues. Other scholars are asked to address the theoretical issues. As curriculum-oriented scholars, however, we cannot write in a vacuum without referring to some of the theoretical issues related to the issue. Thus, we begin this book by presenting a theoretical framework. We, and all who educate African American and other miseducated readers, must focus also on philosophy and the affective, as well as the cognitive, domain because the miseducated suffer not only from the pedagogical aspects of illiteracy but also the social aspects—incarceration, poverty, and unemployment.

For a literacy program to be successful, it must first be based on a strong philosophy and a solid social, cultural, and political foundation. One example is the ideology of "Conscientization" put forth by Paulo Freire (2004), which was the foundation of his literacy program. According to this philosophy, individuals and groups who were unable to read or write were considered victims of society. They were powerless, and they were poor. It was by gaining literacy skills that they became, as Freire says, subjects rather than objects of their cultures. Instead of having decisions about the quality of their lives made for them, they became the decision makers. Freire (1973) found that the people, when motivated by this philosophy, became "more fully human" (p. 55), which sped up their motor and cognitive skills, and thus their literacy skills. Freire also believed in using exciting and generative themes—those social and intellectual issues that excite debate and discussion in a particular culture—as motivation.

Another example is Julius Nyerere's (1968) philosophy of "education for self-reliance," which motivated adult students in his literacy programs. He stated that

> this is what our education system has to encourage. It has to prepare our people to play a dynamic and constructive part in the development of a society in which all members share fairly in the good or bad fortune of the group, and in which progress is measured in terms of human well-being,

not prestige buildings, cars, or other such things, whether privately or publicly owned. Our education must therefore inculcate a sense of commitment to the total community, and help the students to accept the values appropriate to our kind of future, not those appropriate to our colonial past. (p. 273)

Like Freire and Nyerere, we feel it is appropriate to base our collection on a stimulating academic and cultural philosophy. Thus, we have selected Irving Pressley McPhail's "On Literacy and Liberation: The African American Experience" to open the book. The chapter discusses the work of eminent African American scholars and others from developing nations—W.E.B. DuBois, Malcolm X, Paulo Freire, and Cheikh Anta Diop—stressing the base of love for liberation and excellence in the literacy process as seen in the development of many effective African American schools.

Asa G. Hilliard III reminds us of the African contribution to discourse in chapter 2, "Pedagogy in Ancient Kemet." He tells us how the Egyptians emphasized song, proverbs, and stories, debunking the myth that Africans and African Americans are not capable of abstract thinking. Furthermore, Hilliard points out that the use of proverbs is highly documented across the entire African diaspora (Daniel, 1972; Smitherman, 2000). Hilliard also describes other contributions of Egyptian discourse to world civilization, such as the Egyptian Mysteries System, the dialectic Law of Opposites, and the origin of the Seven Liberal Arts.

The articles in Part I offer considerable understanding of the African view of education and its place of importance in the lives of African American students. The African American experience in the United States is a continuation of the journey to intellectual excellence begun in ancient African civilizations. If we are to understand the ways of our students, we must have firm grounding in the places from which they came into existence. The culture and heritage of today's children of color is a clue as to how to approach them and teach them effectively. The information is as relevant as any current listing of best practices or scientifically based research.

## REFERENCES

Daniel, J. (1972, Winter). Towards an ethnography of Afro-American proverbial usage, *Black Lines*, 3–12.

Freire, P. (1973). *Education for critical consciousness.* New York: Continuum.

Freire, P. (2004). *Pedagogy of the oppressed.* (Myra Bergman Ramos, Trans.). New York: Continuum. (Original work published 1970)

Nyerere, J. (1968). *Ujamaa—essays on socialism.* Dar es Salaam, Tanzania: Oxford University Press.

Smitherman, G. (2000). *Talkin' that talk: Language, culture and education in African America.* New York: Routledge.

# CHAPTER 1

# On Literacy and Liberation: The African American Experience

*Irving Pressley McPhail*

I became a reading specialist out of a concern for the role of literacy in social action. For me, reading has always been a liberating experience, a means for allowing the voices of the past to speak to the present and to inform the future. Specifically, the reading of African and African American history has enabled the voices of the past to speak to me personally, to call me by name, to ask me what I have done, what I am doing, and what I am prepared to do to ensure that the slaves, activists, and martyrs did not dream and die in vain.

Distinguished historian and social theoretician Lerone Bennett, Jr. (1985) observed that if

> we approach Black history in the spirit of the men and women who made it, we will hear millions of voices, the voices of the slaves and sharecroppers, the voices of Nat Turner and Harriet Tubman, of Martin Luther King, Jr., and Malcolm X, speaking to us, warning us, telling us how they got over and what we must do to overcome. (p. 27)

The role of literacy is to enable us to hear these voices and to act accordingly (see McPhail, 1987).

O'Neil (1970) made a distinction between practicing *proper* and *improper* literacy: *Proper literacy* enhances a person's capacity for genuine control and rational decision making. *Improper literacy* reduces and destroys it—offering the illusion of control instead of genuine control. One may be able to read and write and yet be improperly literate. O'Neil argues,

> Make a distinction: Being able to read means that you can follow words across a page, getting generally what's superficially there. Being literate means that you can bring your knowledge and your experience to bear on what passes before you. Let us call the latter proper literacy; the former improper. (p. 263)

---

Adapted from a paper presented in 2001 at the 46th Annual Convention of the International Reading Association, New Orleans, LA.

Although some students may be considered functionally literate, they may lack the ability to *do* anything with what they can read. They cannot synthesize or evaluate information at the higher levels necessary to reflect on ideas and make critical decisions that would transform their lives. A true conception of literacy requires enlightened beings capable of social transformational acts that would enable them to be active participants in the human condition rather than passive recipients of social acts in the world (Freire, 1970a, 1970b, 1970c).

## A Freirean Perspective on Literacy

The approach to literacy taken by Freire (1970a, 1970b, 1970c) encompasses the ideal of proper literacy. According to Freire, to become more fully human is to become ever more critically aware of one's world and in creative control of it. The more one engages in conscious action to understand and transform the world—one's reality—in a praxis of reflection and action, the more fully human one becomes. He wrote,

> As we attempt to analyze dialogue as a human phenomenon, we discover something which is the essence of dialogue itself: the word. But the word is more than just an instrument which makes dialogue possible; accordingly, we must seek its constitutive elements. Within the word we find two dimensions, reflection and action, in such radical interaction that if one is sacrificed—even in part—the other immediately suffers. There is no true word that is not at the same time a praxis. Thus, to speak a true word is to transform the world. (1970c, p. 75)

The connection of literacy to liberation made by Freire is captured in his conception of words and process. The *words* that people learn to read and write must, through a process of cooperative human action, stimulate critical examination of oppression and enhance the ability of people to break from this oppression. Liberation is accomplished, in part, by overcoming the shackles of illiteracy. The *process* by which literacy is transmitted and employed in the praxis of critical reflection and transforming action must be democratic and liberating. The literacy process, according to Freire, must be a dialogue characterized by social relations of equality and liberation and reflecting the values of trust and mutual respect. Similarly, Lankshear and Lawler (1989) argued that the literacy that comprises reading and writing words is seen, ultimately, as an intrinsic part of a much larger literacy: the act of "reading" and "writing" the world itself: "'Writing' is the act of creating history, culture, and human being, in the light of 'reading' the text of social reality through the act of critical reflection" (p. 70).

# The African and African American
# Literacy Tradition

As I listen to the voices of the past, I am reminded that the failure to achieve this revolutionary conception of literacy for African American children, youth, and adults today must be considered against the background of the African experience. Some have argued that the strong oral tradition of African people suggests that Africans did not develop writing systems. A more careful review of the archaeological, historical, and epigraphic evidence demonstrates that Black Africans emerged at the dawn of civilization with many writing systems, and that these writing systems were used from ancient times to the present (Bekerie, 1994; Bernal, 1987; Diop, 1955/1974; Osei, 2002; Williams, 1976; Winters, 2004). In fact, southern Ethiopia was the source for most of the papyrus plants from which Black Africans invented paper for purposes of writing (Williams, 1976).

African literacy began in the Sahara over 5,000 years ago. In its original conception, writing was a syllabic system that included hundreds of phonetic signs, which over time was shortened to between 22 and 30 key signs, and used as an alphabet by the Egyptians, Meroites, Phonesians, and Ethiopians (Winters, 2004).

African people used writing systems for essentially two purposes: (1) to help merchants maintain records on business transactions and (2) to preserve religious doctrines or write obituaries (the Proto-Saharan script). Winters (2004) concludes that the role of traditional (oral) historians accounts for the scarcity of documents written for historical preservation among ancient African groups. He argues,

> These historians memorized the histories of their nation and people for future recitation before members of their respective communities. This oral history was often accompanied by music or delivered in poetic verse and remains the premiere source for the history of most African nations even today. (p. 3)

However, we know that writing on paper was only one form of sign and symbol communication in classical African civilization. Communication in Africa took many forms: via woven designs, the shapes and designs of Ashanti gold weights, hair braids, architecture (Churchward, 1910/1978; Schwaller de Lubicz, 1978), and drum sounds (Carrington, 1949/1969). In short, African culture relied heavily on symbols for conveying messages. It is a matter of historical record (Bekerie, 1994; Bernal, 1987; Diop, 1955/1974; Osei, 2002; Williams, 1976) that Black Africans developed the oldest literacy tradition in the world. Moreover, it must be emphasized that the Africans who were brought to the western hemisphere as slaves were literate at that time as demonstrated by the many symbolic representations woven into the social fabric of their diverse cultures. The African slaves could read, write, and speak the language of their respective tribal groups. However, in the western hemisphere, African literacy was either suppressed or destroyed. Because teaching slaves to read and write was a crime, they were prevented from continuing their own educational system or from participating in the White educational system of the colonies.

Consider the following historical account from *Remembering Slavery: African Americans Talk About Their Personal Experiences of Slavery and Emancipation* (Berlin, Favreau, & Miller, 1998), part of which was aired as a two-part radio documentary produced by Smithsonian Productions:

> My name is Tonea Stewart. When I was a little girl about five or six years old, I used to sit on the garret, the front porch. In the Mississippi Delta the front porch is called the garret. I listened to my Papa Dallas. He was blind and had these ugly scars around his eyes. One day, I asked Papa Dallas what happened to his eyes.
>
> "Well daughter," he answered, "when I was mighty young, just about your age, I used to steal away under a big oak tree and I tried to learn my alphabets so that I could learn to read my Bible. But one day the overseer caught me and he drug me out on the plantation and he called out for all the field hands. And he turned to 'em and said, 'Let this be a lesson to all of you darkies. You ain't got no right to learn to read.' And then daughter, he whooped me, and he whooped me, and he whooped me. And daughter, as if that wasn't enough, he turned around and he burned my eyes out!" (p. 280)

Despite this brutality, slaves such as Frederick Douglass secretly taught themselves how to read, and thousands of fugitive slaves escaped and told their stories orally and in writing. Slave narratives, in fact, became a new literary genre.

DuBois (1903/1953), in his classic work *The Souls of Black Folk*, analyzed the identity struggle among African Americans that resulted from a history of slavery and the calculated denial of access to literacy. African Americans saw literacy as a tool for liberation. After the ratification of the 15th Amendment in 1870, which provided specifically that the right to vote shall not be denied or abridged on the basis of race, color, or previous condition of servitude, a new vision of liberty emerged:

> Slowly but steadily, in the following years, a new vision began. It was the ideal of "book-learning." Here at last, Black Americans seemed to have discovered the mountain path to Canaan, the biblical land of freedom. (DuBois, 1903/1953, p. 19)

Literacy became for African Americans a palpable and symbolic goal that led to freedom from slavery and toward the struggle for full citizenship in America.

Once the ban on education was lifted, there was a rapid rise in literacy for African Americans (Bullock, 1970; DuBois, 1973/2001). Perhaps the most dramatic literacy campaign in U.S. history was that led by Septima Poinsette Clark in the southern United States during the first half of the 20th century. The purpose of the campaign was to counter the tactic of denying African Americans the right to vote because of illiteracy, which was produced in the first place because of a ban on teaching.

## Literacy and Activism: The Cases of W.E.B. DuBois and Malcolm X

The sociolinguistic model of literacy (Spolsky, Englebrecht, & Ortiz, 1983) recognizes the legitimizing role that culture plays in the development of a literate citizenry. According to that model, culture has a legitimizing role in the spread of literacy by providing a familiar context for the growth of a new vernacular. New language, terms, technology, and orthography are accepted—not when they are viewed as alien to the existing cultural norms—but when they are integrated into the existing traditional cultural norms of a people. The great scholar and social activist W.E.B. DuBois understood the role of culture in promoting literacy and liberation; he observed that "All art is propaganda and ever must be.... Whatever art I have for writing has been used always for propaganda, for gaining the right of Black folk to love and enjoy..." (as quoted in Lester, 1971, p. 99).

DuBois (1903/1969) advanced the concept of the "Talented Tenth," the view that "the best and most capable youth [of an oppressed people] must be schooled in the colleges and universities of the land" (p. 45). He argued,

> The Negro race, like all races, is going to be saved by its exceptional men. The problem of education, then, among Negroes must first of all deal with the Talented Tenth; it is the problem of developing the Best of this race that they may guide the mass away from the contamination and death of the Worst, in their own and other races. (p. 33)

In describing the new group of educated and gifted African American leaders who came on the scene after emancipation, DuBois observed the following:

> Through political organization, historical and polemic writing, and moral regeneration, these men strove to uplift their people.... These figures illustrate vividly the function of the college-bred Negro. He is, as he ought to be, the group leader, the man who sets the ideals of the community where he lives, directs its thoughts and heads its social movements.... The Talented Tenth of the Negro race must be made leaders of thought and missionaries of culture among their people. (p. 42)

Reading, writing, speaking, listening, and *acting* were the tools used by the Talented Tenth to help African Americans critically examine the state of their oppression and to develop the ability to resist this oppression.

Williams and Ladd (1978) used the term *self-education* to represent the extent to which a culture may restructure those experiences that have historically provided strength, resilience, and unity to nurture the seeds of literacy. The body of knowledge contained in those seeds may be used to liberate that culture and free the individual. Self-education, in that sense, may work in conjunction with the formal modes of education to enhance the entire educative process. African American men and women who possessed the qualities inherent in self-education have contributed much to the voices of the past: Sojourner Truth, Frederick Douglass, Booker T. Washington, W.E.B. DuBois, Mary McLeod Bethune, Carter G. Woodson, Paul Robeson, Marcus Garvey, Lorraine Hansberry, Benjamin Mays, and Martin Luther King, Jr., are cases in point. But El-Hajj Malik El-Shabazz (Malcolm X) represents a classic example of an African American intellectual who utilized Black experience to transform his own life and the lives of millions of people throughout the world.

The story of Malcolm X's acquisition of reading and writing skills behind prison walls remains a seminal study of self-education. While pursuing his newly acquired interest in reading, Malcolm determined that he needed to improve his comprehension skills. Thus, he began to copy the dictionary, page-by-page, learning definitions as he advanced. He began a concerted reading program in Black studies and moved systematically through the classical works in philosophy, religion, history, and economics. Malcolm's growing interest in Elijah Muhammad and the Nation of Islam provided a catalyst for his involvement with books. It was through his readings that Malcolm became more aware of the "deafness, dumbness and blindness that was afflicting the Black race in America" (Malcolm X, 1966, p. 179). To Malcolm, education, ultimately, became "a process of continuous reorganization, reconstruction and transformation of his ideas, experiences, and knowledge" (Williams & Ladd, 1978, p. 278). Malcolm's education was action oriented and goal directed. The need to learn became a personal as well as a group-oriented goal for Malcolm. And literacy provided the tools for his transformation from street hustler to human rights leader. Freire's conception of words and action (praxis) seems to accurately depict the social transformation and human liberation of Malcolm X (1966), who captured the relationship of self-education to action when he observed his own personal liberation through literacy:

> Until I left that prison, in every free moment I had, if I was not reading in the library, I was reading on my bunk. You couldn't have gotten me out of books with a wedge.... Months passed without my even thinking about be-

ing imprisoned. In fact, up to then, I never had been so truly free in my life. (pp. 172–173)

Perhaps Malcolm X's greatest contribution was the momentum he gave to the liberation movements in developing nations with his linkage of African Americans to the struggle of oppressed peoples throughout the world and, especially, to the newly independent nations of Africa. Malcolm X's transformation demonstrates that as the process of self-education evolves, Black activism becomes a decisive factor in the motivation for further learning, hence reinforcing the relationship of literacy to social action, self-education, and liberation.

# From Theory to Practice

Earlier I stated that reading, and specifically the reading of African and African American history, enabled the voices of the past to speak to me personally and to motivate me to appropriate action. As an educator, and most especially as a reading specialist, I have been motivated to seek out the causes of reading failure among low income African American children and to join other progressive educators in pointing the way toward a solution to the literacy crisis in the African American community. I have been guided by the voice of Frederick Douglass who said: "It is idle, a hollow mockery, for us to pray to God to break the oppressor's power, while we neglect the means of knowledge which will give us the ability to break this power. God will help us when we help ourselves" (as quoted in Bennett, 1985, p. 30).

Hoover (1984), in the spirit of Douglass's philosophy, argued that anyone interested in addressing the literacy crisis in the African American community today must use the prior knowledge of African and African American history and the models of Black excellence in the past to advocate and agitate on behalf of literacy for all people, and their scholarship to challenge the established theories and rationales for the failure of African American children to learn to read successfully. Five lines of inquiry and advocacy require our immediate attention if our vision of *proper* literacy is to be realized for African American learners.

## Essential Elements of Best Practice

Foster (1999) reviewed the emerging research literature that defines the essential elements of best practice with African American learners. These essential elements include the teacher's

1. ability to develop productive relationships with students and their parents or guardians;

2. sense of self-efficacy, i.e., the teacher must believe that they motivate students, work productively with them, and teach them;

3. belief that academic achievement results from concerted and consistent effort, not from ability;

4. conception of education that goes beyond cognitive growth and includes the students' social and emotional growth and leadership development;

5. fashioning, promoting, and adhering to a shared set of common values; and

6. grounding of teaching in students' histories—personal, family, political—communities, cultures, and indigenous linguistic abilities, and linking them to processes, school curriculum, and interactions. (p. 14)

## Culture in School Learning

Hollins (1996a) proposed a theory to explain the relationship between culture and instruction, and offered the following rationale for the theory of cultural mediation in instruction:

> The basic premise underlying the theory of cultural mediation in instruction has two components based on the centrality of the students' home-culture in framing memory structures and mental operations. First, teaching and learning are more meaningful and productive when curriculum content and instructional processes include culturally-mediated cognition, culturally-appropriate social situations for learning, and culturally-valued knowledge. Second, the authenticity of schooling is validated for students by the interactions and relationships between adult members of their community and school personnel. (pp. 137–138)

A growing body of literature, written principally by African American scholars and practitioners, is exploring the use of culture in school learning and explicitly describing classroom environments and practices that are effective in teaching African American students to read at all levels, preschool through adult education (Hollins, 1982, 1996b; Hollins, King, & Hayman, 1994; Hollins & Oliver, 1999; Hoover, 1982; Hoover, McPhail, & Ginyard, 1992; Kifano, 1996; Ladson-Billings, 1994; Lee, 1995; McPhail & McPhail, 1999; McPhail & Morris, 1986; Moses, Kamii, Swap & Howard, 1989; Piestrup, 1973; Shade, 1989).

## Effective Schools and Classrooms in Literacy Education

An established research tradition examines the characteristics of schools and classrooms that are effective in teaching African American students.

This research proceeds along two paths: one looking at generic school-based factors and a second examining the characteristics of inner-city schools and classrooms in which African American children are reading at grade level by grade 3. Unfortunately, much of this research is ignored and not utilized effectively in fashioning solutions to the literacy crisis in African American communities.

Edmonds (this volume) pioneered a study of urban public schools that successfully teach poor children. He made the following conclusions regarding the most tangible and indispensable characteristics of effective schools:

> (a) They have strong administrative leadership without which the disparate elements of good schooling can neither be brought together nor kept together; (b) Schools that are instructionally effective for poor children have a climate of expectation in which no children are permitted to fall below minimum but efficacious levels of achievement; (c) The school's atmosphere is orderly without being rigid, quiet without being oppressive, and generally conducive to the instructional business at hand; (d) Effective schools get that way partly by making it clear that pupil acquisition of basic school skills takes precedence over all other school activities; (e) When necessary, school energy and resources can be diverted from other business in furtherance of the fundamental objectives; and (f) There must be some means by which pupil progress can be frequently monitored. These means may be as traditional as classroom testing on the day's lesson or as advanced as criterion-referenced systemwide standardized measures. The point is that some means must exist in the school by which the principal and the teachers remain constantly aware of pupil progress in relationship to instructional objectives.

In what has become the mantra for those who believe that *all* children can learn, Edmonds calls us to action by issuing three now famous declarative statements:

> (a) We can, whenever and wherever we choose, successfully teach all children whose schooling is of interest to us; (b) We already know more than we need to do that; and (c) Whether or not we do it must finally depend on how we feel about the fact that we haven't so far.

Weber (1971) focused specifically on the study of four inner-city schools in which the majority of third graders were reading at grade level. Weber assumed that when all four of the successful schools followed a practice that was not usually found in unsuccessful schools, that practice had something to do with their success. He concluded further that different practices that existed in some, but not all, of the successful schools were not essential to success. Based on these two propositions, Weber accounted for the success of beginning reading instruction in the four successful schools.

Weber identified eight factors common to the four successful schools and not usually present in unsuccessful inner-city schools as success factors. These factors are (1) strong leadership, (2) high expectations, (3) good atmosphere, (4) strong emphasis on reading, (5) additional reading personnel, (6) use of phonics, (7) individualization, and (8) careful evaluation of pupil progress. The nonessential school-level factors are small class size, achievement grouping, high quality of teaching, school personnel of the same ethnic background as the pupils, preschool education, and outstanding physical facilities.

McPhail (this volume) revealed four additional success factors about two of the schools in Weber's study that were not identified by Weber as critical success factors. These include (1) active parental involvement; (2) strong in-service teacher-training components; (3) appropriate use of Black speech, events, and culture; and (4) emphasis on developing racial pride and cultural identity. McPhail also countered Weber's assertions regarding nonessential factors, particularly teacher quality. As we have learned in the section "Essential Elements of Best Practice," effective teachers are *key* to the success of African American learners.

Hoover (1978) concluded that "one of the most striking characteristics of Black and other minority schools where students read at grade level is the use of a structured approach to reading which focuses on the orthographic rules/spelling patterns of English" (p. 760). Hoover correctly observed that the focus on structure does not exclude the organization of a reading and language arts plan that integrates and balances activities from all four language perspectives (reading, writing, listening, speaking) and emphasizes the search for meaning.

Hoover also identified a set of sociopolitical factors that distinguish effective schools, including the use of a group-oriented philosophy, high expectations, strong teacher-training component, supplementary approaches for nonachieving students, use of parents as paid paraprofessionals or as volunteers, and community-based school governance structures (see also Hoover, Dabney, & Lewis, 1990).

In a recent study, Cole-Henderson (2000) examined the organizational structure of schools that successfully serve low income urban African American students. She defined "school organization" or "organizational structure" as "the ways schools are configured, both for the purpose of supporting students' academic and personal growth as well as for sustaining schools as communities of learning" (p. 79). The data for this study were drawn from questionnaire results from principals of nine highly successful urban public schools serving students pre-kindergarten to eighth grade. The schools in the study met the following criteria:

1. On school district and/or state-mandated, nationally normed tests, at least 51% of their students passed with scores at or above grade level in reading and mathematics for at least two consecutive years.

2. They served primarily low income African American students; that is, 51% or more of their student bodies consisted of African American youth.

3. The schools were public, urban, and nonselective. (p. 81)

The successful schools were characterized by the following factors: (1) relatively stable educational environments distinguished by low teacher and student mobility and substantial parental involvement, (2) clear mission statements, (3) strong leadership, (4) collegial climate, and (5) continuous commitment to improvement. Again, the role of the school principal was a key factor. The principals in this study

> reached consensus about what they believe their schools must do and provide to ensure a quality education for all their students....what constitutes outstanding leadership, teacher quality and efficacy, staff development, effective school governance, parent involvement, clarity of school mission, high expectations, school climate and environment, resources, school structure and relationships, and a broad range of outcomes.... (p. 89)

The principals also agreed that to be successful, "urban schools in low income areas must address the needs of the whole child as well as the child's family and community" (p. 89).

## What We Need to Know

Strickland (this volume) contended that "African-American children deserve literacy programs that stress the construction of meaning right from the start," and that "build on and expand their language and culture with a view toward helping them understand and value their heritage and respect the heritage of others." Strickland offered concrete recommendations for improving practice and concluded that

> We can take advantage of a growing body of research that suggests better educational policy and more comprehensive and meaningful approaches to raising the academic achievement of African-American students. The knowledge is available. It is time we demonstrated the commitment to seek a better way.

When considered in the context of culture, politics, and educational policy, the knowledge base for teaching African American students to read is expanded exponentially. At the same time, five critical questions arise:

1. What do teachers need to know about the early learning of African American children in order to frame meaningful curriculum content, identify productive learning and teaching strategies, and create a supportive context for literacy acquisition and development?

2. How do teachers who are effective with African American students develop these behaviors and learn to use effective approaches? Can these effective approaches be taught to others and with what effect?

3. What content and learning experiences in preservice teacher education programs increase the probability that teachers will be able to facilitate literacy acquisition and development for African American students?

4. What new models for in-service teacher development can be designed that are powerful enough to change teachers' attitudes, expectations, and classroom practices in urban classrooms? (See Towner, Hollins, and Labov [2000].)

5. How do we teach African American learners to read and write the world, using classic and contemporary literature to increase intellectual engagement and literate behavior, and simultaneously to move readers toward personal, civic, and communal sociopolitical awareness and action?

## A New Definition of "Back to Basics"

Clearly and unequivocally, the kind of proper literacy called for and required by African American students must transcend teaching to low-level, basic skills and the threat of placing an unintended ceiling on learning. We know, for example, that teaching directly to the test and aligning curriculum directly to the test results in knowledge that is not liberating (Darling-Hammond, 1993; Shepard, 1991). The theories and instructional strategies discussed in this chapter offer powerful alternatives for literacy educators and others committed to helping African American students become more critically aware of their world and in creative control of it. Specifically, the new scholarship in literacy education that more directly links African American culture, information processing, and instruction provides a more powerful alternative from which to transform classroom practice and to increase opportunities for literacy learning. The centrality of culture in literacy learning and the use of literacy as a tool for empowerment and transformation mark a departure from the old paradigms and define the "new back to basics movement" for African American learners.

# A Promise to Keep

The voices of the past speak to all of us of hope, endurance, and daring. Proper literacy remains the key to unlock these voices of the past for those of us in the present. The connection of literacy to social consciousness and the liberation of the mind and spirit has been amply demonstrated through the voices of the past. It remains our responsibility to ensure that every African American child, youth, and adult today and in the future can use literacy as a tool to ensure a life of freedom, justice, and equality.

In closing, I return to the story of Papa Dallas as told to his daughter, Tonea Stewart:

> At that instant, I began to cry. The tears were streaming down my cheeks, meeting under my chin. But he cautioned, "Don't you cry for me now, daughter. Now you listen to me. I want you to promise me one thing. Promise me that you gonna pick up every book you can and you gonna read it from cover to cover. You see, today, daughter, ain't nobody gonna whip you or burn your eyes out because you want to learn to read. Promise me that you gonna go all the way though school, as far as you can. And one more thing, I want you to promise me that you gonna tell all the children my story." (Berlin, Favreau, & Miller, 1998, p. 280)

## REFERENCES

Bekerie, A. (1994). The four corners of a circle: Afrocentricity as a model of synthesis. *Journal of Black Studies, 25*(2), 131–149.

Bennett, L., Jr. (1985, February 25). A living history: Voices of the past speak to the present. *Ebony, 43*(4), 27, 28, 30, 32.

Berlin, I., Favreau. M., & Miller, S.F. (Eds.). (1998). *Remembering slavery: African Americans talk about their personal experiences of slavery and emancipation.* New York: New Press; Washington, DC: Library of Congress.

Bernal, M. (1987). Black Athena: The Afroasiatic roots of classical civilization. New Brunswick, NJ: Rutgers University Press.

Bullock, H.A. (1970). *A history of Negro education in the South, from 1619 to the present.* New York: Praeger.

Carrington, J.F. (1969). *Talking drums of Africa.* New York: Negro Universities Press. (Original work published 1949)

Churchward, A. (1978). *The signs and symbols of primordial man: The evolution of religious doctrines from the eschatology of the ancient Egyptians.* Westport, CT: Greenwood Press. (Original work published 1910)

Cole-Henderson, B. (2000). Organizational characteristics of schools that successfully serve low income urban African American students. *Journal of Education for Students Placed at Risk, 5*(1 & 2), 77–91.

Darling-Hammond, L. (1993). Reframing the school reform agenda. *Phi Delta Kappan, 74* (10), 752–761.

Diop, C.A. (1974). *The African origin of civilization: Myth or reality* (Mercer Cook, Trans.). New York: Lawrence Hill. (Original work published 1955)

DuBois, W.E.B. (1953). *The souls of Black folk.* New York: Blue Heron. (Original work published 1903)

DuBois, W.E.B. (1969). The talented tenth. In *The Negro problem: A series of articles by representative American Negroes of today* (pp. 33–60). New York: Arno Press. (Original work published 1903)

DuBois, W.E.B. (2001). *The education of Black people: Ten critiques, 1906–1960.* New York: Monthly Review Press. (Original work published in 1973)

Foster, M. (1999, July). *Teaching Black students: Best practices.* Paper presented at the meeting of the Commission on Research in Black Education, Working Colloquium, American Educational Research Association, St. Simons Island, GA.

Freire, P. (1970a). The adult literacy process as cultural action for freedom. *Harvard Educational Review, 40*(2), 205–226.

Freire, P. (1970b). Cultural action and conscientization. *Harvard Educational Review, 40*(3), 452–477.

Freire, P. (1970c). *Pedagogy of the oppressed* (Myra Bergman Ramos, Trans.). New York: Herder and Herder.

Hollins, E.R. (1982). The Marva Collins story revisited. *Journal of Teacher Education, 33*(1), 37–40.

Hollins, E.R. (1996a). *Culture in school learning: Revealing the deep meaning.* Mahwah, NJ: Erlbaum.

Hollins, E.R. (Ed.). (1996b). *Transforming curriculum for a culturally diverse society.* Mahwah, NJ: Erlbaum.

Hollins, E.R., King, J.E., & Hayman, W.C. (Eds.). (1994). *Teaching diverse populations: Formulating a knowledge base.* Albany: State University of New York Press.

Hollins, E.R., & Oliver, E.I. (Eds.). (1999). *Pathways to success in school: Culturally responsive teaching.* Mahwah, NJ: Erlbaum.

Hoover, M.R. (1978). Characteristics of Black schools at grade level. *The Reading Teacher, 31,* 757–762.

Hoover, M.R. (1982). A culturally-appropriate approach to teaching basic (and other) critical communication skills to Black college students. *Negro Educational Review, 33,* 14–27.

Hoover, M.R. (1984, May). *Using research in schema theory and Black learning styles to teach reading and composition to linguistically-different college students.* Paper presented at the 29th Annual Convention of the International Reading Association, Atlanta, GA.

Hoover, M.R., Dabney, N., & Lewis, S. (Eds.). (1990). *Successful Black and minority schools: Classic models* (Rev. ed.). San Francisco: Julian Richardson.

Hoover, M.R., McPhail, I.P., & Ginyard, L. (1992). Literacy for miseducated Black adults: The Nairobi method, a culturally appropriate approach. In A.M. Scales & J.E. Burley (Eds.), *Perspectives: From adult literacy to continuing education* (pp. 212–218). Dubuque, IA: William C. Brown.

Jackson, J. (1970). *Introduction to African civilizations.* Secaucus, NJ: Citadel Press.

Kifano, S. (1996). Afrocentric education in supplementary schools: Paradigm and practice at the Mary McLeod Bethune Institute. *Journal of Negro Education, 65*(2), 209–218.

Ladson-Billings, G. (1994). *The dreamkeepers: Successful teachers of African American children.* San Francisco: Jossey-Bass.

Lankshear, C., & Lawler, M. (1989). *Literacy, schooling, and revolution.* New York: Falmer Press.

Lee, C.D. (1995). A culturally based cognitive apprenticeship: Teaching African American high school students skills in literary interpretation. *Reading Research Quarterly, 30,* 608–630.

Lester, J. (Ed.). (1971). *The seventh son: The thought and writings of W.E.B. DuBois* (Vol. 1). New York: Random House.

Malcolm X. (1966). *The autobiography of Malcolm X.* New York: Grove Press.

McPhail, I.P. (1987). Literacy as a liberating experience. *English Quarterly, 20*(1), 9–15.

McPhail, I.P., & McPhail, C.J. (1999). Transforming classroom practice for African American learners: Implications for the learning paradigm. *Removing Vestiges: Research-Based Strategies to Promote Inclusion, 2,* 25–35.

McPhail, I.P., & Morris, P.L. (1986). A new look at reading/communication arts in the inner-city junior high school. *Reading Improvement, 23,* 49–60.

Moses, R.P., Kamii, M., Swap, S.M., & Howard J. (1989). The algebra project: Organizing in the spirit of Ella. *Harvard Educational Review, 59*(4), 423–443.

O'Neil, W. (1970). Properly literate. *Harvard Educational Review, 40,* 260–263.

Osei, O.K. (2002). *Civilization began in Africa.* Kumasi, Ghana, West Africa: Vytall Print Publishers.

Piestrup, A.M. (1973). *Black dialect interference and accommodation of reading instruction in the first grade* (Monograph of the Language Behavior Research Laboratory). Berkeley: University of California.

Schwaller de Lubicz, R.A. (1978). *Symbol and the symbolic: Egypt, science and the evolution of consciousness* (Robert & Deborah Lawler, Trans.). Brookline, MA: Autumn Press.

Shade, B.J.R. (1989). *Culture, style, and the educative process.* Springfield, IL: Charles C. Thomas.

Shepard, L. (1991). Negative policies for dealing with diversity: When does assessment and diagnosis turn into sorting and segregation? In E.H. Hiebert (Ed.), *Literacy for a diverse society* (pp. 279–298). New York: Teachers College Press.

Spolsky, B., Englebrecht, G., & Ortiz, L. (1983). *The sociolinguistics of literacy: An historical and comparative study of five cases* (Final report). Albuquerque: University of New Mexico. (ERIC Document Reproduction Service No. ED236943)

Towner, A.G., Hollins, E.R., & Labov, W. (2000). *African American literacy and culture research project: Executive summary* (U.S. Department of Education, Office of Educational Research and Improvement Award No. R 215 R 980014-98). Hayward: California State University, Hayward.

Weber, G. (1971). *Inner-city children can be taught to read: Four successful schools.* (Occasional Papers No. 18). Washington, DC: Council for Basic Education.

Williams, C. (1976). *The destruction of Black civilization: Great issues of a race from 4500 B.C. to 2000 A.D.* Chicago: Third World Press.

Williams, J.E., & Ladd, R. (1978). On the relevance of education for Black liberation. *Journal of Negro Education, 47,* 266–282.

Winters, C. (2004). *Ancient writing in Middle Africa.* Retrieved August 11, 2004, from http://www.geocities.com/Tokyo/Bay/7051/anwrite.htm

CHAPTER 2

# Pedagogy in Ancient Kemet

*Asa G. Hilliard III*

The surface has been hardly scratched in the study of history of Africa and its people. The rough outlines of that history are beginning to emerge as well-prepared African and African American historians have begun the painstakingly detailed work of documenting the African experience in antiquity. It is hard enough to trace the broad general outlines of the African experience. It is even more difficult to focus in on small aspects of that experience, such as pedagogy, with any degree of clarity. And yet there is the need for us to do precisely that.

Our concern with the connection to our African past is really future oriented. It is not merely for sentimental or aesthetic reasons that we return. While it is true that no one can or should live in the past, it is equally true that all futures are created out of some past. Ancient Africans not only existed, they developed a way of life the remnants of which continue to influence world development. As we view competing designs for human institutions and competing philosophies, it is incumbent upon us to come to that process as fully disciplined and, especially, as creative participants. A review of our past will reveal that no people has a better place from which to start.

It is my task to draw the best possible picture of one small aspect of a total development process of ancient Africans in the Nile Valley region and in the Great Lakes region. Simply put, how did the ancient Africans design and carry out the educational process? What were the aims, the methods, and the contents of ancient African education? The best preserved records of cultural activity are to be found in Kemet (Ancient Egypt). As a result, a great deal of our attention must be focused on that point. However, it is important always to keep in mind the fact that ancient Egypt was, as poet Gerald Massey said, "merely the mouthpiece for a more deeply rooted African birthplace."

Anyone who is familiar with the material on ancient Egypt is well aware of the fact that there exist few if any books on the educational system of Egypt.

Adapted from M. Karenga & J.H. Carruthers (Eds.) (1986), *Kemet and the African Worldview: Research, Rescue and Restoration* [Selected papers of the proceedings of the first and second conferences of the Association for the Study of Classical African Civilizations, 24–26 February 1984, Los Angeles, and 1–3 March 1985, Chicago] (pp. 131–148). Los Angeles: University of Sankore Press.

Consequently the reconstruction of what must have been a highly developed and vast system of education necessarily requires an approach that is highly inferential. Nonetheless, the inferences are not without empirical grounding. For example, the evidence that gives information about the educational system can be found in paintings, monuments, architecture, technology, and above all in the hieroglyphic and demotic writings, which include stories, rituals, songs, and so forth. In addition, the skilled eye can detect in the widespread African diaspora an extensive variety of cultural forms whose antecedents are clear matches to those of the Egyptian and earlier ancient cultural forms. And so we are not short of evidence for the fact that educational systems existed. Rather the task is to sift through a plethora of direct and indirect data in order to reconstruct a picture of the past.

It is important at this point that a few words be said about the general orientation that I consider to be essential to any understanding of the raw data or summarized interpretation of data about ancient Egyptian education. First, in doing our analysis we must always keep in mind the *antiquity* of African culture. Second, and just as important, we must always keep in mind what Cheikh Diop (1978) has referred to as the *unity* of African culture. For to explain the culture, and particularly the educational system of Egypt, we must appeal not only to data in Egypt but to data about education from the cultural antecedents of Egypt, as well as manifestations of the core African culture, not only in the Egyptian part of the diaspora, but in the rest of the continental diaspora and later in the intercontinental diaspora as well.

# History

Briefly let me summarize some of the main points of African ancient history with which most of us are now quite familiar. It is clear now from the archaeological record that the whole body of data supports an African origin for mankind. What is equally important is that the earliest record of what we call civilization developed first in the same areas where the earliest fossil remains of humans are found. That is to say, long before Egypt began, it was Black people in Africa along the southern Nile River valley, close to its source, who produced the first stirrings of "civilization" that can be documented. Albert Churchward (1978) echoes paleoanthropologist Richard Leakey when he says that

> the first Paleolithic man was the pigmy who was evolved in Central Africa at the sources of the Nile or Nile Valley, and that from here all originated and were carried throughout the world. (p. 3)

In fact, Churchward goes further, saying,

> The sources of the Nile—equatorial provinces—where the Great Lakes in the papyrus swamp were their Ta-Nuter, or Holy Land—i.e., "the land of the spirits of Gods," and the chief features of this earthly paradise were repeated in the circumpolar highland. (p. 201)

It was Henri Frankfort (1969), among other students of Egyptian history and culture, who recognized from the evidence that Egypt's historical and cultural antecedents were to be found *south* of Egypt, deeper in the Nile Valley. For example Frankfort tells us,

> The roots of Egyptian unity reach back into the most distant past. The population of the Nile Valley was homogenous, both physically and culturally, as much as a large group can ever be. The evidence of fauna or flint tools suggest that the inhabitants descended in early neolithic times from the surrounding desert plateaus.... We know that the physique of the inhabitants of this valley from the delta deep down in the Nubia remains much the same from predynastic to late historical times. They also shared a common material culture in predynastic times. There are indications that this culture, the Amaration, extended well into Libya and reached the Red Sea in the east. Ansomatic and ethnological resemblances and certain features of their languages, connect the ancient Egyptians firmly with the Hamitic speaking people of East Africa. It seems that the phaoranic civilization arose on this northeast African Hamitic substratum. In any case, the prehistoric inhabitants of the Nile Valley must have possessed a common spiritual culture as a correlate of the homogenous physical and archaeological remains. (p. 16)

Of course we are all familiar with the fact that the very first unification of the two lands was initiated from the south and, as John G. Jackson (1980) has said,

> Egypt's first golden age was initiated by an invasion from Ethiopia, according to Petrie; a conqueror of Sudani founded the third dynasty, and many entirely new ideas entered the country. This new movement culminated the vast schemes of Khufu, one of history's most dominating personalities. With him the lines of Egyptian growth were established and in the course of events and in the course of events became the subject of the written records. (pp. 97–98)

And it is Yosef ben-Jochannan (1971) who often cites the records from the Papyrus of Hunefer where the Egyptians themselves announced that their home was to the south at the *source* of the Nile near the foothills of the "Mountains of the Moon" (or Mt. Kilimanjaro).

Clearly what we are getting is the picture of highly developed civilized behavior long before Egypt began—to the south of Egypt. For example, hieroglyphic writings existed long before the first dynasty in Egypt. Further, the hard evidence from such great monuments as the great "Sphinx" of Giza (or as Africans called it, Hor-Em-Aket) indicates that it was much older than the pyramids and probably much older than Egypt as a nation. As Jackson (1980) states,

> According to Sir Gastone Maspero, the Egyptians made their first appearance on the stage of history about 8000 to 10,000 B.C.... This estimate should not be considered excessive. The ancient statue known as the Great Sphinx has been estimated by another French Egyptologist, Professor Pierre Hippolyte Boussac, to be at least ten thousand years old. There is an inscription of the Pharoah Khufu, builder of the great pyramid, telling how a temple adjoining the Sphinx, which has for generations been buried under the desert sand, was discovered by chance in his reign. This inscription, now in the Boulak Museum in Cairo, informs us that the Sphinx was much older than the Great Pyramid and that the giant statue required repairs during the reign of Khufu. (pp. 95–96)

Citing the evidence once more, we return to Jackson (1980), who observed,

> The Edfu text is an important source document on the early history of the Nile Valley. This famous inscription, found in the Temple of Horus at Edfu, gives an account of the origins of the Egyptian civilization. According to this record, civilization was brought from the south by a band of invaders under the leadership of King Horus. This ruler, Horus, was later deified and became ultimately the Egyptian Christ. The followers of Horus were called "the blacksmiths" because they possessed iron implements. This early culture had been traced back to Somaliland, although it may have originated in the Great Lakes region of Central Africa. In Somaliland, there are ruins of buildings constructed with dressed stone, showing the close resemblance of the architecture of early Egypt. Professor and author G. Brodeur, in his *The Pageant of Civilization*, has conjectured that the ancestors of the southern Egyptians came originally from this region and that they entered the Nile through Nubia and brought with them a well-developed civilization. It is estimated that this migration must have occurred long before 5000 B.C. (p. 93)

Looking again to evidence for a southern origin of Egyptian civilization, we must note the recent evaluation of material found in archaeological digs just before the waters of the Aswan Dam flooded Nubia:

> South of Abu-Simbel, a group of curious conical mounds at Ballana and on the opposite bank of Qostoi, caught their eye, and they decided to make

a trial excavation.... Further mounds were examined with similar results, and eventually at Ballana, the tumulous graves of kings themselves were found. They were tall men, with negroid features. (Drower, 1970, p. 65)

And so it is that establishment Egyptologists, such as Bruce Williams (1980), at the University of Chicago, began to say that Egyptian civilization had a parent, perhaps more than one, and that the most likely candidate for immediate parenthood is the Nubian civilization of Ta-Seti to the south of Egypt. Finally, as Barbara Mertz (1978) has said,

> Let's look to the fair queens of Egypt to begin with. I discussed them in another book, but this point requires repetition. As far as I know, there never was a blond queen of Egypt. The famous fourth dynasty lady, who was believed to be blond or red headed, has been shown to be wearing a yellow headcloth. There never were any other candidates for the description. (p. 13)

What emerges clearly from the evidence is that indigenous Black Africans developed the whole Nile Valley, including Egyptian civilization.

# Culture

Diop's (1978) concept of cultural unity is very important to us. It is a powerful explanatory construct that helps to guide empirical investigation. The concept of cultural unity helps us to bridge Egypt (East Africa) to the rest of Africa to the intercontinental diaspora. It cannot be emphasized too strongly that we are not limited to mere speculation on these points, as Diop's book on the cultural unity of Black Africa has demonstrated. There is abundant evidence for the cultural unity, both in antiquity and in the present. For example, in West Africa,

> Ethnologists who have studied Bozos believed that this tiny island of fishermen came from Egypt 5000 years ago and settled in the Niger basin. They have not moved since or changed their ways, which are derived from the river people of the Nile, under the early dynasties, as is their language. The Bozos have maintained their spiritual independence from Islam and Christianity and kept alive traditions that originated before the fall of Memphis. Watching a Bozo ceremony, the dancer's heads covered with animal masks, is like watching living hieroglyphics. (DeGramont, 1977, p. 30)

I must emphasize that it was the *empirical* evidence that led DeGramont to such a conclusion. Similarly, study of Voodoo religion in West Africa reveals its similarity to ancient Egyptian religion, and to its offspring, European religion.

The role of the mystery named Legba, for example, corresponds to that of Hermes in Helenistic mysteries, so many of their symbols being identical that the analogy cannot be dismissed, either as incidental or as a consequence of what anthropologists term 'convergence'. They comprise the total image of the god, and are furthermore, symbolically consistent, whether rendered in the rites and myths or as interpreted by qualified *Houngans* with a sufficient number of whom Milo Ligaud has been for years well acquainted on the best of terms. In any case, no matter what the explanation may be, the parallel between the myth and cult in contemporary Haiti and those not only of 17th century Africa but over antiquity are undeniable and abundant. (Deren, 1951, p. xi)

We can look at another culture in West Africa. DeGramont, in his book *The Strong Brown God*, was fascinated by the ancient West African city of Djenne, a companion city to Timbuktu in Mali, which he called an "African Venice."

When the river is high it can only be reached by boat, protected by water. Djenne is said to have resisted 99 sieges in the course of its history. If the Pharaoh awoke there today, he would think he was in ancient Egypt. The clay houses have decorated facades with trapezoidal porticos, pointed glens and columns in tow relief. The Mosque, as large as a gothic cathedral, is all inspiring in its use of primitive materials on a monumental scale. The people of Djenne are fishermen and traders attached to their city, seldom leaving it. (pp. 32–33)

It is amazing how often scholars who wish to understand ancient Egyptian culture, especially its religion, are driven to the study of other Black African populations who are descendants of ancient Egyptians or of ancestors in common with the ancient Egyptians. This was expressed explicitly by Sir E.A. Wallis Budge and also by Henri Frankfort (1969) in his book *Kingship and the Gods*, who states,

There are two ways to penetrate behind the words of our text. In the first place, there are alive today in African subgroups of people who are the survivors of that great East African substratum out of which Egyptian culture arose. Among other things we can study how deeply the divine nature of kings affects both the ruler and his subjects. Yet, this evidence requires correction for we are dealing here with savages, who either by tenacity or by inertia, have preserved through several thousand years the remnants of a primeval world of thought, while pharaonic culture was the most developed and most aggressive of its age. (p. 6)

Once again, the essential point to be made here is there is an overwhelming abundance of *empirical* data to show both the historical and contemporary cultural connection between East Africa, including Egypt, and its continental and its intercontinental diaspora.

We need the linguistic terms from Noam Chomsky of "surface structure" and "deep structure" to explain the apparent diversity that exists throughout the African continent and, indeed throughout the diaspora. Foreign explorers have been fascinated by what they considered to be significant differences among Africans, differences in the physiognomy of peoples, in ways of worship, and so forth. However, they have been attracted to the surface structural manifestations. Clearly an impartial investigation based upon empirical facts will demonstrate as Diop (1978) and others such as Thompson and Cornet (1981) and Jahn (1961) have done, that cultural unity is far more significant than is superficial diversity.

If time permitted, it would be instructive to examine the records of African neighbors in what we now call the Middle East, in Asia, and in Europe. In doing this we would see that during the early part of development of civilization the source of civil ideas was almost completely African. Three thousand years of unbroken development along the Nile Valley positioned Africans to have a major influence on the world, an influence that still continues.

# Education

This brings me to my major task, which is to attempt to sharpen our picture of Egyptian education. We are hampered in our attempt to learn about ancient Egyptian education not only by the widespread loss of documentary materials, by the destruction of social institutions and civilizations, including their library records, and by years of prejudice and neglect; but we are also hindered by the fact that some of the most important parts of the educational process were conducted in "secret." Much of the tradition was passed on orally to the prepared initiate.

We are indebted to such writers as George G.M. James (1976), R.A. Schwaller de Lubicz (1977), R.F. Thompson and J. Cornet (1981), Albert Churchward (1978), and others for helping to pull back the veil on some of this "secret" tradition. George James studied the reports of the establishment historians and collected fragments of accepted information, placing them in a new perspective. R.A. Schwaller de Lubicz studied the ruins of the Temple at Luxor and Egyptian symbolic writing and thought. Thompson and Cornet studied cultural patterns of existing Bantu tribal groups, especially their religious practices. Churchward studied the evolution of the use of symbols from their source in the Great Lakes region and Nile Valley to the dispersion of the use of those symbols through the world. What I'm trying to show once again is that there is an *empirical* base for emerging descriptions of an ancient Egyptian educational system.

As we look at ancient Egyptian cultural patterns we see that there was not only a cultural unity *among* apparently diverse groups of people. There was also an essential unity *within* the culture that was reflected in the intimate and harmonious ties between and among education, politics, economics, religion, and so forth. It would make no sense whatsoever to consider the educational process apart from a deep study of the world view and religion of ancient Egypt. Ancient Egyptians lived close to nature, basically as a sedentary population under highly favorable environmental conditions. They were in a position to make repeated observations of natural processes over thousands of years. As clearly as anywhere else in the world, it can be seen in the Nile Valley that nature has regular processes of birth, growth, aging, death, decay, and rebirth. All nature seems to tell the same story. The behavior of the mother Nile was cyclical. Within general limits, this behavior could be predicted. Indeed, the successful predictions of its rise and fall determined the degree to which its bountiful resources could be exploited.

The skies were almost always clear, providing an unparalleled opportunity for long-term systematic observation of the behavior of heavenly bodies. The enduring repetitive cycles obviously made a profound impression upon the ancient dwellers on the Nile. Since the Nile River in Egypt is but a thin ribbon in a vast land with a full population, Egypt is, and from its beginning, was crowded providing the basis for easy transportation up and down the smooth Nile river. The transportation on the Nile was assisted by winds that blow from the north to the south, enabling travelers to take the current downstream to the north and to return aided by the light breezes from the north.

The ancient Egyptians observed movement, change, and life itself. What seems to have impressed them most was the degree to which a grand design appeared to be evident throughout the universe, enabling one who studied any part of the universe to understand the rest of it through the play of analogies. For example, the Nile was a river on the earth and the Milky Way was a "river in the sky." The observation of plant and animal life provided the opportunity to reflect on human life as well as with cycles of birth, growth, death, decay, and rebirth.

A major technology arose in the northern end of the Nile Valley. That technology is reflected in thousands of temples, tombs, pyramids, and in writings and scientific developments and discoveries. The observational technology produced the first zodiac, such as that seen in the Temple of Dendera of in the tomb of Seti I in the valley of the king at Waset (Luxor to the Arabs and Thebes to the Greeks), gives evidence of a long line of development. The construction of the Great Pyramid at Giza, attributed to Pharaoh Khufu, with its 2,200,000 limestone rocks averaging two tons each, some weighing as much as 40 tons, gives ample evidence of a high level of technical development. This is especially true when we realize that until the present time, no one appears to have been able to repeat the feat.

But given these and many other examples of high-level technical developments in Egypt, what is important is not so much the level of technical development as the *philosophical orientation of the users of the technology*. The purpose to which technology was put was to develop a greater understanding of man's relationship to nature and mankind's place in nature. This is in stark contrast to some contemporary expressions about purposes of technology. Today we seem to seek technical developments for the sole purpose of *exploiting* the environment for personal gains in wealth and power. Sometimes the goal of technology is expressed merely as one of helping people or nations to know, but toward *what end?*

At this point we need to return to George G.M. James (1976), who has given an excellent summary description of the Egyptian Mystery System. The ultimate aim of education in Egypt was for a person to become "one with God" or to "become like God." The path to the development of god-like qualities was through the development of virtue. A person was seen as being essentially spiritual whose essence was housed in a finite body. It was the spirit that had an eternal existence. The capacity of a person to become god-like was determined by the degree to which the person was able to overcome certain natural impediments of the body, these were character flaws. Virtue was the antidote to character flaws. But virtue could be achieved only through special study and effort. According to George G.M. James, the following 10 virtues were sought by students in the ancient Egyptian Mystery System:

1. Control of thought

2. Control of action

3. Devotion of purpose

4. Faith in the Master's ability to teach the truth

5. Faith in one's ability to assimilate the truth

6. Faith in our self to wield the truth

7. Freedom from resentment under persecution

8. Freedom from resentment under wrong

9. Ability to distinguish right from wrong

10. Ability to distinguish the real from the unreal

Even a brief study of this list of 10 virtues will reveal just how different it is in character from typical educational objectives with which most of us are familiar. In *Stolen Legacy*, George G.M. James goes into much greater detail to explain and to interpret the meaning of these 10 virtues.

George James also tells us that the center of the higher education system in ancient Egypt was located at the ancient Egyptian city of Waset, which means "the septer," after the town or nome (province) from which this small city sprang. It was sometimes referred to as the city of Amun, which was the name of the great god. Apparently, Waset was so important that it was sometimes simply referred to as "The City." Waset was later given the name Thebes by European invaders, and after that, the name Luxor by the Arab invaders. Various sections of the city of Waset had their own names. One section of the city was called Ipet-Isut, which means "Most Select of Places." Later populations would refer to it as Karnak, where a great temple now stands. Another part of Waset was called the Southern Opet or sanctuary. Later populations would refer to this section as Luxor, the name by which the whole city is now called.

And so, it was at Waset (Thebes or Luxor) at which we find located the oldest records of a university headquarters. We may think of this as the main branch. Speculation places the age of this headquarters as far back as 3000 B.C. There was another "grand lodge" in lower or northern Egypt dedicated to God in the name of Osiris. It was called the Osiriaca. This lodge had branches in other parts of the Egyptian sphere of influence. According to George James, several were located as follows: There was an Ionian Temple at Dydma; there was Euclid's Lodge at Megara, there was Pythagoras's Lodge at Cortona, and there was the Orphic Temple at Delphi.

We begin to get some inkling of the high level of esteem with which Greek and Romans regarded Egyptian civilization by a review of the activities of the Europeans when confronted with African civilization. It is hard to account for the behavior of European conquerors of Kemet except to note that they must have felt themselves to be in the presence of a superior civilization. They tried to imitate it. Kamil (1976) notes that

> The rule of the Ptolemies is noted for its architectural activity and the Greeks conscientiously endeavored to add to the splendor of national buildings after a priest had told Alexander the he was the son of Amon and should revere him. The Romans too repaired ruins and built temples in the traditional style, each retaining something of the earlier grandeur. But it was a losing battle, the past was not to be recaptured. Thebes could hardly hide its well worn wrinkles and a time weathered quality lay over the Metropolis. (p. 18)

Not only were buildings copied, European kings and people joined the African religions in Africa and in Europe. It is this *African religion* of Isis, Osiris, Horus, and Amen (Amon or Amun) that remained one of the major religions of Europe until the national government of Rome installed Christianity as the state religion, after the council of Nicea, nearly 300 years after the death of Christ.

Parenthetically, we can illustrate at this point the close connection between education and religion. We can also show some antecedents of western religion. In doing this, we take our material directly from the remains of the monuments themselves, in this case the Temple of Luxor. As Kamil states,

> The story of the birthroom is depicted in three rows on the left hand wall. From left to right in the lower row the God Khnum molds the infant. Amenhotep and his guardian spirit or Ka, and fashions them on a potter's wheel. The Goddess Isis sits in the presence of Amon. In the center row, Amon is led by Ibis-headed God of Wisdom to the queen's bed chamber, where he approached her to beget the child already moulded by Khnum. The pregnancy and confinement are attended by Bes and Thoueris, the patron deities of childbirth. After the delivery Amon stands with the child in his arms in the presence of Hathor and Mut. On the much damaged top row are the suckling of the infant king, his guardian spirits, and his presentation to Amon by Horus who promised him "million of years like Ra." In the corner the grown Amen-Hotep stands as King. (p. 32)

Here we have then in the 18th dynasty a visual record of the virgin birth of Amen-Hotep. We find the same scene portrayed in the mortuary temple of Hatshepsut. Once again, it is in the birth collonade of that temple.

> The birth Colonnade corresponding exactly to the Punt Colonnade is already mentioned. It was constructed to allay concern about Hatshepsut's right to the throne. The theory of divine origin was above discussion, let alone dispute, and this is shown in a scene of the rams headed Khnum shaping Hatshepsut and her Ka on the potter's wheel under instructions from Amon who has impregnated the queen's mother Ahmose, full with child. She radiates joy, stands dignified in her pregnancy, smiling a smile of supreme contentment as she is led to the birthroom. Unfortunately, most of the scene in which Amon and the queen's mother are borne to the heavens by two goddess[es] seated on a lion headed couch is badly damaged. (Kamil, 1976, p. 32)

The careful listener may wonder why we skipped from a period in the 12th dynasty over as far as the 18th dynasty. It must be noted here that during this period the government of Egypt was in the hands of invading kings, the Hyksos from Asia. However, their reign is less important than it might be for a very simple reason. They seem to have had little to offer to Kemet. As Riefstahl (1964) observed,

Since the Hyksos has scant culture of their own, they readily adopted Egyptian arts, and customs, even to some extent Egyptian religion. The new rulers took over the Titulary of Egyptian kings; like the latter, they were "sons of Re," the ancient Egyptian solar god from which all pharaohs claim descent. In their capitol at Avaris in the Delta, they set up their own thunder god, who was identified with the Egyptian God Seth. Sparse remains indicate that they added to and embellished Egyptian temples, while despoiling others. Though what little survives from the Hyksos periods in the way of art and architecture shows decline in skill, extant papyri indicate that the ancient learning continued undiminished in the temples. (p. 22)

Certain authors have looked at the initiation system that still exists in West Africa. It is good to do this because that system is a direct outgrowth of the more ancient initiation system that was utilized in the Nile Valley. Contemporary information and historical study of the initiation in West Africa reveals that the process operated in the following way. According to Pierre Erny in his book *Childhood and Cosmo* (1973), the following things were included in the initiation process:

1. The initiates were physically segregated from the regular activity of daily life.

2. They retreated from their familiar environment to an environment that enabled them to get more directly in touch with nature. This symbolized a move from the infantile situation into a situation that would allow for more maturity.

3. The initiate joined with other initiated of the same age and shared their lives in common, since the common living experience was also a common learning experience.

4. The initiates were separated from their parents in addition to being separated from the large community.

5. The initiates had to renounce all that recalls the past existence.

6. The initiates were then taught by the old men and old women of the village or town.

7. The initiates frequently went nude or wore clothes made of grass to symbolize the clothes of the first men or women.

8. The initiates underwent purification baths.

9. During the course of initiation a number of tests of audacity, courage, fasting, flogging, hazing, mutations, scarifications were conducted. (The purpose of the test was to give the opportunity for the initiate to

demonstrate a refusal to take life as it is given as a way of opening the mind to beauty, joy and ecstasy.)

10. Initiates learned a new and secret language.
11. Initiates were given new names.
12. The initiation processes symbolize a rebirth.
13. The initiation process included a number of exercises and things to be learned such as physical and military training, songs, dances, how to handle sacred things such as math and tools.

Dadisi Sonyika summarizes the initiation process into seven steps:

1. Separation.
2. Location in a sacred place.
3. Symbolic death and burial.
4. Testing or revelation.
5. Testing.
6. Resurrection (symbolic).
7. Reintroduction or reincorporation of the initiate into the larger community.

It can be seen from Stierlin's study (1978) of I. Schwaller de Lubicz's two-volume work *Her-Bak* (1950) that the West African initiation as described by Sonyika and Erny are congruent with the initiations that are described by I. Schwaller de Lubicz, which are based on the study of documents, carvings, and paintings from ancient Egypt. At its base, initiation is a comprehensive education system. In addition to the narrowly vocational aims, one can discern in the ancient Egyptian and ancient African educational system that the goals were the following:

1. Unity of the person, unity of the tribe, and unity with nature.
2. The development of social responsibility.
3. The development of character.
4. The development of spiritual power.

It was these higher aims that drove the educational process. Vocational skill training was merely a small part of the whole process.

In the ancient Egyptian educational system little thought seems to have been given to the question of the "inept intellectual capacity" of a person. Much more attention was given to character as an impediment or as a facilitator of educational development. While learning obviously was done by individuals, the picture that we get of the method used is that it was a collective rather than an individual effort. The educational process was designed in such a way that it seemed a true rebirth that occurs through a successive series of personal and social transformations.

Initiatives were deeply emersed in a comprehensive process. It was an interactive process. There were interactions among students and interactions between student and teacher. The process was full including much time for stories, examination of signs, symbols, the use of proverbs, the use of songs, dances, and so forth, all combined to convey values and a special view of the world. Teachers or "masters" *modeled* the behavior that they expected the initiates to learn. The masters were alert and in a position to react to and to nurture the direct experience of students in order that they could experience to learn higher level lessons.

At its base, the educational process was a religious process in the broadest sense of that word. The entire living environment was organized and constructed down to the smallest detail as a teaching environment. The architecture was symbolic down to the smallest detail. Even the layout of buildings within a city carried symbolic meaning. Clothing that was worn, names that were given, everything had multi-levels of meaning. This indicated a full-time commitment to the goal of personal *transformation* through education.

The best single description of education in ancient Egypt is given by Isha Schwaller de Lubicz. In two books, she presents her findings through the eyes of an initiate, Her-Bak. Isha Schwaller de Lubicz and her husband R.A. Schwaller de Lubicz spent nearly 15 years in detailed study of the Temple of Luxor and its environs. R.A. Schwaller de Lubicz has written numbers of important books on that work, among them *The Temple in Man* and *Symbol and the Symbolic*. Both Schwaller de Lubiczes tried to "enter into the mentality of the Egyptians" by in-depth study of their records, both written and archeological. In Isha Schwaller de Lubicz's books, almost all narrative is supported by illustrations of temple carvings, drawings, relief carvings, and building configurations, primarily at Luxor and Karnak temples in Waset.

It must be kept in mind that both Luxor Temple and Karnak Temple are built on the site of older temples! For example, the White Chapel, the oldest part of the 18th-dynasty temple at Karnak, is a reconstruction from fragments that were made by crushing the old chapel. The small pieces were then used as "seeds" from which the new Temple of Amon would grow. The fragments were found in the third Pylon of the Temple of Amon. The older temple, the White Chapel, was built by Sesostris during the 12th dynasty (1950 B.C.) as an offering to the great Black God Min (Stierlin, 1978). Both represent extensions of religious and educational practices that were known from the beginnings of Egyptian civilization.

While no one can be certain of all the details of ancient Egyptian culture, one must respect writers such as the Schwaller de Lubiczes who do not stray far from primary sources, as best they can be understood.

## The Aims of Egyptian Education

We must keep in mind that the Egyptians made no separation between "church and state," or for that matter, between religion and life. They lived a totally religious life, just as is the case with traditional African religions today. Therefore, education was religious at its base.

The lower education system, no matter how unstructured, allowed for a natural progress along a path that reached certain choice points. Having started along a path of advanced education, a learner could reach the major choice of his or her life, according to Isha Schwaller de Lubicz, *the choice between leadership and high positions or knowledge and wisdom*. The learner who chose ambition also chose limits. It was said that "ambition does to intuition what weevils do to wheat." On the other hand, for one who was able to sacrifice personal ambition, the act of sacrifice was said to "defend consciousness against the deadly effect of the search for satisfaction." For that person the path leading to wisdom was open. The initiate could reach the Outer Temple or "Peristyle" where *utilitarian* knowledge was mastered. However, once admitted to the Inner Temple the initiate learned about symbols and came to know him or herself. Undoubtedly, as George G.M. James (1976) has so clearly shown, Greek students of the African "mysteries" came to respect this goal, "man know thyself," which has been falsely attributed to the Greek latecomer of latest dynastic time, Socrates. The highest aim of Egyptian education was for one to become God-like through the revelation of one's own "Neter," or how God is revealed in the person.

## Method in Eyptian Pedagogy

Serious education began by putting the initiate on the path of observation of nature. Usually the initiate would be assigned to a master as an apprentice. But the purpose of the apprenticeship was for the student to learn the laws of matter (materials). It was the knowledge of these laws that separated the master craftsman from a mere worker. So, the "observation" of nature was really a participatory observation. Revealed in any craft were nature's laws. During the apprenticeship, the initiate was confronted with problems of conscience. This would allow for the development of a sense of responsibility and judgment. At the end of a successful apprenticeship, the initiate was offered the chance to choose between the two paths, *political power* and *wisdom.*

Heavy use was made of proverbs, songs, and stories. Direct or symbolic lessons were taught through these. It was the fundamental belief in the unity or interconnectedness of all things that made the use of analogies such a powerful pedagogical tool "for *above* is exalted by below" (Reed, 1978, p. 85). The use of proverbs and analogies permeates African and African Diasporan culture to this very day.

Parenthetically, it is interesting that the racist psychologists claim that Black people are not capable of "Level II thinking," the kind of abstract thinking that is reflected in proverbs and analogies. To the contrary, this is our strong suit. It is the mismatch in experiential content between such psychologists and African-Americans that causes them to miss the extensive use of proverbs and analogies among us.

The African reader of ancient Egyptian writings will find familiar methodology in the use of such things as the sayings of Ptahotep, V Dynasty (circa 2350 B.C.):

> Do not be arrogant because of your knowledge, but confer with the ignorant man as with the learned, for the limit of skill has not been attained, and there is no craftsman who has (fully) acquired his mastery. Good speech is more hidden than malachite, yet is found in the possession of women slaves at the millstones. (Simpson, 1972, p. 161)

Then there are the teachings of Kagemni that are contained in the same Papyrus, Prisse, that contains the sayings of Ptahotep:

> [T]he submissive man prospers, the moderate man is praised, the tent is open for the silent man, and the place of the contented man is wide. Do not talk (freely), for the flint knives are sharpen against the one who strays from the road; there is no hastening, except indeed against his misdeed. (Simpson, 1972, p. 177)

The instructions of Amenomope are estimated to have been written during the 18th dynasty just before the Amarna period, possibly during the reign of Amenhotep III. These sayings have close parallels to later Hebrew scriptures in the Book of Proverbs.

> The hot-headed man in the temple is like a tree grown indoors; only for a moment does it put forth roots. It reaches its end in the carpentry shop, it is floated away from its place, or fire is its funeral pyre. The truly temperate man sets himself apart. He is like a tree grown in a sunlit field. But it flourishes, it

doubles its yield. It stands before its owner; its fruit is something sweet, its shade pleasant; and it reaches its end as a statute. (Wilson, 1972, p. 246)

When we look at the Memphite Theology (Lichtheim, 1975), writings that are estimated to have been composed at the beginning of the pyramid age, we see something remarkably similar to the method of Karl Marx, the dialectic, complete with the use of contradictions. In the Memphite Theology, writings on stone at Memphis in Egypt, we find the doctrine of the four elements and the four qualities (James, 1976). This "law of opposites" (the relationship between pairs of elements) sets up the conditions under which creativity occurs. The Pyramid texts also use the principle of opposites in the description of the African "pantheon," or place of "the Gods." Like the later Greek and Roman copies, there was an Ennead—a pantheon of nine Gods, or more correctly, a diagram of nine aspects of the one Great Neter (God).

Atum

Shu (Air)     —     Tefnut (Moisture)

Geb (Earth)     —     Nut (Sky)

Osirus   —   Isis      Seth   —   Nephthys

In early times the Sun God had his own family of gods that was also the supreme council of the gods. This group, which had its chief center at the Temple of the Sun at Heliopolis, was the Ennead, "the Nine," consisting of four interrelated couples surmounted by one common ancestor. This Ennead or "Nine" may be placed in contrast to the "Eight," for "Eight" comprised elements of cosmic disorder, whereas the "Nine" contained only progressive steps of cosmic order: air and moisture, earth and sky, and the beings on earth.

## The Content of Egyptian Pedagogy

I have already referred to George G.M. James's list of curriculum content. Those courses, grammar, rhetoric, logic, arithmetic, astronomy, geometry, and music were the liberating or liberal arts. They supported the quest of the initiate for the highest form of self-knowledge. The initiate would study for *form, name, place,* and *symbol* of things. Having done that, it was believed that the *function* of things would be revealed.

The important thing to remember is that *nature itself,* the environment or the person, was the basic content for study. In addition, the study of nature was facilitated by the study of symbols, stories, proverbs, songs, puzzles, rhythm, and the sacred writings of the Mdw Ntr (hieroglyphics). These studies also gave insight into human nature, which was as shown before, merely the study of one aspect of nature.

# Conclusion

In the final analysis, the ancient Egyptian sought MAAT (truth, justice, and order); to be more correct, I should say that they sought to become one with MAAT, the cosmic order.

Our window on what was a well-developed education system is through ancient Kemet. Even though the best records in antiquity are found in Kemet, the picture is not yet complete. Suffice it to say that ancient Kemet was an African culture and that it shared then and shares now in the greater cultural unity of the African continent and in the diaspora of ancient African people.

A careful study and reconstruction of this aspect of our African past can give guidance to the reconstruction and development of educational aims, methods, and content appropriate to the children of the sun. As Gerald Massey has said,

> Truth is all powerful with its silent power
> If only whispered and never heard about
> But working secretly almost unseen, except in some excommunicated book
> Truth is like lightning with its errand done before you hear the thunder.

HOTEP

## REFERENCES

ben-Jochannan, Y. (1971). *Africa: Mother of Western civilization.* New York Alkebulan Books.

Churchward, A. (1978). *Signs and symbols of primordial man: The evolution of religious doctrines from the eschatology of the ancient Egyptians.* Westport, CT: Greenwood Press.

DeGramont, S. (1977). *The strong brown god: The story of the Niger River.* Boston: Houghton Mifflin.

Deren, M. (1951). *Divine horsemen: The living gods of Haiti.* New York: Delta.

Diop, C.A. (1978). *Cultural Unity of Black Africa: the Domains of Patriarchy and of Matriarchy in Classical Antiquity.* Chicago: Third World Press.

Drower, M. (1970). *Nubia: A drowning land.* New York: Atheneum.

Erny, P. (1973). *Childhood and cosmos: The social psychology of the Black African child.* New York: New Perspectives.

Frankfort, H. (1969). *Kingship and the gods: A study of ancient Near Eastern religion as the integration of society and nature.* Chicago: University of Chicago Press.

Frankfort, H., Irwin, W.A., & Wilson, J.A. (1977). *The intellectual adventure of ancient man: An essay of speculative thought in the ancient Near East.* Chicago: University of Chicago Press.

Jackson, J. (1980). *Introduction to African civilizations.* Secaucus, NJ: Citadel Press.

Jahn, J. (1961). *Muntu: The new African culture.* New York: Grove Press.

James, G.G.M. (1976). *Stolen legacy.* San Francisco: Julian Richardson.

Kamil, J. (1976). *Luxor: A guide to ancient Thebes.* New York: Longman.

Lichtheim, M. (1975). *Ancient Egyptian literature: A book of readings.* Berkeley: University of California Press.

Mertz, B. (1978). *Red land, Black land: Daily life in ancient Egypt.* New York: Dodd, Mead.

Reed, B. (1978). *Rebel in the soul: A sacred text of ancient Egypt.* New York: Inner Traditions International.

Riefstahl, E. (1964). *Thebes in the time of Amunhotep III.* Norman: University of Oklahoma Press.

Schwaller de Lubicz, R.A. (1977). *The temple in man.* Brookline, MA: Autumn Press.

Simpson, W.K. (Ed.). (1972). *The literature of ancient Egypt: An anthology of stories, instructions, and poetry.* New Haven, CT: Yale University Press.

Stierlin, H. (1978). *The world of the pharaohs.* New York: Sunflower.

Thompson, R.F., & Cornet, J. (1981). *The four moments of the sun: Kongo art in two worlds.* Washington, DC: National Gallery of Art.

Williams, B. (1980). The lost pharaohs of Nubia. *Archaeology, 33,* 12–21.

Wilson, J.A. (1972). *The burden of Egypt: An interpretation of ancient Egyptian culture.* Chicago: University of Chicago Press.

# PART II

# Reading Methodologies

Reading has always been important to African Americans. The culture has always stressed excellence in education, as far back as the slave narratives, in which those enslaved Africans who were deemed intelligent were called "double-headed." For example, Cornelius (1991) describes Enoch Golden as a slave who could read and write and "knowed so much" that the other slaves called him a "double-headed negro." Before Enoch died, he confessed that he "been the death o' many negroes 'cause he taught so many to read and write" (p. 78).

Another enslaved African stated,

> None of us was 'lowed to see a book or try to learn. They say we git smarther than they was if we learn anything, but we slips around and gits hold of Webster's old blue-back speller and we hides it till way in the night and then we lights a little pine-torch, and studies that spelling book. (Botkin, 1945, p. 91)

In cabins, "play schools" were organized by the enslaved Africans. Free Black adults gathered in "stealing the meeting" sessions to teach their brothers, sisters, and friends to read (Anderson, 1988, p. 17). To this day, the love of reading and excellence in education are prominent aspects of Black culture (see "What Black Parents Expect From Public Schools," 1994).

Reading methodology is one of the issues in teaching Black students to read. Methodology became a highly discussed issue in the 1800s. The eclectic, or sight-word, method originated in Germany and France and was adopted in the United States by Horace Mann, first secretary of the State Board of Education in Massachusetts in the mid-1800s. He felt that the old ways of teaching reading were boring, and he advocated the whole-word approach so that students could avoid "rows of lank, stark, immovable letters" (Mathews, 1966, p. 77).

In the early 1900s, John Dewey's philosophy of progressive education had a reading component. In his philosophy, the teaching of reading was postponed and the phonics method of reading was replaced with the eclectic approach (Mathews, 1966).

During the progressive education era, which lasted from 1920 to 1970, scholars held little confidence that Black and other poor children could even learn. As one educator stated, "at least a third of the entire school population is incapable of mastering the stock tools of learning (reading and writing) well enough to profit from textbook instruction" (Mathews, 1966, p. 146).

Jeanne Chall (1995), a professor at Harvard University, analyzed 85 studies and concluded that the reason for low literacy rates was that an incorrect reading method was used by most teachers in public schools. In her study, Chall described the various ways children are taught to read. She concluded that the method used by most public schools—look-say/whole-word—was incorrect. And she held that the other approach, the code approach, based on the decoding of words using the most regular patterns, was more effective. During the 1970s, according to Chall, there was a period when both methods—phonics and sight—were used in schools. For examples of this combination, see "Civil Rights Leader Eyes Success of Phonics at Ravenswood" (1970) and Hoover, Dabney, and Lewis (1990).

During the 1980s, however, another sight-word approach became popular—whole language. Whole language stresses literature and endorses memorizing words by sight and guessing at those not recognized. Kenneth Goodman (as cited in Flesch, 1981), one of the major proponents of whole language, endorsed teaching children to read using the "blank" strategy: "Say 'blank' and go ahead. What happens is that if a word is important to the story, about the third or fourth time the kids have got it. Because each successive context gives them more clues" (p. 91). Whole language has at least one positive influence on reading—its emphasis on literature.

A track record of more than 30 years of teaching reading to African American students exists. This record tells us that Black students learn best with a broad-based approach that includes systematic phonics, among other components such as literature, comprehension, spelling, and critical thinking (Chall, 1995; Delpit, 1995; Foorman, Francis, Beeler, Winicates, & Fletcher, 1997; Hoover et al., 1990; McPhail, this volume; Weber, 1971). We endorse this proven approach but include a variety of descriptions of reading methodologies in this section.

Part II opens with Ronald Edmonds's 1979 classic article on the components of an effective school. Although much has been written on the topic since then, little has been added to our collective knowledge on the subject beyond Edmonds's insights. In chapter 4, George O. Cureton discusses a Black learning style in the context of a decoding approach—action reading. In chapter 5, Mary Eleanor Rhodes Hoover endorses phonics and decodable text, among other techniques. In chapter 6, Nancy Ichinaga advocates use of one of the decodable text methods. In chapter 7, Irving Pressley McPhail evaluates Weber's seminal 1971 article on "Four Successful Schools," which proposes a decoding/decodable text approach. All these articles also stress the importance of major reading categories of vocabulary, comprehension, fluency, phonemic awareness, and literature.

Other authors included in this section are Linda B. Akanbi, who emphasizes the use of multicultural literature in chapter 8, focusing on African American themes; Rudine Sims Bishop, who speaks of literacy and literature as "jumping into another world" of liberation in chapter 9; E.R. Marnell Sr. and Bill Hammond, who offer a dual-text strategy for reading in content areas in chapter 10; Charlotte Rose Sadler, who describes a number of useful comprehension strategies in chapter 11; and Dorothy S. Strickland, who in chapter 12 rejects "low-level impoverished basics" in favor of literacy approaches that stress meaning.

In conclusion, as Hoover and colleagues (1990) have noted, we need to stop asking why children don't succeed, and focus on implementing those factors that ensure success.

## REFERENCES

Anderson, J.D. (1988). *The education of Blacks in the south, 1860–1935.* Chapel Hill: University of North Carolina Press.

Botkin, B.A. (Ed.). (1945). *Lay my burden down: A folk history of slavery.* Chicago: University of Chicago Press.

Chall, J.S. (1995). *Learning to read: The great debate.* New York: Wadsworth. (Original work published 1967)

Civil rights leader eyes success of phonics at Ravenswood. (1970, December 3). *Palo Alto Times,* p. 2.

Cornelius, J. (1991). *"When I can read my title clear": Literacy, slavery and religion in the antebellum South.* Columbia: University of South Carolina Press.

Delpit, L.D. (1995). *Other people's children.* New York: New Press.

Flesch, R.F. (1981). *Why Johnny still can't read.* New York: Harper & Row.

Foorman, B.R., Francis, D.J., Beeler, T., Winicates, D., & Fletcher, J.M. (1997). Early interventions for children with reading problems: Study designs and preliminary findings. *Learning Disabilities: A Multidisciplinary Journal, 8*(1), 63–71.

Hoover, M.R., Dabney, N., & Lewis, S. (Eds.). (1990). *Successful Black and minority schools: Classic models.* San Francisco: Julian Richardson.

Mathews, M.M. (1966). *Teaching to read, historically considered.* Chicago: University of Chicago Press.

Weber, G. (1971). *Inner-city children can be taught to read: Four successful schools* (Occasional Papers No. 18). Washington, DC: Council for Basic Education.

What Black parents expect from public schools. (1994, November 7). *Jet,* p. 14.

# CHAPTER 3

# Effective Schools for the Urban Poor

## *Ronald Edmonds*

I t seems only fair that the reader know what biases, if any, inform the summary remarks I plan to make. Equity will be the focus of my discussion. By *equity* I mean a simple sense of fairness in the distribution of the primary goods and services that characterize our social order. At issue is the efficacy of a minimum level of goods and services to which we are all entitled. Some of us, rightly, have more goods and services than others, and my sense of equity is not disturbed by that fact. Others of us have almost no goods and access to only the most wretched services, and that deeply offends my simple sense of fairness and violates the standards of equity by which I judge our social order.

I measure our progress as a social order by our willingness to advance the equity interests of the least among us. Thus, increased wealth or education for the top of our social order is quite beside the point of my basis for assessing our progress toward greater equity. Progress requires public policy that begins by making the poor less poor and ends by making them not poor at all. This discussion of education will apply just such a standard to public schooling. Equitable public schooling begins by teaching poor children what their parents want them to know and ends by teaching poor children at least as well as it teaches middle class children.

Inequity in American education derives first and foremost from our failure to educate the children of the poor. *Education* in this context refers to early acquisition of those basic school skills that assure pupils successful access to the next level of schooling. If that seems too modest a standard, note that as of now the schools that teach the children of the poor are dismal failures even by such a modest standard. Thus, to raise a generation of children whose schools meet such a standard would be an advance in equity of the first order. I offer this standard at the outset to note that its attainment is far more a matter of politics than of social science. Social science refers to those formal experiments and inquiries carried out by sociologists, psychologists, educational researchers, and other academicians whose inquiries are described as seeking the relationship

Adapted from *Educational Leadership* (1979), *37*(1), 15–24. Originally published by CEMREL, Inc.

among school characteristics, pupil performance, pupil family background, and pupil social class. Politics in this case refers to the substantive and procedural bases for deciding the distribution of educational resources, defining the uses to which the schools are to be put and establishing the criteria by which school personnel are to be evaluated.

Specifically, I require that an effective school bring the children of the poor to those minimal masteries of basic school skills that now describe minimally successful pupil performance for the children of the middle class. My subsequent discussion of certain of the literature on school effects must not be taken to mean that whether or not schools are effective derives from matters of research or social science. Such is not the case. Schools teach those they think they must and when they think they needn't, they don't. That fact has nothing to do with social science, except that the children of social scientists are among those whom schools feel compelled to teach effectively.

There has never been a time in the life of the U.S. public school when we have not known all we needed to in order to teach all those whom we chose to teach. The discussion of research literature that follows may illuminate that fact, but it cannot change it.

Weber was an early contributor to the literature on the school determinants of achievement. In his 1971 study of four instructionally effective inner-city schools, Weber intended his study to be explicitly alternative to Coleman et al. (1966), Jensen (1969), and other researchers who had satisfied themselves that low achievement by poor children derived principally from inherent disabilities characterizing the poor. Weber focused on the characteristics of four inner-city schools in which reading achievement was clearly successful for poor children on the basis of national norms. All four schools had "strong leadership" in that their principal was instrumental in setting the tone of the school; helping decide on instructional strategies; and organizing and distributing the schools' resources. All four schools had "high expectations" for all their students. Weber was careful to point out that high expectations are not sufficient for school success, but they are certainly necessary. All four schools had an orderly, relatively quiet, and pleasant atmosphere. All four schools strongly emphasized pupil acquisition of reading skills and reinforced that emphasis by careful and frequent evaluation of pupil progress.

Weber went on to identify and discuss additional reading personnel, phonics, and individualization as important to the instructional success of the four schools. I'll not endorse or pursue these latter Weber findings—first, because subsequent research does not sustain their relevance as it does leadership, expectations, atmosphere, reading emphasis, and assessment; and second, my own research, of which more will be said later, gives greater weight to the variables noted first rather than later. Despite these reservations, my own view is that Weber was essentially correct both in concept and basic research design, considering the relative modesty of his enterprise.

In 1974, the State of New York's Office of Education Performance Review published a study that confirmed certain of Weber's major findings. The state identified two inner-city New York City public schools, both of which were serving an analogous, predominantly poor pupil population. One of the schools was high achieving, and the other was low achieving. Both schools were studied in an attempt to identify those differences that seemed most responsible for the achievement variation between the two schools. The following findings were reported:

- The differences in student performance in these two schools seemed to be attributed to factors under the schools' control.
- Administrative behavior, policies, and practices in the schools appeared to have a significant impact on school effectiveness.
- The more effective inner-city school was led by an administrative team that provided a good balance between management and instructional skills.
- The administrative team in the more effective school had developed a plan for dealing with the reading problem and had implemented the plan throughout the school.
- Classroom reading instruction did not appear to differ between the two schools since classroom teachers in both schools had problems in teaching reading and assessing pupils' reading skills.
- Many professional personnel in the less effective school attributed children's reading problems to nonschool factors and were pessimistic about their ability to have an impact, creating an environment in which children failed because they were not expected to succeed. However, in the more effective school, teachers were less skeptical about their ability to have an impact on children.
- Children responded to unstimulating learning experiences predictably—they were apathetic, disruptive, or absent.

Admittedly, this study has not identified all factors relating to student reading achievement. However, these preliminary findings are consistent with a significant body of other research. While more research should be encouraged, it is even more important that we begin to apply what is already known.

This study has shown that school practices have an effect on reading achievement. At the very least, the children in low achieving schools should have the opportunities available to the children of the high achieving schools. These opportunities, which do not result from higher overall expenditures, are clearly within the reach of any school today. (pp. vi, vii)

For our purposes, these findings reinforce the relevance to pupil performance of the institutional elements of leadership, expectations, and atmosphere. For further evidentiary support of these findings, see the Madden, Lawson, and Sweet (1976) study of school effectiveness in California. In a more rigorous and sophisticated version of the Weber and New York studies, Madden and his colleagues studied 21 pairs of California elementary schools, matched on the basis of pupil characteristics and differing only on the basis of pupil performance on standardized achievement measures. The 21 pairs of schools were studied in an effort to identify those institutional characteristics that seemed most responsible for the achievement differences that described the 21 high-achieving schools and the 21 low-achieving schools. The major findings are the following 10:

1. In comparison to teachers at lower-achieving schools, teachers at higher-achieving schools report that their principals provide them with a significantly greater amount of support.

2. Teachers in higher-achieving schools were more task-oriented in their classroom approach and exhibited more evidence of applying appropriate principles of learning than did teachers in lower-achieving schools.

3. In comparison to classrooms in lower-achieving schools, classrooms in higher-achieving schools provided more evidence of student-monitoring process, student effort, happier children, and an atmosphere conducive to learning.

4. In comparison to teachers at lower-achieving schools, teachers at higher-achieving schools reported that they spent relatively more time on social studies, less time on mathematics and physical education/health, and about the same amount of time on reading/language development and science.

5. In contrast to teachers at lower-achieving schools, teachers at higher-achieving schools report: (a) a larger number of adult volunteers in mathematics classes, (b) fewer paid aides in reading, and (c) they are more apt to use teacher aides for non-teaching tasks, such as classroom paperwork, watching children on the playground, and maintaining classroom discipline.

6. In comparison to teachers at lower-achieving schools, teachers at higher-achieving schools reported higher levels of access to "outside the classroom" materials.

7. In comparison to the teachers of lower-achieving schools, teachers at higher-achieving schools believed their faculty as a whole had less influence on educational decisions.

8. In comparison to teachers at lower-achieving schools, teachers at higher-achieving schools rated district administration higher on support services.

9. In comparison to grouping practices at lower-achieving schools, the higher-achieving schools divided classrooms into fewer groups for purposes of instruction.

10. In comparison to teachers in lower-achieving schools, teachers in higher-achieving schools reported being more satisfied with various aspects of their work. (pp. 4–9)

My own conclusion is that, aside from intrinsic merit, the California study is notable chiefly for its reinforcement of leadership, expectations, atmosphere, and instructional emphasis as consistently essential institutional determinants of pupil performance.

## The Brookover and Lezotte Study

I want to close this part of the discussion with summary remarks about an unusually persuasive study of school effects. In 1977, Brookover and Lezotte published their study *Changes in School Characteristics Coincident With Changes in Student Achievement*. We should take special note of this work partly because it is a formal extension of inquiries and analyses begun in two earlier studies, both of which reinforce certain of the Weber, Madden et al., and New York findings. The Michigan Department of Education's *Report of the 1974–1975 Michigan Cost Effectiveness Study* (1976) and the Brookover et al. study *Elementary School Climate and School Achievement* (1976) are both focused an those educational variables that are liable to school control and important to the quality of pupil performance. In response to both of these studies, the Michigan Department of Education asked Brookover and Lezotte to study a set of Michigan schools characterized by consistent pupil performance improvement or decline. The Brookover and Lezotte study (1977) is broader in scope than the two earlier studies and explicitly intended to profit from methodological and analytical lessons learned in them.

Since the early 1970s, the Michigan Department of Education has annually tested all Michigan pupils in public schools in grades 4 and 7. The tests are criterion-referenced standardized measures of pupil performance in basic school skills. Over time these data were used by the Michigan Department of Education to identify elementary schools characterized by consistent pupil-performance improvement or decline. Brookover and Lezotte (1977) chose eight of these schools to be studied (six improving, two declining). The schools were visited by trained interviewers who conducted interviews and administered questionnaires to a great many of the school personnel. The interviews and questionnaires were designed to identify differences between the improving and declining schools, and which differences seemed most important to the pupil performance variation between the two sets of schools. The following list gives the summary results:

1. The improving schools are clearly different from the declining schools in the emphasis their staff places on the accomplishment of the basic reading and mathematics objectives. The improving schools accept and emphasize the importance of these goals and objectives while declining schools give much less emphasis to such goals and do not specify them as fundamental.

2. There is a clear contrast in the evaluations that teachers and principals make of the students in the improving and declining schools. The staffs of the improving schools tend to believe that *all* of their students can master the basic objectives; and furthermore, the teachers perceive that the principal shares this belief. They tend to report higher and increasing levels of student ability, while the declining school teachers project the belief that students' ability levels are low, and therefore, they cannot master even these objectives.

3. The staff members of the improving schools hold decidedly higher and apparently increasing levels of expectations with regard to the educational accomplishments of their students. In contrast, staff members of the declining schools are much less likely to believe that their students will complete high school or college.

4. In contrast to the declining schools, the teachers and principals of the improving schools are much more likely to assume responsibility for teaching the basic reading and math skills and are much more committed to doing so. The staffs of the declining schools feel there is not much that teachers can do to influence the achievement of their students. They tend to displace the responsibility for skill learning on the parents or the students themselves.

5. Since the teachers in the declining schools believe that there is little they can do to influence basic skill learning, it follows they spend less time in direct reading instruction than do teachers in the improving schools. With the greater emphasis on reading and math objectives in the improving schools, the staffs in these schools devote a much greater amount of time toward achieving reading and math objectives.

6. There seems to be a clear difference in the principal's role in the improving and declining schools. In the improving schools, the principal

is more likely to be an instructional leader, more assertive in his/her institutional leadership role, more of a disciplinarian, and perhaps most of all, assumes responsibility for the evaluation of the achievement of basic objectives. The principals in the declining schools appear to be permissive and to emphasize informal and collegial relationships with the teachers. They put more emphasis on general public relations and less emphasis upon evaluation of the school's effectiveness in providing a basic education for the students.

7. The improving school staffs appear to show a greater degree of acceptance of the concept of accountability and are further along in the development of an accountability model. Certainly, they accept the Michigan Educational Assessment Program (MEAP) tests as one indication of their effectiveness to a much greater degree than the declining school staffs. The latter tend to reject the relevance of the MEAP tests and make little use of these assessment devices as a reflection of their instruction.

8. Generally, teachers in the improving schools are less satisfied than the staffs in the declining schools. The higher levels of reported staff satisfaction and morale in the declining schools seem to reflect a pattern of complacency and satisfaction with the current levels of educational attainment. On the other hand, the improving school staff members appear more likely to experience some tension and dissatisfaction with the existing condition.

9. Differences in the level of parent involvement in the improving and declining schools are not clear cut. It seems that there is less overall parent involvement in the improving schools; however, the improving school staffs indicated that their schools have higher levels of *parent-initiated* involvement. This suggests that we need to look more closely at the nature of the involvement exercised by parents. Perhaps parent initiated contact with the schools represents an effective instrument of educational change.

10. The compensatory education program data suggests differences between improving and declining schools, but these differences may be distorted by the fact that one of the declining schools had just initiated a compensatory education program. In general, the improving schools are not characterized by a high emphasis upon paraprofessional staff or heavy involvement of the regular teachers in the selection of students to be placed in compensatory education programs. The declining schools seem to have a greater number of different staff members involved in reading instruction and more teacher involvement in identifying students who are to be placed in compensatory education programs. The regular classroom teachers in the declining schools report spending more time planning for noncompensatory education

reading activities. The decliners also report greater emphasis on programmed instruction. (Brookover & Lezotte, 1977, pp. 79–82)

## The Search for Effective Schools Project

Before making summary remarks about the policy import of these several studies, I want to say something of my own research, *Search for Effective Schools: The Identification and Analysis of City Schools That Are Instructionally Effective for Poor Children* (Edmonds & Frederiksen, 1978). This discussion will describe our ongoing efforts to identify and analyze city schools that are instructionally effective for poor and/or minority children. I am pleased to note that we have already developed unusually persuasive evidence of the thesis we seek to demonstrate in the research under discussion. Our thesis is that all children are eminently educable and that the behavior of the school is critical in determining the quality of that education.

The Search for Effective Schools project began by answering the question: Are there schools that are instructionally effective for poor children? In September 1974, Lezotte, Edmonds, and Ratner described their analysis of pupil performance in the elementary schools that make up Detroit's Model Cities Neighborhood. All of the schools are located in inner-city Detroit and serve a predominantly poor and minority pupil population. Reading and math scores were analyzed from Detroit's spring 1973 use of the Stanford Achievement Test and the Iowa Test of Basic Skills. Of the 10,000 pupils in the 20 schools in the Model Cities Neighborhood, 2,500 were randomly sampled. With minor variation, the sample included eight pupils per classroom in each of the 20 schools. The mean math and reading scores for the 20 schools were compared with citywide norms. An effective school among the 20 was defined as being at or above the city average grade equivalent in math and reading. An ineffective school was defined as one below the city average. Using these criteria, 8 of the 20 schools were judged effective in teaching math, 9 were judged effective in teaching reading, and 5 were judged effective in teaching both math and reading.

We turned next to the problem of establishing the relationship between pupil family background and building effectiveness. Two schools among the 20, Duffield and Bunche, were matched on the basis of 11 social indicators. Duffield pupils averaged nearly four months above the city average in reading and math. Bunche pupils averaged nearly three months below the city reading average and 1.5 months below the city math average.

The similarity in the characteristics of the two pupil populations permits us to infer the importance of school behavior in making pupil performance independent of family background. The overriding point here is that, in and of itself, pupil family background neither causes nor precludes elementary school instructional effectiveness.

Despite the value of our early work in Detroit, we recognized the limitations of the Model Cities Neighborhood analysis. Our evaluation of school success with poor children had depended on evaluating schools with relatively homogeneous pupil populations. The numbers of schools were too few to justify firm conclusions. Finally, the achievement tests were normative, as was the basis for determining building effectiveness among the 20 schools. Even so, valuable lessons were learned in Detroit from which we would later greatly profit.

The second phase of the project was a reanalysis of the 1966 Equal Educational Opportunity Survey (EEOS) data (Frederiksen, 1975). Our purpose was to answer a number of research questions that required a data base both larger and richer than had been available to use in the Model Cities Neighborhood analysis. We retained our interest in identifying instructionally effective schools for the poor, but in addition, we wanted to study the effects of schools on children having different social backgrounds. Such an inquiry would permit us to evaluate school contributions to educational outcomes independent of our ability to match schools on the basis of the socioeconomic characteristics of their pupils.

Summarizing and oversimplifying results, we found at least 55 effective schools in the Northeast quadrant of the EEOS. Our summary definition of school effectiveness required that each school eliminate the relationship between successful performance and family background. The effective schools varied widely in racial composition, per-pupil expenditure, and other presumed determinants of school quality.

In our reanalysis of the EEOS, separate evaluations of the schools were made for subgroups of pupils of different races and home backgrounds. Schools were found to be consistently effective (or ineffective) in teaching subgroups of their populations that were homogeneous in race and economic condition. These schools were not found to be consistently effective in teaching children of differing economic condition and race. School effectiveness for a given level on Coleman et al.'s (1966) home items scale extended across racial lines. The prime factors that condition a school's instructional effectiveness appear to be principally economic and social, rather than racial.

Without seeking to match effective and ineffective schools on mean social-background variables, we found that schools that were instructionally effective for poor and Black children were indistinguishable from instructionally less effective schools on measures of pupil social background (mean father's and mother's education; category of occupation; percentage of White students; mean family size; and percentage of intact families). The large differences in performance between the effective and ineffective schools could not therefore be attributed to differences in the social class and family background of pupils enrolled in the schools. This finding is in striking contrast to that of other analyses of the EEOS, which have generally concluded that variability in performance levels from school to school is only minimally related to institutional characteristics.

A very great proportion of people in the United States believe that family background and home environment are principal causes of the quality of pupil performance. In fact, no notion about schooling is more widely held than the belief that the family is somehow the principal determinant of whether or not a child will do well in school. The popularity of that belief continues partly because many social scientists and opinion makers continue to espouse the belief that family background is chief cause of the quality of pupil performance. Such a belief has the effect of absolving educators of their professional responsibility to be instructionally effective.

## Basic Skills for All Children

While recognizing the importance of family background in developing a child's character, personality, and intelligence, I cannot overemphasize my rejection of the notion that a school is relieved of its instructional obligations when teaching the children of the poor. I reject such a notion partly because I recognize the existence of schools that successfully teach basic school skills to all children. Such success occurs partly because these schools are determined to serve all of their pupils without regard to family background. At the same time, these schools recognize the necessity of modifying curricular design, text selection, teaching strategy, and so on, in response to differences in family background among pupils in the school.

Our findings strongly recommend that all schools be held responsible for effectively teaching basic school skills to all children. We recommend that future studies of school and teacher effectiveness consider the stratification design as a means for investigating the separate relationship of programs and policies for pupils of differing family and social background. Information about individual student family background and social class is essential in our analysis if we are to disentangle the separate effects of pupil background and school social class makeup on pupil achievement. Moreover, studies of school effectiveness should be multivariate in character and employ longitudinal records of pupil achievement in a variety of areas of school learning.

The Search for Effective Schools project completed its analysis of social class, family background, and pupil performance for all Lansing, Michigan, pupils in grades 3–7. We identified five Lansing schools in which achievement seems independent of pupil social class. The achievement data are local and normative, and state and criterion. We used both sets of data to identify schools in which all pupils are achieving beyond minimum objectives, including most especially those children of low social class and poverty family background. We then gathered similar data for Detroit pupils in the elementary grades in schools whose pupil population is at least 15 percent poor.

Next will be an on-site study, which will compare Lansing's effective schools to its ineffective schools. Our basic notions of the character and origin of effective and ineffective school differences derive from past work in combination with ideas on school effects that I've held for a long time (Edmonds, 1978). On the basis of the review of the literature in this paper and the Search for Effective Schools project's earlier study in Detroit Model Cities and EEOS's Northeast quadrant, I offer the following distinguishing characteristics of schools that are instructionally effective for poor children:

- What effective schools share is a climate in which it is incumbent on all personnel to be instructionally effective for all pupils. That is not, of course, a very profound insight, but it does define the proper lines of research inquiry.

- What ought to be focused on are questions such as, What is the origin of that climate of instructional responsibility? If it dissipates, what causes it to do so? If it remains, what keeps it functioning? Our tentative answers are these: Some schools are instructionally effective for the poor because they have a tyrannical principal who compels the teachers to bring all children to a minimum level of mastery of basic skins. Some schools are effective because they have a self-generating teacher corps that has a critical mass of dedicated people who are committed to being effective for all children they teach. Some schools are effective because they have a highly politicized Parent–Teacher Organization that holds the schools to close instructional account. The point here is to make clear at the outset that no one model explains school effectiveness for the poor or any other social class subset. Fortunately, children know how to learn in more ways than we know how to teach, thus permitting great latitude in choosing instructional strategy. The great problem in schooling is that we know how to teach in ways that can keep some children from learning almost anything, and we often choose to thus proceed when dealing with the children of the poor.

One of the cardinal characteristics of effective schools is that they are as eager to avoid things that don't work as they are committed to implementing things that do.

# Summary

I want to end this discussion by noting as unequivocally as I can what seem to me the most tangible and indispensable characteristics of effective schools: (a) They have strong administrative leadership without which the disparate elements of good schooling can neither be brought together nor kept together; (b) Schools that are instructionally effective for poor children have a climate of expectation in which no children are permitted to fall below minimum but efficacious levels of achievement; (c) The school's atmosphere is orderly without being rigid, quiet without being oppressive, and generally conducive to the instructional business at hand; (d) Effective schools get that way partly by making it clear that pupil acquisition of basic school skills takes precedence over all other school activities; (e) When necessary, school energy and resources can be diverted from other business in furtherance of the fundamental objectives; and (f) There must be some means by which pupil progress can be frequently monitored. These means may be as traditional as classroom testing on the day's lesson or as advanced as criterion-referenced systemwide standardized measures. The point is that some means must exist in the school by which the principal and the teachers remain constantly aware of pupil progress in relationship to instructional objectives.

Two final points: First, how many effective schools would you have to see to be persuaded of the educability of poor children? If your answer is more than one, then I submit that you have reasons of your own for preferring to believe that basic pupil performance derives from family background instead of school response to family background. Second, whether or not we will ever effectively teach the children of the poor is probably far more a matter of politics than of social science, and that is as it should be.

While it may be improbable that our politics will ever bring us to educational equity for the poor, it is inconceivable that the National Institute of Education (NIE) or the American Educational Research Association (AERA) should do so. What I am therefore suggesting is that if you genuinely seek the means to educational equity for all our people, you must encourage parents' attention to politics as the greatest instrument of instructional reform extant. You must not for an instant suggest that social science as practiced in AERA or as subsidized at NIE will advance the equity interests of the poor. I mention AERA and NIE in this slightly disparaging manner for a particular reason. Their contribution to our national discourse on educational equity graphically illustrates my point that the poor are far more likely to be served by politics than by any equity interests to be found in the educational research establishment. That is, social service enterprises such as NIE are not substantively different from the schools whose study has been the object of this paper. Left to their own devices, social services serve those they think they must, and that does not often include the children of the poor. This is not meant to suggest that NIE does not support socially useful projects, carried out by men and women of substance and merit. It is merely meant to suggest that those who get NIE money will, more often than is helpful for our purposes, be White, and of very conventional social science wisdom. Being White and of conventional wisdom is not, of course, an intrinsic disability. However, the combination does preclude repudiation of those of our social science notions that are most pernicious when discussing school reform. Repudiation of the social science notion that family background is the principal cause of pupil acquisition of basic school skills is probably prerequisite to successful reform of public schooling for the children of the poor.

It seems to me, therefore, that what is left of this discussion are three declarative statements: (a) We can, whenever and wherever we choose, successfully teach all children whose schooling is of interest to us; (b) We already know more than we need to do that; and (c) Whether or not we do it must finally depend on how we feel about the fact that we haven't so far.

## REFERENCES

Brookover, W.B., & Lezotte, L.W. (1977). *Changes in school characteristics coincident with changes in student achievement.* East Lansing: Michigan State University, College of Urban Development.

Brookover, W.B., Schweitzer, J., Schneider, J., Beady, C., Flood, P., & Wisenbaker, J. (1976). *Elementary school climate and school achievement.* East Lansing: Michigan State University, College of Urban Development.

Coleman, J.S., Campbell, E.Q., Hobson, C.J., McPartland, J., Mood, A.M., Weinfeld, F.D., & York, R.L. (1966). *Equality of educational opportunity.* Washington, DC: U.S. Office of Education.

Edmonds, R. (1978). Alternative patterns for the distribution of social services. In W. Feinberg (Ed.), *Equality and social policy.* Urbana: University of Illinois Press.

Edmonds, R., & Frederiksen, J.R. (1978). *Search for effective schools: The identification and analysis of city schools that are instructionally effective for poor children.* Cambridge, MA: Harvard University, Center for Urban Studies.

Frederiksen, J. (1975). *School effectiveness and equality of educational opportunity.* Cambridge, MA: Harvard University, Center for Urban Studies.

Jensen, A.R. (1969, Winter). How much can we boost IQ and scholastic achievement? *Harvard Educational Review,* *39*(1), 1–123.

Lezotte, L., Edmonds, R., & Ratner, G. (1974). *Remedy for school failure to equitably deliver basic school skills.* Cambridge, MA: Harvard University, Center for Urban Studies.

Madden, J.V., Lawson, D.R., & Sweet, D. (1976). *School effectiveness study.* Sacramento: California Department of Education.

Michigan Department of Education, Research Evaluation and Assessment Services. (1976). *Report of the 1974–75 Michigan Cost Effectiveness Study.* Washington, DC: Capital Publications.

State of New York, Office of Education Performance Review. (1974). *School factors influencing reading achievement: A case study of two-inner city schools.* Albany: Author.

Weber, G. (1971). *Inner-city children can be taught to read: Four successful schools.* (Occasional Papers No. 18). Washington, DC: Council for Basic Education.

# CHAPTER 4

# Using a Black Learning Style

*George O. Cureton*

Is there such a thing as a Black learning style? Some argue indefatigably that there is not, while others argue just as vehemently that there is. Before we look more closely at this question, let's be sure what we are talking about. What do we mean by "Black learning style"?

Perhaps the term is at fault. What I am talking about is a style of learning for children, primarily in the inner city, primarily members of minority groups, who have traditionally had difficulty with academic school work, especially reading. For a complex of historical, sociological, and economic reasons, a majority of these children are Black.

Those who oppose the idea of a distinct "Black learning style" feel that to suggest a difference in learning style between Blacks and others is to reinforce the insidious myth that inner-city children are inferior. Instead, these opponents tell us, what we are really talking about is motivation. The inner-city child does not have the same motivation as do middle class children.

Yes and no. Motivation is important, in fact, necessary. But it will have little effect until the inner-city child's learning style has been established. Moreover, the type of motivation differs from that of the middle class children, who usually come to school already motivated to a considerable degree. The Jackies, our inner-city children, often do not. So it is important that we understand the type of motivation that turns them on and off to learning, and that we know how to utilize their strengths so that motivation leads to learning. As Riessman (1976) says,

> In everybody's style there are certain strengths. And everybody has an Achilles' heel. In developing a significant change in learning, one must control the Achilles' heel and utilize the strengths. This is the central problem of the strategy of style, especially in its application to the inner-city pupils in our schools.

Adapted from *The Reading Teacher* (1988), *41*, 751–756. Copyright © 1988 by the International Reading Association.

The inner-city Jackies' battle with reading is their Achilles' heel. But this problem may result from overlooking the strengths that the Jackies bring to school. These strengths are not measurable by readiness tests or other criteria usually used to assess readiness, but they can be determined through cognitive-style mapping.

The term *cognitive-style mapping* refers to a process in which individuals are assessed for their most comfortable manner of learning, whether visual or auditory, independent or in a group. Evidence from cognitive-style mapping indicates that inner-city children learn more effectively when physical and oral involvement are present in the learning (Cureton, 1977).

Evidence from teachers confirms this. Although the term *cognitive-style mapping* may be new in educational literature, the practice is not. A group of successful primary-grade teachers from inner-city schools, for example, use the phrase "when and how." By "when," they mean the time at which to introduce a new skill; by "how," they mean the manner in which the skill is presented. To achieve this knowledge of when and how, they have practiced cognitive-style mapping, though not by that name.

## Only on Wednesday

To these teachers, the variables of time and day are very significant in getting inner-city Jackies to react positively to learning a new task. Although these teachers lack scientific data, they do have success to substantiate their assumptions. For example, their experience, and it is considerable, tells them that Wednesday is the best day for teaching new skills. They also want their classes tested on Wednesday. One teacher showed me the results of two tests taken by her class. The results from the first test, given early in the week, showed the class to be below grade in reading. However, when the students took another form of the test on a Wednesday, they came out on grade level. Why Wednesday? I questioned these teachers, but they were unable to supply any real explanation.

The "how" for inner-city teachers varies, of course, from class to class. But one "how" that has worked for many combines, as it were, business with pleasure. If you observe these teachers, it is difficult to determine when the game is over and when learning is taking place. They have chosen to use a phonic approach to teach reading because they have found that their students are better able to cope with a program that is heavily based on phonics than with a program that places more emphasis on sight words. With a phonic program, they can provide more action, more fun, in contrast to the quieter setting of the traditional classroom, a setting that is not characteristic of the inner-city child's daily life.

Inner-city children, although used to talking a great deal, often come to school with a poor auditory set. They are not accustomed to listening for long periods. The "action approach" to learning, which demands continuous participation by the children, also teaches them to listen as they learn, for their participation is in response to questions from the teacher, questions that must be listened to and understood before they can be responded to. That the action approach works, and that acquisition of knowledge takes place, are attested to not only by the teachers' evaluations of their students but also by these children's scores on standardized reading tests.

## Putting Sounds Together

Come with me to a first-grade classroom where the action approach is being used. Today the teacher is developing the concept of blending by having the children slide around the room. This is done to demonstrate physically how letters and sounds are blended together into words. This psychomotor technique makes the concept of blending letters meaningful, especially when the teacher says, "Slide the sounds together." To further reinforce the skill of sliding or blending, the teacher has the children "slide" the initial sounds in their names together to produce a word. For example, Mary–*muh*, Albert–*aah*, Pam–*puh* would produce the word *map*. (In sliding sounds, the teacher always leads the children through three steps: the separate sounds—*muh, aah, puh*; the sounds joined together—*muhaahpuh*; and the word with no distortions—*map*.)

Another way in which the concept of blending is reinforced is to have children slide objects or pictures of objects together on a table. As they slide *soap, apple,* and *money* together, they blend the initial sound of each to make the word "Sam." Teaching the skill of blending in a concrete manner before applying it to letters brings the concept to life and makes it make sense to the children. The transition from object to letter is a natural progression and far less frustrating than starting with putting letters together to make words.

The last stage of the acquisition of blending skills is seen as the class plays a game. The teacher calls out a series of code words and the students synthesize the sounds these code words stand for into words. For example, the teacher calls out, "soap, money, apple, show," and the class responds with the word "smash." The game has two main purposes: to help develop listening skills, and to give students a background—a frame of reference—to call upon when they apply the concept of blending to the abstract symbols of the alphabet. This application happens later, as the teacher systematically replaces the objects with the letters that represent them. Using this concrete approach to blending eliminates the problem most discussed in teaching with a phonetic approach, getting the children to put the sounds together.

As the children master the concrete representations of the alphabet and of letter combinations, the teacher will play the game again, but this time the students will have to write the letters representing the code. Use of the code not only facilitates the decoding process but also aids those children who have difficulty in hearing the difference between similar sounds, for example, between the short *i* and short *e*. The picture of itching (a girl scratching an itch), which represents the short *i* sound, and the picture of another girl named Ethel, which represents the short *e* sound, makes the difference between the two concrete and unforgettable.

During the teaching of skills, this first-grade teacher has everybody in the class participating simultaneously in answering questions. The purpose of this choral response mode is twofold: to keep everyone alert and to build confidence. Children are able to make a wrong response and have it blend in with the correct one—and not be embarrassed—but the response will be right next time. The choral response also gives security to the shy child. Many questions are repeated and responded to several times so that children who are unsure the first time can respond correctly the next.

In this class, both teacher and children stand during the presentation of new skills; the teacher moves around the room, with every eye pinned on her. This strongly teacher-centered approach might be frowned on in some schools as being too authoritarian and uncreative. However, as one teacher put it, "Creativity will become a part of the children's learning styles when they have mastered the basics." Furthermore, it works. The children, far from feeling cramped or frustrated, are eager to learn. The pace and the action of the class and the accomplishment they feel as they acquire new skills and review earlier ones make them look forward to the reading period.

Can individualized reading programs be successful in inner-city schools, where the learning style of the children favors teacher-centered instruction? The answer will depend somewhat on what is meant by individualized programs. Research by Amidon and Flanders (1963) suggests that achievement level is higher where there is interaction between teacher and student. As one of my students declared after a year using an individualized program, "I need a teacher who will make me learn."

The foregoing paragraphs describe a learning style that results in achievement on the primary level in reading. The next question is how to solve the perplexing problems of maintaining this achievement. Research indicates that by the time most inner-city children reach the fourth-grade level, they have lost from a few months to a year in reading. Why?

One reason appears to be the nature of the tests measuring reading achievement. The questions on intermediate-grade tests require critical thinking rather than simple recall. Teachers who have been successful in maintaining inner-city children's reading achievement have, therefore, devoted large portions of time to the development of children's interpretive skills.

One such teacher points out that development of comprehension skills with her inner-city children is a persistent search for "why." In this search, oral discussion is essential. The students must give reasons why one answer is better than another and must defend that answer with proof. The proof may come from the story or from the students' experience. In order that the "give up" syndrome does not creep into the children's desire to go after the problem, the teacher never tells children they are wrong. Instead she responds to the student with something like, "Now that's thinking. But is there another answer even closer to the problem?" (Such a discussion does not always have to be the outcome of a reading lesson. It could also result from work on an oral puzzle, which allows for participation of the entire class.) Such teacher interaction with the students may take a great deal of time, but it is time well spent, for it builds a pattern for students' thinking that will stand by them.

Another way to ensure participation is to have the students act out the passage read. In this way, emotion and feelings can play a role in comprehension.

## Taking Tests

These techniques have been very helpful in building comprehension skills. But many children do not transfer the acquisition of these skills to testing situations. To correct this, we must make students test-conscious and test-wise and point out the "trickery" of some test questions and the ways in which some test authors try to get students to choose wrong answers. Alerting students to these techniques ensures careful reading of each test question and also helps to build critical thinking skills. Again, this is done through teacher-student interactions.

Why so much emphasis on oral interaction between student and teacher? Simply because of the student's oral background. As one student pointed out, he could see the causal relationship in the story better when the choice of best answer was thrashed out by the class. The inner-city student's learning style depends on oral involvement. The student needs to talk out, with the group, the rationale for a particular choice. This oral exchange of reasons and answers also helps to provide the less apt student with strategies for selecting answers. Most "individualized" programs cannot provide this kind of support.

Computer-assisted instruction is a case in point. The machine does not help show why a chosen answer is wrong. The cold response "incorrect read again" leads to guessing—and a disdainful attitude toward the computer. To be sure, some self-directed students using the machine enjoy the instruction it offers and seem to profit from its use. But they feel that they work better at the machines when the classroom teacher is in the laboratory to praise their achievement and to record their progress. Even though the machine keeps an accurate account of their answers, the students want the teacher to write the percent of correct responses in a record book.

Interaction between teacher and student plays a particular role in helping students prepare for standardized tests. When teachers have interacted with the students all through the term before they are tested, students have this action involvement with which to associate in the test-taking situation. As they take the test and choose their answers, they can "hear" the class discussion.

Test taking is something many of us dread, and for the inner-city child it is an especially traumatic experience. An effective way to lessen this fear is to place students in as many testing situations as possible, to give them practice in taking tests. This is particularly needed in the area of reading. In content areas such as mathematics, science, and social studies, students know essentially what the content of the test will be and they can prepare for it. In reading, however, they have no clue as to the content of the passages on which they will be asked questions. This content may be totally unrelated to their daily lives and experience. Thus it seems mandatory to provide ample preparation, again using the teacher-student interaction learning style.

When inner-city students who have been given practice in test-taking situations are given standardized tests they seem to perform better than students who have not had this kind of practice. Perhaps one more reason for this is that these students have learned to work against time. Inner-city students are often disturbed by the pressure of time. Practice reduced this anxiety.

Is there a Black learning style, a learning style especially suited to inner-city students? I believe there is. Use of such a style does not mean lowering standards or expectations, however. It does mean recognizing the students' strengths and utilizing them. Nor are all these students necessarily in the inner city. This learning style has been successful in rural, suburban, and small-city settings with students from many ethnic backgrounds. All of these students, however, share many characteristics of inner-city children.

Teachers must become attuned to the learning style of the many inner-city Jackies so that these students' fullest potential may become visible on standardized tests. This approach is as valuable with secondary school and college age students as it is with beginners. To develop this learning style, the classroom atmosphere should be that of an "ideal marriage" between teacher and student. Such a relationship does not mean that similar ethnic background should be the criterion. It does mean that the attitude of teacher toward students and students toward teacher is of vital importance in developing the full potential of our most talked about students.

## REFERENCES

Amidon, E.J., & Flanders, N.A. (1963). *The role of the teacher in the classroom*. Minneapolis, MN: Amidon and Associates.

Cureton, G.O. (1977). *Action reading: The participatory approach*. Boston: Allyn & Bacon.

Riessman, F. (1976). *The inner-city child*. New York: Harper & Row.

# CHAPTER 5

# Characteristics of Black Schools at Grade Level Revisited

*Mary Eleanor Rhodes Hoover*

We can laugh at the "back to basics" movement...and joke about definitions of literacy and basics. Or we can support the positive side of this basics movement by urging our schools to endorse an Excellence perspective, using the example of successful schools and attempting to duplicate their findings, including the sociopolitical ones. Without an Excellence perspective, the movement may go far to the right, emphasizing only basics, ironclad discipline, and lack of cultural pluralism. (Hoover, 1978a, p. 762)

This prediction, although made more than 25 years ago, appears to be coming to pass. Though the school reform movement is beginning to implement basic skills, widespread illiteracy among Black and other students of color still remains and very little cultural pluralism exists.

As described in the introduction of my 1978 article, schools for Black and other students of color in the United States are generally failures. Sixty-three percent of Black fourth graders and 58% of Hispanics are below basic levels of reading. And 50% of African American high school students read below level (Barton, 2001). According to Smith (1994), African Americans rank two years below Whites, and Kirch (1993) reveals in an adult literacy survey that 75% to 80% of African American adults tested in the lowest percentile, compared to 36% of Whites. The gap in test scores at the lower levels between African American and Hispanic students and White students widens each year; in fourth-grade reading, only one state reduced the achievement gap between White and minority students between the years 1992 to 2000 (Barton, 2001). In 1900, only 23 years after Reconstruction, 50% of African Americans could read and write (Bennett, 1993); today, that figure has grown by only 4%. This illiteracy rate among Blacks is obscene, particularly considering that African Americans' ancestors are responsible, according to Van Sertima (1983), for some of the first written scripts and other major contri-

Adapted from Hoover, M.R. (1978). Characteristics of Black schools at grade level: A description. *The Reading Teacher, 31,* 757–762.

butions to civilization, and that these statistics are so highly related to unemployment, incarceration, and poverty (Center for the Study of Social Policy and Philadelphia Children's Network, 1994).

Successful Black schools (schools identified as having students achieving at grade level on standardized reading tests) have existed for decades, and have been described by numerous scholars (Edmonds, this volume; Hoover, 1978a; Hoover, Dabney, & Lewis, 1990; McPhail, this volume; Sizemore, 1988; Weber, 1971; Wilgoren, 2000). Several reading methodologies have succeeded in teaching reading at high levels to Black students, in spite of Herrnstein and Murray's (1994) belief that no intervention works in teaching Black children to read. Among these methods are Open Court (Foorman, Francis, Beeler, Winikates, & Fletcher, 1997), Direct Instruction (Jones, 1995), Programmed Reading (Bond & Dykstra, 1967/1997; Hoover, 1992; Hoover, Dabney, & Lewis, 1990), and Superliteracy (Hoover & Fabian, 2000; Perry, 1998).

Before describing what these schools and programs have in common in their approaches to teaching reading, it is important to note that they are remarkable because their students score at and above grade level in spite of biased tests. "Grade level" calculations are of course often an inadequate classification system for test score results. In addition, standardized reading tests, which are used to provide grade level scores, are inadequate in that they are often biased (Hoover, Politzer, & Taylor, this volume). Until a culture-fair test is produced, however, low income communities will need newspapers' printouts of test results for accountability purposes.

This article answers the question "What happens in schools where inner-city children do read at grade level?" This question has not been as popular a question as its reverse: "Why don't inner-city children read at grade level?" First, a review of answers to the second question.

## Review of Popular Rationales for Inner-City Children Not Reading at Grade Level

The list of answers to the question "Why don't inner-city children read at grade level?" comprises largely unresearched beliefs regarding the causes of low achievement in reading for minority students. The list was culled from statements made by teachers in approximately 100 workshops across the United States in the last 30 years. The statements of the teachers represent a sifted review of current thinking in education, as they are basically reflections of the views of their mentors—the professors of education; the authors of journal articles, tests, and textbooks; and the directors of the educational research industry.

## Blame-the-Victim Beliefs

*Deficit:* They can't learn to read because

- the parents don't care.

- their IQs are low, showing minimal cognitive skills.

- their language is so broken as to be no language at all.

- they have a language, but it's so restricted that it hinders them in learning.

- they can't think abstractly, so we can teach them only what they can concretely memorize. We must, therefore, stay away from phonics or higher level mathematics for these children.

- they're culturally deprived.

*Difference:* They can't learn to read because

- they're poor. None of the poor can read—in fact, none of the world's poor can read.

- they're emotionally disturbed—their homes are battlegrounds. We must love them and make them whole again.

- their Black language interferes, having different sound–symbol correspondences—we are thus restricted to the use of sight approaches such as whole language.

- they're not motivated and so they forget how to read.

- they're passive and need to be taught how to control their lives.

- they're violent and need counseling and not teaching.

- they're culturally different and the culture doesn't value reading—their peers don't value it; their parents don't value it.

- their self-concepts are too low—we must first improve the self-concept and then they can learn to read.

- they're not sitting next to Whites—Black children must be exposed to Whites before they will be motivated to learn to read.

- they have an oral tradition—we can't expect them to adapt to written material.

- their family structure is different and not responsive to homework needs.

- the readers are not written in Ebonics—Black children must be exposed to readers written the way they talk in order for them to learn to read.

- Black students think academics is "acting White."

- we don't understand their learning styles—most learn better through drill or Gardner's "Interpersonal" intelligence.

**Blame-the-System Beliefs**

They can't learn to read because

- the system is unequal—schooling might as well be forgotten until we change the system to meet the needs of all the people.
- the tests are biased—students are really reading on level if you examine them on unbiased instruments.
- the textbooks are biased—they're filled with racism, sexism, elitism, and ageism.
- the system needs only 15% of its people to be literate—it has never educated all the people.
- the schools and teachers' colleges are not controlled by the members of the community—a business elite controls these institutions.
- poverty creates such dysfunctional families and traumatic conditions that students cannot learn to read.

Specific documentation of these reasons and summaries of research to refute the most damaging of them would require another lengthy article. Suffice it to say, however, that these statements, particularly those that blame the victim, have served to retard the process of providing literacy skills to inner-city children. Most of these reasons are fatalistic and encourage a do-nothing solution to the problem.

Ninety percent of teachers in the workshops mentioned earlier gave blame-the-victim reasons for lack of achievement. Although we can largely discount the deficit reasons, there are, of course, elements of the truth in some of the less exotic difference reasons. Obviously Black and other minority students are different. They have different income levels, different access to opportunity, different lifestyles and chances, different cultures, and different languages. Yet the successful schools described in this article are located in some of the lowest income areas and diverse communities in the country.

A few well-meaning participants in the workshops give blame-the-system reasons for low achievement, reasons that are also accurate in many instances. Certainly Black and other minority students are disadvantaged by the classism, racism, elitism, and poverty conditions in their way of life; by anachronistic legal roadblocks; by irrelevant programs in teachers' colleges that fail to expose teachers to methods of teaching the cognitive and affective skills necessary for reading achievement; and by a philosophy that now endorses highly funded whole-school reforms that do not include the characteristics we list here. The point is that none of these reasons are in themselves the most salient reasons for low achievement in reading among students of color. Some combinations of these reasons are obviously involved; however, some of the most prominent reasons for low achievement, such as the use of an ineffective method—whole language (Delpit, 1995)—are completely omitted.

In the next section I will answer the primary question of this article, "What happens in schools where inner-city children do read at grade level?" The majority of the schools discussed in this article are public elementary schools located in low income neighborhoods. The characteristics of the Black schools, of course, are not all-encompassing. Some spectacular teachers seem to inspire students through any number of motivating devices—from teaching Chinese to using gymnastics. Some of the schools have components not typical of the other programs. For example, one of the schools uses a supplementary neurological approach for its nonachieving students; others use parents either as paid paraprofessionals in the lower income schools or as volunteers in the higher income schools; some use paid or volunteer tutors; and most stress environment and climate improvement.

# Characteristics of Inner-City Schools Where Children Do Read at Grade Level

The characteristics offered here are methods and approaches that have been successful for average teachers with average budgets. The framework for most of these schools is the DuBois philosophy of *vindicationism* (Drake, 1987; Hoover, 1990)—the belief that Black achievement must be vindicated and stressed. This framework rejects the fatalism of the deficit and difference philosophies. It accepts the need to change the inequities in our society, but refuses to deny students the skills of literacy while we're changing the society. Descriptions of the schools are culled from visits, telephone conversations, and the sources listed in the reference section.

## *Management*

The most important characteristic of an effective school for Black readers is the presence of a leader (principal, superintendent, head teacher) who (1) is familiar with, supportive of, and highly informed in regard to the curriculum and philosophy of the school, which, in most cases, was self-initiated; (2) enforces firm and often innovative approaches to classroom, building, and district management; and (3) implements the other successful school characteristics (see Goss, 1990).

Once the catalyst—the principal, superintendent, or board—begins the change to an effective school, the next two most important characteristics are (1) a structured, proven reading methodology and (2) motivation and high expectations. The cognitive and the affective are thus equally involved.

## Structured, Proven Reading Method

A more than 30-year track record for teaching reading to Black students exists, from Chall (1967/1996) to Weber (1971), to my article (1978a) and book (Hoover, Dabney, & Lewis, 1990), to Edmonds (this volume), to McPhail (this volume), and to Foorman et al. (1997). The record is clear: African American students can be taught the decoding aspects of reading at high levels using any one of several phonics-based reading programs, among other methods. These highly structured, intensive approaches are appropriate for students with second dialects or languages in their backgrounds because they are similar to foreign language teaching methods—with students first being exposed to regular patterns (phonics), then passages written in these patterns (decodable text). One student described decodable text in the following way:

> It is a great program because it helps people who can't read that well or can read but need a little help with it. It's a great book because every step you go to has a poem that has all the short vowel sounds (or whatever sounds were in the chapter) in it that's fun to read. (Compton Unified School District Newsletter, 1996, p. 3)

The use of these methods does not exclude the use of comprehension, vocabulary, and study skills approaches, nor does it exclude the use of whole language or some other literature approach to reading as a supplement.

The structure of the English language creates the need for a structured, systematic phonics approach. In Spanish and Ki-Swahili, for example, the vowels *a, e, i, o, u* are always realized or pronounced like the underlined vowels in the sentence El burro <u>sabe mas que</u> tu, Ilicio. In English there are more than 14 different ways to pronounce the letter *o* as in *Spot, mother, look, open,* and *spook.* In fact, English uses 379 letters and letter combinations for 40 sounds, compared to Italian, Turkish, Spanish, or Swahili languages with the same number of symbols as sounds. This complexity would be confusing to any student; students with more than one language in their backgrounds would be particularly in need of a structured approach to reading.

Not all successful schools use systematic phonics or decodable text. Edmonds (this volume) simply recommended stressing basic reading skills. The highest scores, however, appear to be made in phonics (National Institute of Child Health and Human Development, 2000) or systematic phonics schools as seen in Bennett-Kew (Ichinaga, this volume) and recorded in Chall (1967/1996); Weber (1971); McPhail (this volume); Hoover, Dabney, and Lewis (1990); and Foorman, Fletcher, and Francis (2002).

Methodology in itself can be culturally appropriate. We focus on models of teaching that (1) are not only culturally appropriate in terms of the arts and humanities, but also culturally appropriate in that they bring students to high levels of achievement (Hoover et al., 1990); (2) are a constant value in the culture (Cornelius, 1991; Perry, Steele, & Hilliard, 2000), helping to defeat the bell curve (Herrnstein & Murray, 1994) mentality that argues that African American and other students of color are genetically inferior; and (3) strengthen the community's support, in survey after survey, for high levels of literacy for their children ("What Black Parents Expect From Public Schools," 1994).

Another important aspect of methodology is the adoption by the school district of one proven method. To bring an urban, low income district to grade level, as has only happened infrequently—for instance in Kansas City, Missouri, in the 1970s under Robert Wheeler (Doyle, 1970) and the Ravenswood City School District, California ("Civil Rights Leaders Eye Ravenswood," 1970)—the district must use all the characteristics listed here, plus one more: The district must adopt one proven reading method, mainly because urban areas are characterized by much mobility and because it simplifies staff development.

## Motivation and High Expectation

The affective domain, for instance, the use of high expectations for teachers and motivation for students, is realized in a number of ways: multicultural or Afro–Latino-centered affirmations, community speakers, positive slogans, poetry slams, assemblies stressing history, and oratory (Ichinaga, this volume; Wilks, 1990). There is some evidence that emphasis on the affective domain assists in raising self-esteem. Researchers have demonstrated that Black and other students do suffer from lack of self-esteem; that self-esteem, however, is improved to the same level of other students when the students of color are provided with material on their histories, literature, oratory, and other motivating topics (Powell-Hopson & Powell-Hopson, 1988).

The vindicationist philosophy characterizes the Chick School (Cunen, 1996), Shule Mandela (Cannon, 1990), and the Nairobi Day School (Hoover, 1992)—the latter two are now defunct. Students in these schools were exposed to the academic strengths of African and African American cultures in refutation of the usual assumptions that these cultures do not emphasize academics. These strengths are important because they serve to motivate students to achieve (Delpit & Dowdy, 2003). Some examples of these strengths are as follows:

- African Americans' ancestors are responsible, according to Van Sertima (1983), for some of the first written scripts and other major contributions to civilization. Africans invented the oldest written language 5,300 years ago in Egypt (Diop, 1991) and the first scripts—Meriotic, Srakan, Sudanic, and Manding—were invented in Africa (Van Sertima, 1983).

- Africans and African Americans have also contributed to the philosophies of the world. Williams (1976) informs us in his survey of 107 African societies that Africans invented the first philosophies and ideologies of the world, including democracy, as seen in 14 precepts found in the 107 societies; for example, "The people are the first and final source of all power" (p. 171) and "The trouble of one is the trouble of all" (p. 172). This egalitarianism and African communalism is also reflected in the culture of African American families (Hill, 1997).

- African American Language, or Ebonics, has great breadth and depth as seen in its proverbs and syntax. The proverb has been found to be a frequent and preferred genre throughout the African diaspora and highly tied to intelligence (Daniel, 1972; Smitherman, 2000). It is used for a number of purposes—introducing speeches, teaching the young, and revealing the brilliance of the speaker. Proverbs, such proverbs as "The Lord don't like ugly" and "What goes around comes around," obviously can be used for all the listed purposes. Ebonics also has at least two varieties: vernacular and standard (Hoover, McPhail, & Ginyard, 1992; Taylor, 1971).

  As Hilliard (1986; see also chapter 2 of this volume) states,

  > Far from being broken English, Ebonics has a superior strength for measuring intelligence. It is interesting that racist psychologists claim that Black people are not capable of "Level 11 thinking"—the kind of abstract thinking which is reflected in proverbs and analogies. To the contrary, this is our strong suit. It is the mismatch in experiential content between psychologists and African-Americans which causes them to miss the extensive use of proverbs and analogies among us. (p. 144)

  Asante (1991) also describes the strengths of Ebonics, for example, the fact that Ebonics has four perfectives whereas English has only two, and that Ebonics speakers utilize several verbs, while standard English uses a single verb to express a complete action; for example, "I took consideration and joined the church" and the uniqueness of African American harmonizing: "Speak," "Word up," "Amen," and "Ase" as a West African-based speaking response style involving pitch, intonation, and rhythm.

• The culture also produces brilliant young people. Wilson (1992) describes a number of studies indicating that African and African American children test in advance of all other groups on psychomotor and cognitive measures from the ages of birth to two years old.

Much of the current thinking in education places an emphasis on the individual—individualized reading, individualized testing, individualized counseling. One significant characteristic of successful schools for students of color, however, is the use of a group-oriented philosophy. Many of the schools stress the learning style of audience participation (Cureton, 1988; see also chapter 4 of this volume) or group involvement. All the schools have slogans that symbolize the striving for excellence, such as "Our Kids Can Learn," "Children First," "Only the Best." These slogans symbolize and stress group achievement.

Not only are group approaches to motivation used but also group approaches to teaching. Many of the schools encourage a learning style identified as appropriate for minority students, for instance, an audience participatory approach that includes poetry, choral reading, and unison responses (see Cureton, chapter 4 of this volume). A number of schools use the chanting element, for example, Knowledge Is Power Program (KIPP) academy schools (Wilgoren, 2000) and superliteracy schools (Hoover & Fabian, 2000; Hoover, Washington, & Fabian, 2002).

## Staff Development

Workshops for extensive faculty development are critically important. Not only are the students motivated to achieve, encouraged by high expectations and positive attitudes on the part of the staff, but teachers also are expected to achieve. A strong teacher training component is characteristic of most of the programs; it is assumed that teachers can teach and that they want to teach. Goss (1990), of the J.P. Hill School in a low income community in Philadelphia, Pennsylvania, for example, strongly emphasizes the importance of teacher training.

## Monitoring

Frequent assessment of students for assistance rather than for punitive reasons is another important characteristic of Black schools at grade level. As described by a successful principal (Goss, 1990): "The success of any program is dependent to a large degree on a practical workable monitoring system. We installed, among other things, charts to periodically indicate national reading scores and every child's progress in book-level instruction" (p. 12).

## Time

A sufficient amount of time each day for instruction and practice in reading, language arts, and math—generally half a day—is necessary. Time is also important in regard to the initiation of instruction. Many of the schools begin the teaching of reading in preschool and kindergarten (Hoover, 1992; Ichinaga, this volume).

# Conclusion

To update my 1978 statement revisited at the beginning of this chapter, we can laugh at the "school reform" movement and joke about definitions of literacy and basics. Or we can support the positive side of this movement by urging our schools to endorse an excellence/vindicationist perspective, using the example of successful schools and attempting to duplicate their findings, including the motivational ones. Without an excellence/vindicationist perspective, the movement may go far to the right, emphasizing only basics, iron-clad discipline, and lack of cultural pluralism.

Hopefully, as we go forward to implement these characteristics, we will not abandon the culture advocated by so many Black educators. We have learned much since the first version of this article was written in 1978. We have learned that, in addition to the use of a successful reading methodology, culture makes not only an affective contribution but also a cognitive one (Politzer & Hoover, 1976; Powell-Hopson & Powell-Hopson, 1988).

It won't be easy to become an advocate. It won't be easy to openly criticize ourselves, our administrators, and our school boards. It won't be easy to quietly answer references to Black and other minority children as "culturally deprived," "culturally different," "linguistically inferior" with the evidence of their abilities as seen in the successful schools. It won't be easy to abandon the current liberal stance that accepts lack of achievement for minorities with a shrug of the shoulders, and instead to demand what we all want for our children (and what it has been established that low income communities want for theirs)—literacy (Hoover, 1978b; "What Black Parents Expect from Public Schools," 1994). It won't be easy to fight for equal time for vindicationism in the journals, schools of education, the media, and our highly funded educational efforts.

The evidence of these models and methods make it inexcusable that low literacy scores still exist. These models and methods must be examined because they provide answers to the pressing problems in education today: illiteracy, endorsement of vouchers because of the failure of public schools, and lack of rigor in teacher education. In describing the characteristics of the successful schools, a consideration of what works, will give us additional answers to the question of why education isn't working for Black and other students of color. Obviously, if the characteristics described here are effective in schools suffering from the effects of poverty and all the other excuses usually given for lack of achievement, then a major reason for low reading scores is the refusal to implement these characteristics.

By advocating and effecting change, we in education may be able to demonstrate to other responsible institutions—those concerned with unemployment and poor health and medical conditions—that change is possible; that one institution at least—education—is willing to meet the needs of all classes of people; and that our responsibility for a literate population is being addressed.

## REFERENCES

Asante, M. (1991). African elements in African-American English. In J.E. Holloway (Ed.), *Africanisms in American culture* (pp. 19–33). Bloomington: Indiana University Press.

Barton, P.E. (March, 2001). *Raising achievement and reducing gaps. Reporting progress toward goals for academic achievement: On the NAEP report.* Washington, DC: National Education Goals Panel.

Bennett, L., Jr. (1993). *Before the Mayflower: A history of Black America* (6th ed.). New York: Penguin. (Original work published 1964)

Bond, G.L., & Dykstra, R. (1997). The cooperative research program in first-grade reading instruction (The first-grade reading studies). *Reading Research Quarterly, 32,* 348–427. (Original work published 1967)

Cannon, J. (1990, March 3). Shule Mandela teaches more than just 3 Rs. *The Times Tribune,* pp. B1–B2.

Center for the Study of Social Policy and Philadelphia Children's Network. (1994). *World without work: Causes and consequences of Black male unemployment.* Washington, DC: Author.

Chall, J.S. (1996). *Learning to read: The great debate* (3rd ed.). Fort Worth, TX: Harcourt College. (Original work published 1967)

Civil rights leader eyes success of phonics at Ravenswood. (1970, December 3). *Palo Alto Times,* p. 2.

Cornelius, J.D. (1991). *"When I can read my title clear": Literacy, slavery, and religion in the antebellum South.* Columbia: University of South Carolina Press.

Cunen, J. (1996). The end of integration. *Time,* pp. 39, 45.

Cureton, G. (1988). Using a Black learning style. *The Reading Teacher, 41,* 751–756.

Daniel, J. (1972, Winter). Towards an ethnography of Afro-American proverbial usage. *Black Lines,* 3–12.

Delpit, L. (1995). *Other people's children.* New York: New Press.

Delpit, L., & Dowdy, J. (Eds.). (2003). *The skin that we speak: Thoughts on language* and culture in the classroom. New York: New Press.

Diop, C.A. (1991). Civilization or barbarism: An authentic anthropology (Y.-L. Meeme Ngami, Trans.). Brooklyn, NY: Lawrence Hill.

Doyle, P. (1971, March 19). City deprived pupils ahead in reading capabilities. Kansas City Star, p. 18.

Drake, S.C. (1987). Black folk here and there (Vol. 1). Los Angeles: Center for Afro-American Studies, University of California.

Flesch, R. (1981). Why Johnny still can't read. New York: Harper & Row.

Foorman, B.R., Fletcher, J.M., & Francis, D.J. (2002). Preventing reading failure by ensuring effective reading instruction. In S. Patton & M. Holmes, The keys to literacy (pp. 44–53). Washington, DC: Council for Basic Education.

Foorman, B.R., Francis, D.J., Beeler, T., Winikates, D., & Fletcher, J.M. (1997). Early intervention for children with reading problems: Study designs and preliminary findings. Learning Disabilities: A Multidisciplinary Journal, 8(1), 63–71.

Goss, O. (1990). L.P. Hill School. In M.R. Hoover, N. Dabney, & S. Lewis (Eds.), Successful Black and minority schools: Classic models (pp. 11–14). San Francisco: Julian Richardson.

Herrnstein, R., & Murray, C. (1994). The bell curve: Intelligence and class structure in American life. New York: Free Press.

Hill, R.B. (1997). The strengths of African American families: Twenty-five years later. Washington, DC: R & B Publishers.

Hoover, M.R. (1978a). Characteristics of Black schools at grade level: A description. The Reading Teacher, 31, 757–762.

Hoover, M.R. (1978b). Community attitudes toward Black English. Language in Society, 7(2).

Hoover, M.R. (1990). A vindicationist perspective on the role of Ebonics (Black language) and other aspects of ethnic studies in the university. American Behavioral Scientist, 34(2), 251–262.

Hoover, M.R. (1992). The Nairobi Day School: An African American independent school. Journal of Negro Education, 61(2), 201–210.

Hoover, M.R., & Fabian, E.M. (2000). Problem solving—struggling readers: A successful program for struggling readers. The Reading Teacher, 53, 474–476.

Hoover, M.R., Dabney, N., & Lewis, S. (Eds.). (1990). Successful Black and minority schools: Classic models. San Francisco: Julian Richardson.

Hoover, M.R., McPhail, I., & Ginyard, L. (1992). Literacy for miseducated Black adults: The Nairobi Method, A culturally-appropriate literacy approach. In A.M. Scales & J.E. Burley (Eds.), Perspectives: From adult literacy to continuing education (pp. 212–218). Dubuque, IA: William C. Brown.

Hoover, M.R., Washington, E., & Fabian, E.M. (2002). Superliteracy: Patterns for reading. Washington, DC: Onyx.

Jones, J.M. (1995). Educational philosophies: A primer for parents. Milwaukee, WI: Parents Raising Educational Standards in Schools (PRESS).

Kirch, I. (1993). Adult literacy in America. Washington, DC: Office of Educational Research and Improvement, U.S. Department of Education.

National Institute of Child Health and Human Development. (2000). Report of the National Reading Panel. Teaching children to read: An evidence-based assessment of the scientific research literature on reading and its implications for reading instruction (NIH Publication No. 00-4769). Washington, DC: U.S. Government Printing Office.

Perry, T. (1998). On superliteracy. In T. Perry & L. Delpit (Eds.), The real Ebonics debate: Power, languages, and the education of African American children (pp. 205–206). Boston: Beacon Press.

Perry T., Steele, C., & Hilliard, A. (2003). *Young, gifted and Black: Promoting high achievement among African American students*. Boston: Beacon Press.

Phillips, S. (1971). Participant structures and communicative competence: Warm Springs children in community and classroom. In C.B. Cazden, V.P. John, & D. Hymes (Eds.), *Functions of language in the classroom* (pp. 370–394). New York: Teachers College Press.

Politzer, R.L., & Hoover, M.R. (1976). *Teachers' and pupil's attitudes toward Black English speech varieties and Black pupils' achievement*. Stanford, CA: Stanford Center for Research and Development in Teaching.

Powell-Hopson, D., & Powell-Hopson, D.S. (1988). Implications of doll color preferences among Black preschool children and White preschool children. *Journal of Black Psychology, 14*(12), 57–63, 205–206.

Sizemore, B. (1988). The Madison Elementary School: A turnaround case. *Journal of Negro Education, 57*(3), 243–265.

Smith, T.M. (1994). *The condition of education, 1994*. Washington, DC: National Center for Educational Statistics.

Smitherman, G. (2000). *Talkin' that talk: Language, culture, and education in African America*. New York: Routledge.

Snow, C.E., Burns, M.S., & Griffin, P. (Eds.). (1998). *Preventing reading difficulties in young children*. Washington, DC: National Academy Press.

State of the district. (1996). *Compton Unified School District Newsletter, 5*(2), p. 10.

Taylor, O.L. (1971). Response to social dialects and the field of speech. In R. Shuy (Ed.), *Sociolinguistic theory: Materials and practice* (pp. 13–20). Washington, DC: Center for Applied Linguistics.

Van Sertima, I. (Ed.). (1983). *Blacks in science: Ancient and modern*. New Brunswick, NJ: Transaction Books.

Weber, G. (1971). *Inner-city children can be taught to read: Four successful schools*. Washington, DC: Council for Basic Education.

What Black parents expect from public schools. (1994, November 7). *Jet*, p. 14.

Wilgoren, J. (2000, August 16). Seeking to clone schools of success for poor children. *The New York Times*, p. A1.

Wilks, G. (1990). Nairobi schools. In M.R. Hoover, N. Dabney, & S. Lewis (Eds.), *Successful Black and minority schools: Classic models* (pp. 26–31). San Francisco: Julian Richardson.

Williams, C. (1987). *The destruction of Black civilization* (3rd ed.). Chicago: Third World Press.

Wilson, A. (1992). *Awakening the natural genius of Black children*. New York: Afrikan World Infosystems.

# CHAPTER 6

# Bennett-Kew School:
# One School's Turnaround
# in Academic Achievement

*Nancy Ichinaga*

I tell parents (that) if their children can't read it's not their fault. The school hasn't done its job. There are no excuses.

This is a statement I made to the Torrance, California, *Daily Breeze* in February 1990, and I still believe it. I have always believed that the focus in education should be on closing the achievement gap between the affluent and the poor children in the United States.

In the past decades, two types of educational literature have been published on why there is an achievement gap and on how this gap has been closed by many schools in the United States. One type, which unfortunately comprises much of the literature on this topic, still emphasizes that the achievement gap can be explained as the result of the socioeconomic status of the student population. The insinuation is that until the socioeconomics are equalized, the achievement gap will continue to exist. This perspective only crystallizes the prejudice of public opinion about the inferiority of the poor, particularly poor children of color.

The second type of educational literature is generally about different schools and districts that have proven that poor children can learn as well as middle class children. This type of literature is based on the belief that the secret of success is that all children can learn—not only the affluent—and that educators can find ways to teach these children successfully.

My story on how the achievement gap has been closed is often ignored. An article in *Education Week* (Spencer, 2001), which highlights some findings of District 2 in Manhattan, New York, illustrates my point of view. The article chides District 2 for ignoring research and not making distinctions between poor and middle class children in its educational delivery system. District 2 teaches a progressive, integrated curriculum in all its schools. The article points out that middle class children can afford not to be taught in schools, but poor children cannot afford the leisurely and loosely organized curriculum of the district's progressive system. Most poor children know only what is taught in school, and, for that reason, schools in poor urban areas must teach more *intensively* and *extensively*. An intensive standards-based curriculum in poor schools will close the achievement gap. This has been proven time and again by many schools in the United States, and it is too bad that publicity about these successes have been eclipsed by reports that emphasize that the difference in socioeconomics explains the difference in the achievement level of rich and poor children.

# Improving a Failing School

In 1974, I became principal of Bennett-Kew School, a K–3 school in Inglewood, California. At that time the school was made up of 99.9% minority students: 70% Black, 29% Hispanic, and 1% all others. Approximately 70% of students were on the free-lunch program, and 30% received Aid to Families with Dependent Children (AFDC).

Prior to my arrival at Bennett-Kew, the school had ranked at the 3rd percentile in the state's reading test. I told my staff that this ranking meant that either (1) the large majority of the children were mentally retarded, or (2) that the educational program at the school was not working. I asked members of my staff if they were satisfied with the low scores and, if not, what did they plan to do about it? One person's response was, "What did you expect? The kids are all Black!" I strongly rejected that response: I told the staff that I would not tolerate any racist opinion or attitude in the school and that I believed that all children could learn if they were taught.

The teachers quickly supported me and worked together to change the school. They knew what they had to teach, but they did not know how to do it because they had only raw materials. Some tried to create their own materials, but that was unsatisfactory. The teachers and I looked for commercially made, sequenced instructional material and found a programmed decoding series—a phonics-based reading program. We reorganized the entire instructional program to make sure that every teacher had a manageable range of reading levels with flexible reading groups. The program's sequence started at the kindergarten level, so children of all grades in the school participated in it.

The school's state reading scores improved annually from 1974 to 1978. In 1978, third graders scored at the 68th percentile. In 1990, the last year of the state test, third graders scored at the 78th percentile in a combined reading, math, and language test.

# Necessary Steps
# to Create School Success

To create a turnaround, I had to get the teachers to agree to the following ideas:

1. All children could learn to read. Behavioral psychologist B.F. Skinner taught pigeons to read, and our children were surely much smarter than pigeons.

2. It was the teachers' responsibility to teach the children to read. The children had to be taught reading through a direct and systematic method. Skinner's pigeons did not learn to read by chance; they were taught methodically and systematically.

3. Everyone had to teach well if children were to learn and the school's test scores were to go up. If only every other teacher taught well, the good work that one teacher had done would be cancelled out by a poor teacher the next year.

To make a school successful, an administrator must do the following:

1. Make sure that every classroom is teachable and manageable by a teacher who is not superhuman. When the achievement range within a classroom is too wide, teachers need to be encouraged to team-teach. If a class is somehow more difficult than others, then that teacher must be given some help to compensate for having a particularly difficult group. Otherwise, you will have programmed classrooms for failure.

2. Oversee and monitor the entire curriculum, particularly the reading, writing, and math program. Keep a record of each class so that intervention can be done if perceived to be needed. Walk through classrooms with a monitor book to take notes. Check every report card. Check teacher grading and comments to make sure that even report cards are used as tools to make kids more successful.

3. Take the results of the standardized test scores, study them carefully, and plan in-service training sessions based on the test analysis.

4. Take time to give teachers frequent positive feedback or strokes for their hard work and successes, for without them nothing can be accomplished. I compliment teachers often and let them know in as many ways as possible that I appreciate their work.

5. Affirm the belief that schools are created and exist primarily for the education of the children and that educators' jobs exist for this reason.

Understand that what we do is crucial, particularly because our children do come from so-called underprivileged minority groups.

6. Reinforce academic achievement. Display and publish student writing regularly; recognize honor roll students quarterly. Since 1985, the Bennett-Kew sixth graders have been awarded school- and parent-funded scholarships at graduation to encourage serious planning for college.

7. Make sure teachers expect much of their students. Make assignments on a consistent and regular basis and give students immediate feedback following any test or completion of assignments. The most common disciplinary referral of a sixth-grade student is for not completing or returning homework assignments—not active misbehavior.

8. Treat everyone equally. There is no hierarchy at Bennett-Kew—everyone from teachers to the janitorial staff is treated equally: As I recounted to the *Daily Breeze* reporter in 1990, once, when I wasn't satisfied with the way a former janitor cleaned student restrooms, I scrubbed the walls myself.

The emphasis in elementary schools should be on teaching the basic academic skills to its children. Children need to be taught to read using scientifically proven systems that include phonics-based programs and the best of children's literature, so that both the *how* and *what* of reading are addressed.

# Conclusion

In the world of reality, all children do not come to school ready to learn at the same level. However, what they need to master before they are promoted to the next grade level should be clear. At Bennett-Kew, we educators have found that the most successful intervention for students placed "at-risk" must occur as early as kindergarten and grade 1. We created a "junior first grade" to meet the needs of the most needy kindergartners. The junior first grade is really a high-level kindergarten that gives the "gift of time" so students can be successful in school. Our junior first-grade students have generally become successful first graders. Some students eventually are double promoted from grade 4 to grade 6.

Bennett-Kew has changed since the 1970s: The student population, which used to be 70% African American, is now more than 50% Hispanic. The curriculum has not changed much. Because all instruction has been in English, there are bilingual aides in every kindergarten and first-grade class to make sure that children do not miss any instruction. When only 6% of California second-language children were meeting reclassification to fluent speaking level, we were reclassifying about 40% of our students annually. In 1995, the state gave our school a waiver from bilingual education based on the high achievement of our Hispanic children. This vindicated our belief that all children can learn provided they are given the right instruction.

There is no magic in the accomplishments of Bennett-Kew School. Clear goals, with know-how and hard work, are the answers to creating achieving schools. This I know and believe.

## REFERENCE

Spencer, L.C. (2001, February 28). Progressivism's hidden failure. *Education Week*, *20*(24), 29, 32–33. Retrieved September 10, 2004, from http://www.edweek.org/ew/ewstory.cfm?slug=24spencer.h20

CHAPTER 7

# A Critique of George Weber's Study: Inner-City Children Can Be Taught to Read: Four Successful Schools

*Irving Pressley McPhail*

George Weber's (1971) study of four inner-city schools, in which the majority of third graders were reading on grade level, was a forerunner of the new thrust in research in urban education that focuses on the identification and analysis of successful inner-city schools. This classic study will be critiqued in the following areas: (1) the problem, (2) design and methodology, (3) findings, and (4) conclusions.

## The Problem

The soundness of the logic underlying the identification of common factors in the reading programs of successful inner-city schools as the major focus of the study is evident in Weber's discussion of the significance of the problem. Specifically, the existence of schools that were successful in teaching low-income minority students to read suggested that beginning reading achievement in inner-city schools did not have to be as depressed as it usually is. In rejecting the rationales for failure most prevalent during the early 1970s[1]—poor family background and alleged differences in intelligence between low-income minority students and their White middle class counterparts—Weber appears to be endorsing the "Excellence" philosophy. However, Weber stated that "even though in (his) opinion the intelligence of poor children is somewhat lower, on the average, high intelligence is not necessary to learn the relatively simple skill of beginning reading" (1971, p. 528).

The "Excellence" philosophy, as defined by the National Association of Black Reading and Language Educators, rejects the "Deficit" and "Difference" type ideologies in favor of the belief that Black children can learn anything if

From L.M. Gentile, M.L. Kamil, & J.S. Blanchard (Eds.) (1983), *Reading research revisited* (pp. 549–558). Columbus, OH: Merrill. Reprinted with permission of Pearson Education, Inc.

taught, and seeks to propagate those persons and programs that work in teaching Black children. "Deficit" views of Blacks, for example, that a flaw in Black genes is responsible for low reading scores for Blacks, must be rejected. Most "Difference" views of Blacks, for example, that Blacks are so different in their language and culture that they cannot learn, or that they require a "special" nonacademic education, must also be rejected (see Hoover, 1978). Although Weber did not discuss the basis for his opinion on the intelligence of poor children, he did make reference to Jensen's (1969) controversial work, which argues in favor of a "Deficit" view of Blacks. Jensen's theory that the average lower intelligence quotient (I.Q.) score for "American Negroes" (as compared to the averages for Whites and American Orientals) is the result of heredity has been soundly challenged by the overwhelming evidence in support of the influence on I.Q. of social and physical environmental factors (Senna, 1973) and the built-in bias of the I.Q. tests themselves (Ristow, 1978; Williams & Whitehead, 1971; Word, 1974).

By selecting the school as the unit of study, Weber rejected the teacher and the individual class, and the school system, as potential units of study. The school, in contrast to the school system or the classroom, is the basic organizational and institutional unit responsible for providing instruction. Even within school systems, schools enjoy a fairly high degree of autonomy in organizing their instructional programs. Families typically form attachments to, and develop concerns about, their neighborhood school. A child's educational experiences are organized principally around the school, with curriculum and instruction organized and sequenced by grade level within schools, and with a host of extracurricular and other noninstructional activities located in, and organized by, the school. Yet, recent trends in the effective-schools research suggest that factors that distinguish successful schools from unsuccessful schools also seem to distinguish effective classrooms and teacher behaviors from their less effective counterparts. Weber's naivete on this point is discussed later in this article.

Having defined the school as the study unit, Weber next defined *inner-city* and *successful reading achievement*. The criteria established for defining these key terms avoided one major pitfall, yet suggested another pitfall that has made much of the teacher effectiveness and effective-schools research inadequate. Most of this research uses a relative definition of effectiveness, in which schools or teachers are identified as effective if their *average* achievement level is higher than those with comparable school or classroom composition. Such a relative definition could lead to accepting achievement differences between schools and classrooms with low-income students versus those with middle class students. Weber wisely avoided this problem by requiring that inner-city schools, to be defined as successful in reading achievement, achieve a *national* grade norm score as a median and that the percentage of gross failures be low. On the other hand, if one accepts the definition of instructional effectiveness which includes the criterion that the relationship between pupil background and achievement, within the school, approach zero, (then) only research which treats the variance in student achievement (and especially the extent to which such variance covaries with racial, ethnic, and/or social status characteristics of individual pupils) as a topic for investigation will permit identification of alterable school and instructional factors which can reduce the correlation between pupil background and performance. (Cohen, n.d., p. 738)

In this regard, Weber can be criticized for not reporting any differences in student achievement between Black, Puerto Rican, Mexican American, and "other" students in the inner-city schools (P.S. 11, Manhattan; P.S. 129, Manhattan; Ann Street School, Los Angeles), which had more than one ethnic group represented in its student body. Weber's selection of only low-income schools avoided any difficulties arising from the covariation of student achievement and social status characteristics.

Finally, the decision to focus on the third grade was appropriate given the investigator's objective of assessing the children's mastery of the *basic* reading skills covered in the *beginning* reading program, that is, the children's " 'mechanical' ability to read simple American English" (Weber, 1971, p. 530). Yet we know that many schools demonstrate steady growth up to grade 3 and then the achievement curve falls sharply to grade 12. School effectiveness research thus far has not examined instruction in higher level cognitive skills (comprehension, mathematical reasoning) at the elementary level, instruction in writing at the elementary and secondary levels, and instruction in reading and mathematics at the secondary level. Future research, then, needs to identify effective school and classroom instructional practices at higher grade levels, for more complex skills, and in writing, as well as reading and mathematics.

## Design and Methodology

The procedures described by Weber to obtain nominations of successful inner-city schools and to secure permission to visit 17 schools that supposedly met both criteria (type of school and reading success) are clearly described. The reasons why 52 of the second sample of 69 schools selectively dropped out of the project are of particular interest.

The decision to conduct an independent evaluation of reading achievement was most appropriate given the limitations that nationally standardized test results pose in this type of research design. Adequate information pertaining to the design (Cohen, 1969, pp. 67–68) and standardization properties of the reading test developed by Weber (pp. 531–532) is provided in the text , including evidence of a preparatory validation study of the test having been conducted. However, Weber did not provide adequate statistical data about the reliability and validity of the test, that is, correlation coefficients with standardized reading tests. We must, therefore, *assume* that the test possessed adequate reliability and validity.

The purposes for conducting the visits to 17 big city schools and the description of field procedures (observations and interviews) used to collect data are discussed. The field procedures determined the nature of the beginning reading program and, where the school met both the inner-city and reading success criteria, the factors that accounted for the success. However, had Weber been conducting the study today instead of in 1971, he might have used ethnographic monitoring in one or more of the schools that met both criteria (see Dabney, 1983; Rist, 1973; Watkins, 1981; Wilson, 1977).

To summarize, Weber found four schools that met the following criteria:

> (1) they were nonselective public schools in the central areas of large cities that were attended by very poor children, and (2) at the third-grade level, their reading achievement medians equalled or exceeded the national norm and the percentages of nonreaders were unusually low for such schools. (p. 533)

## Findings

Weber assumed that when all four of the successful schools followed a practice that was not usually found in unsuccessful schools, that practice had something to do with their success. He concluded, further, that different practices that existed in some, but not all, of the successful schools were not essential to success. Based on these two propositions, Weber accounted for the success of beginning reading instruction in the four successful schools.

Eight factors common to the four successful schools and not usually present in unsuccessful inner-city schools were identified as success factors: (1) strong leadership, (2) high expectations, (3) good atmosphere, (4) strong emphasis on reading, (5) additional reading personnel, (6) use of phonics, (7) individualization, and (8) careful evaluation of pupil progress. The nonessential school-level factors were small class size, achievement grouping, high quality of teaching, school personnel of the same ethnic background as the pupils, preschool education, and outstanding physical facilities.

Weber's identification of school-level factors that seemed to account for successful beginning reading instruction in low income minority schools carved the path for the later, more sophisticated studies in this area (see Dabney, 1983; Edmonds, this volume; Hoover, 1978). Weber's analysis of success factors did, however, leave out important details about at least two of the four schools that he reported on: Woodland Elementary School and John H. Finley School.

## Selected Success Factors

Silberman (1970) and Thomas (1990) found active parental involvement and strong in-service teacher-training components were major keys in the success of the Finley and Woodland schools, respectively. Also, at Woodland, teachers were trained to be aware of their students' use of Black English Vernacular (BEV) and to accept it, as well as to teach the children to be facile in "standard" English (Thomas, 1990). Weber's description of the role of the "speech improvement" teacher at Woodland did not suggest the bidialectal perspective operative at Woodland that Thomas revealed. Perhaps the bidialectal perspective runs counter to Weber's views on the issue of Black children's language. In an earlier report on one successful inner-city school in Harlem, Manhattan, New York (P.S. 192), Weber (1969) observed that the school "makes no concessions to what has been called by some 'the inner-city English dialect'" (p. 4). Weber reported: "Dr. Gang (principal) says that the school does not worry about it, uses standard English. He comments characteristically that 'the dialect problem' is important only in the educational and sociological literature" (p. 4).

Hoover (1978) found that other successful low-income minority schools put great emphasis on exposure not to BEV but to "Standard Black English" (Taylor, 1971), which uses standard grammar in addition to elements of Black style, speech events, and vocabulary (see McPhail, 1979b; Piestrup, 1973; Smitherman, 1981; Williams & Whitehead, 1971).

At the Finley School, Silberman (1970) observed that "great stress (was) placed on developing pride in children's racial and ethnic identity" (p. 111), a factor that Weber failed to mention.

A somewhat different analysis of the Silberman (1970) and Thomas (1990) observation of active parental involvement in the Finley and Woodland schools argues that characteristics of successful low-income minority schools, such as strong leadership, high expectations, good atmosphere, and so on, are *causally* important, but only in schools that have an adequately socialized student body. That is, there is a conditional relationship in which factors such as those identified by Weber are important *only* if students are prepared to work in schools, but are not powerful enough to overcome the negative effects of students who are unmotivated and who do not receive adequate support and encouragement at home and in their communities. Similarly, schools with well-prepared students may still turn out to be ineffective if they are not doing the things identified in Weber's and others' work. However, evidence suggests that an inadequately socialized student body may, in fact, be resocialized through the exercise of instructional options under the school and classroom's control.

Specifically, research has demonstrated that a literate environment at home produces early readers and children who experience greater reading achievement in school (Durkin, 1966; Sakamoto, 1975; Thorndike, 1973). Yet, Cohen (1968) found that inner-city second-grade students from a *nonliterate* home environment advanced in their reading, language skills, and interest in reading in a school that provided a literate classroom environment. The children in Cohen's experiment were read to daily and encouraged to take part in activities that stimulated interaction. This finding was coupled with the results of three remarkable studies (Levenstein, 1975; Sprigle, 1972; Strickland, 1973) that demonstrated that low-income children who are given experiences, at school or at home, in a cognitively and affectively rich environment, get higher scores on intelligence and reading achievement tests and on measures of affective development. The findings *strongly* suggest that, regardless of socioeconomic status, schools can make the difference in the education of minority children.

Weber's finding of strong leadership as a success factor is also of great interest. In three of the four schools, the strong leadership was provided by the building principal. The brief descriptions of the three principals suggest a leadership style characterized by the ability to manage the instructional program, clarify and emphasize goals, allocate and procure resources, and supervise personnel and program (Barnard & Hetzel, 1976). This view of the principal as a strong *instructional* leader runs counter to the ethnographic study of an elementary school principal by Wolcott (1973) that portrayed the principal as one responding to a multitude of complex forces, many of which had little to do with classroom instruction. Principals who view their ideal role as that of an instructional leader, in fact, seem to spend more of their time managing conflict. Perhaps successful low-income minority schools are effective precisely because they are more tightly managed and more collectively committed to basic skills instruction. This seems logical on its face, though we need to know more about *how* principals exercise instructional leadership in the face of a multitude of complex, competing forces.

Finally, Weber's identification of the use of phonics as a success factor is not surprising. No aspect of reading instruction has been investigated more than the effect of teaching sound-spelling relationships. The major studies have concluded that systematic instruction in sound-spelling patterns increases performance on reading tests through the primary grades (Chall, 1967; Dykstra, 1968). In fact, Hoover (1978) reported that "the use of a structured approach to reading which focuses on the orthographic rules/spelling patterns of English" (p. 760) emerged as one of the *most striking* characteristics of successful low-income minority schools. However, Hoover was correct in observing that the use of phonics does not preclude the use of the language experience approach, for example, at Woodland Elementary School. Recent psycholinguistic research and notions of reading as a language process support the organization of a reading and communication arts plan that integrates and balances activities from all four communication perspectives (reading, writing, listening, speaking) and emphasizes the search for meaning (Botel, 1977; Goodman, 1968).

## Selected Nonessential Characteristics

Weber (1971) identified quality of teaching as a nonessential characteristic. He argued that "outstanding teachers can teach beginning reading successfully with *any* materials and under a wide range of conditions...poor teachers will fail with the best materials and procedures" (p. 701). Weber suggested that the four successful schools were probably favored, somewhat, by the quality of their teaching, but some mediocre and even poor teaching was evident. Weber, in the opinion of this writer, erred in his judgment that quality of teaching is not, in fact, a *primary* causal factor in the success of the four schools.

Until recently, little has been written concerning *exactly* what happens in the classrooms of successful low-income minority schools; however, a relatively well-developed research tradition has demonstrated that the teacher is the most important determinant of students' reading achievement (Bond & Dykstra, 1967; Harris & Morrison, 1969; Harris, 1978). It is not surprising, then, that factors which distinguish successful schools from unsuccessful schools also seem to distinguish effective classrooms from their less effective counterparts: strong leadership, high expectations, good atmosphere, and emphasis on reading. Dabney (1983) summarized the general findings of studies of more effective teaching behavior, which suggest that low-income minority children achieve more in reading when their teacher:

1. assumes the role of a strong leader, using time efficiently and keeping students engaged in task-related activities;
2. organizes students into medium to large groups for instruction;
3. monitors work while being available to answer student-initiated questions;
4. asks low ordered questions, insuring that students experience a great amount of success and have the opportunity to learn sufficient amounts of content;
5. keeps interaction at a low level of complexity, structures lessons so that students are aware of objectives. (pp. 190–191)

McPhail (1979b) also points to the need for teachers to sustain a classroom environment that is warm, friendly, democratic, relatively free of disruptive behavior, and tolerant of linguistic diversity as a critical factor in helping low-income minority children achieve success in reading.

Clearly, there is a need to learn *what* teachers do on a day-to-day basis and *how* they make decisions on the nature of instructional activities; the nature, size, and composition of instructional groups (Weber's comments on achievement grouping were most helpful in this regard); strategies for motivating and rewarding student behavior; and strategies for coping with a considerable diversity of student ability and prior performance within the classroom. Again, the research tool of ethnographic monitoring is likely to prove useful in unraveling these complex issues.

Further, we need to radically redesign preservice teacher education programs that purport to prepare teachers for service in low-income minority schools. Preservice programs should reflect the knowledges and skills identified as successful teacher behaviors generally and, specifically, in the teaching of reading (McPhail, 1981a).

Weber included the ethnic background of the principals and teachers in the category of nonessential characteristics. Given that the leaders of the four schools were, in all but one case, not members of the ethnic group predominant in the school's student population, Weber concluded that "there are far more important matters than the ethnic background of the administrators and teachers in achieving success in beginning reading instruction" (p. 701). To be sure, the competence, attitude, and commitment of the teachers and administrators in low-income minority schools to the teaching of basic skills are more critical than their ethnic backgrounds. Yet, there are powerful reasons to suggest the need for more competent and committed Black, Puerto Rican, and other minority teachers and administrators in low-income minority schools who endorse the "Excellence" perspective.

Rhody McCoy (1970), a leader of the controversial struggle for decentralization and community control of schools in Ocean Hill-Brownsville (Brooklyn, New York) in the late 1960s, has argued,

> Here in New York it's conceivable that a kid can go from first grade all the way through high school and never see a black teacher. If all these kids coming up today still see the white principal, the white district superintendent, the white Board of Education, white State Commissioner of Education, then their only conception is that in order to be successful, and be the boss, you gotta be white. That's not so. At least we don't want these kids to believe that it's so. So we're interested in having success models. (p. 256)

Weber did not include instruction in test-wiseness as a nonessential character-istic or success factor; however, he observed that pupils at the Ann Street School were consciously instructed "in the mechanics of test-taking...it (the school) tests the children frequently, using a variety of tests" (p. 546). The prevalence of test-ing in schools, particularly minimum competency testing as a prerequisite for graduation, has alerted educators to the importance of test-taking skills (Downey, 1977). Limited attention has been focused on the role of test-wiseness in the test performance of minority students (McPhail, 1979c); however, infor-mal reports from classroom teachers who have taught test-wiseness systemati-cally have been encouraging. This informal data, with the limited empirical data on teaching test-wiseness to minority students, suggests that these stu-dents can be taught to be test-wise and can improve their performance as a re-sult. Future research on these hypotheses, and on which skills to teach, is a critical need (McPhail, 1981b).

## Conclusions

The hypothesis of Weber's research study was proven. At least four inner-city public schools existed in the United States whose achievement in beginning reading instruction was far higher than in most inner-city schools. As such, Weber confirmed that the failure of low- income minority children to learn to read is the "fault not of the children or their background—but of the schools" (p. 547). Despite the limitations of the study critiqued above, the work of George Weber will remain a classic study of the assertion that low-income minority chil-dren can learn to read if taught.

### *Note*

1. The issue of language differences was also advanced during this period as a primary causal factor in African American children's reading failure. The reader is referred to Baratz and Shuy (1969), Labov (1972), Laffey and Shuy (1973), McPhail (1975, 1979a), Piestrup (1973), Tolliver-Weddington (1979), Williams (1970), and Williams (1975) for classic discussions of this issue. The characteristics of the African American family also figured prominently in the effort to build a case for the failure of African American learners to achieve in school. The reader is referred to the Coleman Report (Coleman, 1966) and the U.S. Department of Labor, Office of Planning and Research (1965) report on *The Negro Family* for a discussion of deficit views on the Black family, and to Billingsley (1968) and Hill (1972) for a discussion of the strengths and assets of the Black family.

# REFERENCES

Baratz, J.C., & Shuy, R.W. (Eds.). (1969). *Teaching Black children to read.* Washington, DC: Center for Applied Linguistics.

Barnard, D.P., & Hetzel, R.W. (1976). The principal's role in reading instruction. *The Reading Teacher, 29*(4), 386–388.

Billingsley, A. (1968). *Black families in White America.* Englewood Cliffs, NJ: Prentice Hall.

Bond, G.L., & Dykstra, R. (1967). *Coordinating center for first grade reading instructional programs: Final report* (USOE Project No. X-001). Minneapolis: University of Minnesota.

Botel, M. (1977). *Literacy plus.* Washington, DC: Curriculum Development Associates.

Chall, J.S. (1967). *Learning to read: The great debate.* New York: McGraw-Hill.

Cohen, D.H. (1968). The effects of literature on vocabulary and reading achievement. *Elementary English, 45*(2), 209–213, 217.

Cohen, M. (n.d.). *Instructionally effective schools* (Research Area Plan). Washington, DC: National Institute of Education.

Cohen, S.A. (1969). *Teach them all to read.* New York: Random House.

Coleman, J.S. (1966). *Equality of educational opportunity.* Washington, DC: U.S. Department of Health, Education, and Welfare, Office of Education.

Dabney, N. (1983). See how it runs: A successful inner-city school. *Dissertation Abstracts International, 44*(04A), 1042. (UMI No. AA18318158)

Downey, G.W. (1977). Is it time we started teaching children how to take tests? *American School Board Journal, 164,* 27–30.

Durkin, D. (1966). *Children who read early: Two longitudinal studies.* New York: Teachers College Press.

Dykstra, R. (1968). Summary of the second-grade phase of the Cooperative Research Program in primary reading instruction. *Reading Research Quarterly, 4,* 49–70.

Goodman, K.S. (1968). The psycholinguistic nature of the reading process. In K.S. Goodman (Ed.), *The psycholinguistic nature of the reading process* (pp. 13–26). Detroit, MI: Wayne State University Press.

Harris, A.J. (1978, May). *The effective teacher of reading, revisited.* Paper presented at the 23rd Annual Convention of the International Reading Association, Houston, TX. (ERIC Document Reproduction Service No. ED 153 193)

Harris, A.J., & Morrison, C. (1969). The CRAFT project: A final report. *The Reading Teacher, 22*(4), 335–340.

Hill, R.B. (1972). *The strengths of Black families.* New York: Emerson Hall.

Hoover, M.R. (1978). Characteristics of Black schools at grade level: A description. *The Reading Teacher, 31,* 757–762.

Jensen, A.R. (1969). How much can we boost IQ and scholastic achievement? *Harvard Educational Review, 39*(1), 1–123.

Labov, W. (1972). *Language in the inner city: Studies in the Black English Vernacular.* Philadelphia: University of Pennsylvania Press.

Laffey, J.L., & Shuy, R. (Eds.). (1973). *Language differences: Do they interfere?* Newark, DE: International Reading Association.

Levenstein, P. (1975). *The mother–child home program.* New York: Verbal Interaction Project.

McCoy, R. (1970). Why have an Ocean Hill-Brownsville? In N. Wright (Ed.), *What Black educators are saying.* New York: Hawthorn Books.

McPhail, I.P. (1975). *Teaching Black children to read: A review of psycho- and sociolinguistic theories and models.* Philadelphia: University of Pennsylvania. (ERIC Document Reproduction Service No. ED103819)

McPhail, I.P. (1979a, April). *Beyond Black English: Toward an ethnography of communication in the inner-city class-room.* Paper presented at the 24th Annual Convention of the International Reading Association, Atlanta, GA. (ERIC Document Reproduction Service No. ED172178)

McPhail, I.P. (1979b). A study of response to literature across three social interaction patterns: A directional effort. *Reading Improvement, 16*(1), 55–61. (ERIC Document Reproduction Service No. EJ206218)

McPhail, I.P. (1979c). Test sophistication: An important consideration in judging the standardized test performance of Black students. *Reading World, 18*(3), 227–235. (ERIC Document Reproduction Service No. EJ203030)

McPhail, I.P. (1981a, August). *An agenda for urban education: Implications for teacher education from the study of successful low-income minority schools.* Keynote address at the 2nd Annual Conference on Urban Education, Dallas Teacher Education Center Council and Teacher Corps Project, Dallas, TX.

McPhail, I.P. (1981b). Why teach test-wise-ness? *Journal of Reading, 25*(1), 32–38.

Piestrup, A.M. (1973). Black dialect interfer-ence and accommodation of reading in-struction in first grade. *Monographs of the Language Behavior Research Laboratory* (No. 4). Berkeley: University of California.

Rist, R.C. (1973). *The urban school. A factory for failure.* Cambridge: Massachusetts Institute of Technology Press.

Ristow, W. (1978). Larry P. versus IQ tests. *The Progressive, 42*, 48–50.

Sakamoto, T. (1975). Preschool reading in Japan. *The Reading Teacher, 29*(3), 240–244.

Senna, C. (Ed.). (1973). *The fallacy of IQ.* New York: Third Press.

Silberman, C.E. (1970). *Crisis in the class-room: The remaking of American educa-tion.* New York: Random House.

Smitherman, G. (Ed.). (1981). Black English and the education of Black children and youth: *Proceedings of the National Invitational Symposium on the King Decision.* Detroit, MI: Center for Black Studies, Wayne State University.

Sprigle, H. (1972). *The learning to learn pro-gram: Final report.* (ERIC Document Reproduction Service No. ED066669)

Strickland, S. (1973). Can slum children learn? In C. Senna (Ed.), *The fallacy of IQ* (pp. 150–159). New York: Third Press.

Taylor, O.L. (1971). Response to social dialects and the field of speech. In R. Shuy (Ed.), *Sociolinguistic theory: Mater-ials and practice* (pp. 13–20). Washing-ton, DC: Center for Applied Linguistics.

Thomas, J.M. (1990). The Woodland Elementary School. In M.R. Hoover, N. Dabney, & S. Lewis (Eds.), *Successful Black and minority schools: Classic mod-els* (pp. 6–10). San Francisco: Julian Richardson.

Thorndike, R.L. (Ed.). (1973). *Reading com-prehension education in fifteen countries: An empirical study.* New York: Wiley.

Tolliver-Weddington, G. (Ed.). (1979). Introduction. *Journal of Black Studies, 9*(4), 364–366.

U.S. Department of Labor, Office of Planning and Research. (1965). *The Negro family: The case for national action.* Washington, DC: Author.

Watkins, M. (1981). *Teachers' perceptions of parents' roles vs. parents' perception of their roles in children's acquisition of liter-acy for learning.* Unpublished manu-script, University of Pennsylvania.

Weber, G. (1969). How one ghetto school achieves success in reading. *Council for Basic Education Bulletin, 13*, 1–4.

Weber, G. (1971). *Inner-city children can be taught to read: Four successful schools.* (Occasional Papers No. 18). Washington, DC: Council for Basic Education.

Wilcox, P. (1970). Education for Black humanism: A way of approaching it. In N. Wright (Ed.), *What Black educators are saying* (pp. 3–17). San Francisco: Leswing Press; New York: Hawthorn Books.

Williams, F. (Ed.). (1970). *Language and poverty: Perspectives on a theme.* Chicago: Markham.

Williams, F., & Whitehead, J.L. (1971, April). Language in the classroom: Studies of the Pygmalion Effect. *English Record, 21*(4), 108–113.

Williams, R.L. (1972). Abuses and misuses in testing Black children. *Counseling Psychologist, 2*(3), 62–73.

Williams, R.L. (Ed.). (1975). *Ebonics: The true language of Black folks.* St. Louis, MO: Institute of Black Studies.

Wilson, S. (1977). The use of ethnographic techniques in educational research. *Review of Educational Research, 47*(2), 245–265.

Wolcott, H.F. (1973). *The man in the principal's office; an ethnography.* New York: Holt, Rinehart, & Winston.

Word, C. (1974, October). Testing: Another word for racism. *Essence, 5,* 38.

# CHAPTER 8

# Using Multicultural Literature to Create Guided Reading Connections for African American Learners

*Linda B. Akanbi*

Producing engaged proficient readers is the ultimate reading instructional goal of any classroom teacher. Engaged readers are motivated and able to sustain their interest while reading. Proficiency requires being able to read with a high level of accuracy, fluency, and comprehension.

In guided reading instruction, the teacher assists and supports small groups of students in applying reading strategies they have learned as they attempt to read a book independently, monitors their comprehension and reading progress, and provides the tools for students to attain the desired levels of proficiency and beyond. The time spent on actually reading is the key to children making reading gains. The more students read, the more proficiently they will read. Increased reading improves overall literacy development, resulting in better performance on tests of reading comprehension, increased vocabulary levels, enhanced critical-thinking skills, enjoyment of the creative uses of language and art, and exposure to a variety of linguistic models (Harris, Kamhi, & Pollack, 2001). However, as Allington (2002) points out, if children are to read a lot throughout the school day, they will need a rich supply of books that they actually can read and that they will want to read. Books that pertain to the students' own experiences, and that contain characters who are very much like the students themselves, have great potential for producing engaged reading because students will be able to make connections easily.

Making connections, which is based on schema theory, means relating unfamiliar text to one's prior world knowledge or personal experiences. According to Keene and Zimmermann (1997), these connections usually take three forms: text-to-self connections, which occur when a book makes readers think about their own lives or experiences; text-to-text connections, which occur when a new book reminds readers of other books that they have read; and finally, text-to-world connections, which occur when readers use their world knowledge to enhance comprehension of a book. Ideally, books selected for guided reading should allow for such connections to be made. Choosing books that relate to children's cultural experiences, such as Bill Cosby's Little Bill Series (Cosby, 1997– ), which focuses on the African American culture, make these connections easier.

Au (2001) sees multicultural literature as a means of bringing children from diverse backgrounds to high levels of literacy. She speaks of culturally responsive instruction, which includes, according to Au, approaches that build on the strengths that students bring from their home culture instead of ignoring these strengths or requiring that students learn through approaches that conflict with their cultural values. Au says that multicultural literature allows educators to engage students in literacy experiences they find meaningful and motivating. Although Au believes that it is important for students of all backgrounds to read and respond to works of multicultural literature, she feels that the interaction with these texts is especially important for students of diverse backgrounds.

# Benefits of Using Multicultural Materials in the Reading Program

The benefits of using multicultural literature in the reading program are highlighted as follows:

1. Moving toward culturally responsive instruction fosters new literacies that make connections to students' home cultures, allows educators to engage students in literacy experiences they find meaningful and motivating, and provides for a means to the end of bringing children from diverse backgrounds to levels of high literacy.

2. Students can gain insights about themselves and their families, and discover the value of their own experiences.

3. Students who do not share the author's ethnic identity learn that different cultural groups have histories and experiences that, while unique, offer lessons about life to all readers.

4. Multicultural materials have the advantage of making literacy learning immediately rewarding to children of diverse backgrounds (Au, 2001).

In addition, Harris (1990; see also Taylor, 1999) notes the following benefits regarding sharing African American children's literature with students: cognitive development, familiarization with patterns of language, and the stimulation of the imagination.

Conversely, the lack of quality ethnic children's literature in a school reading program can have a negative impact on students' self-esteem as well as their motivation. Sims (1982) argues that when African Americans are excluded from or stereotyped in children's literature, they are not afforded the respect they are due and racism is enforced. According to Harris (as cited in Taylor, 1999), "if African American children do not see themselves in school texts or do not perceive any affirmation of their cultural heritage in those texts, then it is quite likely that they will not read or value schooling as much" (p. 12).

This observation was borne out further in a study by Tyson (1999) who explored the pedagogical implications of the selection of children's literature, as well as how that literature may be used as an instructional tool to increase literacy success and initiate social action with a group of African American fifth-grade boys. The boys were reluctant readers, "turned off" to literature, and scored very low on standardized reading tests. Over the course of an academic year, Tyson met with the boys who attended an urban Midwestern elementary school. According to Tyson, as the boys became friends, they named themselves "the Posse" and became a brotherhood of readers. For the purposes of the project, Tyson chose contemporary realistic fiction, which she defines as picture books that are fictionalized narratives based on socially significant events. One example is the 1995 Caldecott Medal winner, *Smoky Night* (Bunting, 1994), a fictional account of the Los Angeles riots that occurred after three police officers were acquitted of criminal charges for the beating of Rodney King.

Tyson read aloud contemporary realistic fiction to the boys, gathering their responses in both written and oral form. She states that as the boys responded to the texts, they began to discover and supplement the fictional information with factual information. They began to scrutinize and interpret the information through cause and effect, hypothesizing ideas and predictions, inferring or deciphering character traits or identifying authors' purpose, as well as bringing personal insight and their own experience to their literary interpretations. As one can see, these are all higher-order thinking skills.

In terms of making text-to-self or personal connections, Tyson stated that the boys would often say that a character reminded them of family members, friends, sports figures, neighbors, media images, and others who touched their lives. Finally, as the boys responded to the literature as a community of readers, noted the researcher, they began to think about serious problems in their communities and to make suggestions to address those problems.

Choosing a genre of contemporary realistic fiction, which the boys could relate to and that was relevant to their lives, not only motivated these reluctant, low performance readers to become engaged in reading, but sustained their engagement as they constructed meaning as a group. Tyson saw the boys develop literacy understanding, which led to important gains in reading and literacy behaviors that enhanced success with school literacies.

## Guidelines for Evaluating and Selecting Multicultural Materials

Banks (1997) states that one of the best ways to ensure that books accurately portray the perspectives of ethnic groups is to use books written by members of those groups. He has developed the following guidelines for evaluating and selecting multicultural materials for classroom and library use:

1. Certain values, aspirations, and viewpoints are prevalent in American ethnic communities. Books should honestly and accurately reflect those perspectives and feelings, both through characters and in the interpretations of events and situations.

2. Fictional works should have strong ethnic characters. Many books have characters of color that are weak, subservient, and ignorant.

3. Books should describe settings and experiences with which all students can identify and yet should accurately reflect ethnic cultures and lifestyles.

4. Books should contain protagonists with ethnic characteristics, but the characters should face conflicts and problems universal to all cultures and groups. [See the following section on "African American Themes Found in Culturally Conscious Fiction."]

5. Books should contain illustrations that are accurate, ethnically sensitive, and technically well done. Many books have beautiful illustrations but are inaccurate.

6. Ethnic materials should not contain racist concepts, clichés, phrases, or words. This means also being sensitive to subtle stereotypes of ethnic groups. In many current books, subtle ethnic stereotypes are more frequent than blatant ones.

7. Factual materials should be historically accurate. Books that present inaccurate information about ethnic groups confuse students, reinforce stereotypes, and instill misconceptions.

8. Multiethnic sources and basal textbooks should discuss major events and documents related to ethnic history. (pp. 125–126)

In addition to the guidelines above, Banks suggests that teachers determine the age level for which a particular book might be appropriate, along with the characteristics of their class. That is to say, the teacher should bear in mind whether the class is, for example, all African American, all Native American, all Asian American, all White, or ethnically integrated.

# African American Themes Found in Culturally Conscious Fiction

The following themes depict authentic African American sociocultural themes:

1. Emphasis on respect for eldership and for family and community adult role models.

2. Use of affective cues, gesturing, proverbial statements, rhyming and rhythm, and so forth when communicating.

3. A social environment that prioritizes flexible and spontaneous activity or behavior (e.g., spontaneous group formation and change, flexible rule and roles, etc.) rather than firmly structured and regimented activity, social or otherwise.

4. Games and play activities that augment social (human) interaction (e.g., hand games, hopscotch, Double Dutch, etc.) in preferences to activities that encourage interaction with object or independent games or play activities with toys, computerized games, puzzles, and so forth. (Bell & Clark, 1998, pp. 4–5)

Overlapping these themes are six culturally conscious literature elements (Sims, 1982; see also Taylor, 1999): (1) Black English Vernacular, (2) relationships between young and old, (3) extended families, (4) awareness of skin color, (5) tradition of naming, and (6) African American cultural traditions. According to Sims, the primary purpose of culturally conscious literature—in which African American children are major characters, and their culture is not only emphasized but is celebrated—is to allow Black authors to speak to Black children about their lives and themselves. However, by no means are these books to be closed to other children.

# The Little Bill Series

A series of books that meet all the criteria established by Banks (1997), Bell and Clark (1998), and Sims (1982) for being culturally relevant, yet containing situations and themes that all children can relate to, is the Little Bill Series by Bill Cosby (1997– ). The main character, Little Bill, lives in an extended family household in which there are three generations including his younger brother, his parents, and his great-grandmother. The oral tradition in the African American culture is celebrated in the stories, wisdom, and teachings that the older generations in the series pass down to the younger generation. Respect for adults is taught, as well as respect for other human beings. There are implications for character education in almost all of the books in the series. The reading level of the books is 2.0 (second grade); however, the books are appropriate for children ages 6–10.

In the series, Little Bill attends a school where the student population is culturally diverse, and his close associates reflect that diversity, although most of them are minorities. Cultural traditions, such as playing "the Dozens," are portrayed, along with such common childhood experiences as being afraid of the dark. The stories are contemporary, the characters are strong, and the adult characters provide excellent role models for children. The illustrations are very colorful and extremely well done, portraying the ethnicity of the characters convincingly. The illustrations also show Black art in the home.

Working as a reading consultant, I used the Little Bill Series in staff development workshops to teach guided reading as well as to demonstrate guided-reading techniques in third-, fourth-, and fifth-grade classrooms in an urban school in which 99% of the student population was African American. The response of the students was overwhelming. Not only were the students excited and motivated by the books, they were able to make connections to the stories and characters immediately and to become fully engaged in the reading of the stories. The follow-up writing activities allowed the students to create their own literacies using familiar experiences.

I have included figures that present resources for using the Little Bill Series in the classroom. Figures 8.1 shows a story map for the series, and Figure 8.2 offers introductory materials. See Figure 8.3 for a sample lesson plan I developed based on one book from the Little Bill Series, *The Day I Saw My Father Cry* (Cosby, 2000). A teacher may adapt this lesson plan to his or her own literacy objectives.

---

### FIGURE 8.1 Story Map for the Little Bill Series

| | |
|---|---|
| **Author:** | Bill Cosby |
| **Illustrator:** | Varnette Honeywood |
| **Main Characters:** | Little Bill, Mom, Dad (Big Bill), Bobby, Alice-the-Great, Andrew, Michael, Jose, Kiku, Fuschia |
| **Setting:** | School, home, playground |
| **Problem:** | What is the problem in the story? What do the characters have to deal with? |
| **Resolution of the Problem:** | What finally happened? |
| **Theme:** | What can we learn from this story? |

---

## FIGURE 8.2  Introduction to the Little Bill Series

How many of you have ever heard of Bill Cosby? Bill Cosby has written a series of books called the Little Bill Series. I suspect that some of the stories are about him when he was a little boy. Today, we are going to read some of these books. I'll introduce you to each book briefly, and then I'll give each of you one of the books to read on your own. I want you to read softly to yourselves. If you come to a word you don't know, use what you have learned about sounds and word parts to figure it out. But remember, it has to make sense. While you are reading softly to yourselves, I will come around and listen to you read and try to help you figure out any words you don't know. I might ask you some questions about the story, too.

**Little Bill**

Little Bill is a boy in third grade. His friends are in the third grade, too. His friends are Andrew, Jose, Michael, and a girl named Kiku. Then there's Fuschia, who is also his cousin.

Little Bill lives with his mother and father. His father is Big Bill. Little Bill has an older brother named Bobby. Little Bill's great-grandmother lives with them, too. Everybody calls her Alice-the-Great.

Who knows what a great-grandmother is? Do any of you have a great-grandmother? Is she wise? Well, Little Bill's great-grandmother is very wise. She can always help him figure out things when he is worried about something.

So, this is Little Bill's family and his closest friends, his inner circle.

His teacher's name is Miss Murray.

In every story, Little Bill has a problem to solve. I want you to read to find out how he resolves his particular problem. Then, I want you to go to the writing center and make up your story about the same kind of problem and tell how you would resolve it.

## FIGURE 8.3  Lesson Plan for Guided Reading

**Subject Area:** Reading and language arts

**Skills:** Vocabulary, comprehension, critical thinking and problem solving, fluency

**Objectives:**
1. For students to be able to read for a purpose.
2. For students to be able to use prior knowledge to develop empathy with the characters (making connections).
3. For students to develop an understanding of the concept of role model, as demonstrated by their ability to name examples of role models.
4. For students to increase reading fluency.
5. For students to be able to apply what they learned from the story to resolve conflicts.

*(continued)*

FIGURE 8.3 *(continued)*

**Materials:**
*The Day I Saw My Father Cry* by Bill Cosby

**Procedures Before Reading:**
Show the book cover and read the title. Introduce the story briefly, providing just enough of the plot structure (a preview) to arouse the students' curiosity and interest.

Activate the students' prior knowledge by having them to relate similar experiences in their personal lives to the introduction.

Give the students a purpose for reading, for example:

A lot of things can make people cry, can't they? What are some things that can make people cry? (Wait for responses.) Sometimes people cry when they're sad. When someone dies who we love, that makes us sad, doesn't it? But when we remember the good things that a person did, that makes us smile. This is a story about a very special friend of Little Bill's father who passed away. One thing that was so special about him was that he always knew how to break up fights or arguments between Little Bill and his brother or between Little Bill's friends. Read this story to find out how he did this.

**Procedures During Reading:**
Have the students to read the texts softly to them selves. As the read, move around to each child in the group and "listen in" to small sections of the text being read aloud. Assist students who need support in applying strategies for decoding any unfamiliar words.

**Procedures After Reading:**
Discuss the story in terms of the stated purpose.

Have the group to retell the story, making sure there is a beginning, a middle, and an end.

Ask questions pertaining to the plot, theme, and different characters in the story.

Carry out the extension activities (see below).

Students may reread the story by themselves or to a partner to develop fluency.

**Extension Activities:**
*Exploring A Concept.* Explore the concept of role model. Write the term on the board. Discuss what a role model is. Have the students to determine how the character, Alan Mills, was a role model in the story. Ask them if they have any family members, neighbors, friends whom they consider to be good role models. Have the students extend the concept to include members in the community and superstars. Then have them write a story about their favorite role model and tell why this person is their favorite role model.

*Role-Playing.* Have the students role-play scenarios in which a problem has to be resolved. The problem could be one that occurs on the playground, at home, or at school–anywhere that the students and their friends or siblings are involved (e.g., someone cuts in front of other students in the lunch line; a sister and a brother cannot agree on whose turn it is to wash the dishes, etc.). The students can make up their own scenarios. Then let the group decide on an amicable and fair way to resolve the conflict.

# Conclusion

There are many ways to use multicultural literature in the school reading program. The uses are limited only by the teacher's imagination. The advantages are that it makes the curriculum content relevant (especially for children of color), it builds self-esteem, and it improves reading comprehension. The use of the Little Bill books demonstrates only one example of how multicultural literature can be used to enhance the reading abilities of African American learners.

## REFERENCES

Allington, R.L. (2002). What I've learned about effective reading instruction. *Phi Delta Kappan, 83*(10), 740–747.

Au, K.H. (2001, July/August). Culturally responsive instruction as a dimension of the new literacies. *Reading Online, 5*(1). Retrieved October 2, 2001, from http://www.readingonline.org/newliteracies/au/#culturally.

Banks, J.A. (1997). *Teaching strategies for ethnic studies* (6th ed.). Boston: Allyn & Bacon

Bell, Y.R., & Clark, T.R. (1998). Culturally relevant reading material as related to comprehension and recall in African American Children. *Journal of Black Psychology, 24*(4), 455–475.

Harris, J.L., Kamhi, A.G., & Pollock, K.E. (Eds.). (2001). *Literacy in African American communities.* Mahwah, NJ: Erlbaum.

Harris, V.J. (1990). Benefits of children's literature. *Journal of Negro Education, 59*(4), 538–539.

Keene, E.O., & Zimmermann, S. (1997). *Mosaic of thought: Teaching comprehension in a reader's workshop.* Portsmouth, NH: Heinemann.

Sims, R. (1982). *Shadow and substance: Afro-American experience in contemporary children's fiction.* Urbana, IL: National Council of Teachers of English.

Taylor, G.S. (1999). Pass it on: The development of African-American children's literature. *The Negro Educational Review, 1,* 11–17.

Tyson, C.A. (1999). "Shut my mouth wide open": Realistic fiction and social action. *Theory Into Practice, 38*(3), 155–159.

## LITERATURE CITED

Bunting, E. (1994). *Smoky night.* San Diego: Harcourt Brace.

Cosby, B. (1997–). Little Bill books for beginning readers (Series). New York: Scholastic.

Cosby, B. (2000). *The day I saw my father cry* (Little Bill Series). (V.P. Honeywood, Illus.). New York: Scholastic.

# CHAPTER 9

# Working Together for Literacy: Faces of Hope

*Rudine Sims Bishop*

The theme for the 1997 Reading Recovery Conference, Working Together for Literacy, calls to mind the currently popular African proverb, "It takes a village to raise a child." It implies that if we as a society are to bring all our children to literacy, it is going to take all of us—classroom teachers, Reading Recovery teachers, librarians, teacher educators, families, government—the entire professional and nonprofessional "literacy village," so to speak, to make it happen. Working with those children whom the system would give up on—children considered candidates for failure—revaluing them, and helping them to revalue themselves constitute an awesome task, the importance and the enormity of which is underscored, it seems to me, by the recent brouhaha over the Oakland, California, school board resolution on Ebonics (see http://linguistlist.org/topics/ebonics/ebonics-res2.html).

Many of the children in Oakland likely were and are very similar to children who end up in programs such as Reading Recovery. We know, therefore, that the problem Oakland is wrestling with does not reside in the children, but in the failure of the school and the larger community to find ways to initiate those children into what Frank Smith (1987) called "the literacy club," the society of literate people. The problem, as Ladson-Billings (1997) pointed out, is the shocking percentage of those children who have been severely labeled, shunted aside into special education classes, and robbed of the opportunity to reach their full potential. The Oakland School Board resolution was a desperate cry from the community for help in trying to save and liberate a generation of children, for the African American community has historically believed that, in some sense, literacy and liberation go hand in hand.

A recently published picture book highlights the importance of literacy in the life of one individual and, by extension, to a larger community, and offers a launching pad for this article. *More Than Anything Else* (Bradby, 1995), set in

Reprinted with permission from *Journal of Children's Literature* (Spring 1998), *24*(1), 90–97. Originally presented as a speech at the Reading Recovery Conference, Columbus, OH, February 2, 1997.

West Virginia a few years after the Civil War ended, is the story of a young boy who works in the salt mines and longs to learn to read, to know "the secret in those books." He lives in a community of formerly enslaved people, many of whom have had no previous opportunities to learn to read. As he listens to a Black man reading a newspaper to a crowd of people in town, he dreams that he, too, will not only become a reader himself but that he will teach others to read. In response to his almost desperate need to become literate, his mother eventually produces from some unknown place a blue-covered primer from which he tries to teach himself to read. Unsuccessful in his efforts, he seeks out the man he had seen reading the newspaper—a "brown face of hope." With the man's help, he unlocks the secrets of the alphabet, and he is on his way to being a reader. His elation is unbounded: "I shout and laugh like when I was baptized in the creek. I have jumped into another world, and I am saved." Connecting the alphabet to sounds is not enough, however. He needs more, and the newspaper man teaches him to write his name. As he writes the name in the dirt, the identity of the boy becomes known: Booker.

Booker is the famous late 19th- to early 20th-century Black educator Booker T. Washington. Although this story is fictionalized biography, we know that he was born into slavery, a condition that has the potential to squash all hopes and dreams, but that he "held fast to his dreams," and became an educator, the founder of Tuskegee Institute (Alabama), and the most famous and influential African American of his day. The story strongly implies that it was literacy that opened the way for Booker T. Washington.

His story can be both inspirational and instructive, and leads to my first point: In literacy learning and teaching, *what* children read matters as much as *how* they learn they read. When Booker informed his mother that he had to learn to read, she gave him the only help she could. She provided him with what appears to be Noah Webster's (1800) *Blue-Backed Speller*. At the time, it was the most widely available, and probably the most widely used instructional text in the country. It was so popular, in fact, that next to the Bible, it was the book most likely to be found in the average American home. Many accounts of enslaved men and women coming to literacy record their use of the speller. It began with the alphabet, followed by pages of syllables, such as *ab, eb, ib, ob, ub*. It progressed on to words of one, two, three syllables, and so on, implicitly theorizing that word length or syllable length is a valid measure of difficulty. Webster's focus was on pronunciation, and although there are many accounts of people teaching themselves, it is also true that almost all those accounts indicate that, in the beginning, they needed someone who was literate to get them started. When Booker couldn't "catch the tune," he recruited the newspaper reader to be his teacher.

Helping readers "tune in" to the way written language works has traditionally been the role of teachers of beginning reading. The great debates about beginning reading—whether defined as phonics versus whole word, or whole language versus phonics, or couched in the language of an exchange between one former (Barnes, 1997) and five current Reading Recovery teachers (Browne, Fitts, McLaughlin, McNamara, & Williams, 1997)—have been mainly about instructional strategies, about *how* to go about helping beginners to become literate. That is all well and good and these are worthwhile debates, because our experience and knowledge lead us to believe that some instructional strategies are more effective than others. My point, though, is that in our zeal to help children become effective readers and writers, we must not permit the real-life purposes of literacy to become secondary to the means of achieving it. No matter how effective we become at helping children acquire skills and strategies, those skills and strategies are not, in and of themselves, enough. "I have to know more," Booker said in *More Than Anything Else*. "Tell me more."

I would submit that even from the beginning, we need to help children tune in to the power of literacy: the potential for reading and writing to expand our horizons, to help us understand how the world works, and to show us how we as human beings function effectively in various social and cultural contexts. I would suggest, then, that we consider the creators of children's books, both writers and artists, to be important citizens in the village of literacy workers that we call on to help us bring children to reading and writing. It is through transactions with the rich texts these writers and artists create that children learn how to read both the surface features of texts and the meanings beneath and beyond the surface. In *How Texts Teach What Readers Learn*, Meek (1988) demonstrates, through her description of a child reading *Rosie's Walk* (Hutchins, 1969) and other rich picture books, that "the most important single lesson that children learn from texts is *the nature and variety of written discourse*, the different ways that language lets a writer tell, and the many and different ways a reader reads" (p. 21).

But stories not only help children understand how written language works, stories, broadly defined, are fundamental to thinking, to helping children, in fact all of us, to make sense of the world. "Narrative," in the words of Harding (1977), "is a primary act of mind" (p. 12). Story becomes important, then, particularly in early literacy programs because it legitimizes narrative as a way of thinking in a school setting. I am fond of quoting Lloyd Alexander (1981), arguing that story is fundamental to human experience:

> By inventing language, the human race invented story. We can state a fact: "The straw was yellow." Or work magic: "The straw was spun into gold." Story need not be verbal. Pictures can tell a story. Music plays out wordless

dramas, different at every hearing. We can dance a story...but my interest here is in story in the form of language.... In story, the dividing line is not necessarily between fact and fiction. The line, that is, can be stretched very thin. Some fiction claims to be true. We call it history. Some truth claims to be fiction. We call it literature. Both are aspects of story, nonetheless. In the broad sense of the word, story ranges from the book of Job to the report of a street accident. Once we go beyond the simplest declaration of fact to give an account with any degree of complexity, we are obliged to select, arrange, emphasize—to become storytellers. (p. 3)

If story is so basic to language—and Alexander says that by inventing one, humans invented the other—then story is also basic to literacy, and the selection of reading material takes on major significance in reading instructional programs. Two decades ago, Bettelheim (1976), in the introduction to his classic book, *The Uses of Enchantment,* reminded us that "the acquisition of skills, including the ability to read, becomes devalued when what one has learned to read adds nothing of importance to one's life" (p. 4). Thus, there is another reason for *what* children read being as important as acquiring strategies for dealing with the surface features of language: Story, literature, is one of the ways we socialize our children. Even Noah Webster, for all his focus on sounds and syllables, was concerned about the content of the material in his *Blue-Backed Speller.* He was interested in both the moral and nationalistic education of his readers, and the fables and stories included in the speller, as well as the practice sentences learners were expected to read, were all quite moralistic in tone. For example, here are some practice sentences, all in words of one syllable:

Be a good child; mind your book; love your school; strive to learn.
Tell no tales; call no ill names; you must not lie, nor swear, nor cheat, nor steal.
Play not with bad boys. (Webster, as cited in N.B. Smith, 1965, p. 48)

So even for Noah Webster, the *Blue-Backed Speller* was a means to a cultural end. We have, in the best of our children's literature, moved beyond such obvious and overt moralism and didactic intent, but nevertheless, the stories we offer our children tell them a good deal about what and who we value in this society. We are shaped in part by the stories and symbols that we value and that we pass on to our children, which also influence the mores, manners, and attitudes that we develop toward each other. For example, our fantasy literature—folk tales, mythology, other traditional literature, as well as modern fantasy—is one of the vehicles through which we pass on these values. These old stories unambiguously relate what we believe to be the difference between right and wrong, between good and evil. They tell us the kind of behavior that gets rewarded and the kind that gets punished. For example, in many fairy tales, the young person who is hardworking and generous and shares his or her meager belongings is the one who is rewarded with treasure, while the lazy, greedy siblings receive some sort of punishment. It's a variant on the idea that the meek shall inherit the earth.

In stories, readers and writers come face to face with ideas that we are often embarrassed to talk about, such as honor and courage and love and hate and truth. Literature often centers on themes that give insights into a society's values. Let me give you one example: *The Wizard of Earthsea* (Le Guin, 1968) is a classic fantasy with a young hero on a quest for wisdom, identity, and self-knowledge. Its main theme is that we are responsible for the evil we create, and we can only free ourselves by facing it directly. A subtheme is that each choice we make carries with it a concomitant responsibility. When the main character asks to be taught magic he is not yet competent to handle, his teacher tells him:

> You will learn it, when you are ready to learn it. But you must not change one thing, one pebble, one grain of sand, until you know what good and evil will follow the act.... A wizard's power of Changing and of Summoning can change the balance of the world. It is dangerous, that power. It is most perilous. It must follow knowledge, and serve need. To light a candle is to cast a shadow. (p. 29)

That is the kind of truth that could serve not only our children, but our political leaders as well, as technology becomes more and more sophisticated, and our world becomes ever smaller. They have the power not only to change the world, but to destroy it.

So it *does* matter what we offer children as reading material. Let me be clear that I am not suggesting that we use literature to indoctrinate children or that we return to the days of the Sunday School tract. I am suggesting that one of the purposes that literacy can serve is to open to children the world of literature and thereby provide them the means by which they can, as Booker says in *More Than Anything Else,* "jump into another world" and gain insight into what it means to be a decent human being in the world that they inhabit.

*What* children read is also important because good stories nurture the imagination, and that well may be the most important function that literature serves. Imagination leads to invention, to innovation. Albert Einstein himself once said that, for him, imagination was more important than positive knowledge. Neil Armstrong could not have walked on the moon if someone had not imagined that it could be done. In the story, it was Booker's ability to imagine a better life for himself—and for others—that motivated him to learn to read.

For Booker, the whole idea of reading seemed like magic, and in some sense he was right.

Writer and poet Jane Yolen (1981) often reminds her readers or listeners of the connection between wisdom, magic, and imagination, all of which are related to the same root word. As she traces it, the connection begins with a *mage*—a person of great wisdom. A mage could produce *magic*, which was the power to produce surprising phenomena and seemingly unnatural effects. Mages used their magic to produce *images* that passed for reality, that change our understanding of what is real, that push us past our initial perception into the world of *imagination*. Good literature keeps alive the connections between wisdom, magic, and imagination, and it is that connection that will ultimately turn children into readers.

The other major point I want to draw from the Booker story is that literacy can be a source of power and a source of hope. Booker T. Washington was born into slavery, although his birth occurred just about six or seven years before the Civil War ended, so he was free before he was ten. One of the things we know about the era of slavery is that for slave holders and their sympathizers, literacy was considered a threat to their livelihood and their way of life. Frederick Douglass, in his autobiography *The Life and Times of Frederick Douglass* (1881), for example, reported on how his putative master declared that teaching a Black child to read would forever unfit him to be a slave. That is why there were laws forbidding people to teach slaves to read, particularly after a few insurrections in the early 1830s that were led by literate Black men. Such resistance to literacy helped enslaved men and women understand that literacy represented a kind of empowerment. If it did not lead to actual physical freedom (and in many cases it did), it could lead to a sense of self-determination, a sense of being free from ignorance, even a sense of identity as a real person rather than a nonentity—a mere slave. It could lead, in other words, to survival, both physical and psychological. Booker T. Washington understood that literacy was the key to the fulfillment of his dreams, and he was driven, like so many newly freed African Americans, to acquire it at all costs.

And what has all that to do with literacy today? If literacy could help people in bondage survive over a hundred years ago, what can it mean to be denied literacy in today's world? Walter Dean Myers, who has written both picture books and novels for young people, talks frequently about what literacy—and literature—has meant to him (see Bishop, 1990). He grew up in New York City's Harlem. He was young at a time when Harlem was a kinder, gentler place than the one we read about today. He learned to read at home. His mother taught him with *True Confessions* magazine, among other material. So he started school with an advantage, was placed eventually in an advanced class, and attended one of the premier high schools in the city. But as a teenager, he was troubled. He skipped school, hung out with the wrong crowd, and courted disaster. There was one teacher, however, who recognized his talents as a writer and gave him an individualized reading list that became the basis for his literary education. Years later, he did a project that took him into prisons to interview some of the inmates. To his surprise, he discovered that many of the inmates were or had been very much like the person he was as a Harlem teenager. So he asked himself what had made the difference. How was it that young men with virtually the same background could take such different directions? How had Myers been able to escape their fate? His answer was that he had been a reader, and that had made all the difference. Reading had given him a sense of an ideal for which to strive, a recognition that there were numerous possibilities available to him in life.

Another story illustrates the double-edged nature of the power of literacy. My late aunt was born in the rural South at a time early in the 20th century when education for Blacks was a luxury granted to only a few. So at the time, she migrated north to the town where I was born. She was about 30 years old and barely able to read and write. Like most Black women in our town who were employed outside the home, she did domestic work and always felt that her opportunities were extremely limited by her lack of a formal education (as well as by racial discrimination). Then along came a fundamentalist religious group with an offer to study the Bible with her. She accepted the offer and it changed her life—not so much because of their religious teachings, but because, in studying the Bible, they taught her to read it, and in some very real sense it made her free. She took her religion seriously, and she felt she was no longer dependent on some preacher to tell her what the Bible said; she could read it for herself. She felt could make her own moral, ethical, and religious choices. Not only that, but because they also required her to write and gave her practice at doing so, she was no longer dependent on her children or me to help her with other tasks that required literacy. She had gained a degree of control over her own life.

Unfortunately, there is a darker side to the gift of literacy as it was given to my aunt. The people who taught her to read the Bible also taught her that there was only one way to interpret it, only one correct meaning to make of it and, that, of course, was the one chosen by them. They left no room for comparing and sharing meanings with others, for doubting, for constructing her own meaning, or for thinking for herself. Part of the power of literacy is that its liberating effect can be a threat. The power of literacy to free one's thinking can be seen as threatening by members of groups who see the school as a place that alienates their children from their traditional values. And that is one of the reasons that censorship exists. Literacy can also be threatening to people in positions of power in a society that needs an underclass to do its menial work or who would be threatened if the so-called underclass were to become politicized or even radicalized, and begin to seek redress for the grievances it has suffered. At times, I have to wonder if some of the extraordinary political efforts at controlling the methods and materials of literacy teaching, especially in schools that serve the urban poor in the United States, aren't at least subconsciously motivated by the same fear that made it a criminal act to teach a slave to read.

It may be that some people in power are afraid that, if we make the millions of poor children in our inner cities truly literate, they will grow up to hold the United States to its promise—that we all have a right to life, liberty, and the pursuit of happiness. Perhaps they are afraid that if we make them truly literate, they will begin to question why "liberty and justice" are not evenly distributed in a nation purportedly built on the premise that "all men are created equal." Perhaps they are afraid that literate people will begin to understand that the conditions under which they live are not entirely accidental, and not at all inevitable. Perhaps they are afraid that these children will discover the power of the written word. Perhaps they even fear that people who are critically literate will begin to hold the leaders of government responsible for their actions.

In the meantime, there is work to be done. We as literacy advocates need to find ways to convince the powers that be that we should not be spending more money on prisons than on schools. We need to be outraged that in 1990 only 23,000 Black men earned degrees from colleges and universities in this country, while 2.3 million Black men and Black juveniles passed through the nation's jails and prison systems. We need to be outraged that new prisons sometimes have better cafeterias and better libraries than many schools, while too many of our old urban schools are crumbling around our children. We need to be outraged that cities are willing to tax themselves to build new stadiums, while their schools are in receivership.

When we speak of working together for literacy, we have to recognize that it will take the will of the entire national village to raise our children to be literate, productive citizens of a democracy. We have to convince our neighbors, our politicians, and our business leaders that it is in their own best interests to fully fund schools and libraries, to eradicate the inequitable system of funding that ensures that "them that has gets," and leaves the rest with the crumbs. And although it will take longer, we must convince people that the schools cannot overcome by themselves the evils that are foisted on the poor by the larger society. Jonathan Kozol, in *Amazing Grace: The Lives of Children and the Conscience of a Nation* (1995), reported the following statement from a Harlem teenager:

If you weave enough bad things into the fibers of a person's life—sickness and filth, old mattresses and other junk thrown in the streets, and other ugly ruined things, and ruined people, a prison here, sewage there, drug dealers here, the homeless people over there, then give us the very worst schools anyone could think of, hospitals that keep you waiting for ten hours, police that don't show up when someone is dying, take the train that's underneath the street in the good neighborhoods and put it up above where it shuts out the sun—you can guess that life will not be very nice and children will not have much sense of being glad of who they are. Sometimes it feels like we've been buried six feet under their perceptions. (pp. 39–40)

In this richest nation on earth, we have the capacity to change all that, if we could just find the will. Professionals concerned with literacy learning and teaching have the opportunity to make a difference early in the lives of children who might otherwise be lost, to see to it that the children with whom we work understand that life *can* be "nice," and that they can be glad about who they are. For Booker, literacy was the face of hope. And as Katherine Paterson reminded us in her January 25, 1997, speech at the Ohio State Children's Literature Conference, "Children deserve the hope that stories can bring."

A final story offers another symbol of hope, and leads full circle back to my title, "Working Together for Literacy: Faces of Hope." *The Lotus Seed* (Garland, 1993) is the story of a Vietnamese woman who, on the day the emperor lost his throne, managed to take, as a memento, a seed from a lotus pod in the Imperial garden. The seed was a prized possession, and when she escaped from the war and came to the United States, her seed was one of the few possessions that came with her. When her grandson discovered the seed years later, he asked many questions and learned the story of the emperor and the lotus. Curious about a lotus blossom, he stole the seed one night and planted it in the mud near his grandmother's onion patch. His grandmother was distressed, but in the spring, the lotus bloomed, and eventually she was able to give each of her grandchildren a lotus seed to remember her by. For the grandmother, the lotus was "the flower of life and hope," able to survive for many years and, after lying dormant over a fall and winter, still able to emerge in the spring as a beautiful flower, bearing seeds that would generate new symbols of life and hope. Perhaps those who work together for literacy, particularly with children who have been labeled "at risk" of failure in school, are also planting seeds that will eventually bloom, providing access to fuller lives, and keeping hope alive for a whole generation of children. Perhaps for those children such teachers are, like the newspaper reader in the Booker story and the lotus flower in story of the lotus seed, the very faces of hope.

## REFERENCES

Alexander, L. (1981). The grammar of story. In B. Hearne & M. Kaye (Eds.), *Celebrating children's books* (pp. 3–13). New York: Lothrop, Lee & Shepard.

Barnes, B.L. (1997). But teacher you went right on: A perspective on Reading Recovery. *The Reading Teacher, 50,* 284–292.

Bettelheim, B. (1976). *The uses of enchantment: The meaning and importance of fairy tales.* New York: Knopf.

Bishop, R.S. (1990). *Presenting Walter Dean Myers.* Boston: Twayne.

Browne, A., Fitts, M., McLaughlin, B., McNamara, M.J., & Williams, J. (1997). Teaching and learning in Reading Recovery: Response to "But teacher you went right on." *The Reading Teacher, 50,* 294–300.

Harding, B. (1977). Narrative as a primary act of mind. In M. Meek, A. Warlow, & G. Barton (Eds.), *The cool web: The pattern of children's reading* (pp. 12–23). London: Bodley Head.

Ladson-Billings, G. (1997, January). Seminar presented at Ohio State University, School of Teaching and Learning, Columbus, OH.

Meek, M. (1988). *How texts teach what readers learn.* Stroud, UK: Thimble Press.

Paterson, K. (1997, January). Speech presented at Ohio State University Children's Literature Conference, Columbus, OH.

Smith, F. (1987). *Joining the literacy club: Further essays into education.* Portsmouth, NH: Heinemann.

Smith, N.B. (1965). *American reading instruction.* Newark, DE: International Reading Association.

Webster, N. (1800). *The American Spelling Book* (Blue-Back Speller). Boston: Isaiah Thomas and Ebenezer Andrews.

## LITERATURE CITED

Bradby, M. (1995). *More than anything else.* (C.K. Soentpiet, Illus.). New York: Orchard Books.

Douglass, F. (1881). *Life and times of Frederick Douglass: His early life as a slave, his escape from bondage, and his complete history to the present time.* Hartford, CT: Park Publishing.

Garland, S. (1993). *The lotus seed.* (T. Kiuchi, Illus.). San Diego: Harcourt.

Hutchins, P. (1969). *Rosie's walk.* New York: Aladdin.

Kozol, J. (1995). *Amazing grace: The lives of children and the conscience of a nation.* New York: Crown.

Le Guin, U.K. (1968). *The wizard of Earthsea.* (R. Robbins, Illus.). Berkeley, CA: Parnassus.

Yolen, J. (1981). The mask on the lapel. In *Touch magic: Fantasy, faerie and folklore in the literature of childhood.* New York: Philomel.

# CHAPTER 10

# Improving the Reading Comprehension Skills of Urban Students: One High School's Success Story

*E.R. Marnell Sr. and Bill Hammond*

A teacher—mimicking weariness—pushes a handcart loaded with texts and teaching supplies along the quiet corridor of the high school. The teacher makes eye contact with a colleague walking toward the cart. The teachers exchange smiles. One beseeches the other: "Don't these children ever read? Do they even know how to read?" Neither stops to speak. They pass each other with sympathetic looks of commiseration.

The academic performance of students in secondary schools has been a source of concern for many years. Because these years are critical in a student's educational development, and because this may be the last chance for teachers to assist students before they move into the larger and less protective environment of college or the workplace, the sense of urgency is heightened for many educators to provide meaningful instruction and correct the oversights of the previous years. Added to that concern is the poor academic performance that is characteristic of many secondary students, particularly in urban settings.

It was in just such a scenario that the Dual-Text Reading Initiative described in this chapter was born. Southwest DeKalb High School—a large, predominately Black, urban high school in a community adjacent to Atlanta, Georgia—is indicative of the typical environment in which many students are located. What is different about this school is the effort that its faculty and administration made to extend the instructional program to the students through teacher training, modification of instructional resources, and the development of an approach and attitude to instructional delivery. The success described herein is certainly possible to replicate in other communities. The only necessary prerequisites are leadership from the administrators and involvement of the teachers in the planning and development of the program.

# The Dual-Text Reading Initiative

The Dual-Text Reading Initiative was founded on the belief that meaningful information about student performance, scientifically based effective reading strategies for teaching high school content, and teacher training on effective student motivational methods could be incorporated into a simple, straightforward plan for instruction that could be understood and implemented in the classroom. Critical to this process was the need to make certain that methodology was clearly presented to and understood by the teachers. Kennedy (1997) asserts that teachers find it extremely difficult to apply research information that is of poor quality, is communicated poorly, and is lacking in credibility and practicality. In short, the information has to be presented to teachers and others in a "real" and usable form if it is to be understood, accepted, and implemented.

## *The Goal*

The goal of the Dual-Text Reading Initiative as first implemented at Southwest DeKalb High School was to help teachers gain an understanding of the notion of *teaching for understanding*. The conceptual framework for this program drew from the work of Perkins (1992, 1993) and his colleagues at Harvard University's Project Zero (Blythe, 1998; Perkins & Blythe, 1993; Wiske, 1998) and from others (Graves & Graves, 1994; Hogan & Pressley, 1997; Ryder & Graves, 1998; Wiggins, 1989; Wiggins & McTighe, 1998). Although Perkins and his colleagues are primarily associated with the concept of teaching for understanding, the other researchers cited here have contributed to the concept of *scaffolding student learning*. Both concepts were incorporated in the planning, instructions, and training on methodology provided to content area teachers.

Perkins (1992) asserts that, to teach for understanding, students must accomplish three tasks: (1) retain important information, (2) understand topics deeply, and (3) actively use knowledge. These concepts were part of the instruction on which content area teachers in the Dual-Text Reading Initiative based their lessons and instructional approaches. Perkins (as cited in Graves & Graves, 1994) suggests that a substantial amount of teaching should be done in fairly lengthy units that include the following features, which may be delineated into a four-part framework:

1. Generative topics
2. Understanding goals
3. Understanding performances
4. Ongoing assessment

Graves and Graves (1994) assert that students engaged in prolonged investigations of specific topics in content areas need sufficient guidance and direction for learning from teachers. Effecting teacher modeling and active engagement in strategies such as coaching, prompting, and providing meaningful and immediate feedback will help establish the right direction for students to develop their understanding of gaining meaning from text. These measures and others are described by Graves and Graves as "scaffolding."

The Dual-Text Reading Initiative was a deliberate attempt on the part of the teachers and administrators at Southwest DeKalb High School to translate the theories of Perkins, Graves and Graves, and others into meaningful and sustainable practices that would result in improved delivery of instruction and, finally, in improved student understanding and performance.

## Formation and Implementation

The history of the Dual-Text Reading Initiative at Southwest DeKalb High School began in 1998 with school principal Stanley J. Henson and assistant principal E.R. Marnell Sr., one of the authors of this chapter, who were concerned about low reading-skill levels of ninth-grade students. Principal Henson was determined to address the problem by encouraging the teaching of reading through the content areas. He considered the following questions: Can high school teachers using abridged texts aligned to their subjects' basal text (known as *dual texts*) help low-level readers comprehend material more quickly? Will reading-level gains be measurable? Can students transfer reading strategies in abridged text format to the more detailed content textbook? How does a teacher address equity, self-esteem, and behavior?

In keeping with the stated goal of the school—to develop a program to help teachers teach for understanding—it was imperative that the program be designed to increase students' achievement scores. Regardless of academic discipline, all achievement scores are inextricably linked to reading. The emphasis on metacognition—learning to learn—needed to be a significant component throughout the curriculum. Every effort, it was hoped, would provide data by which to benchmark success and guide future efforts.

As part of the solution, the principal also sought to develop an academy structure at the ninth-grade level to emphasize reading as a central component of the instructional delivery system. He assigned two administrators to the ninth-grade academy—one for disciplinary and attendance issues, and the other to coordinate staff development and instructional concerns. Principal Henson gave permission to provide reading-level testing for students to establish a baseline data point.

It was during this stage of program development that school reading specialist Elizabeth Filliat made her proposal. A veteran reading specialist of 20 years, Mrs. Filliat proposed to use her $500 Wal-Mart awards grant, an honor she had received for previous achievement in reading instruction, to establish a dual-text reading program designed for low level readers. She made her decision after preliminary reading-test results showed that the reading levels of nearly half the ninth-grade students entering school in 1998 were below the seventh grade.

Mrs. Filliat's proposal included the use of texts in the Globe Fearon Pacemaker Classic Series—abridged versions of existing basal texts used for ninth graders in science and social sciences (government)—to assist in bringing the grade equivalent (GE) of the lowest readers in a classroom to, at, or near normal ninth-grade reading levels.

Marnell began working with Mrs. Filliat on this program, and was so impressed by her dedication, drive, and experience that he decided to become a reading specialist, too. He realized early in their discussions that he would be called on to develop instruction skills in reading in order to assist in program development for teachers. Additionally, after reviewing his own nearly 10 years of classroom experience, he knew that he was knowledgeable concerning reading techniques that worked, but he wanted to be able to demonstrate these skills to the ninth-grade teachers—to show them how to incorporate the techniques into their instruction—rather than merely request that they use them.

During that first year of program formation and implementation, Marnell also sought to establish interdisciplinary teaching and collaborative learning techniques among the teachers involved in the Dual-Text Reading Initiative.

During the spring of the 1998–1999 school year, two ninth-grade teachers in adjacent classrooms implemented the Dual-Text Reading Initiative. Each of the 15 students showed noteworthy reading level gains. Based on this improvement, the decision was made to continue and expand the project.

The dual-text use was expanded during the second year of the program (1999–2000), and the emphasis on interdisciplinary teaching, as well as collaborative teaching techniques, was also increased. As the school launched the second year of dual-text instruction, Mrs. Filliat, who had been critical to the program's inception, was at retirement, and it fell to Marnell to monitor the project to its conclusion. Mrs. Filliat would remain in contact with school personnel during the first few months of the 1999–2000 school year and function as a consultant. She also would return in June to present a seminar for teachers on dual-text use. The training and orientation sessions would be scheduled for the full complement of academy teachers in the fall.

During the 1999–2000 school year, the Dual-Text Reading Initiative continued with two teams of two teachers each intended to serve approximately 32 students who were identified as reading significantly below grade level. Mrs. Filliat developed specific learning strategies for the teachers and presented them in person and individually for each teacher. A follow-up session was held at the end of the first semester. After training in the use of the dual-text approach, the two sets of teachers shared the original working texts (15 science texts and 8 civics texts) and the teacher resource material and implemented the program weekly for a group of ninth graders whose average reading level was below sixth grade (5.7 GE). (One student, originally identified as reading significantly below grade level, would later test to an eighth-grade GE. This student was the only one to be considered reading on the eighth-grade level when the Dual-Text Reading Initiative began.) A dedicated parent volunteer, along with continued support and encouragement by the reading specialist and reading instruction staff, greatly enhanced the entire project.

The original two ninth-grade teachers shared their dual-text teaching experience with the two new teachers of social science and science. Both sets of teachers were in classrooms adjacent to each other, and all the teachers were part of a ninth-grade instructional and curriculum arrangement whereby planning periods were aligned for daily planning—team and individual.

Each of the four teachers approached the dual-text teaching in his or her own way. Two engaged the parent volunteer as a direct instructor during class time, with the lesson planned around the duality. A third used full-class collaboration techniques, while the fourth engaged in collaborative efforts but discovered much of his original time would be spent in vocabulary building (in context) and word-attack skills followed by writing instruction. (The word-attack exercise begins with dividing a particular word into its prefixes and suffixes, and examining its root word for initial meaning. The teacher assists by refreshing students' knowledge of derivatives of each until a reasonable series of clues develop and become recognized by the students. Then their suggested meanings are applied to the context and the more exacting, precise meaning of the word in its sentence and related story becomes apparent.)

The teachers' comments concerning their experiences are part of this study. The parent volunteer was engaged weekly in two of the four classes and intermittently in the other two classes. The volunteer also would act as liaison between the reading specialist's classroom and the academy teachers to provide proper scheduling, testing, and test reporting, as well as provide continued assistance as needed by the reading specialists for the teachers. The job of interfacing between classroom instructors and the reading instructor allowed Marnell to maintain communication among all involved.

At the beginning of the semester, only one student read on the eighth-grade level. By the end of the semester, 16 of the 26 students read on the eighth-grade level or higher (10 students were at 8.5 GE or above). The average gain of student reading-level grade equivalency was more than two years as measured on the Nelson Reading Test and compared to their eighth-grade Iowa Test of Basic Skills total reading scores (see Table 10.1).

TABLE 10.1  Grade Level Equivalent Gains By Ninth Graders After a Semester of Dual-Text* Instruction (Reading in the Content Area) Applied to Science and Social Science

(Average positive gain: Increase over two grade levels)

| Student | Preinstruction Reading GE | Postinstruction Reading GE |
|---------|---------------------------|----------------------------|
| 001 | 4.6 | 9.0 |
| 002 | 8.3† | 9.0 |
| 003 | 7.0 | 9.9 |
| 004 | 6.4 | 8.5 |
| 005 | 5.5 | 9.0 |
| 006 | 8.5 | 8.0 |
| 007 | 7.8 | 8.7 |
| 008 | 3.9† | 6.3 |
| 009 | 4.8 | 9.0 |
| 010 | 4.3 | 4.6 |
| 011 | 6.6 | 8.9 |
| 012 | 4.4 | 5.4 |
| 013 | 5.4 | 7.0 |
| 014 | 6.3 | 8.4 |
| 015 | 5.5 | 8.8 |
| 016 | 4.4 | 6.4 |
| 017 | 5.1 | 6.4 |
| 018 | 4.9† | 7.5 |
| 019 | 4.3 | 8.7 |
| 020 | 8.8† | 9.6 |
| 021 | 3.7 | 8.0 |
| 022 | 3.5 | 4.6 |
| 023 | 5.9 | 8.5 |
| 024 | 6.2 | 7.9 |
| 025 | 5.4 | 7.8 |
| 026 | 4.4 | 9.6 |
| 027–032 | N/A | N/A |

ITBS scores at the end of the eighth grade determined preinstruction levels.
*Globe Fearon Pacemaker Series
†Indicates no ITBS score available so a separate pretest score was used. Students were entering ninth graders assigned to two teams of teachers who provided instruction using dual texts (basal text and an abridged version). Scores for six students were not available. Postinstruction scores are from the Nelson Reading Test. Tests were administered by the teachers and scored through the reading specialist.

At Southwest DeKalb High School, the design of the ninth-grade academy allows for four core-area teachers (mathematics, language arts, social science, and science) in one four-classroom modular building. The ninth-grade academy itself—with a two-year history of dedication to the reading regimen, interdisciplinary instructional activities, and collaborative teaching techniques—consists of 16 teachers, 4 each in four modules. Each four-teacher team instructs as many of the same students as possible. The teachers are engaged daily in joint planning of individual classroom lessons. The Dual-Text Reading Initiative, then, added an additional cooperative and interdisciplinary effort that was geared to bring lower level readers on to a successful high school learning curve. The second planning session is vital to the dual-text effort; the consideration of methodologies and student needs require the additional planning time.

Based on the reading gains made by the students in these teachers' classes, Principal Henson opted for a complete dual-text program to be implemented in the four core disciplines among the entire entering ninth-grade population in the upcoming school year. The decision would affect all ninth-grade teachers. Increases in student confidence, abilities, and testing results were the central justifications for expansion to the entire ninth grade.

## Teacher Observations

In his second year with the Dual-Text Reading Initiative, social science teacher Ray Maple credited his familiarity with the texts as a distinct benefit:

> I think [dual texts] help with students' reading on the lower levels. [Dual texts] allowed me to get them more involved in the social studies class and with the information I was teaching because they could understand the book a little better. Plus, and most importantly, they got the one-on-one help from the parent volunteer. I think that is what really helped more than anything else.

During class, the parent volunteer worked at the side of the room with five or six students using the lesson plan provided by the teacher. Mr. Maple added,

> She [parent volunteer] was able to get them to read more often, which increased their reading skills and knowledge of the core information. That was the main thing. They could get more out of the (abridged) text, and they really enjoyed it once they got started in small groups. I was in the classroom teaching the rest of the class, and she had 5 or 10 students and could lead them through the same chapters we were on.

Mr. Maple reported that initially student reaction was negative to the dual-text format, and student misbehavior required him to intervene with the dual learners. He added,

> But after a couple of weeks, they got used to it and started to like it. It also helped that the parent volunteer knew assertive discipline techniques. But after that first couple of weeks, there was no problem.
>
> I think the key, too, was that I never wanted them [the lower level reading students] to get away from the basal text. I also didn't want to have them perceive themselves as not part of the class. Overall, the experience was beneficial to everyone.

Mr. Maple made his own tests, which encompassed both the regular textbook and the dual-text series. He recommended that a paraprofessional or reading specialist assist in the room during the dual-text learning. He added that implementing the program places a premium on good classroom management:

> The immaturity level of ninth graders is high—even the mature readers are not socially mature—and the prospect of delay or lack of teacher attention during dual-text learning can create "attention voids" for student misbehavior. The critical element is classroom management. If you don't have that, it's all lost.

The second social studies teacher, Byron Simmons, who was using dual texts for the first time, stated,

> At first the students felt embarrassed. There was marked resistance. They would ask, "Why are you giving us these baby books" and remarks like that. I just told them this was a program to help them read better with greater comprehension of what they are reading, and most of these students know they need to read better. I told them this was just another tool to that end.

Mr. Simmons chose to use his eight books, using collaborative teaching techniques, in groups of four students, each group member sharing in listening or round-robin reading.

> I tried to do peer teaching during the groups, and we continued with that kind of group activity during the semester, too.
>
> I didn't really do what I wanted to do because we only had eight books, but you've got to do what you have to do. Also, the class I worked with had a low reading level on average, and it wasn't long before I realized they lacked some of the fundamentals of reading itself. I think that is also what the dual-text program makes a bit more obvious than a more sophisticated text.

So before we got into using the books, we went back to fundamentals of syntax, grammar, spelling, and word-attack skills. They really didn't know how to syllabicate, to draw meaning from suffixes and prefixes, or have a working knowledge of verb agreement—things like that. In fact, I think I probably spent half of just about every class on one type of basic skill or another.

What really started helping was writing. We started out with trying to write sentences then paragraphs, and I know you can fake it for a while, but we soon got to short answers and essays, and they can't carry one another then. They had to deal with their own knowledge and comprehension skills, then. They have to know what they have read to be able to write about it. We did at least two essays [in class] a week, and I think that really expanded learning the dual text and the regular textbook.

I know we went back and did some elementary things, but as a teacher, you do what you have to do for your kids to do well. It's not only a reflection on them, but you, too. In the beginning, I almost had to *make* them do it. There was a lot of resistance and resentment, and they let you know it. Here I was, a social science teacher dealing with grammar basics, but we had to get through it, and I think that is how they started learning some of the terms we have in our field. The presentation of material and vocabulary in history and government are very hard [for 14- or 15-year-olds], and they had no way of breaking the words down—there was no way they were going to be able to read a book about them.

We ended up doing a lot of word mapping skills. We used SQ3R every day. I presented Cornell note-taking, and I think the combination of those skills, with the first rush of the dual text, then followed up in the regular text reached into their long-term memory. Note-taking and SQ3R—we used a lot of that.

Science teacher Barbara Gofford-Hampton offered commentary as well:

The students responded well to [dual texts] because it allowed them to move at their own pace without feeling frustrated while it didn't hold back students using the regular textbook. Plus, it was nice having the parent volunteer in the room to work with individual students when they needed it. I rather enjoyed working with the dual texts in science.

I could see improvement in students' attitude toward learning and in their reading ability. We had to share books and that was the difficult part. It was also difficult to get the books back and forth to the other module [science teacher] and keeping everything planned, lessons on track, and all the things you have to do in your regular day.

I tried to do some pairing, but it was dependent upon what group (class) I was working with. If I had some higher level readers in a class, we would work in groups of three or four (each with a higher level reader) and that seemed to work. That was better than in just one or two groups where some of them would become overwhelmed, frustrated, then totally disinterested.

At the beginning of the 2004–2005 school year, science teacher Mylinda Weberg wrote,

I have used dual text in my classroom for many years. It is extremely helpful in helping students achieve the objectives. It has a side benefit of increasing their reading comprehension level as well. When I began using dual text, I had a volunteer who would come into my classroom to work with the students who needed extra help reading. I was soon to discover that even the three who scored well on the reading assessment preferred to be able to use the dual textbooks with the rest of their peers.

I made the adjustment to using the dual text with the whole class quickly and easily. A few students would question the need for the extra book. I always tell those students that the dual text is just another way of saying things. If they don't understand it in the regular text, the dual text may explain it where they can understand it. They also have commented that the basal text makes more sense after reading the dual text.

Neither my students nor I consider the dual text to be a lessening of standards. My standards can be much higher because I know they have gotten the basic concept and can move up to application and synthesis rather than struggling through knowledge and comprehension. The dual text allows teachers the opportunity to accomplish many tasks at once. They are teaching the concept, improving reading skills, and differentiating instruction.

I teach my students science. While teaching my students science, I find that I can also teach reading and mathematics. I do not take time out of science to teach reading or math. I combine the skills they need with the concepts to be covered. Dual text allows me to do this in ways the basal text alone does not. First, the dual text meets the students where they are. A student struggling to read fifth-grade–level material cannot make the jump to ninth- or tenth-grade–level material without a bridge. It is not possible. Dual text provides the bridge to these students. They can discover the concept at their reading level. Second, using the basal text after the dual text extends the students' grasp of the concepts and their reading skills. Now that they already have prior knowledge of the concept, the students can focus on comprehending the new words of the basal text. It is wonderful to see the light bulb go on for a student when they realize that the basal text says the same thing as the dual text only with bigger words. Those students can then apply prior knowledge in the acquisition of new science terms.

The dual text also helps address behavior problems. Many behavioral problems in the high school classroom can be attributed to students feeling hopelessly unsuccessful. They don't have the skills they need to achieve, and they know it. They are ashamed to ask for help. They do not want their peers to know they are behind in their skills. They will do things to keep their peers from noticing they don't know the material or that they lack skills. Normally, this comes out as acting out. The dual text allows these students to be successful. Once these students achieve success they are much more motivated to succeed. High school students are starving for success and the more they don't succeed the more they want to succeed. Many times, a student who "doesn't care" is a student who is hopelessly unsuccessful.

Students will learn to use the dual text on their own. It usually only takes a few weeks each before my students start reminding me to start with the dual text. They will also ask to use the dual text on their own if they get confused by the basal text. I can't recall the number of times my students have said, "Can we do this out of the other book first?" or "Can I use the other book before I do this assignment in my textbook?" This is an important life skill. The students need to know that if they don't understand something that they should look to other sources rather than give up immediately.

Dual text is very beneficial to my students. It helps them understand sometimes difficult science concepts. It helps me meet my students where they are in their skills, and helps bridge the gap in those skills. It allows me to differentiate instruction with differentiating between students. It helps cut down on behavior problems, and it teaches students to be persistent in their learning. I love the dual text approach, and I will continue to use it to reach my students.

## Dual-Text Instruction: Epilogue

Kenneth Bradshaw—now in his fourth year as principal at Southwest DeKalb High School—has continued dual-text instruction among entering freshmen. Each ninth-grade teacher—as part of regular instruction—uses the approach in each core discipline. He has done so in the face of economic constraints that brought discontinuance of the formal "academy" model (the academy structure has been reconstituted for the 2004–2005 school year under Superintendent Crawford Lewis); changes in the teaching staff due to attrition, retirement, and realignment; and major reading initiatives at the county level. Dual-text instruction has helped to support the new systemwide reading initiatives under Dr. Lewis's leadership.

Principal Bradshaw has added technologies to dual-text instruction, namely OpenBook Literacy System, a complete language arts package that can be fitted to any grade level or class. This computerized program—available on site and soon to be made available to students for their use at home—has been coupled with dual-text instruction and has shown significant results in its ability to increase student reading levels both as a stand-alone effort and as one coupled with other programs including the Dual-Text Reading Initiative. Principal Bradshaw has supported expansion of PLATO Learning Systems, applied initially to algebra and biology instruction, and CPS Learning Systems (eInstruction), an "immediate teaching moment" tool designed to give constant learning evaluation to teachers and students alike. Each school program is intended to increase participation in the superintendent's major literacy and numeracy campaigns.

Individually, teachers themselves and individual departments are now operating ongoing literacy and numeracy efforts at every grade level, each intended to culminate in helping produce a champion reader and self-learner. It is a measure of the Dual-Text Reading Initiative's adaptability and continuity that teachers find it still a valuable tool to bring entering freshmen into the high school experience. As science teacher Mylinda Weberg notes,

> We worked on the dual text one day, then would move into the regular text—same subject area—the second day, and I think that was useful in bringing the lower level reader up into the higher levels both of the book and in thinking. Dual text—an abridged version with the main points and the regular texts—gave them a chance to digest what they were learning so they could see the cross-referencing and the ways things tie together better.
>
> I think reading in the content area is critically important. Let's face it, science is complicated, and it has its own way of thinking and its own language sometimes, and all of this—most of it, anyway, is new to someone just out of eighth-grade. I think it is critical for students to read, period! Reading in the content area instruction is one way to address content and still teach reading. We need to do both. I think the dual-text program helps us with that.

## The Skilled Comprehenders Pilot Project

In the 2000–2001 school year, a follow-up project was proposed and put in place for sophomores at Southwest DeKalb High School. The Skilled Comprehenders Pilot Project was intended to follow up the Dual-Text Reading Initiative and to demonstrate that shared expertise of faculty among departments coupled with directed learning activities would result in student gains both academically (as measured by successful completion rates of a course) and in reading assessment. Although this one-year project was discontinued when new systemwide initiatives were announced, the experiences of those who participated are presented here both as a tribute to their teaching professionalism and in the hope that others may wish to embark on initiatives of their own.

The Commission on Behavioral and Social Sciences Education (Snow, Burns, & Griffin, 1998) describes skilled comprehenders as having

> superior overall language comprehension, background knowledge that supports intricate use of the language, and fluent word identification skills. They also possess superior metacognitive skills—i.e., they grasp quickly the purpose and meaning of any text and are more capable in their application skills. (p. 128)

In addition to the dual-text approach, key elements of the Skilled Comprehenders Pilot Project were interdisciplinary language arts skills (reading, writing, listening, speaking), collaborative instructional strategies, and modeling. Interdisciplinary engagement included guest speakers (teachers who volunteered to travel to the other school to give lectures in their field) from other curriculum departments.

In the world history class at Southwest DeKalb High School, sophomore students had average reading levels at about sixth grade. It is worth noting that none of the instructional strategies were directed at improving a single score or grade in a particular discipline but at academic success as a whole.

The diversity of the students, their different classes, and their specific needs precluded gearing the approach to one class or another. The instructional approach in the Skilled Comprehenders Pilot Project, which used varied techniques, was also offered to mainstream students in general education classes. The teacher's role was to walk students through the strategies; model how to accomplish tasks; demonstrate how thinking progresses and how to listen, speak, write, and read for different purposes; and to provide lessons to broaden both detailed and global experiences of the students in a learning environment.

As expressed in initial discussions, the teacher and administrator wanted to develop and improve critical reading skills by offering appropriate strategies for each learner on the assumption that every child learns in his or her own way. A package of strategies was devised to incorporate the language arts spectrum.

It was decided that in the four-month course, the teacher, George Cozens, would present the learning and reading strategies. The basics of interdisciplinary activities, collaborative learning techniques, and reading in the content areas were to be guideposts of the activities and strategies.

The project was divided into three 6-week periods: (1) startup, which would include a reading test; (2) comfort zone, which would be a period of intense study-skill and reading-strategy application, whereby students "zone in" on what is working for them; and (3) skills application, which was the final 6 weeks of the 18-week period. Mr. Cozens and the administrators wanted to see if students would adopt what worked for them.

It should be noted here that Mr. Cozens's initial reading test was intended to provide him with a current grade-level equivalent of the students' reading abilities. It would have been unusual to gear a one-semester course for measurement of such a variable. However, for his own purposes and to attempt to validate his observations, Mr. Cozens asked for a final reading test. In fact, a reading-level test was administered at the end of the course, during the school's final exam days, both for the teacher's information and to acquire data on hoped-for comprehension gains. (One section of the test measures Comprehension Grade Equivalents, in addition to vocabulary. Both are combined to form a Total Reading Grade Level Equivalent.) The Comprehension Grade Equivalent data was used because of the shortness of time involved.

During the initial six-week period—the beginning of the school year—a number of students moved through the class due to schedule changes. The 16 students monitored through the semester were in the class from beginning to end.

The effort of the first six weeks was to involve the students in as many thinking skills as could be developed in the short time frame. Mr. Cozens and the administrators were looking for the "hook" of interest in each child, aware that the first six weeks of school are a time of excitement and commitment on the part of students. They arrive at school ready for a successful year and are generally eager to achieve. Project leaders wanted to capitalize on that excitement and momentum even at the risk of overwhelming students, and time would prove that such an outpouring seemed to work in the students' favor. Seizing on the teacher's zeal, the students "soon dropped their initial reluctance and resistance to reading and took ownership of the class. I was amazed," according to Mr. Cozens.

The following reading strategies were used. After the introduction of the class, reading strategies included read aloud, think aloud, paired reading, guided reading, Directed Reading–Thinking Activity (DRTA), silent reading, paraphrasing (verbally), and regular vocabulary-in-context exercises and discussions. The beginning of the course included time management and organizational skills (teacher modeled); Cornell note-taking method (modeled and used throughout the 18 weeks); and in-class program for individual accountability in cooperative learning sessions (modeled and used throughout the semester). In early September, project leaders developed a lesson for following instructions through visualization and moved to visualization of a critical reading exercise (Steven Crane's *The Red Badge of Courage*), coupled with the study technique SQ3R. These study skills would be repeatedly presented throughout the semester.

The writing elements of the first six weeks involved exercises and strategies in paraphrasing and, as the course moved along, sentence construction and essay development. The instructor wrote on the board while the students followed his thinking aloud to model the exercises. A special lesson involved the chairman of the English department, Diane Langston, who agreed to present to the students a one-hour session on types of sentence construction and rationale for their use. Said the teacher,

> It was an ultra-successful lesson. The students realized then that they did not have to rely on how they spoke for the written word. They could shape new ideas and get across their message in a much more mature fashion. After this lesson and several practice sessions the writing improved remarkably.

The second six weeks, the comfort-zone period, was highlighted with more intense practice and individualized attempts to encourage each student's success. The skills-application period, leading to a final exam, placed emphasis on continuing to apply learning skills across the curriculum. Mr. Cozens observed,

> [Students] became less reluctant to do things. At the beginning they were very reluctant, and they resented doing some of the methods, but they soon became comfortable with them—and with each other. They were skeptical about reading, and they started stepping outside their familiar zones because they had to expose themselves to their weaknesses. The cooperative learning techniques and the added emphasis on using skills in their other classes made them participators. They had to participate, and they knew they couldn't just sit there and avoid interaction.
>
> I think the interaction, the cooperative learning strategies, were critical to their behaviors about reading. They started linking what we were doing to their other classes and subjects, and it was obvious to them they were having success.
>
> I could see an improvement in their writing skills, their continuity and clearness of thought in expression of their views during the classroom discussion periods. They could delve into characters in literature; their discussions of life around them were more mature and sophisticated, and their vocabulary was truly more refined.
>
> The writing exercises did take a little more time. After the two language speakers—one in literature and the other in actual sentence formation—they realized they could not write the way they talked with its teen slang and incomplete sentences, improper syntax, etc., and they started attempting to write in complete thoughts. I think this was also critical for their listening skills development. All of this started showing up in the increase of quality of work, whether it was short answer, essays, or paraphrasing. We never stopped the Cornell note-taking, and every day we used SQ3R for something, and I believe that kept things improving as well.
>
> We used SQ3R nearly every day until everyone was comfortable in taking a paragraph in and of itself and pulling from it what they needed. I had

known of this technique for a long time, but I had never insisted it be used all the time. After awhile, it was second nature to them. So was SQ3R. Now, when they read something they don't quite understand, instead of just turning aside, they take the technique—or one of the other techniques—and it helps them grasp more fully what they are reading.

It got to where they were not only comprehending what was written, but I could see Bloom's taxonomy at work right before my eyes. At the end they were evaluating—determining whether they agreed or disagreed with what they were reading and why. They were moving right through analysis, comparing, synthesizing, then evaluating. In short, I thought the techniques got them past the general-knowledge level and into the higher levels of thinking in a hurry.

Toward the end of the semester, they were conscious of their grades in other classes to the point they would discuss study skills, ways approaching problems, and even show me some of their good results. What started out as dragging them into the reading techniques ended up with, I guess what I would say, was student ownership of the class. In September, I would have to coax and encourage, and by November they were arriving prepared well enough to know exactly what was expected of them and why, and cooperation was one of the hallmarks of this group. It was a great experience for me and I think they all learned something about themselves as well.

There were several students who showed remarkable improvements in the academic area. One student arrived in August refusing to read aloud; by November the same student was leading discussions and reading aloud with excellent diction, inflection, and paraphrasing. I think a lot of that confidence came from our class and many of the speaking activities we had coupled with certain read-alouds. There's something else to know, too, about that student. She had a great deal of home support for the reading class. I know her parents played a major role in her gains. Incidentally, she tested in September at a reading level of seventh grade and took a reading test in January—a more difficult test, I thought—and rated at the post-high school level in total grade equivalent. We had some measurable gains with others, too, as I'm sure you will point out in the chart. But the growth I saw in their confidence, their positive changes in attitudes and behaviors toward learning, reading, and each other, and the increased sophistication of their work and just their general desire to do well was the real benefit, I think.

### Reading in the Content Area: Measurement and Application

This sophomore world history class used the Skilled Comprehenders approach during most of the school year (pretest in November, with a posttest in May). The Nelson Reading Test was used to determine grade-equivalent total reading levels. The teacher administered the test, with scoring by the reading specialist. The average positive gain in reading level would be nearly two years.

A selection of reading critical comprehension and study skills were presented during the class. Use of the Skilled Comprehenders package is at the judgment of the instructor and should be based on the needs of the students. The entire approach is linkage: linking the disciplines and linking the aspects of the language arts (listening, speaking, writing, reading). Support strategies that involve guest speakers play a key role in expanding the student's own classroom experiences. The activities reinforce interdisciplinary strategies and collaborative learning techniques.

One colleague and expert in history presented the topic "Where do we get these ideas?" The chairman of the science department presented the topic "Scientific developments and its links to history." He brought with him a historical perspective on science and a blood-typing activity that kept the students enthralled and active. It was the first time the class had ever heard him speak, and several days afterward he reported that one student requested to be scheduled in his advanced chemistry course.

A master English teacher presented a walk-through of grammar, syntax, and sentence construction applied to answering short answers and essays in world history. A skim-scan-scour lesson plan was provided in this study as an example of a strategy dealing with difficult material. He noted, "It will take planning and practice at first, but it is useful to model this type of academic skill to the students." He did. Other strategies included daily use of graphic organizers, illustrating vocabulary activities (art, diagrams, cartoons), ongoing vocabulary development exercises, Cornell note-taking, SQ3R repeatedly, and critical reading strategies.

This teacher, Mr. F, also presented several strategies on silent reading. The initial reaction of the students to silent reading was "shock." The teacher said, "They said I was supposed to tell them what they need to know. They had apparently not often read content in class silently (and then been asked to retell and paraphrase) before. It was amusing, but they caught on." Silent reading was presented several more times during the school year. The purpose of silent reading was to remove any oral reading constraints, to allow students personalized time to read at their own pace and in their own way, then to discuss the various aspects of the material among themselves.

Mr. Cozens said that at the beginning of the year, he was not clear "where all this was leading." As the school year ended, he recorded some of his observations about the Skilled Comprehenders Pilot Project: "The variety of activities seemed analogous to a 'shotgun approach' where you try lots of different things in hopes that something will work, and then you have the difficulty of determining the effectiveness of the various activities." He suggested having teachers focus on two or three strategies to use on a regular basis, but the pilot project's intention was to allow students to select from the strategies available. Project leaders have not had a full discussion on his suggestions. Mr. Cozens also suggested regular meetings, planning sessions, and mutual encouragement among instructors to share their experiences and techniques for bringing reading in the content area as a natural part of the curriculum.

## *Teacher Observations*

Dr. L., a 27-year teaching veteran and Ph.D. in literature, commented,

> During the first semester, Mr. Marnell came to me and said, "Dr. L., I want you to give a lecture to Dr. C.'s class on the European Renaissance." He continued talking, but I really didn't hear him because I was thinking, "What! How can I fit this in to everything else I have to do! Help!!"
>
> I stood there shaking my head "yes," trying to catch up with what he was saying. I finally realized two things—one, he wasn't giving me a choice, and two, the program really did sound exciting.
>
> Over the next few weeks, I thought about my high school and college students and how much difficulty they were having in moving beyond simple comprehension of whatever they were reading—how few of them made the connection between and among other disciplines and real-life experiences. How dull and uninteresting many of them felt the subject matter presented to them because they could not see any linkage between the classroom and real life. How unprepared and uninspired most of my students were.
>
> As I read over my lecture notes to prepare for what I thought would be my only lecture, little seeds of acceptance and doubt found fertile ground in my mind. I wasn't sure these young people in Dr. C.'s class were ready for a lecture that demanded critically listening and responding orally and in writing on a much high level than they had ever experienced. Could they see and understand the way in which writers were influenced by the historical, social, political, and economic events of their time? More importantly, could they link that with today's world and articulate it in oral and written forms? But if the program did work, what a wonderful head start for these young people!
>
> I had an absolute blast in Dr. C.'s class. The students were so well prepared. *They listened, they took notes, and they asked intelligent questions, they made connections!* [Emphasis is Dr. L.'s.] I had an epiphany while lecturing. Quite often instruction takes place, but learning doesn't. Learning was taking place that day.

Within the lecture, I had given the answers to all but one question in the evaluation (guest lecturers bring their own evaluation forms as part of the written portion of their appearance). When Dr. C. gave that test, the students knew exactly what answer I had left out. It was wonderful. They *all* had listened to carefully, and had taken such good notes that it was easy for them to do well.

I did one more lecture for Dr. C.'s class second semester on the Industrial Revolution and its impact on literature, especially nonfiction writers. Once again, same results.

By the way, both teachers took notes during my lectures. This was a wonderful way to demonstrate the importance of note taking to the students. Quite often, by modeling a skill we touch students in a special way.

By this time, I really understood what "Skilled Comprehenders" meant. It wasn't just reading instruction or comprehension, although that is a vital part of anyone's life in the 21st century. What it really means is that an individual has enough knowledge, strategies, skills, and experiences to be a lifelong learner; a person who can and will accept the challenges of the century in which fundamental changes will alter the way in which we all live out our lives.

Connections and linkage between and among the disciplines must take place in order for civilization to continue. When students take ownership for their own learning, the process begins. Socialization, civility, sensitivity, all will become important to an individual who sees his or her role in the world as a positive one.

Positive comments and individual verbal feedback were also reported from the history teacher, science teacher, and English instructor who presented in the Skilled Comprehenders Pilot Project.

An administrator's advisory: Choose those teachers who can commit. Not all have schedules to allow them to present.

## *Expanding the Skilled Comprehenders Project*

The Skilled Comprehenders Pilot Project was applied in one classroom. Marnell gave demonstrations of its techniques in both a special education classroom and an advanced Latin classroom. The participants believe the strategies work, and there is now a small nucleus of experienced teachers capable and willing to reach out to their students with new techniques—and all these teachers are veteran educators—most with advanced degrees.

At this writing, it may be worthwhile to attempt more skilled comprehenders projects to allow students to select the most successful working methods by which they can refine their own learning skills as well as their self-confidence and self-esteem, and their future contributions to society. The time involved for planning and implementing such a program and the numerous challenges presented to the administration in implementing this approach can be daunting. However, the ultimate outcomes—greater student achievement and improved teacher satisfaction and instructional delivery, as reported here—are surely worth the effort.

# Conclusion

The strategies used in the Dual-Text Reading Initiative and the Skilled Comprehenders Pilot Program were neither unique nor new. Perhaps a distinction might be that portions of the know-how, details of the plan, and impetus for implementation were at the administrative and reading-specialist level. The encouragement and approval of the projects came from—notably—the school system's director of reading instruction, the principals, the assistant principals of instruction, and the area executive directors. The reading specialist was instrumental in the inauguration of the Dual-Text Reading Initiative. The successes and gains, though, were obtained through the efforts of the classroom instructors. For it is in the classroom where theory becomes practice. The true credit belongs to these teachers.

Many variables—various home, community, and educational factors—remain unaccounted for. These case studies have focused only on effort (attempted) and results measured. The Dual-Text Reading Initiative produced measurable and significant reading level gains heretofore unknown to content area teachers.

**REFERENCES**

Blythe, T. (1998). *The teaching for understanding guide.* San Francisco: Jossey-Bass.

Graves, M.F., & Graves, B.B. (1994). *Teaching reading in the 21st century.* Boston: Allyn & Bacon.

Hogan, K., & Pressley, M. (Eds.). (1997). *Scaffolding student learning: Instructional approaches and issues.* Cambridge, MA: Brookline.

Kennedy, M.M. (1997). The connection between research and practice. *Educational Researcher, 26*(7), 4–12.

National Assessment of Educational Progress. (1999). *Reading report card for the nation and states.* Washington, DC: U.S. Department of Education.

Perkins, D. (1992). *Smart schools: From training memories to educating minds.* New York: Free Press.

Perkins, D. (1993). Teaching for understanding. *American Educator, 17*(3), 8, 28–35.

Perkins, D., & Blythe, T. (1993). Putting understanding up front. *Educational Leadership, 51*(5), 4–7.

Ryder, R.J., & Graves, M.F. (1998). *Reading and learning in content areas* (2nd ed.). Upper Saddle River, NJ: Merrill.

Snow, C.E., Burns, M.S., & Griffin, P. (Eds.). (1998). *Preventing reading difficulties in young children.* Washington, DC: National Academy Press.

Wiggins, G. (1989). The futility of trying to teach everything. *Educational Leadership, 47*(3), 44–48, 57–59.

Wiggins, G., & McTighe, J. (1998). *Understanding by design.* Alexandria, VA: Association for Supervision and Curriculum Development.

Wiske, M.S. (Ed.). (1998). *Teaching for understanding: Linking research with practice.* San Francisco: Jossey-Bass.

# CHAPTER 11

# Reading Comprehension Strategies for Struggling Middle School Learners

*Charlotte Rose Sadler*

I n my experience of 17 years as an educator, primarily working with African American students and students with a variety of cultural backgrounds, I have found that to be truly effective with diverse populations, teachers should have some multicultural education, gain insight regarding cultural backgrounds, and understand the various learning styles of each of their students. The reading comprehension strategies discussed in this chapter can be effective with all middle school learners, regardless of background. The manner in which the strategies are delivered and the specific examples used with the strategies should be tailored to the students who are being taught.

## Middle School Students' Struggles With Reading Comprehension

The issue of middle school students who are struggling with reading comprehension has ventured beyond the reading classroom and into the content area classrooms. Teachers of content area subjects such as math, science, social studies, and even English often feel that it is not their responsibility to teach reading comprehension skills to students at the middle school level. They feel that it is something for the reading teacher to deal with or, often, that it should have been taught in the elementary school and is not their problem. If this mindset were to prevail, the outcome would be middle school students who fail to comprehend the text, fall further and further behind, and move on to become high school students with an even dimmer hope of acquiring the reading skills needed to succeed academically.

Middle school students are not just a larger version of elementary school students. The differences in these years include major changes socially, emotionally, intellectually, and physically. Students who cannot read well in middle school often *know* they cannot read well, and recognize that their peers are also aware of this fact. At an age when social acceptance is important, being "labeled" as struggling readers often makes it more difficult for these students to seek or accept the assistance needed to help improve their reading skills. Students do not want to feel they have been singled out. If, however, the assistance provided to struggling readers is done through strategies that are useful to *all* students, the struggling readers will be more apt to embrace these strategies that may improve their comprehension skills. Although it is important to respect and recognize differences in individuals, it is also of value to show how some strategies can be useful to all.

Although it would be beneficial, teachers in the middle school do not have to have intensive training in reading in order to help struggling readers. Three things, however, are necessary. First, teachers must truly recognize that many middle school students struggle with comprehending grade level text. Second, teachers must have a willingness to accept that it is their responsibility to teach the material to the students. If a lack of comprehension is an issue, teachers must find a way to break through that barrier in order to teach the content to students. Third, teachers need to be willing to seek out and use strategies in their classroom. They must be committed to trying a variety of strategies until they find the ones that help their students to fully comprehend the material.

## Reading Comprehension Strategies for Middle School Learners

Many comprehension strategies work well with middle school students. It is my experience that implementing comprehension strategies will not only help struggling readers, but also will benefit readers who are able to comprehend on and above grade level text. These students may find strategies that are especially useful to them individually at the present time or may retain strategies that can be used in the future. The strategies also provide a welcome change to traditional instruction that involves reading the text and answering the questions at the end of each section or chapter.

Comprehension strategies available to middle school students vary, depending on the type of text being read and what is being assessed in the reading. Several strategies will be presented here that tend to be effective with middle school students, and especially struggling students, in both reading and in the content areas. These strategies are divided into groups based on their primary goal. The goals include checking for understanding, fostering cooperative learning, connecting to previous knowledge, improving organization, promoting independent learning, and teaching to learning style.

## Checking for Understanding

In almost every classroom, one of the primary goals is to check for understanding. The teacher wants to know if the student truly understands the material that has been covered. Numerous strategies are available, including Clink and Clunk, Interactive Read-Alouds, and Paraphrasing/Summarizing. These strategies can be adapted for use with African American learners through the manner in which they are delivered and the examples that are used.

**Clink and Clunk** (Vaughn & Klingner, 1999) strategy allows the teacher and the student to differentiate between information that the student knows well and information that needs to be covered in more depth. The students create two columns on a sheet of paper and label them "Clink" and "Clunk." On the Clink side, they list information that they clearly understand regarding the material that has been covered. On the Clunk side, they list information that they do not clearly understand. In some cases, the teacher may want to provide the students with a list of topics and have them place the topics under the appropriate column, showing their level of understanding. The information under the Clunk column can be covered in more depth through teacher-directed instruction or through allowing students who understand the information to explain it to the class. Allowing students to explain concepts in their own language or dialect can provide greater understanding to other students in the class, rather than focusing on the textbook or the language that the teacher is using. This will assist in making concepts "clink" for the students. The object is to have all information go into the Clink column, showing that all students clearly understand the material that was covered.

**Interactive Read-Alouds** (Barrentine, 1996) is a strategy that assesses understanding throughout the reading of text. Questions should be prepared before the lesson begins. As the text is being read aloud, questions are posed periodically to determine if the students understand the text that is being covered. Interactions with the students, both personally and interpersonally, are encouraged. This strategy is uncomplicated and provides immediate feedback. This strategy works well with students who tend to be more verbal; however, it is still beneficial to those who may not participate directly, but who are able to gain information and insight through listening to the conversation.

**Paraphrasing/Summarizing** (Gunning, 1996; Katims & Harris, 1997; Vacca & Vacca, 1989) is a strategy that is especially effective for middle school students. First, it is extremely important that this strategy be modeled for the students. Then they may attempt to use the strategy with guided practice. Finally, they are encouraged to independently practice the strategy. The strategy involves reading a paragraph or short section and having the students summarize the information in their own words. The teacher should be assessing if the students are relaying the important points in the reading. Paraphrasing and summarizing are also useful in writing reports and doing research because students must learn to write information in their own words. As with Clink and Clunk, allowing students to put information into their own words can be helpful in assessing that the material has been comprehended, and it allows students to translate the concepts to make them easier to understand for others.

## Fostering Cooperative Learning

A second goal of many teachers is to foster cooperative learning. This strategy is especially effective at the middle school level because it appeals to the social nature of the students. It is my experience that struggling readers often learn better in social and cooperative settings. Four effective strategies that are based on cooperative learning include Circle-Seat-Center, Jigsaw, Partner Prediction, and Think-Pair-Share/Think-Pair-Square.

**Circle-Seat-Center** (Ivey, 1999) allows students to work in three rotating groups cooperatively and also addresses a variety of learning styles. Once the course material has been covered, students are divided into three groups, and each group is given an assignment of Circle, Seat, or Center. Those in the Circle group sit together with the teacher and cover information aloud regarding the text. This is helpful for auditory learners. Those in the Seat group work either individually or with their group to cover information using worksheets and study sheets. This is helpful for visual learners. The Center group works on specific projects related to the text, either individually or with their group. The projects may include creating timelines, games, or charts. This focuses students on tactile learning. Students rotate so that they particpate in all three groups, thereby giving them the opportunity to learn using various learning styles. In order to be effective, the teacher must assess the information presented by individual students in order to determine their individual level of comprehension.

**Jigsaw** (Aronson, 1997; Hendrix, 1999) is a cooperative learning strategy that allows the students to learn from one another. This strategy is highly effective but requires specific directions when it is initially implemented. Groups of three to six students are placed in teams. Each team member is given a specific topic on which to become an "expert." The teams split up and students locate members from other teams that have their same topic. They work together in topic groups, determine the information that is most important, then return to their teams to share the information they have learned. After the students have become familiar with the strategy, they should be able to determine what information is important. Assessment for this strategy may be done through discussion or written responses.

**Partner Prediction** (Buehl, 1997) is a strategy that allows students to work together and predict what will happen next in the text. After reading a short section, students should discuss with a partner what they feel will happen next and why. If a struggling reader is having difficulties with prediction, partner them with a reader who is strong with prediction. This will allow the struggling reader the opportunity to see how the process of prediction works. The teacher can assess this strategy through discussion, observation, or quizzes.

**Think-Pair-Share/Think-Pair-Square** (Banikowski & Mehring, 1999; Bromley & Modlo, 1997) is a cooperative strategy that allows students to work together in checking for comprehension. After reading the text, students think about what they already know, decide what it reminds them of, and determine what might happen next. Students will choose Pair and Share (two students) or Pair and Square (four students) to discuss what they have thought about. This strategy allows the students to learn from one another and can be assessed through discussion or quizzes.

## Connecting to Previous Knowledge

According to Lewis (1999), middle school students learn more when they feel connected to what they are reading. Ivey (1999) states that having a real purpose for reading is extremely important for struggling middle school readers. There are many strategies that help readers connect with previous knowledge. Three of these strategies include Anticipation Guide, Directed Reading Activity (DRA), and ReQuest.

**Anticipation Guide** (Banikowski & Mehring, 1999; Gunning, 1996; Herber, 1978; Vacca & Vacca, 1989) is a strategy that works best with topics that require information in order to develop opinions. This strategy begins with the teacher listing three or more debatable statements about a topic that is going to be studied. Students are asked to identify whether they agree or disagree with each statement. As they are reading the text, they should find statements to support their views. After reading the text, the students are asked if they maintain their original view or if they have changed their opinion. There are certain things that need to be considered in an Anticipation Guide, including analyzing and determining main ideas; writing in short declarative statements; writing the statements in a format that will encourage anticipation and prediction; discussing the students' predictions and anticipations before reading; having students evaluate the statements according to the author's intent and purpose; and contrasting the predictions with the author's intended meaning. This strategy is motivational in that it gives the students a purpose for reading and allows them to use prior knowledge to make their predictions.

**Directed Reading Activity** (DRA) (Cochran, 1993; Gunning, 1996; Vacca & Vacca, 1989) is a strategy that helps struggling readers to find a purpose in what they are reading. First, the teacher establishes a purpose for reading, builds background, and motivates the students. This may involve going over vocabulary terms or unfamiliar concepts. This is especially useful in math because it is explained that the information they will be learning will be used in their day-to-day lives—especially in making purchases and paying bills. Once students see a purpose in what they are reading, it makes the material more meaningful. Next, the students are asked to read the text silently. Finally, the teacher should reinforce and extend ideas through follow-up activities such as a demonstration, speeches, questions, or a quiz. The follow-up activity serves as an assessment for the teacher in determining the students' comprehension of the topic.

**ReQuest** (Gunning, 1996; Manzo, 1969; Vacca & Vacca, 1989) encourages students to build on previous knowledge and consider what might be important in the assigned reading. For example, before reading a story that deals with family dynamics, students might discuss their knowledge regarding the various types of family structures (such as single parents, guardianships, extended families, traditional families, etc.) and how each might play a role in how a person might react in various situations. In this strategy, students are able to write questions about things they do not understand and the text is broken into short sections so it is not overwhelming to the students. After a selection of text has been assigned, have students read the first paragraph or short section and think of questions to ask regarding the topic. Students are then to ask their questions and use the text to answer. Following this, the teacher should ask some higher level questions that have been prepared. This procedure is used throughout the selection with a question-answer session at the end of each section. Discussion is an easy way to assess comprehension.

## Improving Organization

Organizational skills are important and are strongly developed in the middle school years. The process of organizing information often helps struggling readers better comprehend the information they are reading. Three very effective organization strategies that work well with middle school students include Expectation Outline, K-W-L (Know-Want to Know-Learned), and ORDER.

**Expectation Outline** (Vacca & Vacca, 1989) is an organizational strategy that is also useful as a study guide. The teacher begins by creating an outline, leaving several blanks that will be filled in by the students as the text is being read.

Some information should already be provided on the outline to give the students a guide. As students fill in the outline, the teacher can assess if they are comprehending the desired information. After students have done this a few times, they may be able to create their own outlines in the future.

**K-W-L** (Know-Want to Know-Learned) (Banikowski & Mehring, 1999; Gunning, 1996; Jeffrey, 1997; Ogle, 1986, 1994; Warren & Flynt, 1995) connects to previous knowledge and gives the students a purpose for reading. Before reading, students are asked to brainstorm about the assigned topic. They create a list with three columns. Under the first column (Know), they write what they already know about the topic. Under the second column (Want to Know), they create questions they would like answered. During reading, the students are to refer to their questions and try to find answers. Then, under the third column (Learned), they will fill in information they have learned. This strategy is most effective when the teacher models it on the board a few times before having the students do it individually. Instructors may make an assessment by comparing the Want to Know and Learned columns to see if the students were able to find out the information they wanted to learn about.

**ORDER** (Bulgren & Scanlon, 1998) can be used with any subject area and assists students with organizing and reviewing information. The steps involved include [O]pen your mind and take notes; [R]ecognize the structure of the text; [D]raw a visual organizer such as an outline, map, or chart; [E]xplain the organizer to others; and [R]euse it as a study guide. Teachers should model this strategy several times and have students assist in completing the organizers before they are required to do one on their own. The visual organizer and the act of explaining the organizer to others help students to determine ways to categorize information. It is a strategy that can eventually be used independently.

## Promoting Independent Learning

Perhaps one of the most valuable goals in teaching is to promote independent learning. It is possible to provide students with strategies that they can use on their own in the future. At first, however, these strategies must be taught and used in the classroom. Three highly effective strategies that promote independent learning are Question-Answer-Relationship (Q-A-R), SQ3R, and Think-Aloud.

**Question-Answer-Relationship** (Q-A-R) (Banikowski & Mehring, 1999; Gunning, 1996; McIntosh & Draper, 1996; Pearson & Johnson, 1978; Raphael, 1982; Swanson & De La Paz, 1998) is a strategy that assists struggling readers in recognizing the various places where answers to questions may be found. The "places" may be physically located in the text or metaphysically located through prior knowledge of the reader. These places include Right there—in a single sentence in the text; Putting it together—in several sentences in the text; On my own—using a student's background knowledge; and Writer and me—using a combination of information from the text and the reader's background. An example of questions that might be asked in a short story include the following:

Right there: What is the setting?

Putting it together: Why was the character upset?

On my own: In what situation have you been upset?

Writer and me: Is there anyone who reminds you of the character in the story? Who and why?

As the text is being read, the teacher uses text questions or creates questions about the material that is being covered. Students then determine what information is needed to answer the question. Once students know where the answer is found, they are more able to answer the question and hopefully will continue to use this strategy with future questions. This is an excellent strategy for struggling middle school students because it gives them a variety of ways to find information and helps them to recognize that some information is directly stated and some is inferred.

**SQ3R** (Gunning, 1996; Robinson, 1961) is a strategy that takes time but is effective in improving comprehension because it breaks the text into manageable parts. The teacher begins by teaching the students the following steps: [S]urvey—look through the chapter for an overall idea of the topic; [Q]uestion—turn each heading into a question; [R]ead to answer the questions; [R]ecite—at the end of each section, try to answer the questions without looking back; do not take notes until the entire section is read; [R]eview what you have read—go over all of the questions and try to answer them. This strategy should be modeled using information that has been previously covered in order to help the students understand the steps. The level of comprehension can be determined by assessing the students' responses during the Recite and Review parts of the strategy. This strategy is successful because it keeps the text from becoming overwhelming. Instead of focusing on the text as a whole, the student is able to focus on one step at a time.

**Think-Aloud** (Gunning, 1996) is a very valuable strategy because it helps students to understand the thought processes associated with silent reading. The teacher models this strategy. As a short selection is read aloud, the teacher talks about their thoughts regarding the selection and discusses what they understand and what they need to learn more about. Students are then invited to do the same as they read selections. This strategy helps the struggling reader to see how different individuals think while they are reading and may assist them in their own comprehension skills. Questions such as "Why is the character acting as he or she is?" "What may have happened to cause this character to be in this place at this time?" "What would you do?" allow the African American reader to realize that others may be bringing their personal experiences into play as they attempt to fully comprehend what is happening in the story and that not every answer is found word for word in the text.

## Teaching to Learning Style

African American students, like all students, have a variety of learning styles. Some students learn best visually, some through auditory means, and others through tactile methods. Teaching to these various learning styles can be very beneficial to both struggling readers and those who are able to comprehend on or above grade level text. A variety of strategies are available; these include Draw a Picture, Journal, and Visual Adjuncts.

**Draw a Picture** (Banikowski & Mehring, 1999) is a visual strategy that helps students to organize and conceptualize what a text is about. After students have read a selection, have them draw a simple picture about the text. Guidelines may be given at first to help the student by providing questions for them to visually answer. For example, when studying aspects of life in Ancient Egypt, students may choose to draw a pyramid depicting the various parts of life for Egyptians (e.g., listing the gods at the top, the pharaoh next, and the workers on the bottom), then write short descriptions with each part of the pyramid. Following this, the students are asked to write a short summary paragraph that will be used in assessing their level of comprehension.

**Journal** (Di Pillo & Sovchik, 1997; Vacca & Vacca, 1989) allows students to independently think through the information that is being taught and allows the teacher to independently assess each student. Teachers initiate this strategy by giving a prompt to the students that is instructional, contextual, reflective, or other. For example, after reading a short story, the following questions may be asked: What is the setting in this story? What feeling is the main character expressing? How would you react in this situation? Students are then given five to eight minutes to write about the prompt. As the journals are turned in, the teacher can assess their comprehension and may choose to respond to students individually.

**Visual Adjuncts** (Craig & Yore, 1996) uses the visuals that are provided in the text to help students better comprehend the information that is being covered. These visuals include charts, graphs, pictures, maps, and more. These visual parts of the text are often overlooked and are most useful when the teacher discusses them in detail and assists the students in clarifying, enriching, or reinforcing concepts that are covered in the text. Although this strategy is useful for African American students and provides additional information in comprehending text, it is especially valuable for all struggling readers who learn visually.

# Conclusion

Although several specific comprehension strategies have been described here, there are still many more available. Teachers, depending on their goals, teaching styles, and the subjects being taught, can find strategies to assist struggling readers of all backgrounds in their classroom. Often the strategies that teachers use can be varied and enhanced to be more effective for their classroom. Using examples that relate to students' backgrounds, experiences, and cultures makes the strategies more meaningful and effective, especially for African American students and other diverse populations. There is a satisfaction and sense of accomplishment that is felt when struggling readers have made a significant step toward truly comprehending what they have read. As a teacher, there is no greater reward than seeing students' eyes light up with the realization that they finally comprehend what was once previously unclear to them.

## REFERENCES

Aronson, E. (1997). *The jigsaw classroom: Building cooperation in the classroom* (2nd ed.). New York: Longman.

Banikowski, A.K., & Mehring, T.A. (1999). Strategies to enhance memory based on brain-research. *Focus on Exceptional Children, 32*(2), 1–16.

Barrentine, S.J. (1996). Engaging with reading through interactive read-alouds. *The Reading Teacher, 50,* 36–43.

Bromley, K., & Modlo, M. (1997). Using cooperative learning to improve reading and writing in Language arts. *Reading & Writing Quarterly, 13*(1), 21–35.

Buehl, D. (1997, September). Loud and clear. *The Reading Room*. Retrieved March 3, 2000, from http://www.weac.org/News/SEPT97/read.htm

Bulgren, J., & Scanlon, D. (1998). Instructional routines and learning strategies that promote understanding of content area concepts. *Journal of Adolescent & Adult Literacy, 41*(4), 292–302.

Cochran J.A. (1993). *Reading in the content areas for junior high and high school.* Boston: Allyn & Bacon.

Craig, M.T., & Yore, L.D. (1996). Middle school students' awareness of strategies for resolving comprehension difficulties in science reading. *Journal of Research & Development in Education, 29*(4), 226–238.

Di Pillo, M.L., & Sovchik, R. (1997). Exploring middle graders' mathematical thinking through journals. *Mathematics Teaching in the Middle School, 2*(5), 308–314.

Gunning, T.G. (1996). *Creating reading instruction for all children* (2nd ed.). Boston: Allyn & Bacon.

Hendrix, J.C. (1999). Connecting cooperative learning and social studies. *Clearing House, 73*(1), 57–60.

Herber, H.L. (1978). *Teaching reading in the content areas.* (2nd ed.). Englewood Cliffs, NJ: Prentice Hall.

Ivey, G. (1999). Teaching struggling middle school readers. *Education Digest, 65*(2), 60–65.

Jeffrey, C.R. (1997). K-W-L learning journals: A way to encourage reflection. *Journal of Adolescent & Adult Literacy, 40*, 392–393.

Katims, D.S., & Harris, S. (1997). Improving the reading comprehension of middle school students in inclusive classrooms. *Journal of Adolescent & Adult Literacy, 41*, 116–123.

Lewis, A.C. (1999). Getting real about middle school reading. *Changing Schools in Long Beach, 3*(2), 11–14.

Manzo, A.V. (1969). The ReQuest procedure. *Journal of Reading, 13*(2), 123–126, 163.

McIntosh, M.E., & Draper, R.J. (1996). Using the question-answer relationship strategy to improve students' reading in mathematics texts. *Clearing House, 69*(3), 154–162.

Ogle, D.M. (1986). K-W-L: A teaching model that develops active reading of expository text. *The Reading Teacher, 39*, 564–570.

Ogle, D.M. (1994). Assessment: Helping our students see their learning. *Teaching Pre-K–8, 25*(2), 100–101.

Pearson, P.D., & Johnson, D.D. (1978). *Teaching reading comprehension.* New York: Holt, Rinehart & Winston.

Raphael, T.E. (1982). Question-answering strategies for children. *The Reading Teacher, 36*, 186–190.

Robinson, F. (1961). *Effective study* (Rev. ed.). New York: Harper.

Swanson, P.N., & De La Paz, S. (1998). Teaching effective comprehension strategies to students with learning and reading disabilities. *Intervention in School & Clinic, 33*(4), 209–218.

Vacca, R.T., & Vacca, J.L. (1989). *Content area reading* (3rd ed.). Glenview, IL: Scott, Foresman.

Vaughn, S., & Klingner, J.K. (1999). Teaching reading comprehension through collaborative strategic reading. *Intervention in School & Clinic, 34*(5), 284–292.

Warren, J.S., & Flynt, S.W. (1995). Children with attention deficit disorder: Diagnosis and prescription of reading skills deficits. *Reading Improvement, 32*(2), 105–110.

# CHAPTER 12

# Educating African American Learners at Risk: Finding a Better Way

*Dorothy S. Strickland*

E ven before they enter school, at least one third of the nation's children are at risk for school failure. The deck is stacked against them, not because of anything they have done or failed to do. Most of these youngsters live in poverty, and they are members of a minority group. A large proportion of them are African American. The fact that they are poor is the key reason they are at risk for failure. Indeed, children from middle class Black families academically outperform poor children, regardless of ethnicity (Hodgkinson, 1991). Although education cannot solve all the societal problems that poor, African American children face, it remains an important and powerful weapon against poverty and crime. It is becoming increasingly obvious that whether or not these children become literate has a profound effect on all our lives. For these children, the successful application of what is known about the teaching and learning of literacy is of critical importance. In this article, I bring that knowledge together with my very deep concern for a group of children who are in desperate need of our help.

## New Trends in Literacy Instruction

Throughout the United States, teachers and administrators are thoughtfully re-examining the assumptions underlying their literacy programs. Dramatic changes have taken place in many individual classrooms and schools. In some cases massive reforms have been initiated across entire school districts. The changes appear under the heading of various holistic and process-oriented terms, such as literature-based curriculum, integrated language arts, language across the curriculum, whole language, and emergent literacy (Allen & Mason,

From *Language Arts* (1994), 71(5), 328–336. Copyright © 1994 by the National Council of Teachers of English. Reprinted with permission.

1989; Cazden, 1992; Edelsky, Altwerger, & Flores, 1991; Hiebert, 1991). Among the changes in evidence are the following:

• *Increased attention to writing and its relationship to reading.* Students in these classrooms write every day. The writing does not stem from a series of teacher-based assignments to be collected, corrected, and returned. Rather, it is grounded in the ongoing activities of the classroom and the interests of individual students. Students are helped to see their writing through the entire process of prewriting, drafting, revising, editing, and publishing (Farnan, Lapp, & Flood, 1992; Jensen, 1993; Shanahan, 1990).

• *Greater use of tradebooks or library books rather than the more traditional reliance on textbooks.* Children in these classrooms read and are read to every day. Sharing and responding to literature are fundamental to all aspects of the curriculum. The reading aloud continues long after children are fluent, independent readers. Textbooks remain important as *one* of many resources for learning literacy and learning through literacy. Response to literature takes many forms: Personal reflection, group discussions, writing, art, and drama may act as a means of reformulating children's understanding and interpretations of texts. Poems, stories, and informational texts are discussed in terms of their content, their literary qualities, and the art of writing. Students are encouraged to apply what they learn about the author's craft to their own writing (Cullinan, 1992; Huck, 1992; Norton, 1992).

• *Greater student choice in what they read and write in the classroom.* Teachers encourage children to share in the decision making regarding choice of topics to write about and materials to read. Making thoughtful selections and decisions is considered to be a valuable part of students' literacy development (Calkins, 1986; Cambourne, 1987; Wells, 1986).

• *Greater integration of oral language and literacy across all subjects in the curriculum.* Literacy learning is viewed as a key element of every aspect of the curriculum. Reading, writing, speaking, listening, and reasoning are integral to every subject throughout the day (Lipson, Valencia, Wixson, & Peters, 1993; Pappas, Oyler, Barry, & Rassel, 1993).

## Dissenting Voices

These ideas and their applications are continually gaining acceptance and applicability where mainstream, "typical" learners predominate. There is disagreement, however, about how these principles and practices might relate to more diverse populations. Some educators have expressed their concern about the effect of holistic practices on the reading and writing achievement of learners considered to be at risk for school failure, particularly when those learners are Black.

Delpit (1988), an African American educator, has complained about the lack of a display of power and authority in process-oriented classrooms: "The teacher has denied them access to herself as the source of knowledge necessary to learn the forms they need to succeed" (p. 288). She stresses the need for teachers to be explicit, "both with what you're trying to communicate and why that information is important to the task at hand" (as quoted in Teale, 1991, p. 541), particularly when they are teaching across cultures, as is often the case in schools where African American children are prevalent.

Others have questioned the value of holistic approaches to any learners considered to be at risk for failure in school. When questioned by *The Washington Post* regarding practices associated with young children's emergent literacy and the whole language approach, Chall (1991) responded, "the new approach is particularly harmful for below-average children or children at risk of failure because of poverty or learning problems" (p. A16). More recently, Chall expressed similar concerns, directing them specifically at what she perceives to be a lack of appropriate phonics instruction in programs that engage in holistic approaches. Once again, she is concerned for "especially those who are at risk" (as quoted in Willis, 1993, p. 8).

Still others express concern about the change process itself. MacGinitie (1991) warns that advocates of holistic approaches are doomed to repeat the failures of the past if they are not more specific in their descriptions of what they propose. "Those who seriously wish to improve education must do more than describe a classroom atmosphere; they must describe how the atmosphere can be achieved and maintained and how people function within it" (p. 57).

Delpit, Chall, and MacGinitie are highly respected scholars whose words require serious consideration. Perhaps even more importantly, their concerns are shared by many well-intentioned, caring parents and teachers of African American children. Unfortunately, when these views are expressed by those less well informed or less well intentioned, two very fundamental but faulty assumptions often underlie them. One is rooted in learning; the other, in teaching.

First there is widespread belief, whether tacit or explicit, that African American children are inherently less capable than most other learners. Indeed, many Black children are at risk for failure, but the risk is neither inevitable nor inherent (Heath, 1983; Shepard, 1991). Second, the traditional view of "teacher as source of knowledge and power" remains highly prevalent, not only among the general public, but among many educators as well. Effective teachers are far more than repositories and dispensers of information. Their primary goal is to help children become independent learners. They share power in order to empower. Even Delpit (1988) concedes that "the teacher cannot be the only expert in the classroom. To deny students their own expert knowledge is to disempower them" (p. 288).

Effective teachers also regard the direct instruction of strategies (with their attendant underlying skills) as fundamental to the "new" approaches outlined above. At the same time, however, they reject instruction that relies heavily on merely transmitting, "explicitly," a body of information from a single viewpoint or relaying only one way to solve a problem or address an issue. While such instruction may be explicit and clear, it risks denying the strengths that diverse views and cultural frameworks bring to the classroom. Moreover, effective teachers take care not to reduce explicit teaching merely to "telling." They know that modeling and demonstrating are key to being explicit (Duffy, Roehler, & Rackliffe, 1986).

Still, it behooves those of us who espouse new approaches to heed MacGinitie's admonition to be clear about what we advocate and to relate new practice to the many traditional practices that should be preserved. Indeed, Chall's concerns may be well founded in classrooms where basic principles of holistic education are not well understood and only in evidence at a superficial level. Fortunately, there is a growing body of literature written, not only by university theorists and researchers but also by classroom teachers and teacher-researchers, in which classroom environments and practices are explicitly described and related to theory (see Atwell, 1987; Chew, 1991; Feeley, Strickland, & Wepner, 1991; Routman, 1991, among others).

It is not surprising that some are skeptical about the new approaches to helping children learn literacy. For many educators, shifting to a new paradigm or to a new way of thinking is difficult under any circumstances. It may be virtually impossible when old ideas are tenaciously held, regardless of new evidence. For others, the reservations are guided by a healthy and informed skepticism. Their expressions of concern should be welcomed and reflected upon by all those working to help African American children become literate. They serve as a reminder of the constant need to reexamine our changing beliefs and practice.

## Basic Skills: Pros and Cons

In the past, the educational problems of at-risk African American children have received a great deal of attention. The administration of President Lyndon Johnson brought about widespread attempts at school reform. Most of the resulting efforts were characterized by highly structured, isolated skills instruction in reading, with little or no attention given at all to instruction in writing. In schools where low student achievement was persistent, the emphasis was placed on increasing test scores in reading and math; and, for the most part, that focus remains today (Strickland & Ascher, 1992).

Oddly enough, the initiation of these "basic skills" reforms had a positive side. Applied skillfully, the conventional ways of responding to the educationally disadvantaged did improve student performance on standardized tests. This improved performance was especially true in the elementary grades. It demonstrated that when schools rallied around a common purpose, were goal oriented, and were given explicit help to achieve those goals, students would learn what was taught. For some, this improvement may have been the first real evidence that these students were capable of learning. Higher performance proved to be a morale builder for students and teachers alike. When administrators and teachers saw their efforts pay off, they felt good about themselves and their clients—the students they served. And, the community also felt a sense of pride (Knapp & Turnbull, 1990).

There was also an ominous and negative side to this, however. As the definition of what it means to be literate in our society becomes more demanding and more complex, the constraints of this type of teaching become increasingly evident. Teaching to low level, basic skills apparently places an unintended ceiling on learning. Those rising test scores, the pride of a school district, begin to level off, and children actually appear to stop learning. In an effort to increase test scores at any cost, many schools may spend excessive amounts of time and effort aligning curriculum to the test and valuable instructional time teaching directly to the test. Focusing so much attention on tests and so little on true instructional reform tends to yield benefits that are both limited and temporary (Darling-Hammond, 1993b; Shepard, 1991).

The really important message in all this, however, lies well beyond what the test scores reveal. When students are repeatedly served a diet of low level, impoverished basics, they accumulate a kind of knowledge that is neither empowering nor self-improving. Students may conscientiously take in the information dispensed to them, and they may spout it back on cue. But, they are frequently left not knowing how to use that information, how to learn on their own, to think for themselves, solve problems, and critique their own work and the work of others.

## A Better Way

Fortunately, some promising instructional alternatives exist. Building on the work of previous researchers, contemporary investigators have broken fresh ground to create new paradigms for the way we view children's literacy development and the way adults can best help them learn. Much of what has been learned applies to all children regardless of race or socioeconomic level. Several major principles seem to stand out regardless of the learner variables present. Whether the learners be high achieving or at risk, inner-city poor or affluent suburban, second language, or native speakers, certain learner characteristics are maintained:. These characteristics will be discussed in the following sections.

## Literacy Learning Starts Early and Continues Throughout Life
(Goodman & Goodman, 1979; Teale & Sulzby, 1986;
Woodward, Harste, & Burke, 1984)

African American children deserve early literacy programs that are framed from an emergent literacy perspective. Such programs would capitalize on the fact that, like all other children, African American children enter school eager to learn and to please the responsive adults around them. They are aware of the print in their environment: their names, the names of siblings, the logos and slogans from fast food restaurants, and various other signs representing environmental print.

Recommendations

1. Avoid readiness tests that screen children out. Implement instructional strategies and systematic observational techniques that allow children to demonstrate what they do know. Use what is learned to build their linguistic awareness and expand their knowledge about the world.

2. Create learning environments that give children confidence that they can learn and let them know *by your actions* that you believe they can learn.

3. Initiate family literacy programs in which adults and children approach literacy learning as a cooperative social experience. At the very least, such programs would make books and other materials available to parents for reading to and with their children.

4. Seek out information from parents about their perceptions of their children as learners, and their educational goals and concerns as a family. Let parents know you value whatever literacy experiences they give to their children. View home and school as making different but interdependent contributions to the child's total education.

5. Start coordinated school and social service intervention programs early and make them ongoing. The purpose should be to prevent failure and promote accelerated achievement rather than merely to remediate problems.

6. Treat instruction in phonics as an important part of beginning reading and writing, but not a precursor to it. View phonics for what it is—one of several enablers (including word meanings and sentence structures) to success in literacy. Nothing more! Nothing less! Allow neither students nor their parents to think they are receiving instruction in reading when they are merely receiving instruction in phonics. Emphasize sound-symbol relationships during the reading of interesting, predictable texts and during writing through children's own attempts at spelling.

## Literacy Learning Is Used to Make Meaning Out of Our World
(Donaldson, 1978; Smith, 1982; Wells, 1986)

African American children deserve literacy programs that stress the construction of meaning right from the start. As with every other aspect of their learning, these young children are attempting to make sense of the world around them. Print is simply one of the many curiosities in the world about which they are eager to learn.

Recommendations

1. Take care to see to it that the tasks students are given make sense to them. Keep in mind that low level, rote tasks tend to make less sense than tasks that require reasoning and reflective thought (Resnick, 1987).

2. Select instructional materials that employ whole texts, including a wide variety of fiction and nonfiction. Avoid meaningless drills on isolated skills delivered in the form of workbooks and worksheets.

3. Integrate instruction in the language arts so that students connect learning how to spell with proofreading a composition, expanding their vocabularies with comprehending stories and informational books, authoring and responding with what they do as writers and readers, and so on.

4. Foster inquiry-based curricula, in which individuals and groups of children pose questions and seek to answer them. Allow the teaching of literacy to be largely driven by needs arising from the content and questions that children are curious about—for example, learning how to conduct a good interview during the study of personal health in order to learn what nurses do. Even when content foci are preset by a fixed curriculum, independence and motivation can be fostered by allowing children to pose their own questions within the sphere of the content they are required to study.

## Literacy Learning Takes Place
## Through Active Involvement and Use
(Lindfors, 1987; Wells, 1986)

African American children deserve literacy programs that recognize that knowledge is not merely an accumulation of assorted facts absorbed like a sponge. Knowledge is constructed by active minds and grounded in life experience.

Recommendations

1. Plan instructional activities that involve children in a high degree of critical thinking and problem solving. For example, postreading activities based on student-generated questions and observations related to key ideas in a text are more likely to stimulate active response and involvement than those that simply require students to answer a preset list of teacher-generated questions.

2. Help students use talk as a means of mediating what they are attempting to understand. Engage students in literature study groups, collaborative group discussions, partner activities, and research groups. Rather than attempting to keep students quiet, plan activities where talk is channeled and used along with reading and writing as a tool for learning.

3. Employ collaborative group learning strategies and peer teaching methods to promote active learners. Approaches that emphasize the fact that everyone in the classroom is both a teacher and a learner help increase student involvement and tend to promote active learning.

4. Keep instruction as close to the point of use as possible. Expand the definition of direct instruction to go beyond conveying information to an entire group of students in a pre-ordered way. Include the demonstration of strategies for individuals and groups of students that they actually need to complete a given task. Both the how and the why of a strategy are made explicit when the need is clearly understood.

## Literacy Learning Is Influenced
## by One's Language and Cultural Background

African American children deserve literacy programs that build on and expand their language and culture with a view toward helping them understand and value their heritage and respect the heritage of others. They deserve teachers and administrators who value diversity and recognize its presence in every child (Au, 1993).

Recommendations

1. Never use a child's dialect, language, or culture as a basis for making judgments regarding intellect or capability. Competence is not tied to a particular language, dialect, or culture.

2. Learn as much as you can about students' language and cultural backgrounds. Avoid making sweeping generalizations based on skin color or surnames. There is a high degree of variability within every cultural group. Learn as much as you can; then keep an open mind.

3. Give students literature that reflects a wide diversity of cultures. Take special care to see to it that African American children are familiar with literature by and about African Americans as well as with the writers and illustrators themselves.

4. Encourage standard English through exposure to a variety of oral and written texts and oral language activities. Keep in mind that while competence in standard English is a worthy goal for all children, it must not mean a rejection or replacement of one language and culture with another. Rather, it should be viewed as language expansion and enrichment of the students' home language to include standard English, giving them the opportunity and the *choice* to communicate with a broader speech community (Galda, Cullinan, & Strickland, 1993).

## *Literacy Learning Is Influenced by Social Context*
(Cazden, 1992; Moll, 1990; Scribner & Cole, 1981)

African American children deserve opportunities to learn in contexts that reflect what is known about the social nature of literacy and literacy learning. This requires administrators and teachers who know how to establish supportive and responsive contexts for learning. According to Darling-Hammond (1993a), "the problems of equity are constrained by the availability of talented teachers, by the knowledge and capacities those teachers possess, and by the school conditions that define how that knowledge can be used" (p. 754).

Recommendations

1. Foster a sense of community and interconnectedness within each classroom and throughout each school. Keep schools and classes small enough, or divide them into manageable units, so that individual students feel known and recognized as participants in a community, and closer student-teacher relationships are more likely to develop.

2. Avoid long-term ability grouping and tracking. These deny equitable access to learning opportunities (Epstein, 1985; Oakes, 1985). Seek alternatives such as flexible grouping practices, which may include some short-term ability grouping and cooperative learning instructional methods that treat diversity as a valued resource.

3. Create large, uninterrupted blocks of time for language arts instruction, during which no children leave the classroom for special activities. Short time periods lead to a one-size-fits-all instruction, in which every student is assigned precisely the same tasks and given the same amount of instructional support and time to complete them. Large time frames foster integrated learning and allow for differentiated instruction, thus fostering true educational equity.

4. Give incentives to attract the very best teachers available and provide ongoing professional development focused on empowering teachers to make instructional decisions. Emphasize classroom observation—how to assess what students are learning and use it to plan accordingly.

5. Encourage ongoing professional development such as teacher networks that operate as voluntary support groups. Professional networks allow teachers to organize their own staff development efforts so that ideas close to the classroom may be discussed in a risk-free atmosphere of mutual support. Avoid placing all resources in one-shot staff-development days, and be wary of intensive "training" programs on narrowly construed, highly prescriptive models of instruction.

# Conclusion

For most educators, the ideas offered here are neither new nor revolutionary. In fact, some would argue that these suggestions are appropriate for any child, regardless of ethnicity, socioeconomic status, or intellect. And, that is precisely the point. We now know enough about the learning and teaching of language and literacy to offer some basic principles to guide instructional decision making for the education of every child. Perhaps the greatest value of these principles and recommendations is that they are learner centered and thus adapt to and support all learners, no matter who they are.

Teachers who work with large numbers of African American children in situations where failure is chronic may wonder how these ideas will help them deal with diversity. Having placed so much emphasis on how their students are different from others, they may be confused by the suggestion that there are "universal" principles of learning and teaching from which all children may benefit. They want advice specific to the needs of the children they teach. This is highly understandable. Yet, these teachers should know that the ideas offered here are not meant to suggest a one-size-fits-all curriculum. They in no way negate the fact that there are great differences among the children we teach. Respecting and building on these differences is an important part of what good teachers do. The differences we face in schools, however, go far beyond those distinctions commonly made *between* various ethnic groups. There are important differences among children *within* ethnic groups and linguistic communities, even among those who live at the poverty level. These include children's interests, experiential backgrounds, abilities, and motivation. These differences may be overlooked by teachers who come to the teaching situation with preconceived ideas about how certain children learn and behave. Moreover, when the curriculum fails to value each learner's unique background, there is a risk that important individual characteristics may never be revealed as potential building blocks for instruction.

Dawn Harris Martine, a second-grade teacher in Harlem, New York City, once told me that she could trace at least a dozen different national origins among her group of 26 children. More than half her students had very recent roots in several countries in Africa, the Caribbean, and Central America, as well as various parts of the United States. Yet, she said, to most people they simply look like any other group of African American kids. To Dawn, the differences were very important and helped shape the curriculum and the ways in which she interacted with each child.

What, then, should teachers know that is specific to these youngsters? Teachers who work with these children should enter the classroom informed as much as possible about the broader population from which these children come—both from reading the relevant literature and from first-hand experiences with others who belong to that population. They should also learn as much as they can about the immediate community and the families of these children. They should use what they learn as a framework for understanding who and where their learners are. At the same time, they should use the principles described here to develop a literacy curriculum that is both rigorous and learner centered. Most importantly, they should avoid assigning preconceived characteristics and attributes to any child, bearing in mind the need to suspend judgment and respect each as an individual.

Harris (1993), a philanthropist and child advocate, recounts a parable about some people picnicking beside a river:

> Suddenly, they see an enormous number of babies being carried down the river by the current. Their first impulse is to jump in and pull out as many of the babies as possible. But they keep coming, and the rescuers can't save them all. Finally, someone is smart enough to run up the river to see who is pushing them in. (p. 30)

As teachers of the language arts, we sometimes feel like those rescuers—attempting to "save the children" despite overwhelming forces beyond our control. Indeed, the responsibility for helping African American students, or any other students who are at risk for educational failure, is not ours alone. The problems are serious and demand the attention of everyone—the home, the school, and the community.

Nevertheless, there is a great deal that we *can* do. We can work as individuals and within professional and civic organizations to effect social policy change, and we can work with students and their parents to achieve better mutual support between home and school. Most importantly, we can take advantage of a growing body of research that suggests better educational policy and more comprehensive and meaningful approaches to raising the academic achievement of African American students. The knowledge is available. It is time we demonstrated the commitment to seek a better way.

## REFERENCES

Allen, J.B., & Mason, J.M. (Eds.). (1989). *Risk makers, risk takers, risk breakers: Reducing the risks for young literacy learners.* Portsmouth, NH: Heinemann.

Atwell, N. (1987). *In the middle: Writing, reading, and learning with adolescents.* Portsmouth, NH: Heinemann.

Au, K.H. (1993). *Literacy instruction in multicultural settings.* Fort Worth, TX: Harcourt College.

Calkins, L.M. (1986). *The art of teaching writing.* Portsmouth, NH: Heinemann.

Cambourne, B. (1987). *The whole story.* Sydney: Primary English Teaching Association.

Cazden, C.B. (1992). *Whole language plus.* New York: Teachers College Press.

Chall, J.S. (1991, May 13). Armed with pen and lots to say. *The Washington Post,* p. A16.

Chew, C.R. (Ed.). (1991). *Whole language in urban classrooms.* Roslyn, NY: Berrent.

Cullinan, B. (Ed.). (1992). *Invitation to read: More children's literature in the reading program.* Newark, DE: International Reading Association.

Darling-Hammond, L. (1993a). *Federal policy options for Chapter 1: An equity agenda for school restructuring.* New York: National Center for Restructuring Education. (ERIC Document Service No. ED364625)

Darling-Hammond, L. (1993b). Reframing the school reform agenda. *Phi Delta Kappan, 74*(10), 752–761.

Delpit, L.D. (1988). The silenced dialogue: Power and pedagogy in educating other people's children. *Harvard Educational Review, 56*(3), 280–298.

Donaldson, M. (1978). *Children's minds.* Glasgow, Scotland: William Collins Sons.

Duffy, G.O., Roehler, L., & Rackliffe, G. (1986). How teachers' instructional talk influences students' understanding of lesson content. *The Elementary School Journal, 87*(1), 3–16.

Edelsky, C., Altwerger, B., & Flores, B. (1991). *Whole language: What's the difference?* Portsmouth, NH: Heinemann.

Epstein, J.L. (1985). After the bus arrives: Resegregation in desegregated schools. *Journal of Social Issues, 41*(3), 23–43.

Farnan, N., Lapp, D., & Flood, J. (1992). Changing perspectives in writing instruction. *Journal of Reading*, 35(7), 550–557.

Feeley, J.T., Strickland, D.S., & Wepner, S.B. (Eds.). (1991). *Process reading and writing: A literature-based approach*. New York: Teachers College Press.

Galda, L., Cullinan, B.E., & Strickland, D.S. (1993). *Language, literacy and the child*. Fort Worth, TX: Harcourt College.

Goodman, K.S., & Goodman, Y.A. (1979). Learning to read is natural. In L.B. Resnick & P.A. Weaver (Eds.), *Theory and practice of early reading* (Vol. 1, pp. 137–154). Hillsdale, NJ: Erlbaum.

Harris, I.B. (1993, Spring). Education—Does it make a difference when you start? *Aspen Quarterly*, 5, 30–52.

Heath, S.B. (1983). *Ways with words: Language, life, and work in communities and classrooms*. Cambridge, UK: Cambridge University Press.

Hiebert, E.H. (Ed.). (1991). *Literacy for a diverse society*. New York: Teachers College Press.

Hodgkinson, H. (1991). Reform versus reality. *Phi Delta Kappan*, 73(1), 8–16.

Huck, C. (1992). Literature and literacy. *Language Arts*, 69, 520–526.

Jensen, J.M. (1993). What we know about the writing of elementary school children. *Language Arts*, 70, 290–294.

Knapp, M.S., & Turnbull, B.J. (1990). *Better schooling for the children of poverty: Alternatives to conventional wisdom*. Washington, DC: US Department of Education.

Lindfors, J.W. (1987). *Children's language and learning*. Englewood Cliffs, NJ: Prentice Hall.

Lipson, M.Y., Valencia, S.W., Wixson, K.K., & Peters, C.W. (1993). Integration and thematic teaching: Integration to improve teaching and learning. *Language Arts*, 70(4), 252–263.

MacGinitie, W.H. (1991). Reading instruction: Plus ça change.... *Educational Leadership*, 48(6), 55–58.

Moll, L.C. (Ed.). (1990). *Vygotsky and education*. New York: Cambridge University Press.

Norton, D.E. (1992). *The impact of literature-based reading*. New York: Macmillan.

Oakes, J. (1985). *Keeping track: How schools structure inequality*. New Haven, CT: Yale University Press.

Pappas, C., Oyler, C., Barry, A., & Rassel, M. (1993). Focus on research: Collaborating with teachers developing integrated language arts programs in urban schools. *Language Arts*, 70(4), 297–303.

Resnick, L.B (1987). The 1987 presidential address: Learning in school and out. *Educational Researcher*, 16(9), 13–20.

Routman, R. (1991). *Transitions: From literature to literacy*. Portsmouth, NH: Heinemann.

Scribner, S., & Cole, M. (1981). *The psychology of literacy*. Cambridge, MA: Harvard University Press.

Shanahan, T. (Ed.). (1990). *Reading and writing together: New perspectives for the classroom*. Norwood, MA: Christopher-Gordon.

Shepard, L. (1991). Negative policies for dealing with diversity: When does assessment and diagnosis turn into sorting and segregation? In E.H. Hiebert (Ed.), *Literacy for a diverse society* (pp. 279–298). New York: Teachers College Press.

Smith, F. (1982). *Understanding reading*. New York: Holt.

Strickland, D.S., & Ascher, C. (1992). Low income African American children and public schooling. In P.W. Jackson (Ed.), *Handbook of research on curriculum* (pp. 609–625). New York: Macmillan.

Teale, W.H. (1991). A conversation with Lisa Delpit. *Language Arts*, 68, 541–547.

Teale, W.H., & Sulzby, E. (1986). *Emergent literacy: Writing and reading.* Norwood, NJ: Ablex.

Wells, G. (1986). *The meaning makers: Children learning language and using language to learn.* Portsmouth, NH: Heinemann.

Willis, S. (1993, November). Whole language in the '90s. *Update*, pp. 1, 5, 6, 8.

Woodward, V.A., Harste, J.C., & Burke, C.V. (1984). *Language stories and literacy lessons.* Portsmouth, NH: Heinemann.

# PART III

# Cultural Considerations

The impact of the cultural background of African American students on teaching and learning has long been a source of debate and controversy. Should teachers take into account the culture of a student when planning instruction or evaluating a student's academic performance? To what extent do African American students display a preference for a certain type of instruction, and, if so, what are the characteristics of that learning style? Can learning styles be measured and are the results relevant to teaching of African American students?

In the minds of many readers, questions probably still exist regarding the necessity for incorporating cultural learning styles information into classroom practice: Does it really matter? If it does, will it make a significant difference in improving the performance of students? Is there research regarding which practices are most effective and should be incorporated into my classroom?

Heredia (1999) has suggested that the concept of cultural learning styles is rooted in learning styles theory. The fundamental concept to be adhered to, according to Irvine and York (1995), is that designing educational experiences, curriculum, and instruction that match the student learning styles may improve academic achievement. It is this premise that much of the work on matching learning styles to ethnic groups is based (Worthley, 1987). Indeed, cultural considerations are critical to the selection of instructional resources and approaches to instructional delivery in the classroom. Guild (2001) has asserted that the relationship of values of the culture in which a child is currently living, or from which a child has roots, and the learning expectations and experiences in the classroom are directly related to the child's school success academically, socially, and emotionally.

The amount of research (Clarkston, 1983; Gilbert & Gay, 1989; Hale-Benson, 1986; Hilliard, 1989; Irvine & York, 1995; Shade, 1989; Willis, 1989) on the preferred learning patterns of African American children is significant. Hale (2001) suggests that the culture of African American students does have a profound impact on their learning and achievement. The lack of understanding and, in some cases, commitment to their learning by teachers is one reason why the achievement gap between these children and others still exists. Hale suggests that the solution lies in the classroom, in the nature of the interaction between the teacher and the child.

Although many African American scholars and researchers, including the ones represented in this section, do recognize that the cultural learning styles of the African American child is worthy of examination when planning for instruction, there also is a skeptic (Frisby, 1993) who argues that the notion of a Black cultural learning style is seriously flawed. Frisby suggests that developing a perspective that African American children need to be educated differently from other children has, in many ways, contributed to the continuing gap in academic performance that exits today. As Guild (2001) points out, "Even as we acknowledge that culture affects learning styles, we know that distinct learning styles patterns don't fit a specific cultural group" (p. 12). Dunn (1997) also points out that researchers have clearly established that there is no single or dual learning style for the members of any cultural, national, racial, or religious group.

Part III provides perspectives on the issues related to the culture of African American students and offers practical suggestions for incorporating knowledge about a student's cultural background into the instructional delivery system. All the articles in Part III deal with cultural considerations that must be included as teachers prepare to teach African American children to read. The articles represent a blending of research and effective classroom practices. They are intended to help broaden the perspectives of classroom teachers on the impact of a student's culture as they prepare to teach, especially as related to African American students. In chapter 13, Lisa Delpit examines the impact of a child's language and culturally responsive teaching. Kelli Harris-Wright, in chapter 14, explores literacy development through oral language. Effective instructional strategies for African American students are presented by Sharroky Hollie in chapter 15. Barbara J. Shade discusses the cognitive learning style of African Americans as a variable in school success in chapter 16. In chapter 17, Etta Ruth Hollins, Linda R. McIntyre, Charles E. DeBose, Kimberly S. Hollins, and Arthurlene G. Towner discuss literacy development in the primary grades. In chapter 18, Wanda M. Brooks identifies linguistic features and a component of providing successful instruction for African American middle school learners. Carol D. Lee highlights culturally based literary interpretative skills for African American high school students in chapter 19.

As has been shown in the research cited previously, the culture of a student plays a considerable role in his or her ability to learn in the classroom. Despite this information, relatively little has been written for or demonstrated to teachers on effective methods of incorporating the cultural strengths of their students into classroom instruction. More often, the preferred learning styles, patterns of behavior, and general school behaviors of African American students have been sources of conflict and punishment by many dedicated but uninformed teachers.

The editors of this book hope that the information presented in Part III will stem the tide of conflict in the classroom and, instead, provide teachers of these students of color with clear and precise information to be incorporated into their classrooms, helping to make both teacher and student successful.

## REFERENCES

Clarkson, J. (1983). Urban learning styles. In J.M. Lakebrink (Ed.), *Children's success in school* (pp. 115–139). Springfield, IL: Charles C. Thomas.

Dunn, R. (1997). The goals and track record of multicultural education. *Educational Leadership, 57*(7), 74–77.

Frisby, C.L. (1993). One giant step backwards: Myths of Black cultural learning styles. *School Psychology Review, 22*(3), 535–557.

Gilbert, S.E., & Gay, G. (1989). Improving the success in school of poor Black children. In B.J.R. Shade (Ed.), *Culture, style, and the education process: Making schools work for racially diverse students* (pp. 275–283). Springfield, IL: Charles C. Thomas.

Guild, P.B. (2001, October). Diversity, learning style and culture. *New Horizons for Learning.* Retrieved February 20, 2004, from http://www.newhorizons.org/strategies/styles/guild.htm

Hale, J.E. (2001). *Learning while Black: Creating educational excellence for African American children.* Baltimore: Johns Hopkins University Press.

Hale-Benson, J.E. (1986). *Black children: Their roots, culture, and learning styles.* Baltimore: Johns Hopkins University Press.

Heredia, A. (1999). *Cultural learning styles.* Washington, DC: ERIC Clearinghouse on Teaching and Teacher Education. Retrieved October 5, 2004, from http://library.educationworld.net/a12/a12-166.html

Hilliard, A.G. (1989, January). Teachers and cultural styles in a pluralistic society. *NEA Today, 7*(6), 65–66.

Irvine, J.J., & York, D.E. (1995). Learning styles and culturally diverse students: A literature review. In J.A. Banks & C.A. McGee Banks (Eds.), *Handbook of research on multicultural education* (pp. 484–497). New York: Macmillan.

Shade, B.J. (1989). Influences of perpetual development on cognitive style: Cross ethnic comparisons. *Early Childhood Development & Care, 51,* 137–155.

Willis, M.G. (1989, February). Learning styles of African American children: A review of the literature and interventions. *Journal of Black Psychology, 16*(1), 47–65.

Worthley, K.M. (1987). *Learning style factor of field dependency/independency and problem solving strategies of Hmong refugee students.* Unpublished master's thesis, University of Wisconsin–Stout.

CHAPTER 13

# Ebonics and Culturally Responsive Instruction: What Should Teachers Do?

*Lisa Delpit*

T he "Ebonics Debate" has created much more heat than light for most of
the country. For teachers trying to determine what implications there
might be for classroom practice, enlightenment has been a completely
nonexistent commodity. I have been asked often enough recently, "What do
you think about Ebonics? Are you for it or against it?" My answer must be neither. I can be neither for Ebonics or against Ebonics any more than I can be for
or against air. It exists. It is the language spoken by many of our African
American children. It is the language they heard as their mothers nursed them
and changed their diapers and played peek-a-boo with them. It is the language
through which they first encountered love, nurturance, and joy.

On the other hand, most teachers of those African American children who
have been least well served by educational systems believe that their students' life
chances will be further hampered if they do not learn Standard English. In the
stratified society in which we live, they are absolutely correct. While having access
to the politically mandated language form will not, by any means, guarantee economic success (witness the growing numbers of unemployed African Americans
holding doctorates), not having access will almost certainly guarantee failure.

So what must teachers do? Should they spend their time relentlessly "correcting" their Ebonics-speaking children's language, so that it might conform to
what we have learned to refer to as Standard English? Despite good intentions, constant correction seldom has the desired effect. Such correction increases cognitive
monitoring of speech, thereby making talking difficult. To illustrate, I have frequently taught a relatively simple, new "dialect" to classes of preservice teachers.
In this dialect, the phonetic element *iz* is added after the first consonant or consonant cluster in each syllable of a word. (*Maybe* becomes *miz-ay-biz-ee* and *apple*
becomes *iz-ap-piz-le*.) After a bit of drill and practice, the students are asked to

From *Rethinking Schools* (1997), *12*(1), 1–7. Copyright © 1997 Lisa Delpit. Reprinted with permission.

tell a partner in "iz" language why they decided to become teachers. Most students only haltingly attempt a few words before lapsing into either silence or into Standard English. During a follow-up discussion, all students invariably speak of the impossibility of attempting to apply rules while trying to formulate and express a thought. Forcing speakers to monitor their language typically produces silence.

Correction may also affect students' attitudes toward their teachers. In a recent research project, middle school, inner-city students were interviewed about their attitudes toward their teachers and school. One young woman complained bitterly, "Mrs.___ always be interrupting to make you 'talk correct' and stuff. She be butting into your conversations when you not even talking to her! She need to mind her own business." Clearly this student will be unlikely to either follow the teacher's directives or to want to imitate her speech style.

## Group Identity

Issues of group identity may also affect students' oral production of a different dialect. In a study of phonologic aspects of Pima Indian language, Nelson-Barber (1982) found that, in grades 1–3, the children's English most approximated the standard dialect of their teachers. But surprisingly, by fourth grade, when one might assume growing competence in standard forms, their language moved significantly toward the local dialect. These fourth graders had the competence to express themselves in a more standard form, but chose, consciously or unconsciously, to use the language of those in their local environments. The researcher believes that, by ages 8–9, these children became aware of their group membership and its importance to their well-being, and this realization was reflected in their language. They may also have become increasingly aware of the schools's negative attitude toward their community and found it necessary—through choice of linguistic form—to decide with which camp to identify.

What should teachers do about helping students acquire an additional oral form? First, they should recognize that the linguistic form a student brings to school is intimately connected with loved ones, community, and personal identity. To suggest that this form is wrong or, even worse, ignorant, is to suggest that something is wrong with the student and his or her family. To denigrate your language is, then, in African American terms, to "talk about your mama." Anyone who knows anything about African American culture knows the consequences of that speech act!

On the other hand, it is equally important to understand that students who do not have access to the politically popular dialect form in this country are less likely to succeed economically than their peers who do. How can both realities be embraced in classroom instruction?

It is possible and desirable to make the actual study of language diversity a part of the curriculum for all students. For younger children, discussions about the differences in the ways television characters from different cultural groups speak can provide a starting point. A collection of the many children's books written in the dialects of various cultural groups can also provide a wonderful basis for learning about linguistic diversity (see Clifton, 1973; Edler, 1981; Green, 1959; Jacobs & Rice, 1983; Yukon-Koyukkuk School District, 1979–), as can audiotaped stories narrated by individuals from different cultures, including taping books read by members of the children's home communities. Mrs. Pat, a teacher chronicled by Heath (1983), had her students become language "detectives," interviewing a variety of individuals and listening to the radio and television to discover the differences and similarities in the ways people talked. Children can learn that there are many ways of saying the same thing, and that certain contexts suggest particular kinds of linguistic performances.

Some teachers have groups of students create bilingual dictionaries of their own language form and Standard English. Both the students and the teacher become engaged in identifying terms and deciding upon the best translations. This can be done as generational dictionaries, too, given the proliferation of "youth culture" terms growing out of the Ebonics-influenced tendency for the continual regeneration of vocabulary. Contrastive grammatical structures can be studied similarly, but, of course, as the Oakland, California, Standard English Proficiency Program (Oakland Unified School District , 1996) suggests, teachers must be aware of the grammatical structure of Ebonics before they can launch into this complex study.

Other teachers have had students become involved with standard forms through various kinds of role-play. For example, memorizing parts for drama productions will allow students to practice and get the feel of speaking Standard English while not under the threat of correction. A master teacher of African American children in Oakland, Carrie Secret, uses this technique and extends it so that students video their practice performances and self-critique them as to the appropriate use of Standard English (Miner, 1997). (But I must add that Carrie's use of drama and oration goes much beyond acquiring Standard English. She inspires pride and community connections that are truly wondrous to behold.) The use of self-critique of recorded forms may prove even more useful than I initially realized. California State University Hayward Professor Etta Hollins has reported that just by leaving a tape recorder on during an informal class period and playing it back with no comment, students began to code-switch—moving between Standard English and Ebonics—more effectively. It appears that they may not have realized which language form they were using until they heard themselves speak on tape.

Young students can create puppet shows or role-play cartoon characters—many superheroes speak almost hypercorrect Standard English! Playing a role eliminates the possibility of implying that the child's language is inadequate and suggests, instead, that different language forms are appropriate in different contexts. Some other teachers in New York City have had their students produce a news show every day for the rest of the school. The students take on the personae of famous newscasters, keeping in character as they develop and read their news reports. Discussions ensue about whether televison news anchor Tom Brokaw would have said it that way, again taking the focus off the child's speech.

Although most educators think of Black language as primarily differing in grammar and syntax, there are other differences in oral language of which teachers should be aware in a multicultural context, particularly in discourse style and language use. At Harvard University, Michaels and Cazden (1986) and other researchers identified differences in children's narratives at "sharing time." They found that there was a tendency among young White children to tell "topic-centered" narratives—stories focused on one event—and a tendency among Black youngsters, especially girls, to tell "episodic" narratives—stories that include shifting scenes and are typically longer. While these differences are interesting in themselves, what is of greater significance is adults' responses to the differences. Cazden (1988) reports on a subsequent project in which a White adult was taped reading the oral narratives of Black and White first graders, with all syntax dialectal markers removed. Adults were asked to listen to the stories and comment about the children's likelihood of success in school. The researchers were surprised by the differential responses given by Black and White adults.

## Varying Reactions

In responding to the retelling of a Black child's story (refer to Cazden, 1988), the White adults were uniformly negative, making such comments as "terrible story, incoherent" and "[n]ot a story at all in the sense of describing something that happened." Asked to judge this child's academic competence, all of the White adults rated her below the children who told topic-centered stories. Most of these adults also predicted difficulties for this child's future school career, such as, "This child might have trouble reading," that she exhibited "language problems that affect school achievement," and that "family problems" or "emotional problems" might hamper her academic progress.

The Black adults had very different reactions. They found this child's story "well formed, easy to understand, and interesting, with lots of detail and description." Even though all five of these adults mentioned the "shifts" and "associations" or "nonlinear" quality of the story, they did not find these features distracting. Three of the Black adults selected the story as the best of the five they had heard, and all but one judged the child as exceptionally bright, highly verbal, and successful in school.

This is not a story about racism, but one about cultural familiarity. However, when differences in narrative style produce differences in interpretation of competence, the pedagogical implications are evident. If children who produce stories based in differing discourse styles are expected to have trouble reading, and viewed as having language, family, or emotional problems, as was the case with the informants quoted by Cazden, they are unlikely to be viewed as ready for the same challenging instruction awarded students whose language patterns more closely parallel the teacher's.

Most teachers are particularly concerned about how speaking Ebonics might affect learning to read. There is little evidence that speaking another mutually intelligible language form, per se, negatively affects one's ability to learn to read (Sims, 1982). For commonsensical proof, one need only reflect on nonstandard English-speaking Africans who, though enslaved, not only taught themselves to read English, but did so under threat of severe punishment or death. But children who speak Ebonics do have a more difficult time becoming proficient readers. Why? In part, appropriate instructional methodologies are frequently not adopted. There is ample evidence that children who do not come to school with knowledge about letters, sounds, and symbols need to experience some explicit instruction in these areas in order to become independent readers (see Hoover, 1997). Another explanation is that, where teachers' assessments of competence are influenced by the language children speak, teachers may develop low expectations for certain students and subsequently teach them less (Sims, 1982). A third explanation rests in teachers' confusing the teaching of reading with the teaching of a new language form.

Cunningham (1976/1977) found that teachers across the United States were more likely to correct reading miscues that were "dialect" related ("Here go a table" for "Here is a table") than those that were "nondialect" related ("Here is a dog" for "There is a dog"). Seventy-eight percent of the former types of miscues were corrected, compared with only 27% of the latter. She concludes that the teachers were acting out of ignorance, not realizing that "here go" and "here is" represent the same meaning in some Black children's language.

In my observations of many classrooms, however, I have come to conclude that even when teachers recognize the similarity of meaning, they are likely to correct Ebonics-related miscues. Consider a typical example:

Text: Yesterday I washed my brother's clothes.

Student's Rendition: Yesterday I wash my bruvver close.

The subsequent exchange between student and teacher sounds something like this:

Teacher: Wait, let's go back. What's that word again? [Points at *washed.*]

Student: *Wash.*

Teacher: No. Look at it again. What letters do you see at the end? You see *e-d.* Do you remember what we say when we see those letters on the end of the word?

Student: "ed"

Teacher: OK, but in this case we say "washed." Can you say that?

Student: Washed.

Teacher: Good. Now read it again.

Student: Yesterday I washed my bruvver...

Teacher: Wait a minute, what's that word again? [Points to *brother.*]

Student: *Bruvver.*

Teacher: No. Look at these letters in the middle. [Points to *brother.*] Remember to read what you see. Do you remember how we say that sound? Put your tongue between your teeth and say "th"...

The lesson continues in such a fashion, the teacher proceeding to correct the student's Ebonics-influenced pronunciations and grammar while ignoring that fact that the student had to have comprehended the sentence in order to translate it into her own language. Such instruction occurs daily and blocks reading development in a number of ways. First, because children become better readers by having the opportunity to read, the overcorrection exhibited in this lesson means that this child will be less likely to become a fluent reader than other children that are not interrupted so consistently. Second, a complete focus on code and pronunciation blocks children's understanding that reading is essentially a meaning-making process. This child, who understands the text, is led to believe that she is doing something wrong. She is encouraged to think of reading not as something you do to get a message, but something you pronounce. Third, constant corrections by the teacher are likely to cause this student and others like her to resist reading and to resent the teacher.

Language researcher Robert Berdan (1980) reports that, after observing the kind of teaching routine described above in a number of settings, he incorporated the teacher behaviors into a reading instruction exercise that he used with students in a college class. He put together sundry rules from a number of American social and regional dialects to create what he called the "language of

Atlantis." Students were then called upon to read aloud in this dialect they did not know. When they made errors he interrupted them, using some of the same statements and comments he had heard elementary school teachers routinely make to their students. He concludes,

> The results were rather shocking. By the time these Ph.D. candidates in English or linguistics had read 10–20 words, I could make them sound totally illiterate.... The first thing that goes is sentence intonation: they sound like they are reading a list from the telephone book. Comment on their pronunciation a bit more, and they begin to subvocalize, rehearsing pronunciations for themselves before they dare to say them out loud. They begin to guess at pronunciations.... They switch letters around for no reason. They stumble; they repeat. In short, when I attack them for their failure to conform to my demands for Atlantis English pronunciations, they sound very much like the worst of the second graders in any of the classrooms I have observed.
>
> They also begin to fidget. They wad up their papers, bite their fingernails, whisper, and some finally refuse to continue. They do all the things that children do while they are busily failing to learn to read.

The moral of this story is not to confuse learning a new language form with reading comprehension. To do so will only confuse the child, leading her away from those intuitive understandings about language that will promote reading development, and toward a school career of resistance and a lifetime of avoiding reading.

Unlike unplanned oral language or public reading, writing lends itself to editing. While conversational talk is spontaneous and must be responsive to an immediate context, writing is a mediated process that may be written and rewritten any number of times before being introduced to public scrutiny. Consequently, writing is more amenable to rule application—one may first write freely to get one's thoughts down, and then edit to hone the message and apply specific spelling, syntactical, or punctuation rules. My college students who had such difficulty talking in the "iz" dialect found writing it, with the rules displayed before them, a relatively easy task.

## Conclusion

The teacher's job is to provide access to the national standard as well as to understand the language the children speak sufficiently to celebrate its beauty. The verbal adroitness, the cogent and quick wit, the brilliant use of metaphor, the facility in rhythm and rhyme, evident in the language of Jesse Jackson, Whoopi

Goldberg, Toni Morrison, Henry Louis Gates, Tupac Shakur, and Maya Angelou, as well as in that of many inner-city Black students, may all be drawn upon to facilitate school learning. The teacher must know how to effectively teach reading and writing to students whose culture and language differ from that of the school, and must understand how and why students decide to add another language form to their repertoire. All we can do is provide students with access to additional language forms. Inevitably, each speaker will make his or her own decision about what to say in any context.

But I must end with a caveat that we keep in mind a simple truth: Despite our necessary efforts to provide access to Standard English, such access will not make any of our students more intelligent. It will not teach them math or science or geography—or, for that matter, compassion, courage, or responsibility. Let us not become so overly concerned with the language form that we ignore academic and moral content. Access to the standard language may be necessary, but it is definitely not sufficient to produce intelligent, competent caretakers of the future.

## REFERENCES

Berdan, R. (1980). Knowledge into practice: Delivering research to teachers. In M.F. Whiteman (Ed.), *Reactions to Ann Arbor: Vernacular Black English and education.* Arlington, VA: Center for Applied Linguistics.

Cazden, C.B. (1988). *Classroom discourse: The language of teaching and learning.* Portsmouth, NH: Heinemann.

Cunningham, P.M. (1976/1977). Teachers' correction responses to Black-dialect miscues which are nonmeaning-changing. *Reading Research Quarterly, 12,* 637–654.

Heath, S.B. (1983). *Ways with words: Language, life, and work in communities and classrooms.* Cambridge, UK: Cambridge University Press.

Hoover, M.R. (1997). Ebonics: Myths and realities. *Rethinking Schools, 12*(1), 17.

Michaels, S., & Cazden, C.B. (1986). Teacher–child collaboration on oral preparation for literacy. In B. Schieffelin (Ed.), *Acquisition of literacy: Ethnographic perspectives.* Norwood, NJ: Ablex.

Miner, B. (1997). Embracing Ebonics and teaching Standard English: An interview with Oakland teacher Carrie Secret. *Rethinking Schools, 12*(1). Retrieved January 3, 2004, from http://www.rethinkingschools.org/archive/12_01/ebsecret.shtml.

Nelson-Barber, S. (1982). Phonologic variations of Pima English. In R. St. Clair & W. Leap, (Eds.), *Language renewal among American Indian tribes: Issues, problems and prospects.* Rosslyn, VA: National Clearinghouse for Bilingual Education.

Oakland Unified School District. (1996, December 18). *Standard English proficiency program.* Oakland, CA: Author.

Sims, R. (1982). Dialect and reading: Toward redefining the issues. In J. Langer & M.T. Smith-Burke (Eds.), *Reader meets author/Bridging the gap* (pp. 222–236). Newark, DE: International Reading Association.

## LITERATURE CITED

Clifton, L. (1973). *All us come cross the water.* New York: Holt, Rinehart, & Winston.

Edler, T. (1981). *Santa's Cajun Christmas adventure.* Baton Rouge, LA: Little Cajun Books.

Green, P. (aided by A. Abbott). (1959). *I am Eskimo—Aknik my name.* Juneau, AL: Alaska-Northwest.

Jacobs, H., & Rice, J. (1983). *Once upon a Bayou.* New Orleans, LA: Phideaux.

Yukon-Koyukuk School District, AL. (1979–). Alaska Biographical Series. North Vancouver, BC, Canada: Hancock House.

CHAPTER 14

# Building Blocks
# for Literacy Development:
# Oral Language

*Kelli Harris-Wright*

One day after reviewing our school district's assessment data in the areas of reading and English, my supervisor asked a question that was supposed to be a rhetorical one. The question was, "Why can't our kids read?" Although I knew the question was rhetorical, I replied, "They need language to be good readers." My statement created a context for dialogue and discussion between my supervisor and me that would probably benefit other educators, teachers, and parents who are really serious about helping kids learn to read.

All educators believe that learning to read is probably the single, most important skill that students should acquire. All other skills and learning that are required for success in school, employment, and daily living depend on the ability to read. Contemporary views of literacy development include the ability to understand and exchange meaning by listening, speaking, writing, reading, and using viewing skills (Greer, 2002). What are the foundational skills, concepts, and abilities that lead to early success in learning literacy? What kinds of behaviors should parents, caregivers, teachers, and principals be modeling, teaching, and monitoring from birth to age 4 or 5? How do first-language learning experiences and sociocultural factors influence literacy development in the preschool years? Educators, caregivers, and parents should know and have the answers to these and other questions to facilitate the development of oral language skills that are necessary prerequisites for early success in learning to read.

## Acquiring Language

The ability to learn to read and read well begins with the sense of hearing (Cutting & Pisoni, 1978). From birth, the infant has an uninterrupted period of listening to sounds in the environment from nature, people, the household, and all contacts within his or her trajectory. All other senses in the infant are working actively to make sense of the world. The meanings in facial features and gestures from those who interact with the infant are being archived into visual memory by the baby for later retrieval and reference. The infant begins to associate meaning with the mood, tone, and emotional states of people when they communicate with one another and with the infant. The baby learns to associate meaning with intonation patterns used in speech, tone of voice, rate of speech, and words that others use when they communicate. Through human interaction and socialization, babies, toddlers, and preschoolers learn the communication rituals and routines of the various environments to which they are exposed (Chomsky, 1965). During this interaction, it is imperative that all who come in contact with young children actively produce words, phrases, and meaningful sentences to describe actions and interactions, so that children can learn to associate words with the objects, actions, gestures, and intonations being used (Muma, 1978). Language is learned and the mental lexicon or vocabulary develops through this interaction.

During this interaction, a child's early success in being able to hear and use school-like language depends on exposure to hearing and seeing language produced and used in school-like ways (Wyatt, 2001). The distinction between hearing and using language only for social purposes versus hearing and using language in school-like ways is one of the major reasons why some African American children often have difficulty learning to read for school purposes. Sbarra and Pianta (2001) analyzed primarily Caucasian teachers' ratings of 181 African American and 359 Caucasian children within the first two years of public school in the southern United States. The ratings depicted behavior and social skills and competence-related skills. The teachers' ratings suggested that, over time, African American children did not demonstrate more problem behaviors or difficulty in maintaining peer and social skills. However, the ratings strongly indicated that African American children were failing to make gains necessary for success in school-related learning.

Understanding the importance of language skills to the development of literacy, I made it a priority to provide many languages experiences for my daughter when she was an infant and toddler. While driving in my car with my infant daughter, I would often get strange looks from people. Because she was not in sight of other drivers but was in my hearing and viewing range, people would look at me at traffic lights or at the gas pump because I always appeared to be talking to myself. It probably did look strange to others, but I was sure enough about the value of spoken language that I kept talking to my daughter even though others might have thought that I was off! My talk sounded something like this,

Mommy's gonna get you out of the car and put you in the grocery cart 'cause we're going into the store to get some food. Here we go up...over into the basket. Oops!! Sorry, I just knocked off your hood. Lemme put it back on.

The use of language in this social way was just that literal, and I repeated it over and over again with her. When I read stories to my daughter, I was conscious about using all beginning, middle, and ending sounds of the words in the stories. This allowed her to hear the language—of reading aloud based on what the tone of the story required—and that the language of reading a story could sound different from casual conversation. Do we tell mothers as they leave the hospital to talk with their babies in this way? Do pediatricians give such literal advice? Do daycare providers talk like this when they are feeding and diapering and interacting with babies? Have we told fathers to talk to their babies in this way?

# Defining Language

So, what is language? It is thought and cognition, and it also can be thought of as a system of symbols. Spoken or written words act as symbols that allow us to refer to something, someone, some place, or some event, whether it is directly present or not. Language allows people to refer to ideas and thoughts in the past, present, or future. Definitions of language further describe that it develops within historical, political, social, and cultural contexts; that it is rule governed; and that it has a minimum of five components (Catts & Kamhi, 1999): (1) phonological, (2) morphological, (3) semantic, (4) syntactical, and (5) pragmatic.

The *phonological* component refers to the system of sounds and features (phonetics) that make up a particular language, how the sounds can be used in different word positions, and how the sounds can be sequenced and combined into words. The *morphological* component refers to how meaning can be made and changed in small units, as in the addition of prefixes or suffixes. An example of morphological influence can be illustrated with the verb *walk*. The meaning of the word can change with the addition of *ed* at the end to create *walked*. In the English language, this morphological change transforms meaning to signal a reader or listener that the action happened in the past. Other languages show this past-tense relationship in different ways, but a morphological system is still in place even when the language is different.

The *semantic* component includes word meanings, combinations of words to create meaning, word associations, and the influence of context on meaning. The *syntactical* component refers to the rules for combining words to form phrases, sentences, and larger units of connected speech or writing. For example, it is typical in English to say or read the sentence "She wore a red dress." In Spanish, however, the words of the same sentence appear in the following order: "She wore a dress red." This example demonstrates how the rules of syntax function for two different languages.

The *pragmatic* component pertains to the rules for using language in various settings and social contexts based on the speaker-listener or writer-reader relationship. It includes, but is not limited to, the rules for beginning and ending a conversation, entering a conversation when someone else is talking, greetings, requesting information, degrees of familiarity, giving an account, telling a story, nonverbal skills, tone of voice, and asking questions. Pragmatic rules of language, like all language rules, must be learned through experience and interaction. Pragmatic rules are highly influenced by sociocultural, educational, and experiential factors.

The ability to acquire the five components or systems of language is innate and universal in all human beings unless an infant has a significant pathology. Even in the presence of pathologies, most infants and children can still acquire some language skills (Kamhi & Catts, 1989). Oral language in infants begins at birth when the baby begins to make eye contact with the speaker (understanding), coos with vowel sounds such as *a-a-a* and *o-o-o*, and produces differentiated cries, such as for hunger or pain (expression). (See chapter Appendix A for ages and stages of language and speech development in general American English. These stages are critical for success in speech, language, and literacy development for all children who are learning language.)

# African American English

Children will acquire the five components of language, but how they acquire them depends on how language is used at home with family members, friends, and sociocultural and socioeconomic contexts (Wyatt, 2001). Sociocultural and speech-language community information becomes critical when we consider our responsibilities as educators in facilitating literacy acquisition with African American children who may learn to hear and speak language with some of the rule-governed features of African American English (AAE) or dialect (Wyatt, 2001; Williams & Wolfram, 1977). Research has shown that until about the age of 3, there appear to be few differences between the language development of African American children from AAE speaking backgrounds compared to that of children from backgrounds where general American English is heard and spoken (Cole, 1980; Stockman, 1986). (It is beyond the scope of this chapter to present an exhaustive description of the historical, political, economic, and sociocultural origins of AAE or any other nonstandard dialect, but further information can be found in *The Bantu-Speaking Heritage of the United States* [Vass, 1979] and *The Education of Blacks in the South, 1860–1935* [Anderson, 1988]. Chapter Appendix B presents features of AAE and U.S. Southern White Nonstandard English [SWNE] as described previously by Williams and Wolfram [1977]. These descriptions are still considered comprehensive to date and have been further expanded by Thompson et al. [2004] and Wyatt [1995]. Educators who teach African American students who use patterns of AAE primarily for academic purposes should devote some time to explore how AAE and Standard American English [SAE] are more alike than different in terms of grammatical and phonological characteristics [see Wyatt, 1995].)

More recent data has shown that if an African American child speaks with any of the feature patterns associated with AAE, such use is likely to be habitual by age 4 (Craig & Washington, 1998). Craig and Washington compared the dialect patterns and frequency of use among 66 African American children who were 5 and 6 years old in kindergarten in the public schools of Detroit, Michigan. None of the children was in special education, and half qualified for free or reduced lunch based on annual family income. There were 30 girls and 36 boys, and teacher and parent reports indicated that all were developing normally. The examiner communicated conversationally with children in free-play situations of 15 to 20 minutes. Children chose from sets of toys to play with that included (1) Barbie and Ken with a Burger King, (2) action figures with props, and (3) the Fisher-Price schoolhouse. The researchers found that all 66 children exhibited some use of AAE. However, the two important influences on AAE features and the frequency with which it was used were socioeconomic status and gender. African American children from low socioeconomic households used more AAE features than African American children from middle income households. This finding has been corroborated in a previous study (see Wyatt, 2001). Craig and Washington also found that boys used more features of AAE than girls, and that boys used these features more frequently than girls. Although the sample size in this study was small, it is still important to consider because it substantiated what most of us knew as educators but had not read in research or did not feel comfortable saying. Instructional implications from the Craig and Washington study augment the urgency with which teachers must learn how to help African American preschoolers and older students become *bidialectal* concurrently as they develop literacy skills for school purposes.

In models and varieties of language, the term *dialect* can be used to refer to any variation of the standard form of a language. This means that all languages have dialects that have evolved over time and through interactions among many different people who have come together for various reasons: political, historical, economic, educational, and social.

*Bidialectal* language use means that a person has metalinguistic awareness, or a conscious command and control over use of both the dialectal form and the standard language form. Metalinguistic awareness includes the ability to use existing language skills for thought and the acquisition of additional language skills.

For African American students who speak AAE and are in school, this means that they must learn to know when to apply the rules of use for standard English and when to use AAE. That is, they must learn to use standard English based on the context for listening, speaking, reading, and writing. This ability to move between both forms is called *code-switching*, *dialect shifting*, or *bidialectalism*. The context for communication and language use includes the nature of the relationship between the speaker and listener or reader and writer, the setting, the purpose, and the tone or mood (Harris-Wright, 1987, 1999a). Bidialectal skills also mean that learning the standard features of a language does not come at the eradication of the dialectal form (Harris-Wright, 1987). The dialectal form must be maintained because it serves an important social-solidarity function among highly familiar people, such as family and friends. The dialectal form is often a literary element that can be studied and discussed as authors intended the writing to be, and excellent examples can be found in the work of Patricia McKissack. Bidialectal skills can be taught directly to students who need them for literacy development and academic purposes (Thompson et al., 2004). The rationale for teaching bidialectal skills must be communicated to parents. Bidialectal skills are often needed for employment reasons.

## Direct Teaching

In most preschool environments, it is typical for the teacher to establish classroom rules and expectations that students have to learn to live by during school. Preschool is also a good time to develop rules that tell children which literacy skills will be learned and why they must learn them. Because the addition of SAE is often not an option in preschool classrooms where children use AAE, teachers must learn to listen carefully to the oral communication patterns that children use. Teachers must be able to respond to children's use of AAE with SAE by speaking, writing, or reading within the context of learning that is going on in the classroom at any moment. Teachers can model, demonstrate, discuss, and compare and contrast in oral form the differences between the SAE variety and the AAE variety at the phonological, morphological, syntactical, grammatical, and pragmatic levels. The teacher's response must be shared with children in a tone of voice that is pleasing, encouraging, accepting, and void of punitive or negative undertones or facial expressions.

A wonderful piece of literature for introducing the concept of respect and appreciation of differences to young children and the need for rules can be found in the book *The Land of Many Colors*, written by a class of preschoolers at the Klamath County YMCA Family Preschool (1993) in Klamath Falls, Oregon. Teachers can use this book to introduce the reasons for rules and how they benefit everyone when everyone contributes to the development of the rules. The inherent lesson is the importance of positive interdependence. Gunning (1988) offers other excellent resources for beginning readers. Teachers should ask children to describe and share some rules that they live by in their homes. Teachers should write the rules as they are described and tell children that every spoken word can be written with letters from the alphabet. Inherent in the teachers' talking and writing are the development of important emergent literacy skills for students: (1) the ability to understand text-to-self, text-to-world, and text-to-text meaning; (2) awareness of word boundaries, letters, spellings, and phonics; and (3) general print awareness. Teachers should maintain paper, dry-erase boards, magnetic boards, and writing utensils in all areas of the room, but especially at large-group time to encourage preschoolers to write their own rules so they can talk about them with the group.

When it is time for the teacher to present the rule for how students will talk and share during impressionability time—when listeners, who may not know the speaker personally or know much about the topic, learn how much the speaker knows—the teacher models orally an example of SAE that will be contrasted with its AAE correlate. For example, the teacher might say,

> When it is time for me to show someone how much I know at school or on my job, this is impressionability time. I talk, walk, and use my voice and face in a way that shows how much I know. Listen and look at me now: "I know that I can write the rules that our class made." Did you hear how clear and crisp my words sounded? I said all of my beginning, middle, and ending sounds in the words that I used. Listen again [repeat]. Now listen to me when I use the same words differently. The teacher can repeat the sentence again and substitute the initial consonant /d/ for the /th/ in the word *that* to use an AAE feature in comparison to the SAE phonological feature.

The teacher should

- allow the children to comment on how the two sentences sounded;
- write their comments and ask them to think of a sentence that they can try to say in two different ways;
- allow the students to take turns sharing their two sentences; and
- tell them that they sometimes will need to speak during impressionability time, and sometimes they may not have to speak that way if it is not

a time to show someone how much you know or if the listener already knows you well or your topic.

Because use of some AAE features is a part of the first language-learning experiences of many African American children, teachers should refrain from any negative or punitive reference regarding the use of AAE features. Negatives will only deter children's learning and building on the kinds of language skills that they need for success in school. The task is to describe, demonstrate, and compare and contrast different language rules in various contexts, with emphasis on the nature of the speaker–listener or writer–reader relationship.

The teacher should have children identify suitable impressionability times–such as at church or at school, when answering a teacher's question about a story at large-group time–as well as when it is not impressionability time, such as play time and lunch time or informal group work time. Validating and shaping all student responses will build the concept of school speech and home speech. The rationale is that students and teachers talk and communicate at home with family and friends in one way, and at school we talk and communicate in another way or sometimes in both ways, depending upon the context. This is because school is primarily where academic information is learned and students demonstrate how well academic information has been learned. The teacher should define *academic* both verbally and by writing. Students can describe some academic things that are learned at school that may not be learned at home and the converse. Teachers also should develop the expectation among students that each child is an individual and will bring different experiences to school that can be valued and shared by all. Subsequently, each child will talk and communicate differently, which is okay too, but all students will add other ways of talking to their speaking and writing. This concept must be reviewed each day in the context of large- and small-group time and modeled by the teacher.

## Responding to AAE Use in Context

Assume that you are teaching large-group instruction, and ask children to respond to a comprehension question based on a portion of text that has been read. You ask the question, "Where is Trina's hat?" A student answers, "Trina hat is under the bed." What do you say as a follow-up response to this student's answer? As the teacher, you are responsible for providing literacy support in academic-like ways, so you must respond. Assume that the semantic information in the student's response is correct. To facilitate academic language skills at the morphosyntactic level, restate the response with an affirmative and pleasing tone of voice to signal that the content of the response was correct, but as you restate the response, provide the possessive marker so that the child can *hear* the standard-variety rule used in a context that has meaning. When you say the "s" to signal the addition of the SAE possessive marker, you will place more vocal intonation on the "s" so that the child can hear the acoustic signal for this marker. Your speech should sound conversational in nature, not slow, deliberate, or stilted.

Children will learn to add SAE to their communication skills in the same manner that they learned the AAE variety: through conversational speech, social interaction, and engagement in meaningful academic work with people who are speaking, reading, and writing with SAE in appropriate contexts. Every time a teacher hears or sees that a child needs an SAE rule, a pragmatic rule, or a nonverbal rule, it should be taught in the context in which it is needed through modeling and demonstration. All rules should be spoken and written as much as possible so that children can continually see the connection between spoken and written language. New rules for language use are not acquired as readily by children through worksheets, dittos, and other passive forms of learning (Cohen, 1995). Many students who speak and use AAE already have experienced numerous paper-driven learning experiences with little or no addition of academic-like patterns of language for speaking, writing, or reading. Teachers need to become more cognizant of the need to develop language skills in children in more diverse ways beyond paper-driven experiences. Excellent descriptions of how to do this are available (see Tate, 2003). Research supports successful curriculum design and implementation for teaching and responding to students in the aforementioned manner (Adler, 1993; Harris-Wright, 1987, 1993, 1999a, 1999b).

Patty, Maschoff, and Ransom (1996) have indicated that the first stage of emergent literacy is oral language. In this stage it is imperative to build foundations for further literacy development by expanding children's knowledge of words and word relationships; teaching about language and how print is talk written down; introducing sound-discrimination activities, such as rhymes; teaching sound–symbol correspondence; reading picture, pattern, and predictable books; and by writing. In facilitating the foundation for success in learning to read, teachers of African American children must ensure that they have the oral language competence to model language so children can add the standard forms that they need.

## REFERENCES

Adler, S. (1993). *Multicultural communication skills in the classroom.* Boston: Allyn & Bacon.

Anderson, J.D. (1988). *The education of blacks in the south, 1860–1935.* Chapel Hill: University of North Carolina Press.

Catts, H.W., & Kamhi, A.G. (Eds.). (1999). *Language and reading disabilities.* Boston: Allyn & Bacon.

Chomsky, N. (1965). *Aspects of the theory of syntax.* Cambridge, MA: MIT Press.

Cohen, P. (1995). Understanding the brain: Educators seek to apply brain research. *Education Update, 37*(7).

Cole, L.T. (1980). A developmental analysis of social dialect features in the spontaneous language of preschool children. Doctoral dissertation, Northwestern University. *Dissertation Abstracts International, 41*(06), 2132B.

Cutting, J., & Pisoni, D. (1978). An information-processing approach to speech perception. In J. Kavanagh & W. Strange (Eds.), *Speech and language in the laboratory, school and clinic* (pp. 38–71). Cambridge, MA: MIT Press.

Greer, E. (2002, February 6). Implications for scientific based evidence approach in reading. [Transcript]. Washington, DC: U.S. Department of Education. Retrieved October 7, 2004, from http://www.ed.gov/nclb/methods/whatworks/research/page_pg7.html

Gunning, T.G. (1988). *Best books for beginning readers.* Boston: Allyn & Bacon.

Harris-Wright, K. (1987). The challenge of educational coalescence: Teaching nonmainstream English-speaking students. *Journal of Childhood Communication Disorders, 11*(1), 209–215.

Harris-Wright, K. (1993). Appendix I: DeKalb Bidialectal Communication Program. In S. Adler (Ed.), *Multicultural communication skills in the classroom* (pp. 173–176). Boston: Allyn & Bacon.

Harris-Wright, K. (1999a, September). *Program for bidialectal development in a USA school district.* Paper presented to the Annual Conference of the Australian Linguistic Society. Perth, WA: University of Western Australia.

Harris-Wright, K. (1999b). Enhancing bidialectalism in urban African American students. In C. Adger & O. Taylor (Eds.), *Making the connection: Language and academic achievement among African American students* (pp. 53–60). Washington, DC: Center for Applied Linguistics; McHenry, IL: Delta Systems.

Kamhi, A., & Catts, H. (1989). *Reading disabilities: A developmental perspective.* Boston: Little, Brown.

Klamath County YMCA Family Preschool. (1993). *The land of many colors.* (R. Pocock, Illus.) New York: Scholastic.

Muma, J. (1978). *Language handbook: Concepts, assessment and intervention.* Englewood Cliffs, NJ: Prentice Hall.

Patty, D., Maschoff, J.D., & Ransom, P.E. (1996). *Reading resource handbook for school leaders.* Norwood, MA: Christopher-Gordon.

Sbarra, D.A., & Pianta, R.G. (2001). Teacher ratings of behavior among African American and Caucasian children during the first two years of school. *Psychology in the Schools, 38*(3), 229–238.

Stockman, I.J. (1986). Language acquisition in culturally diverse populations: The Black child as a case study. In O. Taylor (Ed.), *Nature of communication disorders in culturally and linguistically diverse populations* (pp. 117–155). San Diego, CA: College-Hill Press.

Tate, M. (2003). *Worksheets don't grow dendrites: 20 instructional strategies that engage that brain.* Thousand Oaks, CA: Corwin Press.

Thompson, C.A., Craig, H.K., & Washington, J.A. (2004). Variable production of African-American English across oracy and literacy contexts. *Language, Speech and Hearing Services in Schools, 35*(3), 269–282.

Vass, W.K. (1979). *The Bantu-speaking heritage of the United States.* Los Angeles: Center for Afro-American Studies, University of California.

Washington, J.A., & Craig, H. (1998). Socioeconomic status and gender influences on children's dialectal variations. *Journal of Speech, Language, and Hearing Research, 41*(3), 618–626.

Williams, R., & Wolfram, W. (1977). *A linguistic description of social dialects.* Bethesda, MD: American Speech-Language-Hearing Association.

Wyatt, T.A. (1995). Language development in African American English child speech. *Linguistics and Education, 7,* 7–22.

Wyatt, T.A. (2001). The role of family, community, and school in children's acquisition and maintenance of AAE. In S.L. Lanehart (Ed.), *Sociocultural and historical contexts of African American English.* Philadelphia: John Benjamins.

# APPENDIX A
## Approximate Ages and Stages of Speech
### and Language Development Birth to Age 4 (American English)

| Age | Understanding | Expression | Speech |
|---|---|---|---|
| 0–3 months | Makes eye contact with speaker. | Coos with vowel sounds (aaa, ooo); different cries for pain and hunger. | |
| 6 months | Localizes source of sound and responds to name. | Repeats syllables (mamama, bye bye bye). | |
| 9 months | Follows simple commands, gestures (give me the toy, put that down).<br><br>Understands names of simple objects.<br><br>Understands "no." | Vocalizes in strings of different syllables (babamama).<br><br>Shakes head "no."<br>Begins to imitate sounds and syllables. | |
| 12 months | Follows one-part instruction (put block in cup). | First true word emerges. | Begins producing environmental sounds (car engine, dog barking). |
| 18 months | Understands 250 words.<br><br>Follows 2-part directions.<br><br>Identifies 1–4 body parts.<br><br>Recognizes names of many objects. | Vocabulary varies between 15–50 words.<br><br>Some two-word phrases such as "want juice," "all gone." | Inconsistently uses consonants such as /p/, /b/, /m/, /w/, /h/, especially at beginning of words. |
| 2 years | Identifies simple picture of objects.<br><br>Identifies 5–6 body parts.<br><br>Follows a variety of two-part directions.<br><br>Recognizes the names of most common pictures and objects. | Vocabulary of 150–250 words and 2- and 3-word phrases. | Speech is about 50% understandable.<br><br>No longer omits consonant sounds at the end of words.<br><br>Uses consonant sounds like /p/, /b/, /m/, /n/, /w/, /h/. |

*(continued)*

| Age | Understanding | Expression | Speech |
|---|---|---|---|
| 2 ¹/₂ years | Identifies pictures of actions.<br><br>Recognizes 3 colors.<br><br>Identifies objects by function (What do we use to comb our hair?").<br><br>Understands 400 words. | Vocabulary about 500 words with 3-word phrases.<br><br>Produces some grammatical or morphological endings (plural –s, ing); "is," "the," "a."<br><br>Normal stuttering is common. | Uses consonants like /t/, /d/, /ng/, /f/, /y/. |
| 3 years | Completes 3-part directions.<br><br>Understands "who?", "where?"<br><br>Understands some adjectives (big/little, hot/cold).<br><br>Understands 800 words.<br><br>Understands complicated sentences. | | Has vocabulary of 800–1,000 words and 3- to 4-word sentences.<br><br>More elaborate grammar (pronouns, past tense verbs, negation, wh-question).<br><br>Speech should be 80% understandable.<br><br>Should produce sounds like /k/, /g/, /sh/. |
| 4 years | Follows 4-part directions.<br><br>Knows adjectives of size and color.<br><br>Comprehends physical needs (what do you do when you're hungry?).<br><br>Understands 1,800–2,000 words. | Has vocabulary of 1,200–1,500 words and uses 4- to 5-word sentences minimally.<br><br>Uses complex sentence structures.<br><br>Normal stuttering is no longer common.<br><br>Can express feelings.<br><br>Answers many types of questions. | Speech about 90% understandable.<br><br>Uses consonants like /j/, /ch/, /s/, /z/, /l/, /v/. |

Adapted from *How does your child hear and talk?* [Brochure]. Rockville, MD: American Speech-Language-Hearing Association.

## Major Phonological and Grammatical Characteristics
## and Similarities of Black English (B) and
## Southern White Non-Standard English (SWNS)

| Features | Descriptions | Examples | B | SWNS |
|---|---|---|---|---|
| Consonant cluster reduction (General) | Deletion of second of two consonants in word final position belonging to same base word. | "tes" (test) | X | X |
| | Addition of past-tense (-ed) morpheme to a base word resulting in a consonant cluster reduction. | "rub"(rubbed) | X | X |
| | Plurals of reduced-consonant clusters assume phonetic shape of words ending in sibilants (s,z,sh,zh) and affricants (ch, j) | "dresses" | X | X |
| The /θ/ phoneme (i.e., the voiceless th sound in words such as "thumb") | / f / for /θ/ between vowels and in word final position | "nofin" (nothing) "Ruf" (Ruth) | X | |
| The /ð/ phoneme (i.e., the voiced th– sound in words such as "the") | / d / for /ð/ in word initial position | "dis" (this) | X | |
| | /v / for /ð/ between vowels and in word final position | "bavin" (bathing) "bave" (bathe) | X | |
| The /r/ and /l/ phonemes | Deletion preceding a consonant | "I be early" (I'll be early) | X | |
| The /b/, /d/, and /g/ phonemes | Devoicing at the end of a syllable, with lengthening of preceding vowel | "buut" (bud) | X | |
| Vowel nasalization (pronunciation of vowels with a nasal quality) | Deletion of final nasal consonant at the end of stressed syllables, with preceding vowel nasalized | "maa" (man) | X | |
| Unstressed initial syllables | Deletion of stressed initial syllables | "member" (remember) | | X |
| The /str/ consonant or /ask/ clusters | /skr/ for /str/ | "skreet" (street) | X | X |

*(continued)*

| Features | Descriptions | Examples | B | SWNS |
|---|---|---|---|---|
| Past tense forms | Past-tense morpheme (-ed) not pronounced because of consonant cluster reduction rule | "finish" (finished) | X | |
| Completive aspect with "done" | "Done" plus a past form denotes an action started and completed in the past | "I done tried" (I have already tried) | X | |
| Remote time construction with "been" | "Been" to denote an action having taken place in the distant past | "I been finished" (I have been finished for a long time.) | X | |
| Third-person singular Present-tense markers | (-s) absent | "He walk" (He walks) | X | |
| | "has" and "does" absent in third person construction | "She always do funny things" (She always does funny things.) | X | |
| | Hypercorrect additions (-s) | "I walks" (I walk) | X | |
| Future tense forms | Use of "gonna" | "She gonna go" (She is going to go.) | X | X |
| | "gonna" reduced to 'mgna, 'mana, 'mon, and 'ma | "I'mgna go" "I'mana go" "I'mon go" "I'ma go" (I am going to go.) | | X |
| Invariant "be" | "Be" to describe a recurring or habitual event or behavior | "I be tired at night" (I am usually tired at night.) | X | |
| A + verb + ing | "a" prefixed to certain verbs with the (-ing) participial form | "He woke up a screamin'." (He woke up screaming.) | | X |
| Absence of forms of the copula (to be) | "is" absent in forms where it can be contracted | "He a man" (He's a man.) | X | |
| | "are" absent where it can be contracted | "You good" (You're good.) | X | |
| Double modals | Co-occurrence of selected modals such as might could, might should, etc. | "I might coulda' done it." (I might have done it) | X | X |

*(continued)*

| Features | Descriptions | Examples | B | SWNS |
|---|---|---|---|---|
| Intensifying adverbs | use of intensifiers, i.e., "right", "plumb" to refer to completeness | "right large" (very large) | X | X |
| Negation | "aint't" for have/has, am/are, didn't | "He aint't go home" (He didn't go home) | X | |
| Multiple negation | placement of a negativized form of verbal auxiliary before the main verb of a phrase having a negative marker | "Couldn't nobody do it" (Nobody could do it) | X | |
| | placement of a negative marker in the noun phrase in a previously negative | "Nobody didn't do it" (Nobody did it) | X | |
| | negative concord across clause boundaries | "There wasn't much I couldn't do" (There wasn't much I could do.) | X | |
| Possessive | absence of final (-s) possessive marker | "The girl hat" (The girl's hat) | X | |
| Plural | absence of suffixes (-s) or (-es) | "She took five book" (She took five books.) | X | |
| | absence of plural suffixes to reference weights and measures | "Two pound" (Two pounds) | | X |
| | regular plurals with irregular nouns | "two foots" (Two feet) | X | X |
| Relative Clauses | deletion of relative pronouns | "That's the dog it me" (That's the dog that bit me.) | X | X |
| Questions | same interrogative form for direct and indirect questions | "I wonder was she walking?" (I wonder if she was walking.) | X | X |
| Existential "it" | "it" for "there" | "It's a store on the corner" (There's a store on the corner.) | X | X |
| | "they" for "There" | "They's money here" (There's money here.) | | X |
| Pronouns | use of objective pronouns as subjects | "Him ain't playing" (He ain't playing.) | X | |

Source: Williams & Wolfram (1977). Reprinted with permission.

# CHAPTER 15

# Acknowledging the Language of African American Students: Instruction That Works

*Sharroky Hollie*

After decades of failing many African American students, particularly in literacy, the American school system is still in search of instructional methods that positively affect the academic achievement of these students. One would think that, after over 30 years of linguistic research on African American students and reading issues (Adger, Christian, & Taylor, 1999), these students would be acknowledged as Standard English learners (SELs) (LeMoine, 1999). SELs are students for whom Standard English is not native and who speak a home language that differs from Standard English in all the dimensions of language. One would really think that after the Oakland, California, Ebonics controversy of 1997 and beyond, the literacy community would be seriously interested in, or at least curious about, the possibility of an alternative to traditional reading/language arts teaching that inherently attempts to eradicate African American Language (AAL). It is estimated that 80% to 98% of African Americans speak AAL (Dillard, 1972; Smitherman, 1986).

African American SELs are not recognized as such by the system, meaning classroom teachers, district administrations, curriculum developers, or policymakers. At the beginning of the 21st century, after nearly 40 years of research on the matter, many African American SELs will walk into classrooms and be discreetly taught in most cases, and explicitly told in others, that the language of their forefathers, their families, and their communities is bad language, street language, the speech of the ignorant and uneducated. They will be "corrected" and told that their "she be" should be "she is" and they will be reminded that two negatives in a sentence equals a positive, even though in their language the use of multiple negatives is allowed. This unfortunate but frequent scenario will occur in too many American classrooms.

Adapted from *English Journal* (2001), *90*(4), 54–59. Copyright © 2001 by the National Council of Teachers of English. Used with permission.

Their negative experience in the American classroom is all too common and cliché. These students are trapped in classrooms where their language is systemically devalued via unresponsive curricula and inadequate instruction. Many teachers continue to hold low expectations and have limited understandings about African American culture and language, not recognizing that these students arrive at school speaking a language that differs from the language of instruction phonologically, morphologically, syntactically, semantically, and pragmatically. In sum, a great number of African American SELs are continuing to underachieve when there are viable instructional alternatives at hand.

# Academic English Mastery Program

Instructional alternatives are being explored with success in classrooms and schools in Los Angeles through the work of the Academic English Mastery Program (AEMP), a comprehensive language awareness program designed to serve the linguistic and cultural needs of African American, Mexican American, Hawaiian American, and Native American students who are not proficient in Standard English. Teachers infuse into the curriculum research-based instructional strategies that facilitate the acquisition of Standard English in its oral and written form without devaluing the home language and culture of these students. The primary goal of the program is for students to master Standard English and, in the process, experience increased enriching literacy opportunities and greater academic achievement. Teachers in approximately 60 schools throughout Los Angeles receive intensive professional development in the philosophy, the pedagogy, and the expert classroom application of five instructional strands, which are discussed in detail later in this chapter:

1. Strategic and purposeful use of culturally relevant literature

2. Systematic and consistent use of contrastive analysis

3. Building on cultural styles and behaviors

4. Increasing academic vocabulary through prior knowledge and schema

5. Creating a conducive learning environments for SELs

Students who have studied in AEMP classrooms have shown successful trends in their writing, based largely on an evaluation by the Los Angeles Unified School District (Maddahian & Sandamela, 2000). In that evaluation, the AEMP students outperformed a control group on the Language Assessment Measure, a test designed specifically for AAL speakers. Both groups participated in pre-

and post-tests, and although both groups made gains between the two tests, there was a significant difference between the experimental and control group on the posttest, with the AEMP students achieving higher scores. In praise of AEMP, Smitherman (1986) says,

> By far the most concentrated and comprehensive classroom practices embracing a philosophy of multilingualism are those in the Academic English Mastery Program. Since 1991, AEMP, designed for grades K–8, has used a historical, linguistic, cultural approach, and a philosophy of additive bilingualism to teacher language and literacy skills to students whose primary language is in the Ebonics family. (p. 12)

Prior to learning about the classroom application of the five instructional strands, teachers need to appreciate and to understand more deeply the linguistic heritage of African American students. The general ignorance and gross misunderstandings about the historical development of the languages of SELs are the source of negative attitudes held by many teachers. Teachers who have limited knowledge of, or who devalue, the language, the culture, and experiences of SELs convey messages that negatively affect classroom performance (LeMoine, 2001). The first step for many teachers is learning about the history, language development, and linguistics. After learning about these topics, many teachers question why they had not received such information in teacher education programs.

## A Linguistic History of AAL: Four Schools of Thought

What teachers learn philosophically is that the debate about the legitimacy of AAL is not germane to classroom instruction at all. Teachers who are linguistically responsive acknowledge first that African American SELs, as well as other SELs, come to school speaking a language or linguistic form that may be dissimilar but is no less valuable than Standard English and Academic English. The teacher's acceptance of this difference is key to powerful teaching and powerful learning in the classroom for SELs. Teachers' beliefs that their African American students' language has a cultural history and a linguistic foundation, what poet Claude McKay called "Spoken Soul," give cause for them to treat their students differently—positively.

The linguistic history of Spoken Soul of African American SELs falls into four broad linguistic schools of thought: (1) the ethnolinguistic theory or afrocologist view, which postulates that language that evolved with the enslaved

Africans is a direct derivation of West African languages; (2) the transformationalist view, which consider what African Americans speak to be a dialect of the English language; (3) the Creolist view, which asserts that Black English is a pidgin language that developed at the beginning of the slave trade (Rickford & Rickford, 2001); and (4) the original view, the deficit perspective, which labels AAL as inferior speech based on cognitive deficiency and articulatory abnormal processes in African Americans.

Looking at the four perspectives on a continuum, the ethnolinguistic view gives AAL the most credence. It credits the West African languages' structure as the basis for its existence, with an English vocabulary overlaying the deep grammatical structure. Robert L. Williams (1972), known as the "Father of Ebonics," defined Ebonics as

> the linguistic and paralinguistic features which on a concentric continuum represent the communicative competence of West African, Caribbean, and United States slave descendants of African origin. Ebonics includes the various idioms, patois, argots, ideolects [sic] and social dialects of these people. (p. 100)

In essence, Ebonics is an umbrella term that refers to the "language family" spoken by the enslaved Africans throughout the African Diaspora, which historically included enslaved Africans in Jamaica (Jamaican Patois), the Caribbean (Caribbean dialects), Brazil (Black Portuguese), Guyana (Dutch Pidgin), and parts of Latin American (Africanized Spanish). Put simply, wherever enslaved Africans were taken throughout the world, a variation of Ebonics exists today. For Africans in America, the Ebonic form is AAL.

Next on the continuum is the Creolists' view. According to this perspective, the linguistic origin of the enslaved Africans resulted from the pidgin trade languages. Many of these languages, such as Haitian Creole French and Jamaican Creole English, are common in the Caribbean islands. Rickford and Rickford (2001) point out that these languages do show African influence, consistent with the previous theory. The difference is the speakers demonstrate simplified existing patterns of African languages. Dillard (1972) says that as early as 1705 enslaved Africans were speaking several varieties of English. He identified three such varieties: (1) West African Pidgin English, (2) Plantation Creole, and (3) Standard English. He contended that the language variety spoken by enslaved Africans was determined by their place of origin and their status and length of stay on the plantation.

The third postulate comes from the transformationalists or dialectologists who see it very differently from the other two perspectives. Whereas the ethnolinguistic and Creolist perspectives give credit to the linguistic origins of West Africa, the dialectologists simply define Black English as a variation of English like any other variation. Rickford and Rickford (2001) write that enslaved Africans learned English from White settlers and that they did so relatively quickly and successfully, retaining little trace of their African linguistic heritage. Therefore, many features of nonstandard English are seen as imports from the dialects spoken by colonial English, Irish, and Scotch-Irish settlers.

The perspective farthest removed from African origin is known as the deficit perspective, which explains Ebonics' existence as a result of cognitive and anatomical deficiencies in the enslaved Africans. In 2005, not much needs to be said about this perspective. Ebonics is seen as a result of cognitive feebleness on the part of Blacks or, worse, insufficient brain mass. According to the view, the type of speech the enslaved Africans spoke was due to their anatomical and physiological deviations. LeMoine (1999) laments this as a racist view that held African tongues were too thick and their lips too full for articulatory proficiency. This deficit perspective differs greatly from all the perspectives and is, in fact, linguistically unsound. In general, continent Africans are multilingual, speak no less than two or three languages, and many of these languages contain very fine, intricate, and complex range of sounds.

The point not to be missed by teachers, especially in literacy education, is that all four theories acknowledge that African American SELs speak in a way that is different from Standard English. Yet, many educators still covertly hold the deficit perspective in attitude and treatment of students. Only linguists, who study language as a science, make the finite language distinctions when it comes to specific terms and their definitions. Educationally, these terms connote that SELs, whether they be African American, Mexican American, Native American, or Hawaiian American, come to school "language different or diverse," not language deficient. The resolution on Ebonics passed by the Linguistic Society of America, a society of scholars engaged in the scientific study of language, emphatically states the point:

> The variety known as "Ebonics, African American Vernacular English" (AAVE), and "Vernacular Black English" and by other names is systematic and rule-governed like all natural speech varieties.... The systematic and expressive nature of the grammar and pronunciation patterns of the African American vernacular has been established by numerous scientific studies over the past 30 years. Characterizations of Ebonics as "slang," "mutant," "lazy," "defective," "ungrammatical," or "broken English" are incorrect and demeaning.... What is important from a linguistic and educational point of view is not whether AAVE is called a "language" or "dialect," but rather that its systematicity be recognized. (Perry & Delpit, 1997)

# AAL Acknowledgment
# and Classroom Application

Rickford (1999) cites ample support that language-awareness teaching can positively affect students' language and literacy learning. He says, "There is experimental evidence both from the United States and Europe that mastering the standard language might be easier if the differences in the student vernacular and Standard English were made explicit rather than entirely ignored" (p. 87). Taylor (1989) compared two groups of students, one being taught traditionally and the other using the language awareness approach, and found that the latter group of students showed a 59% reduction in their use of AAL in writing. The students in the traditional classroom actually increased their use of AAL by 8.5%. Simpkins, Holt, and Simpkins (1977) reported that students who used Bridge readers, transitional readers, and Standard English readers gained 6.2 months on the Iowa Test of Basic Skills. In addition to the experimental research cited by Rickford and others, there is classroom anecdotal evidence that supports this alternative to traditional literacy instruction.

In *Tapping the Potential: English and Language Arts of Black Learners* (Brooks, 1985), published by the National Council of Teachers of English (NCTE), a variety of instructional methodologies and activities directly address the specific use of AAL within Standard English learning: "Properly taught by persons understanding their strengths, varying backgrounds, potential for learning, and who take into account historical, socioeconomic, psychological, and linguistic barriers, Blacks not only can but do learn like any other group" (p. 2). Brooks also points out that Carter G. Woodson, in his apocalyptic *Mis-education of the American Negro*, first published in 1933, writes that teachers were trained "to scoff at the Negro dialect as some peculiar possession of the Negro which they should despise" (p. 8). These teachers were not directed to study the background of the language and its linguistic history. The approach of practicing language awareness teaching has been successfully practiced in Georgia, Illinois, North Carolina, and Tennessee (Rickford & Rickford, 2001).

# Powerful Teaching
# and Powerful Learning in Los Angeles

Based on the results from the 2004 California Standards Test, the achievement gap persists despite catchy phrases, multiple conferences with redundant themes, and a federal mandate, No Child Left Behind, to close the gap. In grade 4 in reading and language arts, the number of White and Asians students who are scoring at the proficient and above levels nearly doubles the number of African American students. In secondary schools in reading and language arts, only 20% of the African American students read at a proficient or advance level, versus 50% at the proficient or advance level with White and Asian students. In comparison, results from classrooms that follow a culturally and linguistic responsive approach as outlaid by the Academic English Mastery Program show a different trend. The most impressive results come from the Culture and Language Academy of Success Elementary School (CLAS), whose scores compared almost evenly with White and Asian populations. Over 50% of the students at CLAS are reading at or above the proficient level. CLAS is located in a working class neighborhood of Los Angeles. Its student population is 100% African American. CLAS is an exemplary schoolwide model of teachers subscribing deeply to the philosophy and pedagogy of AEMP and utilizing the five aforementioned instructional strands. It is believed that these are the ingredients of success for the students at CLAS and in AEMP in general when implemented highly (Hollie, 2001).

1. *Strategic and Purposeful Use of Culturally Relevant Literature.* It is old news that use of authentic literature in the classroom, providing time for reading, and providing for opportunities to be read to benefit students linguistically and culturally (LeMoine, 2001). For SELs, access to culturally relevant literature, books that reflect their cultural and familial experiences are important. Use of such texts provides a mirror and a window for these students. They can see themselves reflected in the pages authentically through fictionalized accounts or in real-life situations. They can identify with characters that look like them, do activities they do, eat the foods they eat, play games they play, celebrate the same holidays they celebrate, and talk like they talk. But they can also see outside of themselves as well. These cultural situations become bridges for creating new knowledge and understandings about other places, other cultures, and other situations. Use of culturally relevant literature serves as a point of reference for SELs.

However, unsophisticated or inconsistent use of culturally relevant literature can be just as dangerous as no use at all. Successful teachers are strategic and purposeful in their daily use of this literature. They incorporate strategies that allow students to read aloud in a variety of ways and provide them opportunities for choice reading. They read aloud to students on a daily basis. Students are given ample opportunities to discuss what they have read and to critically examine the literature, sometimes in comparison to mainstream titles. Specific titles are chosen for their use of the language in particular so students can do linguistic analyses that validate and affirm home language. Popular African

American literature that uses AAL accurately includes works by Virginia Hamilton, Langston Hughes, Julius Lester, Camille Yarborough, and others. These texts provide comparisons and contrasts with the language they read and the language they speak, as well as Standard English.

*2. Systematic and Consistent Use of Contrastive Analysis.* Metalinguistic awareness, thinking about one's language use and how language works, is a necessary skill in language and literacy development for all students (Levine, 2002). Linguistically responsive teachers provide opportunities for SELs to engage in metalinguistic analyses of their own language, so students will understand how their language differs from Standard English in phonology, morphology, syntax, and vocabulary. Contrastive analysis, comparing and contrasting the linguistic structure of two languages, is an effective strategy for these types of analyses. Contrastive analysis increases the ability of students to recognize the differences between standard English and other language structures, leads to more proficient editing and revision during the writing process, increases proficiency in the target language, and, most importantly, validates and affirms home language in the context of learning different language structures such as the language of school. Teachers, who implement contrastive analysis systematically and consistently, must have a deep knowledge in AAL and its system of rules, sounds, and meanings.

*3. Building on Cultural Styles and Behaviors.* Cultural styles are an undeniable dynamic in any classroom. How teachers view these cultural styles affects instruction. Many times the cultural styles of African American students are seen as deviant, which is a factor in the well-documented statistics of disproportionate suspensions and expulsions with African American and Latino students. Hilliard (this volume) and others have demonstrated that these behaviors are not deviant but different, particularly in the context of the culture of school. Hilliard says that experimental evidence proves that SELs have distinct ways of processing information, interacting, communicating, and learning. These ways typically do not match the behavior that is expected in school, leading to teachers' deficit thinking and lowered expectations (LeMoine, 1999).

Teachers who build on the cultural styles of African students recognize their expressive and sociocentric nature as a positive in the classroom. These teachers facilitate learning situations that validate such styles but also lead students towards the expected behavior of school. The goal is for students to have an appreciation and acceptance of both situations and then learn situational appropriateness. Strategies that incorporate high-movement content materials and high movement contexts play a large role in instruction in these classrooms.

This includes using literature with plots and with characters involved in physical movement such as performing arts. Use of common strategies with African American SELs, like role-playing, reader's theater, and performance-related activities, can have uncommon results: positive.

4. *Increasing Academic Vocabulary Through Prior Knowledge and Schema.* SELs arrive at school with vocabularies that are rich culturally and linguistically. Where they are usually limited is in their use of academic vocabulary. One of the best ways to build academic vocabulary—a gatekeeper to success in school—is to build on the conceptual knowledge and vocabulary that SELs bring from the cultural-linguistic context of their home and community environments (LeMoine, 1999). In doing so, teachers activate prior knowledge and rely on schema theory. The theoretical underpinning of both of these constructs is that new learning effectively takes place when connections are made to what the learner already knows. Vocabulary instruction in classrooms of SELs is comprised of a variety of strategies that are based in building on the culturally rich vocabulary and using it as bridge to acquiring academic vocabulary. For teachers in the Academic English Mastery Program and the Culture and Language of Success, this means having the students create personal thesauruses and personal dictionaries. These tools assist students in making explicit connections between their personal vocabularies and the academic vocabularies they are acquiring.

5. *Creating Conducive Learning Environments for SELs.* Learning environments that are conducive to SELs have classroom libraries that include culturally conscious literature, magazines, and newspapers. Many of the classrooms in the Los Angeles program have print-rich environments. The use of listening centers with culture folklore, storytelling, and books on tape provide the models for the language of school and the use of cultural centers that featured African and African American cultural artifacts and games. In addition, obviously, cultural images of heroes, iconic figures, and famous people should be a part of the learning environment. Less obvious though is the use of images that represent youth culture, which might include presenting community members as heroes, focusing on hip-hop culture in particular, and showcasing personalities who are more generationally connected to the students.

The combined use of the five instructional strands in the classroom creates an overall situation in the classroom and schools that affects achievement, as evidenced by AEMP and CLAS in Los Angeles. Use of one or two strands in isolation or practiced infrequently will not make the difference for these students. Teachers who demonstrate consistent, quality use of all strands and the strategies therein offer increased proficiency in Standard English reading and writing for African American SELs.

# Concluding Thoughts

How does the teaching that occurs in the Academic English Mastery Program become systematic? In the classroom, this generally means that the teacher views the language of African American SELs as rule-governed and the acquisition of language as natural, complex, and meaningful. According to Brooks (1985), this specifically means that teachers structure instructional, meaningful conversations for students; respond with modeled language and learn to have conversation (talking with, not to, children). It means an increased understanding of language and how it develops and changes, establishing a respect for AAL as a linguistic system that reflects a culture, and demonstrating to students the belief that they are capable of handling two or more linguistic entities.

Professional development has to be centered on the five instructional strands, especially in the areas of linguistics and language development. The content needs to focus on increasing teacher's knowledge and awareness about linguistic variety and the characteristic linguistic features or rules of African American language. Administrators are encouraged to support teachers in ways that allow them to have confidence about using the language awareness approach. Last, policymakers and the public have to give programs like AEMP an opportunity to work within classrooms and schools. There has to be a collective admission that the system is not working for these students and, more crucially, demonstrate a willingness to do what is responsive to the needs of SELs.

## REFERENCES

Adger, C.T., Christian, D., & Taylor, O.L. (Eds.). (1999). *Making the connection: Language and academic achievement among African American students* [Proceedings of a conference of the Coalition on Language Diversity in Education]. Washington, DC: Center for Applied Linguistics.

Brooks, C. (Ed.). (1985). *Tapping potential: English and language arts for the black learner.* Urbana, IL: Black Caucus, National Council of Teachers of English.

Dillard, J.L. (1972). *Black English: Its history and usage in the United States.* New York: Random House.

Hollie, S. (2001). *African American students as standard English language learners: An alternative approach.* Unpublished doctoral dissertation, University of Southern California.

LeMoine, N. (1999). *English for your success: A language development program for African American children.* Saddle Brook, NJ: Peoples Publishing Group.

LeMoine, N. (2001). *Language variation and literacy in African American students*. In J.L. Harris, A.G. Kamhi, & K.E. Pollock (Eds.), *Literacy in African American communities* (pp. 176–187). Mahwah, NJ: Erlbaum.

Levine, M. (2002). *A mind at a time*. New York: Simon & Schuster.

Maddahian, E., & Sandamela, A. (2000). *Linguistic Affirmation Program 1998–1999: Evaluation report* (Publication No. 781). Los Angeles: Los Angeles Unified School District, Program Evaluation and Research Branch.

Perry, T., & Delpit, L. (Eds.). (1997, Fall). The real Ebonics debate: Power, language and the education of African American children. [Themed Issue]. *Rethinking Schools, 12*(1). Retrieved October 8, 2004, from http://www.rethinkingschools.org/archive/12_01/12_01.shtml

Rickford, J.R. (1999). *Language diversity and academic achievement in the education of African American students: An overview of the issues*. In C.T. Adger, D. Christian, & O. Taylor (Eds.), *Making the connection: Language and academic achievement among African American students* (pp. 1–29). Washington, DC: Center for Applied Linguistics.

Rickford, J.R., & Rickford, R.J. (2001). *Spoken soul: The story of Black English*. New York: John Wiley & Sons.

Simpkins, G.A., Holt, G., & Simpkins, C. (1977). *Bridge: A cross-cultural reading program*. Boston: Houghton Mifflin.

Smitherman, G. (1986). *Talkin and testifyin: The language of black America*. Detroit: Wayne State University Press.

Taylor, H. (1989). *Standard English, Black English, and bidialectalism: A controversy*. New York: Peter Lang.

Williams, R.L. (1972). *Ebonics: The true language of Black folks*. St. Louis, MO: Institute of Black Studies.

Woodson, C.G. (1990). *The mis-education of the Negro*. Trenton, NJ: African World Press. (Original work published 1933)

# CHAPTER 16

# Afro-American Cognitive Style: A Variable in School Success?

*Barbara J. Shade*

The most important issue facing Afro-Americans today is the task of promoting the educational success of Afro-American youth. At first glance, this statement seems a gross exaggeration. After all, today more Afro-Americans than ever before are attending and completing high school. More members of the group are enrolled in colleges, universities, and professional schools, and, subsequently, more Afro-Americans are securing jobs throughout the occupational structure. However, if one examines the statistics and situation closely, one notes these increases have not been of sufficient magnitude to reduce the unequal proportions of Afro-Americans found in the lower end of the social competence continuum.

Among the reasons promoted for this state of affairs is the concept that, as a group, Afro-Americans lack the ability to acquire the skills and knowledge necessary to perform the required societal tasks. Evidence for this point of view is cited from studies in the educational arena that compare scores of ethnic groups on intelligence and achievement tests or teacher evaluations via grades. Unfortunately, although there is a preponderance of evidence that many Afro-American youth are capable of performing on these measures of educational achievement (reviewed by Shade, 1978), there is also a consistent pattern of lower performance on these success indicators by Afro-Americans as a group (Ogbu, 1978; Wright, 1970).

When skin color is not a consideration, social scientists are apparently prepared to concede that individuals or groups who are dissimilar in age, social class, environment, sex, or other factors can legitimately differ in grades, scores on standardized tests, or other performance measures. However, when the issue of Afro-American difference is introduced, inferiority rather than diversity becomes the explanatory base.

From *Review of Educational Research* (1982), *52*(2), 219–244. Copyright © 1982 by the American Educational Research Association. Reprinted with permission.

In recent years, this inferiority explanation has been replaced with the adaptational-survival premise. Proponents of this thesis suggest that Afro-Americans developed a parallel culture in response to their isolation through discrimination, slavery, and ghettoization. Using the various elements of African culture patterns they were able to retain while acquiring others from the Europeans with whom they had contact, Afro-Americans developed an approach to life that assisted in their survival.

In addition to the unique communicative patterns, family structures, art forms, and worldview, these theorists contend that Afro-Americans also developed a culturally specific method of organizing and processing information. This processing strategy apparently proved an effective adaptational tool in social situations. However, Cohen (1969) and others have concluded that this culturally specific strategy differs from the one required in the typical educational setting. The result is an information processing strategy conflict that works to the disadvantage of Afro-Americans in school settings and limits their access to other areas of society. This paper will explore this possibility.

# Cultural Foundations of Afro-American Thought

Do Afro-Americans process information from the environment differently than do other groups? Based on his observations of Afro-Americans, Hilliard (1976) would answer affirmatively. He suggests that Afro-American people (a) tend to view things in their environment in entirety rather than in isolated parts; (b) seem to prefer intuitive rather than deductive or inductive reasoning; (c) tend to approximate concepts of space, number, and time rather than aiming at exactness or complete accuracy; (d) prefer to attend to people stimuli rather than nonsocial or object stimuli; and (e) tend to rely on nonverbal as well as verbal communication. The reason for these differences is found within Afro-American culture.

*Culture* is a rather abstract term but generally is defined as the rules members of a particular group use to govern the interaction with each other and the environment. Berry (1976) considers culture to be a way of life or a learned pattern of behavior that is unique to a group of people. Cohen (1974) defines it as a process of adaptation. The general view of Afro-American culture is that it is a distinct pattern of thinking, feeling, and acting that has developed as a way of adapting to color discrimination. Charles Keil (1966) suggests that this pattern is an "experiential wisdom" that provides Afro-Americans a unique outlook on life, or worldview.

All groups of people seem to have a *weltanschauung,* or worldview, that serves as the philosophical underpinnings of their behavior. This view seems to focus on meeting the demands and challenges presented by people and social situations in ways that will preserve their physical, spiritual, or psychological integrity. Manifestations of this approach show up particularly in interpersonal relationships and social perceptions.

The Afro-American weltanschauung is that the people within one's environment should be approached with caution, wariness, and a sense of distrust. This idea is vital to the survival of a group of people who live in an urban society and in a society with dislikes predicated on skin color. It is, as Perkins (1975) points out, a way of insuring that the individual does not become a victim. Attempting to prohibit victimization also requires developing the ability to manipulate the system or individuals with whom one comes in contact in order to achieve certain desired goals. Therefore, it is not surprising that a distrustful and manipulative point of view seems to pervade the Afro-American community. In fact, it appears that individuals who are a part of Afro-American culture are taught at an early age to be wary of people and systems within their environment (Halpern, 1973; Shade, 1978; Wubberhorst, Gradford, & Willis, 1971).

This lack of trust and suspiciousness often shows up on measures of personality. McClain (1967) found, for example, that Afro-American college students in the South were more likely to be more suspicious and apprehensive than Whites in the standardization sample of the 16PF personality form. Similar findings were reported for lower class hardcore-unemployed Afro-Americans (Triandis, 1976), for those in prisons (Berman, 1976), and for those in counseling (Wright, 1975). Although the subjects of many of the studies were people having problems, the idea of distrust or having a healthy suspicion of others seems to be considered a trait rather typical of Afro-Americans in general (Halpern, 1973; White, 1980). These findings suggest that there is a basic cultural consensus as to what represents trustworthiness, and as several authors point out, Afro-Americans appear to determine this quality on nonverbal behavior rather than on verbal cues (Roll, Schmidt, & Kaul, 1972; Switkin & Gynther, 1974; Terrell & Barrett, 1979).

Yarian (1974) suggests that heroes as cultural emblems of a group of people are also excellent indications of the group's perspective of the world. Within Afro-American folklore and music, there are the tales of the animal or slave trickster who manages to talk or literally trick his oppressors or captors into letting him escape. Other heroes are those who are just so tough and formidable that they bully their way through life, even if it requires violence. Perhaps, however, the most prevalent hero is the one Levine (1977) calls "the moral hard man," who beats society using society's own rules. Within Taylor's (1980) typology of Afro-American heroes, this "moral hard man" might well be the "splendid performer," the "man of integrity," the "independent spirit," or the "group leader."

As part of this people awareness and need to control the environment, or perhaps as a result of it, Afro-Americans seem to develop a unique affective or personal orientation that manifests itself in attention to social cues, subjective meanings attached to words, preference for social distance, and sustained use of nonverbal communication. These characteristics are discussed in turn below.

## Afro-American Social Cognition

In studies in which groups were compared on their attentiveness to cues in the faces of other people, Afro-Americans were found to focus on very different cues than Euro-Americans and, subsequently, developed different recognition patterns. In a study using Black and White females, Hirschberg, Jones, and Haggerty (1978) found that the Afro-American subjects paid much more attention to the affective characteristics of the pictures of male faces than to the physical characteristics. In other studies of these phenomena, it was found that although both groups seem to pay closer attention to the faces of people of their own racial group (Chance, Goldstein, & McBride, 1975; Galper, 1973; Luce, 1974), Afro-Americans seemed better at discerning emotions displayed by individuals regardless of their race (Gitter, Black, & Mostofsy, 1972).

Not only are Afro-Americans better at attending to facial cues, they also appear to detect different social reactions and nuances. A study done by Hill and Fox (1973) of a military situation found that Afro-American and Euro-American squad leaders had entirely different perceptions about the climate and interrelationships of the people in their squads. Euro-American squad leaders reported more of a perceived need to give reprimands to subordinates of their own race and better performance ratings to subordinates of other racial groups. Afro-American squad leaders did not make these types of distinctions and also reported perceptions of better relationships between themselves and their subordinates.

A similar study conducted in a school environment (Wittmer & Ferinden, 1970) reported similar differences in interpersonal perceptions. When teachers were questioned about staff relationships in a recently desegregated school, Afro-American teachers indicated a perception of more teacher-to-teacher conflict than Euro-American teachers. At the same time, they reported having a better rapport with the nonacademic staff as well as with the students. As in the previous situation, racial differences in perceptions of social interactions seemed to polarize with Afro-Americans responding more to the people in the situation and the Euro-Americans responding more to the task requirements.

This difference is also found in studies of the social meanings assigned to words. Landis, McGrew, Day, Savage, and Saral (1976) asked groups of Afro- and Euro-American middle class and hardcore-unemployed males to respond to a word list on a semantic differential scale. Regardless of class, racial differences emerged in the values attached, emotional reactions generated, and the potency assigned to the words. For example, the most highly valued words for Afro-Americans, but not for Euro-Americans, are quality-of-life words such as *progress, success, future,* and *money.* Words having the most positive response and value for Euro-Americans, but not for Afro-Americans, were words such as *marriage, work,* and *hope.* In the personal relationship category, words such as *truth, respect,* and *sympathy* were valued highly by Afro-Americans whereas Euro-Americans preferred such words as *love.* On the other hand, Euro-Americans responded with more emotion and negativism to words such as *battle, danger, trouble, crime,* and *confrontation,* whereas Afro-Americans showed neutrality.

In another study of differences in social perceptions, Szalay and Bryson (1973) found that words representing themes of racial integration, individual needs, and social problems were perceived as having higher value by Afro-Americans, whereas Euro-Americans preferred word domains representing various "isms," national loyalty, and health concerns. The response variation apparently represents differences in attached affective meanings.

Perhaps the area in which differences in interpersonal style are most evident is that of social distance. Social distance involves the expanding and contracting physical space surrounding the individual (Liebman, 1970). The perception of social cues, ideas, and attitudes is affected by the amount of physical separation demanded by the individual for social interaction. Those who permit individuals to come close gather one sort of information, whereas those who demand greater separation receive other types of cues (Hall, 1966). The result is a manifestation of different social-cognitive behavior.

Studies using adult samples noted a closer social distance preference among Afro-Americans. Bauer (1973) found this to be true for college students, as did Hall (1966), Connally (1974), and Liebman (1970). Willis (1966) reported the opposite finding for older Afro-American adults; however, the significance level chosen for potential error determination was extremely high. Thus, this finding had a high probability of being a chance occurrence based on the situation and probably should be disregarded.

When compared to other ghettoized, high involvement groups, Afro-Americans showed little difference in social distance requirements, at least in a street-meeting situation (Jones, 1971). However, in a study by Baxter (1970), Afro-Americans seemed to prefer greater social distance than Mexican Americans. As the dyads were observed watching animals in a zoo, this study would appear to be measuring the degree to which individuals faced each other rather than face-to-face social distance measured in other studies; if this is the case, then the Baxter findings are not inconsistent with the trends previously noted.

The differences noted for Afro-Americans on this dimension seem to depend on the situation in which the proxemic research was conducted. In studies of children in grades 1–4, Afro-Americans tend to stand closer for purposes of communication than other ethnic groups observed (Aiello & Jones, 1971; Duncan, 1978; Jones & Aiello, 1973). Scherer (1974) studied the same age group using photographs of interacting dyads. Although no significant difference was found, the trend was in the expected direction. However, Zimmerman and Brody (1975) observed fifth- and sixth—rade students and found that Euro-American children of this age group permitted closer social distance than Afro-American children. Unlike subjects in other studies, these children did not know each other and came to the experimental situation from different neighborhoods. The fact that this study was done in a laboratory situation rather than a naturalistic setting, as were the others, probably accounts for the difference in the results. Inasmuch as children of this age range are somewhat leary of strangers, regardless of race (Halpern, 1973), the children probably would display this by standing farther apart. In a later study, the closer personal space among Afro-American elementary school children was found again (Willis, Carlson, & Reeves, 1979).

## Socializing Influences on Cognition

The differences in perception of the world, of people, and of events is indicative of the unique socialization experiences of Afro-Americans. In her studies of the Afro-American socialization patterns, Young (1970, 1974) found that child training mechanisms of the Afro-American kinship group seemed to emphasize attending to cues and developing behavior that is compatible with learning to survive. As they receive status-oriented and inconsistent discipline, children learn to judge and adjust to moods of people in authority. At the same time, there exists a respect for the child as an individual, which permits the maintenance of a strong sense of an independent self. This type of socialization pattern is found throughout the Afro-American community and is found particularly in families that are part of a kinship network.

The Afro-American kinship network is a multigenerational social network of relatives, friends, and neighbors (Aschenbrenner, 1973; MacAdoo, 1977; Martin & Martin, 1978; Stack, 1974). Although previously viewed as a less than desirable structure, recent research efforts have found it beneficial in that this network acts as a buffer for Afro-Americans against negative ecological forces and serves as a cultural facilitator and mediator. Through this network, Afro-American individuals and their nuclear family system are able to give and receive emotional, physical, psychological, and social support.

As members of this kinship system, Afro-Americans are urged and trained in the concept of collective responsibility, to respond to the authority of a dominant family figure, and, at the same time, to seek and move toward independence (Aschenbrenner, 1973; Martin & Martin, 1978). The amount of independence, however, seems to depend on the economic plight of the network. As in the earlier Barry, Child, and Bacon study (1959), the greater the need for mutual support for financial and economic survival, the greater the pressure for kinship support and less independence.

The mother–child relationship within the Afro-American family and the kinship or extended family system seem to have an effect on children in several areas that are particularly significant in the development of their information processing preference. As already noted, there appear to be a concentration and particular stress on interpersonal relationships. In addition, Young (1974) notes that the socialization techniques tend to frustrate the child's interest in the "object world." In fact, it appears that by the age of 2, children have been refocused to people stimuli rather than nonhuman stimuli. When Yarrow, Rubenstein, Peterson, and Jankowski (1971) examined this preference of Afro-American infants for humans as opposed to inanimate objects, they found that the two aspects of the environment were strikingly independent.

Carpenter, Tecce, Stechler, and Friedman (1970) also examined the response style of Afro-American infants by exposing them to three types of stimuli: the mother, a mannequin, and an abstract picture. The authors noted that the mother, as the most familiar stimulus, received less of the child's attention than the other two items. This response was interpreted to be the result of familiarity and less of color. Of the other two presentations, it was noted that these infants attended more and/or for a longer period to the mannequin or human-like face than the abstract stimuli. One must wonder if this also represents a finding of person-over-thing orientation.

Although their study was not oriented to the examination of racial differences per se, Lewis and Wilson (1972) did examine the mother-child relationship of 32 twelve-week-old infants of which a large portion was Afro-American. They found that lower socioeconomic mothers were more likely to touch their children, hold them, and smile at them; these behaviors were interpreted as exhibitions that would strengthen the attachment bond rather than institute "distancing." Distancing behaviors were interpreted as those that help the child separate *self* from the immediate environment and move toward the achievement of representational thought. Bruner, Olver, and Greenfield (1966) describe this developmental phenomena of distancing as an important progression for cognitive growth. As children move from the stage in which action and objects are fused to the point of being able to represent objects independent of the actions taken toward them, they are developing their memory and abilities for representational thought. More important, they are setting the stage for learning to handle abstract concepts.

Young (1974) also noted another information processing difference in that Afro-American children apparently are taught to concentrate on many stimuli at one time rather than learning to concentrate on one. Boykin (1979) refers to this as "behavioral verve." He found that when presented with information requiring some type of problem-solving performance, Afro-American children did markedly better if the formats had high variability. The author concluded that Euro-American children seemed to have been socialized to tolerate monotony or unvaried presentation of material. Afro-American children, however, required a great deal of stimulus variety.

When one considers the position of Afro-Americans in society, it seems clear that this variation in cue perception and an orientation to interpersonal relatedness is vital. As sociologists within the community point out, Afro-Americans require a special antenna that helps them differentiate between situations and people. By being able to determine certain emotions, attitudes, and needed behaviors, Afro-Americans can determine which situations or people are friendly and which are hostile. Being able to do this is a matter of psychological and physical survival. However, this particular thinking style may also have an effect on Afro-American cognitive development.

## Afro-American Style of Knowing

How do children come to know the world? Scholars who have examined this question suggest that the process involves perception, memory, and learning to handle various ideas, images, and concepts. Although there are obviously some universal commonalities in the process, there are also some individual and group differences. As Cole and Scribner (1974) point out, a child's method of perception, memorization, and thinking are inseparably bound to the patterns of activity, communication, and social relations of the culture in which the individual is socialized.

The relationship between culture and the cognitive development of the individual has become a familiar and provocative theme in cross-cultural psychology. However, although this relationship is accepted for differentiating western and nonwestern cultures, it is not widely applied to subcultures within American society. Rather than agree to the idea that the differences found in cognitive approaches might be related to a subcultural strategy, researchers generally promote the idea that ethnic differences and genetic makeup create the variation.

An example of this approach is found in a study by Lesser, Fifer, and Clark (1965). In this study, four specific ethnic groups were examined using tasks that required different cognitive processes such as verbal memory, concept formation, numerical memory, and spatial relationships. The results indicated that each of the four ethnic groups, regardless of the difference in performance due to socioeconomic status, displayed a distinct pattern. Of the four groups, Afro-Americans were high on the verbal task but lowest of the four on the space conceptualization task. A similar finding emerged in a replicated study (Stodolsky & Lesser, 1967). In a similar study, Leifer (1972a) compared Afro-Americans to three other ethnic groups on the Lowenfeld Mosaic, Geometric Figures Task, Incomplete Man, and Verbal Fluency Tasks. Again, distinct ethnic group patterns in performance emerged.

Such studies are used as indications of ethnic differences in cognitive growth. Recently, however, some anthropologists and psychologists have used these results to infer that groups of people differ in the kinds of differentiations and inferences they make because they are trained to pay differential attention to different aspects of the environment. Rather than view these differences as ethnic variations in native ability, these scholars have chosen to study them as variations in cognitive style.

Over the years, scholars have identified a myriad of terms, definitions, and concepts that have come to be labeled *cognitive style*. This term represents a superordinate construct that accounts for individual preferences in various cognitive, perceptual, and personality dimensions that influence differences in information processing. As one examines the literature in the area, however, it is noted that these styles can be placed into approximately three categories: Category 1 includes those emphasizing visual-spatial preferences; Category 2 includes those that are more concerned with strategies for concept attainment and thus focus on categorization and abstraction preferences; Category 3 seems oriented more toward personality, ways in which the individual views and responds to information about the world or environment. As Kogan (1971) points out, these styles vary in the amount of empirical substantiation available, the philosophical underpinnings, the methodological sophistication developed, and the situational implications to which they apply.

The question of whether there is a specific cognitive style that can be attributed to being an American of African descent cannot be definitively answered at this time. However, there does appear to be a racial difference in each of the dimensions subsumed under the cognitive style construct. Let us examine the research in each of these areas.

# Afro-American Perceptual Style

A person's perceptual problem-solving strategy represents the method through which an individual gathers and translates information from the environment. Although all sensory modes are involved in this process, visual perception seems to be the one most often included in the cognitive style investigations. No doubt this emphasis is the result of the high visual orientation of American culture.

The area most often studied in the examination of the perceptual aspect of cognitive style is the concept of field-dependence/field-independence, or field articulation. This concept, as developed by Witkin and his associates, denotes the ability of an individual to visually structure or select and use relevant information embedded in a larger interrelated context (Witkin, Dyk, Paterson, Goodenough, & Karp, 1962). Individuals who are unable to distinguish necessary parts in order to solve the problem are said to be more global and interrelated in their approach to visual information and are classified as *field-dependent persons*. Individuals who can abstract the necessary parts from the totality of the material regardless of the distracting elements in the visual field are said to be *field independent*.

The amount of literature in this area using Afro-American subjects is extremely small and is found largely in unpublished dissertations. In the few studies available, Afro-Americans seem to tend toward the field-dependent end of the continuum.

Perney (1976) tested 40 sixth-grade children (age 12) equally divided between race and sex using the Embedded Figure Test (EFT). Not only were sex differences present, but racial differences also existed, with Afro-Americans exhibiting significantly more field-dependence than Euro-Americans. Although no difference was found on the same test for boys of similar age in the study done by Karp, Silberman, and Winters (1969), racial differences were found in the Block Design Subtest of the Wechsler Intelligence Scale for Children (WISC), a test that correlates highly with the EFT. Again, as in the other study, Afro-Americans were more field dependent, whereas the Euro-Americans tended toward field-independence. Using the concept of body differentiation as measured by the Rod-and-Frame Test, Rameriz and Price-Williams (1974) found a similar relationship between race and field-dependence. Afro-American and Mexican American children in the fourth grade seemed to prefer the field-dependent approach, whereas Euro-Americans demonstrated a field-independent preference.

In studies in which the age dimension is not controlled, mixed findings are generally reported. Ritzinger (1971) examined a racially mixed group of children ages 6 to 11 who agreed to participate in a child development research project. Based on the scores obtained on the EFT, Euro-American children appeared to be much more differentiated than the Afro-American children. These racial differences seemed to disappear when socioeconomic class was controlled. In the report of her comparison of racial groups from the third, fourth, fifth, and ninth grades, Schratz (1976) indicates no racial differences in the preadolescent group but significant differences in the adolescent group. Again, the result indicated less perceptual differentiation among Afro-Americans. Racial group differences on the field-dependent/independent continuum were also found in eighth-grade boys (Gamble, 1971) and in the high school males examined by Barclay and Cusumano (1967); the mean age of the students in this study was 15.4.

Whether this variation in field orientation continued into adulthood is not known. In one study in which college students between the ages of 16 and 21 were studied using the EFT, no racial differences in field articulation ability were found (Schmultz, 1975). However, the comparison group consisted of Italian Americans whose cognitive performance patterns seem similar to Afro-Americans (Leifer, 1972b). In studies done by this author, racial differences were found in college students at the beginning of their first year of college, but not when the junior or third year of college had been reached (Shade, 1981); where differences existed, Afro-Americans were more field dependent.

In studies in which Afro-American adult subjects were used and no racial comparisons made, both field-independent and field-dependent individuals were identified. However, the designation of individual styles was based on the scores of the sample using the median as the dividing point. It is, therefore, difficult to tell whether the subjects designated were really field independent or merely less field dependent than others in the sample (Birnback, 1972; Chepp, 1975; Shansky, 1976).

In spite of the observed inconsistencies, a pattern seems to emerge that suggests that Afro-Americans have a field-dependent cognitive style. Jones (1978) seems to agree, as will be noted in the discussion on personality style.

## Afro-American Conceptual Style

In every environment, individuals are confronted with more information than they are capable of handling. Individuals develop approaches to scanning and focusing on particular elements of the information and for abstracting information that classifies the ideas, objects, or situation. The cognitive-style preferences placed in this category examine how people attend to and structure a situation. Also examined are the attributes or relationships most often used in classifying objects or concepts.

Ascertaining the pattern dominating Afro-Americans on this dimension, as with perceptual style, is difficult because evidence is very limited. Carlson

(1971) investigated the perceptual organizing preferences of a racially mixed group of middle class children, ages 5–9. The results indicated that Afro-American children seemed to have difficulty placing visual material into the more discrete groupings. In another study (Hansley & Busse, 1969), Afro-American children, ages 5–8, were tested on their ability to visually structure an unstructured field. They were asked to name pictured objects both randomly arranged on a card and arranged in a triangle. Using the number of omissions and commissions, the researchers concluded that the card on which the pictures were placed in a spatial relationship proved easier for the children than the one on which the pictures were randomly arranged.

Abstraction style denotes the categorizing preference of individuals, not their capacity to develop concepts (Gibson, 1969; Wallace, 1965). Those individuals who tend to be analytical are prone to group-various stimuli based on the similarity in specific elements. Relational individuals seem to perceive the information on the basis of various thematic or functional relationships. When Sigel, Anderson, and Shapiro (1966) studied the categorizing behavior of middle and lower socioeconomic-status Afro-American children, they found significant class differences. Although relational responses were used by the middle class children, they were more likely to use descriptive-analytical responses based on physical attributes of the objects or pictures. Lower class children, on the other hand, produced more relational responses based on the use of the objects or thematic relationships. The authors explained the difference between the two groups as the result of the increasing differentiating ability of the middle class to view the object world in a more objective manner.

In addition to class differences, racial differences also have been noted. Orasanu, Lee, and Scribner (1979) examined Afro-American and Euro-American first and fifth graders and found that although economic status had an effect on categorizing behavior, ethnicity was also responsible for differences. Afro-American children tended to sort lists on a functional basis, whereas Euro-American children used the more descriptive taxonomic approach. This difference in style, however, did not affect successful completion of the task.

Gamble (1971) also found racial differences in categorization style. In this study, which compared Afro- and Euro-American advantaged and disadvantaged groups from rural, urban, and suburban environments, few differences emerged when class was controlled. However, among the disadvantaged group, the White suburban and White rural groups exhibited not only greater field-independence but also a more analytical categorizing style than the Black urban children. In this study, as in the one conducted by Wilde (1973), the more advantaged children appeared to have a different differentiating system than those from the lower classes, regardless of race.

Simmons (1979) suggests that any comment about racial difference in categorizing responses must include a consideration of the cultural salience of the stimuli presented. Kogan (1971) agrees. His review and analysis suggest that the strategy selected seems to be a function of the interaction between age and the nature of the stimulus. In addition, methodologies used make it difficult to distinguish whether individuals are using the relational style because it is their accustomed style or because it seems to fit the task.

An accompanying concept, and perhaps the most investigated using Afro-American subjects, is the dimension of conceptual tempo. Again, individually preferred modes are evident. In processing information, many individuals are slow to respond, waiting until they gather all the information possible and consider the validity of the solution; these individuals are considered to be *reflective* responders. On the other hand, many persons respond immediately to what is presented without regard to potential errors; these individuals are labeled *impulsive*. Although it is generally assumed that Afro-Americans are more impulsive than other groups (Kagan, 1966), there is a lack of evidence to support this view.

In a study of this dimension by Zucker and Stricker (1968), Afro-Americans were reported to be more impulsive than Euro-Americans in their approach. In this study racial differences were confounded by class differences in that only middle class subjects were Euro-Americans and only lower class subjects were Afro-Americans. Even though this was the case in the Fisher (1968) study as well, no differences were found in conceptual tempo.

When they controlled race in the study of this dimension, Mumbauer and Miller (1970) found only class differences. In a study in which class was controlled, Reiss (1972) found no differences between races. Although most findings do suggest that the lower class tends to have a higher percentage of impulsive responders, the distribution of reflective-impulsive style individuals seems to more carefully delineate the successful versus the nonsuccessful student (Messer, 1976: Mumbauer & Miller, 1970; Reiss, 1972).

The lack of consistent patterns in this area suggests that perhaps this dimension is not associated with race or with a culturally specific approach, but is defined only by the rate of individual development.

# Afro-American Personality Style

The recognition of the interrelationship of the perceptual, conceptual, and personality systems is demonstrated in the research of the various advocates of cognitive-style dimensions. Although the field-dependence/field-independence construct essentially measures the perceptual style of an individual, Witkin and Goodenough (1977) have been able to demonstrate a relationship between stylistic preference and various adapting styles individuals use. These response styles are placed essentially on an interpersonal as opposed to an impersonal continuum and are described in terms of the individual's personality.

In studies of the relationship between field articulation and personality style, field- independent individuals have been found to be impersonal in that they were less interested in people and more interested in things. They also demonstrate a preference for nonsocial situations and for physical as well as psychological distancing, and they have the ability to work independently. One might well describe the field-independent style as a prototype of Riesman's (1950) inner-directed personality or Miller and Swanson's (1958) entrepreneurial type.

Field-dependent individuals, however, seem to demonstrate a preference for interpersonal relationships. This preference is manifested through a strong interest in other people, a need and desire to be physically close to people, a preference for social situations, and attentiveness to social cues. These individuals have been identified as particularly well suited for working in cooperative, humanistic situations. In fact, one might describe them as Riesman's (1950) other-directed personality or Miller and Swanson's (1958) bureaucratic personality type. Perhaps the most prominent trait of each of these types is that individuals with this stylistic preference seem to depend heavily on external referents for guidance and information in novel or ambiguous situations and for help in problem solving.

In spite of the fact that Afro-Americans appear to be more externally oriented, which would be consistent with their apparent preference for field-dependence, studies of the locus of control do not verify this. Among the first studies looking at ethnic differences in this dimension was the one by Battle and Rotter (1963). In this study, middle class Blacks and Whites were compared with lower class Blacks and Whites. When social class was controlled, no significant differences were found. However, when middle class Euro-Americans were compared with lower class Afro-Americans, a significant difference emerged, with Euro-Americans being more internally oriented and Afro-Americans more externally oriented. Unfortunately, this difference is often reported as a racial difference rather than an economic role difference.

Scott and Phelan (1969) studied unemployed adult males between the ages of 20 and 28; and although racial differences did emerge in the same directions found in the Battle and Rotter (1963) study, these differences may still be a function of the economic role of the groups. Gurin and her associates (Gurin & Epps, 1975; Gurin, Gurin, Lao, & Beattie, 1969) noted that Afro-Americans seem to have a higher ability than others to differentiate between situations in which they have control and those in which other people have the most influence. Studies by

DuCette and Wolk (1972) and Kinder and Reeder (1975) seem to support this. Thus, the differences found by Scott and Phelan may reflect the greater understanding of unemployed Afro-American males about their situation and epitomize the Afro-American view of the world.

Jones (1978) examined the relationship between field-dependence and personality traits for Afro-Americans and found that those identified by Witkin and Goodenough (1977) did not correspond to those exhibited by Afro-Americans. Although the young adults did tend to be more field-dependent than their Euro-American counterparts in the study, they exhibited a different interpersonal behavior profile. They were more dominant and socially poised, tended to adhere to more fundamental religious beliefs, were concerned about impulse control, and were power oriented, skeptical, and cynical. They also demonstrated a psychological toughness. On the other hand, they were also less risk-oriented, less adventuresome, and more socially conforming than the White students in the sample. Jones suggests that the personality implications for field-dependence may vary for Afro-Americans.

The factor that seems to most affect an individual's adaptation to the environment or personality style is the belief system from which the person operates. The studies in this area are generally oriented toward assessing response patterns as indicators of belief systems. The basic premise underlying these studies is that every person evaluates information received from any situation from a unique perspective. The result is that individuals or groups use their belief systems to distort the world or to narrow it as deemed necessary. Rokeach (1960) referred to this as an open versus closed mindedness and attempted to correlate the idea with that of field articulation. Kelly (1955) identified the style as a part of personal construct formation, while Bieri (cited in Goldstein & Blackman, 1978) referred to it as cognitive complexity versus cognitive simplicity. Regardless of the stylistic label, the basic philosophy suggests that if a person has an open mind, then new ideas, new experiences, tolerance of ambiguous situations, and the need for additional information before making a judgment are part of the individual's typical approach to the world. On the other hand, individuals operating within a closed belief structure would tend to be rigid and perhaps stereotypical in their thoughts, intolerant of new or ambiguous experiences, and probably make important judgments based on little information.

As with other aspects of cognitive style, this dimension also has a cultural base. Inasmuch as the cultural base of Afro-American belief systems seems oriented toward surviving in a color-rejecting world, it is not surprising that the cognitive styles identified in this dimension seem oriented toward this type of environmental interaction. Although empirical evidence has yet to be collected, Harrell (1979) identified a continuum of Afro-American response styles that appear to range from those with a relatively closed approach to those with a high degree of openness relative to their ability to handle race-related structures. The styles, as specified by Harrell (1979), are as follows:

Style 1. *Continued Apathy.* This style is characterized by the recognition that racism does exist and has damaging effects on the individual. However, no plan of action is proposed and a passive or reactive posture is assumed.

Style 2. *Seeking a Piece of the Action.* With this style there is a consuming cognitive commitment to making oneself a marketable commodity for the system. The belief system exhibited, while recognizing the existence of racism, is clearly oriented toward achievement within the system. The behavioral choices include the striving for excellence and competence in various spheres of life.

Style 3. *Counter-Culture Alternatives.* This particular cognitive style stresses a counter-culture solution for difficulties and seeks the type of action that is personally rewarding.

Style 4. *Black Nationalistic Alternative.* The cognitive style represented by this belief system emphasizes total group unity, cohesiveness, and ethnocentrism. Action choices are oriented toward achieving these goals.

Style 5. *Authoritarianism.* The orientation toward authoritarianism supports rigidity and intolerance of ambiguity in the individual's cognitive organization (Goldstein & Blackman, 1978), but most of all, the individual becomes highly dependent on authority figures to determine responses to the world. Action choices are determined more by authority than by the individual.

Style 6. *Cognitive Flexibility.* This cognitive style represents an approach that includes the recognition of the situation, the need for change, but an openness for new, different, and creative strategies for handling problems and situations. The response style depends on the situation.

Although the dominance of any of these styles might occur with some particular historical event, such as the Civil Rights Movement, which obviously fostered and promoted a preponderance of Styles 3 and 4, it would appear that all these patterns are present within the Afro-American community (McCord, Howard, Friedberg, & Harwood, 1969). Of the three cognitive style dimensions examined, this one appears to exhibit the most diversity within the Afro-American community.

As previously indicated, the question of whether there is a specific cognitive style that can be attributed to Afro-Americans cannot be answered unequivocably at this time. However, there does appear to be a racial difference in the visual-perceptual approach to the environment with more Afro-American samples demonstrating a tendency toward field-dependence, but with perhaps different personality traits than usually found in field-dependent persons. There also appears to be a difference in categorizing behavior oriented more toward the thematic and functional approach than toward specific attributes of the objects categorized. In addition, there appears to be a personality style based on a belief system that concentrates on interracial relationships. What must be determined is whether these trends are evident in all strata of the Afro-American community or merely in certain groups. Of equal importance is the need to determine whether these styles of perceiving, organizing, and interpreting information exhibited by Afro-Americans are those which are expected and accommodated within the American educational system.

## Cognitive Style and the Schooling Process

Participants in the schooling process are generally stratified by age and provided with a specified material content that is thought to be appropriate for them. To determine how well each has mastered the information, participants are then given tests designed to measure the expected learnings. Based on the scores of the individuals on these instruments, classroom assignment and future exposure to certain content is determined. Because these allocations often determine future occupation, education, and social mobility, concern is generated about the variability of individuals and groups on these measures.

Group differences on these measures generally are explained on the basis of variation in intelligence, reading level, chronological age, motivation, or social class. Recently, though, educators have begun to consider the possibility that some of the differences might be due to variations in information processing approaches. As this possibility gains credence, interest in cognitive-style research burgeons.

For the most part, cognitive-style proponents have concentrated their efforts on validating the construct rather than exploring the implications of style for education (Kogan, 1971; Simmons, 1979). However, there are some data available on the interaction of cognitive styles and test-taking ability and the influence of cognitive styles on concept attainment and skill development. In addition, theorists also have tried to translate the stylistic preference idea into a learning style construct with particular emphasis on the effect of various styles on pupil-teacher interaction.

The results of these explorations indicate that students in the educational enterprise are most successful if their information processing approach has the following characteristics:

1. An attention style that focuses on the task itself, rather than on the people in the situation.

2. An abstraction ability that separates ideas and concepts into parts and reweaves them into a unified whole.

3. A perceptual style that leads to the abstraction of both obvious and nonobvious attributes that seemingly link things, ideas, or principles.

4. A perceptual style that facilitates the extraction of important information embedded in distracting influences.

5. A long attention span with prolonged concentrating ability.

6. An attending preference for verbal cues rather than nonverbal cues.

7. A reflective rather than an impulsive response style in problem solving.

8. A highly differentiated or analytical thinking style that leads to abstract and logical reasoning.

Cohen (1969), who did the seminal work in this area suggests that this pattern represents a psychologically differentiated cognitive style that is particularly beneficial in a school setting. The style is in fact reinforced by the content of the school curricula, questions, and solutions desired on achievement and intelligence tests, and it is promoted by the use of current teaching methods.

This proposition was substantiated by other investigators. In their reviews of the relationships between various cognitive styles and indicators of success within the educational process, Kogan (1971) and Coop and Sigel (1971) found correlations favoring the analytical, field-independent, conceptually abstract, reflective student. Although the authors agree that this type of individual might be dysfunctional in other settings, they note that the students with this particular stylistic approach seem to perform well in schools.

This trend is also evident within the Afro-American population. Riley and Denmark (1974) found that Afro-Americans who were field-independent performed better on I.Q. tests, and Busse (1968) found that field-independent Afro-American males performed better on problem-solving tasks. Wilde (1973) examined the relationship between conceptual style and school success and found that those Afro-Americans who were more analytical were more likely to perform better in school. These same trends have been found on learning tasks and achievement test performance (Chepp, 1975; Ferrell, 1971; Schratz, 1976; Schwartz, 1972).

The relationship between cognitive style and academic achievement has also been found in the content area of reading. Stuart (1967) found that good readers, regardless of race or sex, tended toward a field-independent perceptual style, while poor readers were more field dependent. In another study, Petersen and Magaro (1969) found that field-dependent students took longer to master a reading-type task than field-independent students. As in test performance, the learners with a psychologically differentiated cognitive style seemed to excel.

This point of view is supported by Zamm (1973) in his examination of the reading skills of Afro-Americans. According to Zamm, reading requires visual and auditory discrimination as well as the ability to perceptually organize symbolic patterns and space. In addition, the student must be able to make a series of differentiated yet integrated responses. In other words, the child who is most successful in developing reading skills probably has a differentiated, analytical method of handling information processing rather than a global, nonanalytic approach.

The consistency of the relationship of style and school success also holds for the studies of other identifiable cognitive styles. Afro-Americans who tend to be more reflective in their approach to work in order to make fewer errors have a better performance score on measures of achievement than those who are impulsive (Harrison & Nadelman, 1972; Reiss, 1972; Wilde, 1973). In a study by Vinson (1974) using the conceptual style system of Harvey, Hunt, and Schroder (1961), Afro-Americans who were flexible in thinking and were abstract learners had higher grades than those classified as concrete learners. Although the difference was not significant and could have occurred by chance, the authors suggest that it does demonstrate a preference by teachers for individuals who essentially epitomize the model student in stylistic preference.

Although all scholars of stylistic tendency have not chosen to study Afro-Americans, the available evidence could lead to the conclusion that the difference in school success is attributable to the use of sociocentric, field-dependent, non-analytic categorizing information processing strategies by many Afro-Americans. Because this style is not the strategy preferred in an educational setting, then racial differences would occur. Of course, other factors must be considered.

First, we must wonder whether these stylistic tendencies are more prominent in the lower class than the middle class, which experiences more school success. It is a common assumption that lower class children function at a different level on cognitive tasks than middle to upper class children. However, the literature in this area does not permit us to make any definitive statement about level of functioning in relation to Afro-American cognitive style. Although some studies report socioeconomic differences (Gamble, 1971; Gill, Herdtner, & Lough, 1968), most find no differences (Karp et al., 1969; Palmer, 1970; Rameriz & Price-Williams, 1974; Reiss, 1972; Ritzinger, 1971). In those studies that matched cognitive style with achievement, it appeared that successful students, regardless of socioeconomic status, developed a more differentiated approach to processing information.

Second, if class is not a major determinant, is it possible that sex differences account for findings of different cognitive-style tendencies? Inasmuch as Afro-American females tend to have more success in school than do males (Shade, 1978), sex may be an important distinction. Sex differences in cognitive style have been reported for most groups (Kogan, 1976; Witkin, Moore, Goodenough, & Cox, 1977); however, whether sex differences exist within the Afro-American sample cannot be determined from the available evidence. Although differences between Black females and Black males on some cognitive-style measures were reported in studies by Schratz (1976) and Perney (1976), other studies reported no sex differences (Gill et al., 1968; Harrison, 1979; Ritzinger, 1971; Seitz, 1971). Sex differences are not often reported in the developmental literature for Afro-Americans and, when they are, the direction of the differences is mixed. A recent pilot study done with college students using the EFT and the Kohs Block Design found racial differences but no sex differences for either Afro-American or Euro-American college students in this sample (Shade, 1981).

Third, the lack of substantive evidence in the other areas suggests that we must also consider the possibility that the differences noted in cognitive style are preferential differences in visual-spatial orientation *only*; Serpell (1976), in fact, suggests that we are not talking about cognitive style but about a perceptual style.

## Cognitive Style or Perceptual Style?

Differences in spatial-perceptual functioning influencing cognitive performance have been found in several studies of Afro-American information processing. In a study by Pierce-Jones and King (1960), both Afro- and Euro-American adolescents were given four tests. Two of the tests required the subjects to use the verbal mode of processing information, and two required the visual mode. The authors report that Afro-American youth did significantly better or were at least equal to Euro-Americans on the verbal synthesizing material but were very poor on the visual tasks.

In 1970 Farnham-Diggory pursued this avenue of inquiry through three small studies in which Afro-American and Euro-American children, ages 4–10, performed three synthesis tasks. The material required the children to coordinate symbolic material with certain concepts and arrive at an inference. When verbal material was involved, racial differences did not emerge. However, when visual symbolic material was used, Afro-Americans did not perform as well as Euro-Americans. The author concluded that perhaps Afro-Americans have some spatial or visual information processing difficulty and then proceeded to remediate the difference through a training program. She found that when the distracting visual cues were removed from the presented material and substituted with memorized cues, the performance of Afro-American children improved tremendously and approached the level of the Euro-American children.

These perceptual differences are most evident in performance on the Wechsler scales, which seem to be the most commonly used measures of intelligence when racial comparisons are made. Cohen (1957, 1959) examined the WISC and Wechsler Adult Intelligence Scale (WAIS) scales and found three major cognitive factors present in these instruments. Factor I is labeled Verbal Comprehension, which is found in the vocabulary, information, and comprehension subtests. Factor II is the Attention-Concentration element measured largely by the Digit Span, Arithmetic, and Coding subtests. Factor III is the Analytical or Spatial Perceptual aspect of the tests and is found in the Picture Completion, Block Design, and Object Assembly subtests.

The perceptual difference in performance on Cohen's (1959) Factor II (attention-concentration) and Factor III (spatial-perceptual ability) is, of course, most evident in the research by Jensen (1969), which examined racial differences in performance on basic learning tasks. Jensen's Level I tasks included Digit Span and serial-rote or paired-associate learning tasks. As reported by Goodenough (1976) and in studies by Rohwer (1971), Bridgeman and Buttram (1975), Guinaugh (1971), and Elkind and Deblinger (1969), group differences were not apparent on these attention-concentration tasks. However, on the Level II task represented by the Raven's Progressive Matrices, a visual-perceptual synthesizing test, Afro-Americans did poorly. Similar findings were reported by the other authors (Bridgeman & Buttram, 1975; Elkind & Deblinger, 1969; Guinaugh, 1971; Rohwer, 1971).

Other studies have emphasized group differences on performance tasks. In 1954, Young and Bright did a study of 81 southern U.S. Afro-American children using the WISC. Although younger children seemed to perform better on all tests than the older group, when compared to the standardization sample, Afro-Americans obtained significantly lower scores on the performance subtests, that is, the Block Design and Object Assembly Picture Vocabulary tests. Similar findings were reported by Davidson (1950) on an adult sample.

Teahan and Drews (1962) examined the difference in Afro-American performance on verbal and performance tasks from a regional perspective. Although high on the comprehension and similarities tests, both northern- and southern-based Afro-American children scored significantly lower than the standardization group on the Vocabulary and Block Design tests. The southern sample had a much wider gap between the verbal and performance quotients.

In a study of racial differences in intellectual performance, Burnes (1970) compared middle and lower class Afro-Americans with middle and lower class Euro-Americans also using the WISC. Although the differences between socio-economic classes were considerably more significant than those between races, the analysis of the subtest results showed much more racial variation on the Block Design, Object Assembly, Coding, and Maze subtests. Cole and Hunter (1971) reported similar findings for social classes.

In a more recent study of racial differences, Vance and Hankins (1979) administered the WISC-R to Afro- and Euro-American students matched on intelligence quotient (I.Q.) and sex. Black males in the sample performed considerably better than White males on the information and verbal subtests; no female differences were noted. Black scores on the performance tasks, particularly Coding, however, were much lower than scores for Whites.

This evidence, of course, has been cited numerous times as indicating an Afro-American perceptual defect. However, as Mandler and Stein (1977) point out, this hypothesis seems to be supported by little evidence. In their review of the evidence, Mandler and Stein (1977) noted that Afro-American children consistently had lower scores on the Block Design test. The authors, however, were unwilling to attribute this solely to the hypothesis of a perceptual defect because of the various cognitive functions that have been determined to affect test performance. For example, perceptual style alone does not influence all tasks, only certain ones.

Witkin and Goodenough (1977) suggest that this is indeed the case and that perceptual styles manifest themselves differently in various situations. When the solution depends on taking the critical element out of context, one style is useful; this type of differentiation does not seem to matter in tasks requiring short-term memory or recall. For example, Witkin and his associates (1962) found that field-independent subjects obtained much higher scores on Cohen's (1959) Factor III subtests. Similar findings were reported by Goodenough and Karp (1961), Kagan, Moss, and Sigel (1970), and Rameriz (1973) for analytically oriented individuals. Scores for field-independent and analytical individuals were better when the tests required perceptual differentiation.

In the examination of performance on tests involving Cohen's (1959) Factor II, no differences between the perceptually differentiated and perceptually diffuse individuals were found, particularly on the Digit Span subtest (Goodenough, 1976; Robinson & Bennink, 1978). In his review of studies demonstrating the relationship between learning and memory and field articulation, Goodenough (1976) concluded that field-independent individuals are no better than field-dependent individuals at associative learning as found in paired-associate, digit memory, or serial-rote learning tasks. Robinson and Bennink

(1978) examined this same relationship and found that while field-independent individuals tended to process the information more efficiently, there was no difference in the two perceptual problem-solving strategies when comparing actual performance on a memory test. Thus it appears that while the differentiated perceptual style is required in spatially oriented tasks, in general, this style seems to have little relationship to performance in attention-concentration tasks.

## Cultural Style and Learning

It appears that the issue of performance concerns a multifaceted processing strategy, not just one dimension. Therefore, we are concerned with *cognitive style*. It seems very possible that the differences in performance that relate to the school context and that continue to be found are the result of a culturally induced difference in Afro-American cognitive or perceptual style preference that emphasizes a *person* rather than an *object* orientation. Although this style is probably of tremendous advantage in social and interpersonal situations, it may be antithetical to school success. In fact, Kogan (1971) points out that "one might in fact legitimately claim that a cognitive style which facilitates fine articulation and sensitivity to social situations is for many purposes more highly adaptive than a style contributing to a better articulation of the physical setting" (p. 253). If this assumption is correct, the modifiability of the style as emphasized by Kogan (1971) would not be the focus of educational change. Instead, some efforts might be made as suggested by Cureton (this volume) and Slaughter (1969) to change the instructional methods used with Afro-American children and teach to this culturally induced style. However, would this make a difference in school success?

Bloom (1976) points out in his examination of the individual characteristics that affect school learning that every learner brings to the task a prior history of learning. This experiential background sets the stage for how well the student is able to learn from adults and under what conditions, the work habits to be used in the tasks, the attention to be paid to task demands, and a set of likes or dislikes about school, subjects, people, ideas, or other items that might be included in the school program. For Afro-American learners, these entry characteristics seem to consist of a preference for people-oriented situations and for spontaneous and novel stimuli and situations, an ability to understand nonverbal communication, and a highly affective orientation toward ideas, things, situations, and individuals (Akbar, 1978; Hale, 1981).

Rychlak and many of his students examined the influence of what many call affective entry characteristics to determine how these characteristics affect verbal learning, in particular, and performance on intelligence and personality tests. In the early studies of affective factors and learning using elementary and college students Rychlak (1975, 1981) and Rychlak, Hewitt, and Hewitt (1973) found that Afro-Americans were more likely to learn and remember trigrams for which they had expressed a positive preference; for Euro-American students, this affective assessment had no effect. This finding was not present in a study by August and Felker (1977) when self-concept was entered as a variable. In this study of fifth graders stratified by race and class, Euro-American students recalled liked words better than the Afro-Americans; in fact, Afro-American children with a high self-concept recalled more disliked words. Unfortunately, no real conclusion can be drawn from this inconsistency because the task used in the studies was changed. We find again, as did Simmons (1979) and Franklin (1979), that the task and situation seem to affect the stylistic preferences that emerge. In spite of this difficulty, Rychlak (1981) presented as part of his logical learning theory a proposition that affection is a specific factor in learning and enters not only into verbal learning but also into performance on intelligence and personality tests.

As one examines other studies in search of the relationship between stylistic preferences and learning, it becomes difficult to dismiss the importance of this interaction by merely indicating difficulty with the measuring instruments. Silverstein and Krate (1975), for example, examined students in a central Harlem, Manhattan, school, and found that they could classify over half those students as "ambivalents." The primary characteristics of ambivalent students were that they needed, and rather aggressively sought, teacher attention, nurturance, and acceptance. When this was not given, or not granted in sufficient quantity, the children became frustrated and angry or disruptive. The authors saw the students as needing constant encouragement, recognition, warmth, and reassurance in order for them to continue participating in the schooling process.

A similar situation was noted by St. John (1971) in an ethnographic study of teacher effects on achievement. After several analyses of the data, it became very evident that Afro-American children demonstrated improved conduct, higher attendance records, and a belief in the teacher if taught by a child-oriented teacher. Characteristics of a child-oriented teacher included a demonstration of kindliness, optimism, understanding, adaptability, and general warmth. The traits seemed to be those of a more affectively oriented teacher rather than a task-oriented instructor.

Although Cureton (this volume) identifies this as a learning-style preference for action-oriented teaching, this need for interpersonal contact seems to underlie the approach described in this essay about teachers who are able to increase the reading achievement of Afro-American students. Again, the author describes an intense, group, rather interpersonal approach, which differs significantly from the traditional individually oriented, seatwork, quiet-room teaching usually advocated. It thus seems that the group consciousness, cooperative, sociocentric, and affective orientation that seems to underlie Afro-American culture has an effect on learning the presented material.

Unlike the deficit theory approaches, which blame the victim for lack of success, the focus of a stylistic approach to learning requires the identification of diversity within the educational setting. This suggests that indeed all children are not alike, cannot be treated in the same manner, or exposed to the same instructional methodologies. It does, however, assume that all children probably can learn the same content and information if we are willing to fit it to their particular cognitive and affective behaviors.

To identify differences related to Afro-Americans is, of course, a controversial issue; regardless of the disclaimers, values of good or bad, inferior or superior, are so ingrained in our society that the issue will still lead to reinforcement of stereotypes. In fact, as we examine this issue even more closely, it could very well lead again to the nature-nurture issue assuming a major portion of the discussion. However, if we are to engage in an educational revolution aimed at promoting the success of a larger percentage of the Afro-American population, it is an area that must be explored.

## Conclusion

In a society where access to social goods seems to be highly dependent on a high rating within the educational arena, it becomes impossible to ignore the continued presence of a large percentage of Afro-Americans in the lower end of the success continuum. If one adheres to the philosophy of inferiority, then this pattern is of little concern. However, when one accepts the premise that Afro-Americans have the same potential as other groups, it is necessary to question the reason for this continued phenomenon.

As the area of cognitive psychology and the study of individual differences promotes new perspectives, it becomes evident that individuals may not learn in the same manner and may in fact develop rather diverse cognitive strategies for processing information. Examination of this possibility further suggests that each situation may promote the need for certain types of strategies or styles and those individuals who fail to acquire the preferred styles end up in difficulty. A review of the literature suggests that successful functioning within the current school context requires cognitive strategies that are described as sequential, analytical, or object oriented. An examination of the culture or lifestyle and worldview of Afro-Americans, however, portrays strategies designed to foster survival and, therefore, tends to be rather universalistic, intuitive, and, more than that, very person oriented. It is postulated that an enhanced ability in social cognition may work to the detriment of individuals within an object-oriented setting such as the school. To verify these assumptions requires strong and methodologically rigid empirical studies.

## Note

This paper was funded by the Wisconsin Research and Development Center, University of Wisconsin-Madison, which is supported in part by a grant from the National Institute of Education (Grant No. NIE-G-81-0009). The opinions expressed in this paper do not necessarily reflect the position, policy, or endorsement of the National Institute of Education.

## REFERENCES

Aiello, J.R., & Jones, S.E. (1971). Field study of the proxemic behavior of young school children in three subcultural groups. *Journal of Personality & Social Psychology, 19*(3), 351–356.

Akbar, N. (1978). *Cultural expressions of the African American child.* San Francisco: Black Child Development Institute. (ERIC Document Reproduction Service No. ED179633)

Aschenbrenner, J. (1973). Extended families among Black Americans. *Journal of Comparative Family Studies, 4,* 257–268.

August, G.J., & Felker, D.W. (1977). Role of affective meaningfulness and self-concept in the verbal learning styles of White and Black children. *Journal of Educational Psychology, 69*(3), 253–260.

Barclay, A., & Cusumano, D.R. (1967). Father absence, cross-sex identity and field-dependent behavior in male adolescents. *Child Development, 38,* 243–250.

Barry, H., Child, I., & Bacon, M. (1959). Relation of child training to subsistence economy. *American Anthropologist, 61,* 51–63.

Battle, E.S., & Rotter, J. (1963). Children's feelings of personal control as related to social class and ethnic group. *Journal of Personality, 31,* 482–490.

Bauer, E. (1973). Personal space: A study of Blacks and Whites. *Sociometry, 36,* 402–408.

Baxter, J.C. (1970). Interpersonal spacing in natural settings. *Sociometry, 33,* 444–456.

Berman, J.J. (1976). Parolees' perception of the justice system: Black White differences. *Criminology, 13,* 507–520.

Berry, J.W. (1976). *Human ecology and cognitive style: Comparative studies in cultural and psychological adaptation.* New York: Halstead Press.

Birnback, S. (1972). *Motivation, cognitive style, and attitude change: An investigation of the relationship between external motivation, non-external motivation, field dependence-independence, sex, and attitude change.* Unpublished doctoral dissertation, New York University.

Bloom, B.S. (1976). *Human characteristics and school learning.* New York: McGraw Hill.

Boykin, A.W. (1979). Psychological/behavioral verve: Some theoretical explorations and empirical manifestations. In A.W. Boykin, A.J. Franklin, & J.F. Yates (Eds.), Research directions of Black psychologists. New York: Russell Sage Foundation.

Bridgeman, B., & Buttram, J. (1975). Race differences on nonverbal analogy test performances as a function of verbal strategy training. *Journal of Educational Psychology, 67*(4), 586–590.

Bruner, J.S., Olver, R.R., & Greenfield, P.M. (1966). *Studies in cognitive growth: A collaboration at the Center for Cognitive Studies.* New York: Wiley.

Burnes, K. (1970). Patterns of WISC scores for children of two socioeconomic classes and races. *Child Development, 41,* 493–499.

Busse, T. (1968). Establishment of flexible thinking factor in fifth grade boys. *Journal of Psychology, 69,* 93–100.

Carlson, J.S. (1971). Some relationships between class inclusion, perceptual capabilities, verbal capabilities, and race. *Human Development, 14*(1), 30–38.

Carpenter, G.C., Tecce, J., Stechler, G., & Friedman, S. (1970). Differential visual behavior to human and humanoid faces in early infancy. *Merrill Palmer Quarterly: Journal of Developmental Psychology, 16*(1), 91–108.

Chance, J., Goldstein, A., & McBride, L. (1975). Differential experience and recognition memory for faces. *Journal of Social Psychology, 97,* 243–253.

Chepp, T. (1975). *The relationship of cognitive style to the attainment of success among selected disadvantaged, young adult Black males.* Unpublished dissertation, Catholic University of America, Washington, DC.

Cohen, J. (1957). Factorial structure of WAIS. *Journal of Consulting Psychology, 21,* 283–290.

Cohen, J. (1959). The factorial structure of the WISC. *Journal of Consulting Psychology, 23,* 285–299.

Cohen, R. (1969). Conceptual styles, culture conflict and nonverbal tests of intelligence. *American Anthropologist, 71,* 828–856.

Cohen, Y. (1974). Culture as adaptation. In Y.A. Cohen (Ed.), *Man in adaptation: The cultural present* (2nd ed.). Chicago: Aldine.

Cole, M., & Scribner, S. (1974). *Culture and thought: A psychological introduction.* New York: Wiley.

Cole, S., & Hunter, M. (1971). Pattern analysis of WISC scores achieved by culturally disadvantaged children. *Psychological Reports, 29*(1), 191–194.

Connally, P.R. (1974). *An investigation of the perception of personal space and its meaning among Black and White Americans.* Unpublished doctoral dissertation, University of Iowa, Iowa City.

Coop, R.H., & Sigel, I.E. (1971). Cognitive style: Implications for learning and instruction. *Psychology in the Schools, 8*(2), 152–161.

Davidson, K.S. (1950). A preliminary study of Negro and White differences on form I of the Wechsler-Bellevue Scale. *Journal of Consulting Psychology, 6,* 489–492.

DuCette, J., & Wolk, S. (1972). Locus of control and levels of aspiration in Black and White children. *Review of Educational Research, 42,* 493–504.

Duncan, B. (1978). The development of spatial behavior norms in Black and White primary school children. *Journal of Black Psychology, 5,* 33–41.

Elkind, D., & Deblinger, J. (1969). Perceptual training and reading achievement in disadvantaged children. *Child Development, 40,* 11–19.

Farnham-Diggory, S. (1970). Cognitive synthesis in Negro and White children. *Monographs of Society for Research in Child Development, 35*(2), 84.

Ferrell, J.G. (1971). *The differential performance of lower class, preschool, Negro children as a function of the sex of E, sex of S, reinforcement condition, and level of field dependence.* Unpublished dissertation, University of Southern Mississippi, Oxford.

Fisher, R.L. (1968). Thinking style and socioeconomic status. *Perceptual and Motor Skills, 26,* 825–826.

Franklin, A.J. (1979). Cultural content of materials and ethnic group performance in categorized recall. In A.W. Boykin, A.J. Franklin, & J.F. Yates (Eds.), *Research directions of Black psychologists.* New York: Russell Sage Foundation.

Galper, R.E. (1973). Functional race membership and recognition of faces. *Perceptual and Motor Skills, 37*, 455–462.

Gamble, J.F. (1971). *Cognitive and linguistic style differences among educationally advantaged and disadvantaged eighth-grade boys.* Unpublished doctoral dissertation, University of Tennessee, Knoxville.

Gibson, E.J. (1969). *Principles of perceptual learning and development.* New York: Appleton-Century-Crofts.

Gill, N.T., Herdtner, T., & Lough, L. (1968). Perceptual and socioeconomic variables, instruction in body orientation and predicted academic success in young children. *Perceptual and Motor Skills, 26*, 1175–1184.

Gitter, A.G., Black, H., & Mostofsy, D. (1972). Race and sex in the perception of emotion. *Journal of Social Issues, 28*(4), 63–78.

Goldstein, K.M., & Blackman, S. (1978). *Cognitive style: Five approaches and relevant research.* New York: Wiley.

Goodenough, D.R. (1976). The role of individual differences in field dependence as a factor in learning and memory. *Psychological Bulletin, 83*(4), 675–694.

Goodenough, D.R., & Karp, S.A. (1961). Field dependence and intellectual functioning. *Journal of Abnormal and Social Psychology, 63*, 241–246.

Guinaugh, B.J. (1971). An experimental study of basic learning ability and intelligence in low socioeconomic-status children. *Child Development, 42*, 27–36.

Gurin, P., & Epps, E. (1975). *Black consciousness, mobility and achievement: A study of students in historically Black colleges.* New York: Wiley.

Gurin, P., Gurin, G., Lao, R., & Beattie, M. (1969). Internal-external control in the motivational dynamics of Negro youth. *Journal of Social Issues, 25*(3), 29–53.

Hale, J. (1981). Black children: Their roots, culture and learning styles. *Young Children, 36*, 37–50.

Hall, E. (1966). *The hidden dimension.* New York: Doubleday.

Halpern, F. (1973). *Survival: Black/White.* New York: Pergamon Press.

Hansley, C., & Busse, T. (1969). Perceptual exploration in Negro children. *Developmental Psychology, 1*, 446.

Harrell, J.P. (1979). Analyzing Black coping styles: A supplemental diagnostic system. *Journal of Black Psychology, 5*, 99–108.

Harrison, A., & Nadelman, L. (1972). Conceptual tempo and inhibition of movement in Black preschool children. *Child Development, 43*(2), 657–668.

Harrison, W.O. (1979). Relationship between cognitive style and selective attention in Black children. In A.W. Boykin, A.J. Franklin, & J.F. Yates (Eds.), *Research directions of Black psychologists.* New York: Russell Sage Foundation.

Harvey, O.J., Hunt, D., & Schroder, H. (1961). *Conceptual systems and personality organization.* New York: Wiley .

Hill, W.H., & Fox, W.M. (1973). Black and White marine squad leaders' perceptions of racially mixed squads. *Academy of Management Journal, 16*, 680–694.

Hilliard, A. (1976). *Alternatives to IQ testing: An approach to the identification of gifted minority children.* Sacramento, CA: California State Department of Education.

Hirschberg, N., Jones, L., Haggerty, M. (1978). What's in a face: Individual differences in face perception. *Journal of Research in Personality, 12*, 488–499.

Jensen, A.R. (1969). How much can we boost IQ and scholastic achievement? *Harvard Educational Review, 39*(1), 1–123.

Jones, E.E. (1978). Black-White personality differences: Another look. *Journal of Personality Assessment, 42*, 244–252.

Jones, S., & Aiello, J. (1973). Proxemic behavior of Black and White first, third, and fifth grade children. *Journal of Personality and Social Psychology, 25*(1), 21–27.

Jones, S.E. (1971). A comparative proxemic analysis of dyadic interaction in selected subcultures of New York City. *Journal of Social Psychology, 84*, 35–44.

Kagan, J. (1966). Reflection-impulsivity: The generality and dynamics of conceptual tempo. *Journal of Abnormal Psychology, 71*, 17–24.

Kagan, J., Moss, H., & Sigel, I. (1970). Psychological significance of styles of conceptualization. In *Cognitive development in children: Five monographs of the Society for Research in Child Development.* Chicago: University of Chicago Press.

Karp, S.A., Silberman, L., & Winters, S. (1969). Psychological differentiation and socioeconomic status. *Perceptual and Motor Skills, 28*, 55–60.

Keil, C. (1966). *Urban blues.* Chicago: University of Chicago Press.

Kelly, G.A. (1955). *The psychology of personal constructs.* New York: Norton.

Kinder, D.R., & Reeder, L.G. (1975). Ethnic differences in beliefs about control. *Sociometry, 38*, 261–272.

Kogan, N. (1971). Educational implications of cognitive styles. In G.S. Lesser (Ed.), *Psychology and educational practice.* Glenview, IL: Scott Foresman.

Kogan, N. (1976). Cognitive styles in infancy and early childhood. Hillsdale, NJ: Erlbaum.

Landis, D., McGrew, P., Day, H., Savage, J., & Saral, T. (1976). Word meanings in Black and White. In H.C. Triandis (Ed.), *Variations in Black and White perceptions of the social environment.* Urbana: University of Illinois Press.

Leifer, A. (1972a). Ethnic patterns in cognitive tasks. *Proceedings of the Annual Convention of the American Psychological Association, 7,* 73–74.

Leifer, A. (1972b). Mosaics of disadvantaged Negro and White preschoolers compared. *Journal of Genetic Psychology, 121*(1), 59–63.

Lesser, G.S., Fifer, G., & Clark, D.H. (1965). Mental abilities of children from different social class and cultural groups (Serial No. 102). *Monographs of the Society for Research in Child Development, 30*(4), 1–115. Chicago: University of Chicago Press.

Levine, L.W. (1977). *Black culture and Black consciousness.* New York: Oxford University Press.

Lewis, M., & Wilson, C. (1972). Infant development in lower class American families. *Human Development, 15*, 112–127.

Liebman, M. (1970). The effects of sex and race norms on personal space. *Environment and Behavior, 2*, 208–246.

Luce, T.S. (1974). The role of experience in interracial recognition. *Personality and Social Psychology Bulletin, 1*, 39–41.

MacAdoo, H. (1977). *The ecology of internal and external support systems of Black families.* Paper presented at the Conference on Research Perspectives in the Ecology of Human Development, Cornell University, Ithaca, NY.

Mandler, J.M., & Stein, N.L. (1977). The myth of perceptual defect: Sources and evidence. *Psychological Bulletin, 84*, 173–192.

Martin, E., & Martin, J.M. (1978). *The Black extended family.* Chicago: University of Chicago Press.

McClain, E.W. (1967). Personality characteristics of Negro college students in the South: A recent appraisal. *Journal of Negro Education, 36*(3), 320–325.

McCord, W., Howard, J., Friedberg, B., & Harwood, E. (1969). *Lifestyles in the Black ghetto.* New York: Norton.

Messer, S.B. (1976). Reflectivity-impulsivity: A review. *Psychological Bulletin, 83*, 1026–1052.

Miller, D.R., & Swanson, G.E. (1958). *The changing American parent: A study in the Detroit area.* New York: Wiley.

Mumbauer, C.C., & Miller, J.O. (1970). Socioeconomic background and cognitive functioning in preschool children. *Child Development, 41*(2), 471–480.

Ogbu, J.U. (1978). *Minority education and caste: The American system in cross-cultural perspective.* New York: Academic Press.

Orasanu, J., Lee, C., & Scribner, S. (1979). Development of category organization and free recall: Ethnic and economic group comparisons. *Child Development, 50*(4), 1100–1109.

Palmer, F.H. (1970). Socioeconomic status and intellective performance among Negro preschool boys. *Developmental Psychology, 3*(2), 1–9.

Perkins, E. (1975). *Home is a dirty street: The social oppression of Black children.* Chicago: Third World Press.

Perney, V.H. (1976). Effects of race and sex on field dependence-independence on children. *Perceptual and Motor Skills, 42,* 975–980.

Petersen, S., & Magaro, P. (1969). Reading and field dependence: A pilot study. *Journal of Reading, 12*(4), 287–294.

Pierce-Jones, J., & King, F.J. (1960). Perceptual differences between Negro and White adolescents of similar symbolic brightness. *Perceptual and Motor Skills, 11,* 191–194.

Rameriz, M., III. (1973). Cognitive styles and cultural democracy in education. *Social Science Quarterly, 53,* 895–904.

Rameriz, M., III, & Price-Williams, D. (1974). Cognitive styles of children of three ethnic groups in the United States. *Journal of Cross-Cultural Psychology, 5*(2), 212–219.

Reiss, E.W. (1972). The influence of race and social class upon the measurement of intelligence, cognitive style, and direct learning ability. Unpublished doctoral dissertation, Ohio State University, Columbus.

Riesman, D. (1950). *The lonely crowd; a study of the changing American character.* New Haven, CT: Yale University Press.

Riley, R.T., & Denmark, F. (1974). Field independence and measures of intelligence: Some reconsiderations. *Social Behavior and Personality, 2,* 25–29.

Ritzinger, F.C. (1971). Psychological and physiological differentiation in children six to eleven years of age. Unpublished doctoral dissertation, Washington University, St. Louis, MO.

Robinson, J.A., & Bennink, C.D. (1978). Field articulation and working memory. *Journal of Research in Personality, 12,* 439–449. (ERIC Document Reproduction Service No. ED174032)

Rohwer, W.D. (1971). Learning, race and school success. *Review of Educational Research, 41*(3), 191–210.

Rokeach, M. (1960). *The open and closed mind: Investigations into the nature of belief systems and personality systems.* New York: Basic Books.

Roll, W.V., Schmidt, L.D., & Kaul, T.J. (1972). Perceived interviewer trustworthiness among Black and White convicts. *Journal of Counseling Psychology, 19*(6), 537–541.

Rychlak, J.F. (1975). Affective assessment, intelligence, social class, and racial learning style. *Journal of Personality and Social Psychology, 32,* 989–995.

Rychlak, J.F. (1981). Logical learning theory: Propositions, corollaries, and research evidence. *Journal of Personality and Social Psychology, 40,* 731–749.

Rychlak, J.F., Hewitt, C.W., & Hewitt, J. (1973). Affective evaluation, word quality and the verbal learning styles of Black versus White junior college females. *Journal of Personality and Social Psychology, 27*(2), 248–255.

Scherer, S. (1974). Proxemic behavior of primary school children as a function of their socioeconomic class and subculture. *Journal of Personality and Social Psychology, 29*(6), 800–805.

Schmultz, T.C. (1975). *The relationship of ethnicity to field-dependence and adjustment.* Unpublished doctoral dissertation, University of Rhode Island, Kingston.

Schratz, M.A. (1976). *Developmental investigation of sex differences in perceptual differentiation and mathematic reasoning in two ethnic groups.* Unpublished doctoral dissertation, Fordham University, New York.

Schwartz, E.N. (1972). *The effect of field dependence-field independence upon the word recognition ability of second grade subjects.* Unpublished doctoral dissertation, Hofstra University, Hempstead, NY.

Scott, J.D., & Phelan, J.G. (1969). Expectancies of unemployable males regarding source of control of reinforcement. *Psychological Reports, 25*(3), 911–913.

Seitz, E.K. (1971). *The relationship between cognitive abilities and impulse control in Project Head Start children.* Unpublished doctoral dissertation, New York University.

Serpell, R. (1976). *Culture's influence on behavior.* London: Methuen.

Shade, B.J. (1978). Social-psychological characteristics of achieving Black children. *Negro Educational Review, 29*(2), 80–86.

Shade, B.J. (1981). Racial variation in perceptual differentiation. *Perceptual and Motor Skills, 52*(1), 243–248.

Shansky, C.R. (1976). *The personality correlates of hypertension and field dependence in Black women.* Unpublished doctoral dissertation, Illinois Institute of Technology, Chicago.

Sigel, I.E., Anderson, L.M., & Shapiro, H. (1966). Perceptual categorization of lower and middle class Negro preschool children. *Journal of Negro Education, 35,* 218–229.

Silverstein, B., & Krate, R. (1975). *Children of the dark ghetto: A developmental psychology.* New York: Praeger.

Simmons, W. (1979). *The role of cultural salience in ethnic and social class differences in cognitive performance.* Unpublished doctoral dissertation, Cornell University, Ithaca, NY.

Slaughter, C.H. (1969). Cognitive style: Some implications for curriculum and instructional practices among Negro children. *Journal of Negro Education, 38,* 105–111.

St. John, N. (1971). Thirty-six teachers: Their characteristics and outcomes for Black and White pupils. *American Educational Research Journal, 8*(4), 635–648.

Stack, C. (1974). *All our kin: Strategies for survival in a Black community.* New York: Harper.

Stodolsky, S., & Lesser, G. (1967). Learning patterns in the disadvantaged. *Harvard Educational Review, 37*(4), 546–593.

Stuart, I.R. (1967). Perceptual style and reading ability: Implications for an instructional approach. *Perceptual and Motor Skills, 24,* 135–138.

Switkin, L.R., & Gynther, M. (1974). Trust, activism and interpersonal perception in Black and White college students. *Journal of Social Psychology, 94*(1), 153–154.

Szalay, L., & Bryson, J.A. (1973). Measurement of psychocultural distance: A comparison of American Blacks and Whites. *Journal of Personality and Social Psychology, 26,* 166–177.

Taylor, J. (1980). Dimensionalization of racialism and the Black experience: The Pittsburgh Project. In R. Jones (Ed.), *Black psychology* (2nd ed.). New York: Harper.

Teahan, J., & Drews, E.M. (1962). A comparison of northern and southern Negro children on the WISC. *Journal of Consulting Psychology, 26,* 292.

Terrell, F., & Barrett, R. (1979). Interpersonal trust among college students as a function of race, sex, and socioeconomic class. *Perceptual and Motor Skills, 48,* 1194.

Triandis, H.C. (Ed.). (1976). *Variations in Black and White perceptions of the social environment.* Urbana: University of Illinois Press.

Vance, H.B., & Hankins, N. (1979). A preliminary study of Black and White differences on the revised Wechsler Intelligence Scale for Children. *Journal of Clinical Psychology, 35*(4), 815–819.

Vinson, A. (1974). An investigation concerning personality characteristics, classroom climate and academic achievement. *Journal of Negro Education, 43,* 334–338.

Wallace, J.G. (1965). *Concept growth and the education of the child.* Slough, Bershire, UK: National Foundation for Educational Research in England and Wales.

White, J.L. (1980). Toward a Black psychology. In R. Jones (Ed.), *Black psychology* (2nd ed.). New York: Harper.

Wilde, J.E. (1973). *A descriptive analysis of children's cognitive styles: Conceptual tempo and preferred mode of perceptual organization and conceptual categorization.* Unpublished doctoral dissertation, Claremont Graduate School, Claremont, CA.

Willis, F., Carlson, R., & Reeves, D. (1979). The development of personal space in primary school children. *Environmental Psychology and Nonverbal Behavior, 3,* 195–204.

Willis, F.N. (1966). Initial speaking distance as a function of the speakers' relationship. *Psychoanalytic Science, 5,* 221–222.

Witkin, H.A. (1964). Origins of cognitive style. In C. Scheerer (Ed.), *Cognition: Theory, research, promise.* New York: Harper.

Witkin, H.A., Dyk, R.B., Paterson, H.F., Goodenough, D.R., & Karp, S.A. (1962). *Psychological differentiation.* New York: Wiley.

Witkin, H.A., & Goodenough, D. (1977). Field dependence and interpersonal behavior. *Psychological Bulletin, 84,* 661–689.

Witkin, H.A., Moore, C.A., Goodenough, D.R., & Cox, P.W. (1977). Field dependent and field independent cognitive styles and their educational implications. *Review of Educational Research, 47,* 1–64.

Wittmer, J., & Ferinden, F. (1970). Perception of school climate: Comparison of Black and White teachers within the same schools. *Journal of the Student Personnel Association for Teacher Education, 9*(1), 1–7.

Wright, N., Jr. (Ed.). (1970). *What Black educators are saying.* New York: Hawthorn Books.

Wright, W. (1975). Relationships of trust and racial perceptions toward therapist-client conditions during counseling. *Journal of Negro Education, 44*(2), 161–169.

Wubberhorst, J., Gradford, S., & Willis, F. (1971). Trust in children as a function of race, sex, and socioeconomic group. *Psychological Reports, 29*(3), 1181–1187.

Yarian, S. (1974). *The comic book hero, a cultural fantasy.* Unpublished doctoral dissertation, Adelphi University, Israel.

Yarrow, L., Rubenstein, J., Peterson, F.A., & Jankowski, J.J. (1971). Dimensions of early stimulation and their differential effects on infant development. *Merrill Palmer Quarterly: Journal of Developmental Psychology, 18,* 205–218.

Young, M.F., & Bright, H.A. (1954). Results of testing 81 Negro rural juveniles with WISC. *Journal of Social Psychology, 39,* 219–226.

Young, V.H. (1970). Family and childhood in a southern Negro community. *American Anthropologist, 72,* 269–288.

Young, V.H. (1974). A Black American socialization pattern. *American Ethnologist, 1,* 405–413.

Zamm, M. (1973). Reading disabilities: A theory of cognitive integration. *Journal of Learning Disabilities, 6*(2), 95–101.

Zimmerman, B., & Brody, G. (1975). Race and modeling influences on the interpersonal play patterns of boys. *Journal of Educational Psychology, 67,* 474–489.

Zucker, J., & Stricker, G. (1968). Impulsivity-reflectivity in preschool Head Start and middle class children. *Journal of Learning Disabilities, 1,* 578–584.

# CHAPTER 17

# Literacy Development in the Primary Grades: Promoting a Self-Sustaining Learning Community Among Teachers

*Etta R. Hollins, Linda R. McIntyre, Charles E. DeBose, Kimberly S. Hollins, and Arthurlene G. Towner*

Teaching is a complex multidimensional process that requires specialized knowledge of the learners, the learning process, pedagogy, and pedagogical content knowledge. Learning to teach is a continuous process that requires reflection on one's own practice, dialogue and collaboration with colleagues, and the acquisition and production of new knowledge about the multidimensional process of teaching. In this discussion we present a review of the literature on professional development for teachers in urban schools and report on research introducing a design for promoting a self-sustaining learning community aimed at supporting teachers in developing the "habits of mind" necessary for improving literacy acquisition and development for urban African American students attending a low-performing, high-poverty elementary school. The underlying assumption is that teachers develop a cognitive schema for their work that must be attended to in order to foster sustainable changes in teaching practices.

The majority of the teachers in the participating school for this study were African American. This shared racial identity should not be taken to mean that they shared a common culture with the children, nor does it mean that in cases where the teachers and the children shared a common culture that the teachers had actualized tacit cultural knowledge to facilitate classroom learning. The teachers in this study were the products of traditional teacher education programs. In these programs, prospective teachers are taught about culture, but not necessarily how to apply knowledge of culture in the teaching process; and rarely are they taught to apply their own cultural knowledge in teaching children with whom they share a common culture. In this study we employed an internal model with a five-step inquiry process that supports teachers in reflecting on their own practices and collaborating with colleagues to identify and implement new approaches to meet the challenges they face in their classrooms. Over the course of two years, there is evidence that the teachers in our study were empowered to reflect publicly on their own practice, learn from their observations of children, and learn from one another. Furthermore, there is evidence that the African American teachers in our study were empowered to draw upon their own cultural knowledge to better understand the African American children they teach.

The aim of the study was to investigate an approach to developing a self-sustaining learning community that will enable teachers to foster high academic achievement in literacy for African American students in kindergarten through fourth grade. A self-sustaining learning community is one in which teachers engage in ongoing teacher-directed collaboration focused on improving classroom practices. Based on our review of the literature, the approach in this study appears to be unique in that it is focused on developing a self-sustaining learning community that involves changing teachers' habits of mind or how they think about conducting their work, rather than focusing on behaviors and pedagogical knowledge or pedagogical content knowledge.

## Review of the Literature

This review of the literature describes studies of professional development programs that focus on methods for addressing the needs of inner-city teachers and learners.

A search was conducted for journal articles published from 1990 to 2001 with the descriptors "inservice teacher education and urban education," using several databases, including the Education Resources Information Center (ERIC), Social Sciences Abstracts, Sociological Abstracts, and PsycInfo. The 49 articles that resulted from the search were then reviewed to confirm that they included a discussion of an urban inservice teacher training program, delineated the specific outcomes of the program, described the context of the study, and provided a discussion of the content and process of the approach. Of the 49 articles reviewed, only 7 met all four criteria.

The seven identified articles can be grouped into three categories: (1) first-year teacher support programs, (2) subject-specific programs, and (3) teacher collaboration programs. The research on first-year teacher support programs investigates methods for improving teacher effectiveness, teacher attitudes, and teacher retention rates. The research on subject-specific programs investigates methods for improving teachers' ability and willingness to teach specific subject matter. The research on teacher collaboration programs investigates self-reflection and cross-visitation as methods of improving teaching and learning.

## First-Year Teacher Support Programs

Several of the research studies described various approaches to inservice teacher education that focused on creating induction programs to provide first-year teachers with the skills, attitudes, and behaviors essential for survival in urban multicultural settings (Smith 1989/1990); developing practices that will sustain teachers beyond the first year (Murphy, Colvin, & Morey 1990); and creating peer support and collegiality—all opportunities to promote a successful first-year teaching experience and improve teacher retention rates, especially among minority teachers in urban settings.

According to Smith (1989/1990), first-year induction programs can be used to effectively recruit, support, and retain first-year minority teachers in an urban multicultural setting. An evaluative questionnaire, designed by the Public Education Association, with both structured and open-ended questions and informal interviews, was used to determine the first-year teachers' and interns' attitudes toward the induction program. First-year teachers highly valued the mentor conferences, reciprocal classroom visits, and faculty support. They reported feeling that it made a difference in their attitudes toward teaching. In September 1986, 32 first-year teachers (22 of them "Black or Hispanic" [p. 45]) entered the first-year induction program in Community School District 4 in East Harlem, New York. Of this group, 30 returned in both September 1987 and September 1988. This multifaceted first-year induction model was highly effective at supporting and retaining first-year teachers in an inner-city school district.

Murphy, Colvin, and Morey (1990) report that new teachers can be trained to become thoughtful practitioners capable of engaging in reflective thought about their classroom experiences. Researchers analyzed 190 critical incident summaries written by 25 new teachers over a nine-month period during the 1988–1989 school year. During the first semester of the program, the researchers found that 40% of the critical incidents focused on teaching successes whereas 60% focused on problems. These numbers improved during the second semester when 46% focused on teaching successes whereas 54% focused on problems. When the new teachers' critical incident summaries were classified according to Donald A. Schon's (1987) categories of reflective practice, 97% were descriptive, 88% were analytical, 36% identified alternative strategies, and 23% were evaluative. Murphy et al. conclude that writing critical incident summaries and case reports, along with an individualized professional development plan, classroom observations, seminars, and workshops can effectively promote thoughtful reflection by first-year teachers.

## Subject-Specific Programs

The challenge of how to improve teaching and learning in inner-city schools has been approached from many different perspectives. Several studies and reports have shown that teacher development efforts focused on particular curriculum content can improve teachers' willingness and ability to teach specific subject matter (Hausman & Ruzek, 1995) and improve student learning outcomes (Allen & Lederman, 1998; Villasenor & Kepner, 1993). Programs designed to train teachers to effectively teach specific subject matter can be extensive and require a substantial time commitment. Programs range from weeklong workshops to 200 hours of training. Many of the programs require large staff and ample budgeting. The program design ranges from simple workshop-based approaches to highly structured teaching academies designed to train teachers to teach a single subject.

**WORKSHOPS.** Villasenor and Kepner (1993) describe a study of students in a large midwestern U.S. urban school district that uses a weeklong workshop followed by a review session and two support sessions to introduce teachers to Cognitively Guided Instruction (CGI) principles and related research. In this study the CGI teachers outperformed the non–CGI teachers on every measure. Eighty-two classroom observations were conducted in experimental and comparison classrooms to analyze the teacher's instruction methods. CGI teachers applied a mix of whole-group, medium-group, and small-group instruction; communicated frequently with the students, consistently asked them to explain the processes used to arrive at a particular result; and did not use skills worksheets as a learning tool. Non–CGI teachers were observed explaining, demonstrating, and providing examples. They did not ask students to explain how they solved a problem, and students spent 50 to 70% of their time working alone on skills worksheets. The CGI students outperformed the non–CGI students in their ability to solve word problems and recall number facts.

Hausman and Ruzek (1995) describe a three-year teacher development program that incorporated five training periods, workshops, special training sessions, on-site specialists, a resource center, and community involvement to improve health education. Interviews, surveys, and participant observations were used to determine the effect of the health education training program on teachers' perceived willingness to teach the health curricula and to determine the relationship between feelings of preparedness and actual teaching practices. Hausman and Ruzek found "a positive significant relationship" (p. 85) between reported feelings of preparedness and willingness to teach the health curricula. Teachers reported teaching more health lessons after participating in the program. They also found a positive, significant relationship between teachers' feeling of preparedness and their willingness to teach sensitive subjects. "The more comfortable teachers felt, the more sensitive subjects they reported having taught" (p. 85). Teachers who participated in this subject-specific training program reported that they became more willing to teach sensitive health education subjects and taught them more often.

**TEACHERS ACADEMIES.** Allen and Lederman (1998) described a program that provided instruction and support for teachers in mathematics and science, as well as training for leadership development teams and teams of parents and community members. Over a three- to four-year period, teachers participate in 160 to 190 hours of guided instruction in mathematics and science, 10 hours of individualized implementation support, and 40 hours of collaborative curriculum planning. They also received 20 hours of technology planning per year for three years and up to 60 additional hours of optional technology classes were available. Leadership development teams, composed of the principal, three teachers, and two parents, received 190 hours of professional development in the first year and another 200 hours over the next two years. Teams of parents and community members practiced leadership development skills for 90 hours the first year and for 65 to 70 hours in each of the next two years. There were also annual parent institutes. These researchers found marked improvement in third- and sixth-grade students' performance in mathematics on standardized tests.

## Teacher Collaboration Programs

Several studies on improving teacher performance have focused on teacher-dependent rather than external expert-dependent approaches to teacher development. These methods of teacher development include various approaches to teacher collaboration (Lytle & Fecho, 1991) and self-inquiry (Lewison, 1999). The approaches range from using self-reflective writing and study groups at a single school to using institute-trained teacher consultants to promote collaboration across entire school districts. Two articles describing studies on teacher collaboration met the requirements for inclusion in this review of the literature.

They presented data on the effectiveness of cross-visitation and self-reflective journal writing to improve teaching and learning.

**SELF-REFLECTION.**  Lewison (1999) described a yearlong inquiry project that included attending study group meetings, reading theoretical articles, and keeping professional journals as a way to improve the teaching of writing at the elementary level. Lewison found that although the teachers did not value the journal writing activity and their participation was limited, 7 of the 13 teachers "found many positive aspects to journal writing" (p. 523). One teacher reported that she found journal writing cathartic and enjoyable. Another teacher found journal writing a useful tool for applying what she had read in articles to her lesson plans. A third found that her resistance to journal writing increased her empathy for students who had difficulty with journal writing, and she adjusted her teaching methods to address this issue.

**CROSS-VISITATION.**  Lytle and Fecho (1991) described a teacher collaboration program that included teacher training in intensive summer institutes, participation in monthly support meetings, and class visitation once or twice a month. This cross-visitation project is designed to decrease teacher isolation by encouraging teacher collaboration on language, literacy, and learning within schools and throughout school districts.

Lytle and Fecho (1991) analyzed data from 14 extensive interviews with the teacher consultants, as well as project-related writings, including essays in project publications and summer institute applications. In response to their inquiry about what teacher consultants were learning by implementing a cross-visitation program in a large urban school district, three themes emerged: (1) benefits and risks of leaving their classrooms to visit other teachers' classrooms; (2) problems associated with other teachers and administrators casting them in the role of expert, rather than collaborator; and (3) logistical obstacles to implementing districtwide collaboration. These researchers found that teacher collaboration through districtwide cross-visitation can alleviate teacher isolation, resulting in a change in teachers' attitudes and increased enthusiasm for teaching, but participants must overcome various obstacles.

## Summary of Literature Review

Each of these seven studies reported a professional development approach that was labeled *successful.* They provided data that gave evidence of teacher change, increased teacher retention rates, and/or student improvement. Five of the seven studies in this literature review reported a change in teacher attitudes, perceptions, or skills. Two of these studies were designed to support first-year teachers and, as a result, increase first-year retention rates. According to Speck and Knipe (2001), "successful professional development must focus on conditions for improving student learning and achievement. Student success is the ultimate aim and outcome of well-planned professional development" (p. 8). (See also Guskey, 2000; Joyce & Showers, 1995.) Only two of the seven studies in this review of the literature reported an effect on student achievement. Both studies fall into the subject-specific programs category. It is not clear whether either of these studies resulted in teachers' ability to sustain learning outcomes over a significant period of time.

# Rationale for This Study

The findings from this literature review and published reports on the academic performance of African American students suggest the need for additional studies of professional development approaches designed to enhance teachers' ability to improve the academic performance of urban students, to sustain the learning gains over time, and to participate in collaboration among colleagues. According to Moats (1999) in a paper titled *Teaching Reading is Rocket Science* published by the American Federation of Teachers, 60 to 70% of African American and Mexican American students in public schools are poor readers. The report further points out that 30% of poor readers are from college-educated families. The National Assessment of Educational Progress (NAEP, 2000) report on fourth-grade reading achievement by race/ethnicity, 1992–2000, shows that the percentage of African American students at or above the basic level was 33% in 1992, 31% in 1994, 36% in 1998, and 37% in 2000. In comparison, the percentage of white students performing at or above the basic level was 71% in 1992, 71% in 1994, 73% in 1998, and 73% in 2000. The reading achievement gap between African American and white students has remained relatively constant over the nine-year period.

In contrast to these reports of low academic performance for African American students, there are reports of high performing, high poverty, urban schools (see Jerald, 2001; Johnson & Asera, 1999). Additionally, researchers have identified the practices of teachers believed to be successful with low-income African American students (Foster, 1997; Ladson-Billings, 1994). These teaching practices need further study to determine the specific link to African American students' academic performance. There is a need to develop an approach to professional development that will assist teachers in identifying and recognizing productive practices for facilitating literacy development for African American children. The African American Literacy and Culture Research Project was an effort towards this end.

# The African American Literacy
# and Culture Research Project

The African American Literacy and Culture Research Project was a three-year study that evolved from collaboration between a local university and a large urban school district. The study investigated (a) approaches to professional development designed to enhance teachers' ability to facilitate literacy acquisition and development for African American children, (b) the use of instructional materials that build upon and extend African American children's language usage to facilitate literacy acquisition and development, and (c) a parent involvement model to support African American children's literacy development. This discussion will address one aspect of the African American Literacy and Culture Research Project, the internal, professional development model designed to enhance teachers' ability to facilitate literacy acquisition and development for urban African American children.

## *Research Setting*

Phyllis Wheatley Elementary School, the participating school in this research study, is located in a large urban school district in California. The Center City School District is nestled within a large community with over 300,000 residents. The school district consists of more than 50,000 students and 2,600 teachers and instructional assistants in 94 schools. African Americans are the majority of the people of color in the Center City School District. The demographic profile of the Phyllis Wheatley School is similar to that of the district. Of the approximately 300 students enrolled in kindergarten through fifth grade, 91% were African American. The school is situated within a predominantly working class community. Most of the students enrolled in the school were from the immediate community. Others were within two blocks of a Center City bus stop. During the 1998–1999 school year, the Phyllis Wheatley School had 15 classroom teachers: 9 African American females, 3 African American males, 2 European American females, 1 European American male, and an African American female principal.

The Phyllis Wheatley Elementary School, like other urban schools, is characterized by ongoing changes. For example, during the 1997–1998 school year, Wheatley's teaching staff was 50% African American, 36% European American, and 14% Asian. During the 1998–1999 school year, 80% of the teachers were African American. In contrast, the percentage of African American students remained at 91%, and Asians, Hispanics, and European Americans made up 9% of the school's student population.

The increase of African American teachers in situations where African American students are the majority may be expected by some educators and scholars to have a positive influence on learning because of a shared cultural and experiential background. But sharing the same racial identity does not necessarily mean sharing the same culture. Where African American children and teachers share the same culture, the teachers bring to the context of the school cultural knowledge they have acquired through their own early socialization that has the potential for providing an advantage for the children's learning. However, the use of this knowledge is not cultivated in most teacher preparation programs, and many African American teachers have not yet learned how to link their cultural knowledge and pedagogical practices to facilitate learning for children from their own culture.

## Description of Methodology

**PARTICIPANTS.** The participants for this study were selected on the basis of their location in an urban elementary school serving predominantly underachieving African American students in kindergarten through the fourth grade. The participating school was viewed as representative of urban elementary schools serving similar populations based on comparable standardized test scores and other demographic characteristics. The principal and teachers within the selected schools were invited to be participants in the study; however, participation was not mandatory or required. All individuals, the school, the school district, and the city in the study were assigned pseudonyms to maintain anonymity.

The participants in this study were 12 teachers in kindergarten through fourth grade. Among these teachers were 10 African Americans and 2 European Americans, of whom 9 were women and 3 men. Two teachers held emergency credentials. Class size was approximately 20 children, of whom approximately 90% were African American.

**QUALITATIVE METHODS.** The research methodology in this study was primarily qualitative, with quantitative data used as one indication of impact on students' academic performance. The qualitative data collection included interviews, tape recordings, field notes, and informal conversations. The researchers involved in this study have had extensive experiences within urban settings and within the African American culture. Thus, the researchers bring to the study a "phenomenological sensibility" and a "concern for constitutive social practice" that is consistent with an ethnomethodological approach (Denzin & Lincoln, 1998, p. 11). This better positioned the researchers to participate in the process, facilitate study groups, and document the actions and dialogue of the participants.

Qualitative procedures were employed to gather and analyze the data. Dialogue during the study group sessions was recorded, transcribed, and analyzed for emerging themes; field notes were analyzed to complement and substantiate the observations and discussions; and interviews added a third source of data for comparing, contrasting, and confirming the results of the analysis. The triangulation of data from these sources supported the findings in this study.

**QUANTITATIVE DATA.** Quantitative data were used as one measure of the impact of the intervention procedure on learning outcomes for students. The quantitative data for this study included performance on the Stanford Achievement Test, 9th edition (1996). Test scores from spring 1998 served as baseline data for comparing gains in the subsequent two years. The percentages of students testing at the 25th, 50th, and 75th percentile on the Stanford Achievement Test in reading/language arts at the selected schools were compared to district averages as a means of determining progress.

## Intervention Procedure

The primary goal in the study of the internal model for teacher development was to investigate the potential of a structured dialogue study-group problem-solving approach, where teachers rely on collaboration and within-group directed inquiry for consistently improving literacy acquisition and development among urban African American children, and the potential usefulness of this approach for developing a self-sustaining learning community. The structured dialogue approach in this study was a five-step process where teachers engaged in (1) delineating challenges, (2) identifying approaches for meeting challenges, (3) implementing selected approaches, (4) evaluating implementation, and (5) formulating theory to guide future practices. Positive indications for the potential usefulness of the internal teacher development model is the documentation of changes in teachers' habits of mind or how they think about their work with urban children, and improvement in the children's academic performance in reading acquisition and development. An indication of the sustainability of this model is the emergence of leadership from within the group.

The steps in the process are designed for completion over several meetings. For example, at the first meeting, teachers identified challenges and specified those over which they have influence or control and shared successes at meeting some of the challenges. At the next meeting, teachers continued with the next step in the process, identifying approaches for meeting the challenges. In the first year of the project, a graduate student served as a facilitator for the study group meetings, which were held biweekly. During the study group meetings, the facilitator's role was to encourage the group to maintain focus by restating the topic under discussion, raising a question for clarification, summarizing major points or accomplishments, or describing the next steps necessary in the process. The same graduate student documented the discussion at study group meetings and conducted classroom observations.

## Results

The structured dialogue approach used as a format for study group meetings is reflected in the categories used in our analysis of the data. These categories included (1) delineation of the challenges the teachers faced in their teaching, (2) identification and implementation of a new approach to meet the challenges, (3) evaluation of the new approach, (4) role transmutation, and (5) continuous dialogue on successful approaches. Three of the categories appear in our analysis of both years of the study. The remaining categories only appear in the second year of the study. The powerful influence of the structured dialogue format is supported in field notes and interviews with the participants.

## First-Year Study Group Meetings

**DELINEATION OF CHALLENGES.** At the first study group meeting, the teachers identified multiple challenges to improving African American children's literacy acquisition and development. Generally, teachers were concerned with students' academic achievement and behavior, the curriculum content and lesson planning, parent involvement, leadership and management of the school, and multiple competing demands on their time. They prioritized their concerns and shared their own experiences in meeting the challenges they identified. For example, a third-grade teacher used his gardening experience to engage students in reading and writing activities. Students planted and harvested a garden and documented the process as part of their writing experience. Also, the students read about plants and gardening. This teacher felt the gardening experience enriched the students' learning and improved their academic performance.

Another third-grade teacher observed the importance of student collaboration: "What's really positive for me is when the students work together and help each other." The teacher created a math game in which several students collaborated to complete math-related challenges. The students were able to complete the game successfully and explain their strategy to other students in the class.

During the discussion of their own successes, some teachers recognized the need for additional information about their students in order to understand how to meet the students' needs. They believed knowledge of test scores, suspension rates, parental information, learning propensities, and values and perceptions would enable them to incorporate students' background knowledge into the curriculum. Some teachers requested scholarly articles on urban children's cultural and academic development for this purpose.

Over the next four study group meetings, teachers analyzed and discussed the information gathered. Initially, during these complex discussions, teachers vacillated between accepting research and presenting arguments rejecting the research findings. At times, the teachers appeared uncomfortable with alternative explanations for students' behavior and learning outcomes. Several times this led to blaming the parents for the children's poor performance. One teacher reported an account of a school in New York:

> The population of the school is representative of a lot of inner-city schools.... It was about 98% African American.... Because they had the lowest test scores in the state of New York, one of the things they did...[was] parents had to come in and...receive workshops on what happened at the school. They were shown how to instruct their children...to come to school with the very basics. Parents were required to do that.

The principal attended the study group sessions and occasionally helped refocus the teachers when they began to digress from the purpose of the sessions: improving African American students' literacy. In this instance, she described a speaker at a recent workshop who argued that if teachers would implement the many methods suggested for improving students' learning, they would achieve positive results. This refocused the teachers on the information they needed to improve their understanding about how to raise students' academic performance. The teachers seemed more willing to accept published research during the fourth study group meeting. There was a very meaningful discussion of a scholarly journal article (Gilmore, 1985) that appeared to help teachers recognize the relationship between cultural practices and effective teaching strategies. The dialogue involved a discussion of a school in which African American children were not allowed to participate in an Academics Plus Program because of an "attitude" they were perceived to display when participating in practices associated with their culture. Gilmore described one example of a game that African American children played on the schoolyard that was characterized by rituals with stylized movements accompanied by rhythmic chants. Some European American teachers viewed this game as sexually suggestive and inappropriate. Children were discouraged from playing the game. Those who persisted were denied admission to the Academics Plus Program.

Initially, the teachers in the study group disagreed on the issues in the Gilmore article. After different perspectives were shared, a consensus seemed to emerge that children should not be punished for bringing cultural rituals to school. Some teachers began to discuss the potential value of incorporating cultural practices into instruction. One teacher shared that her students had taken a poem from the classroom and created a dance in a fashion similar to students in Gilmore's study: "They had a caller and she would do the lead and the other girls would follow. She would spell something out...they were all learning...the ones that didn't learn, they would mock the leader." This was consistent with what the author referred to as a literacy behavior. Adding poetry to dance incorporates literacy. Gilmore suggested that African American children's games employing poetry and dance are cultural tools that can be used for teaching and learning.

One teacher questioned whether this cultural behavior was appropriate for the classroom. Another teacher responded, "When do you cut off behaviors that children learn in their culture and deny them access to literacy because of the way that they behave out of their culture?" In addition, this teacher questioned who should make decisions that determine what is culturally appropriate and what standards should be used. Although this discussion appeared to bring new insight to the teachers, it did not lead to a formal progression to the next step of selecting an approach for implementation.

The teachers continued to explore the link between cultural practices and effective teaching strategies over several study group sessions. At one meeting the teachers discussed Michaels's (1981) article describing an African American narrative style (topic associated) as compared to a European American narrative style (topic centered). The teachers were unfamiliar with this way of thinking about approaches to storytelling and had difficulty conceptualizing the logic of the topic-associated narrative style.

**IDENTIFICATION AND IMPLEMENTATION OF A NEW APPROACH.** After exploring culture and the role it plays in effective teaching strategies, the teachers began to focus on identifying and implementing an approach to some of the challenges they identified during the earlier study group sessions. At the 10th meeting, the teachers began to design an approach to language arts instruction that involved letter writing, a poetry project, and class books, which employed the writing process. The dialogue was rich and positive during this planning process. There was discussion of the values that could be taught through the writing process, as well as form and function. The teachers decided to integrate certain values into their language arts instruction. They agreed to implement a new writing project beginning with the principal of honesty.

The implementation of the writing project was in competition with multiple demands on the teachers' time, including preparing the students for and administering the Stanford Achievement Test, which was an especially high priority for Wheatley School because of its status as a low performing school. In spite of time limitations, the teachers were able to implement the project, although not as completely as they had anticipated.

**EVALUATION OF THE NEW APPROACH'S IMPLEMENTATION.** Evaluation of the implementation of the approach was informal. Teachers discussed the strategies they used to implement the project. According to the teachers, the students' responses to the project were positive. The activities in the project appear very commonplace for teaching language arts; however, teachers seemed to glean support from each other during the implementation process and occasionally provided suggestions for strategies to facilitate students' learning.

## Second-Year Study Group Meetings

In the second year of the study, there was a new study group facilitator. With the new facilitator, the first meeting consisted of a review of the goals and procedures for the study group. The principal and teachers expressed their concerns about not accomplishing all of their goals during the first year's study group meetings. The teachers were reassured that they were empowered to determine the direction of the discussions in ways that would help meet their goals and improve classroom practices.

**ROLE TRANSMUTATION.** During the third meeting, much of the facilitation role was assumed by the principal, and the facilitator settled into the role of participant observer and record keeper. This process is referred to as *role transmutation* because of the significant change when the principal moved from skeptic to facilitator of the study group meetings. The teachers made a similar change that was apparent in the interest and enthusiasm of their spirited discussions about successes and challenges, which typically lasted well beyond the one hour set aside for the study group and required little or no prompting or direction. A good deal of the discussion at one session followed a third-grade teacher's sharing of a successful method she had developed to help students understand comprehension questions at the end of assigned readings. The principal commented about how the purposes of the study group were consistent with efforts underway at the school to improve test scores and other measures of student achievement.

At the end of one session, the group had identified a significant concern with teaching and learning in the areas of comprehension, vocabulary, decoding, and inferences. The principal asked the teachers to teach a lesson in one of the areas before the next meeting and be prepared to share their experience. She asked the facilitator to recommend some articles or books on teaching reading to African American children.

**CONTINUOUS DIALOGUE ON SUCCESSFUL APPROACHES.** The teachers continued to share a variety of successful methods, materials, and activities, including a visualization technique that helps children understand what they read; manipulation of sight words on flash cards, having children change them by adding prefixes and suffixes or changing the initial consonant to make a new word; a big-word-challenge activity in which students use a dictionary to find polysyllabic words and learn to sound out big words, and a word worm, which serves as a pocket for words that children can use as a resource for learning vocabulary. The teachers were encouraged at the end of the session to implement one of the ideas shared in their classroom.

## Qualitative Data

The analysis of the qualitative data from both the first and second year of the project lend support to the potential usefulness of a structured dialogue approach to study groups for fostering the habits of mind and classroom practices that improve literacy acquisition and development for African American students. The fact that the principal at Wheatley School was eager to take the facilitator role and used the approach from the intervention for the project seems particularly promising.

## Quantitative Data

A three-year analysis of students' scores on the Stanford Achievement Test, 9th edition, was used as a quantitative indicator of the possible connection between changes in teachers' habits of mind, classroom practices, and the academic performance of students. Scores on the Stanford Achievement Test for spring 1998 served as baseline data.

Over all, at Wheatley School, the greatest gains were made with the poorest readers in the second and third grades. In 1998, 45% of second graders scored above the 25th percentile as compared to 64% in 1999, and 73% in 2000. This increment represents a 28% overall gain. Districtwide, 48% of second graders scored above the 25th percentile in 1998, 61% in 1999, and 56% in 2000, an overall gain of 12%. Second graders gained 15% in the 50th percentile over the same period at Wheatley, and 6% districtwide. In 1998, 32% of Wheatley's third graders scored above the 25th percentile, 52% in 1999, and 63% in 2000. This overall gain equals 31%. Districtwide, 42% of third graders scored above the 25th percentile in 1998, 59% in 1999, and 51% in 2000—an overall gain of 9%. Third graders gained 13% in the 50th percentile over the same period at Wheatley, and 6% districtwide. We believe these data indicate that the internal model for professional development has potential for influencing teaching practices that improve learning for African American students.

## Summary and Conclusions

Over the course of the project, we documented the discussions during study group meetings in which the five-step process for the internal teacher-development model was employed. These discussions revealed the progression of teachers' thinking from the beginning of the project to the end—about the students they teach, their life conditions, motivation and values, and about themselves, and their own identity. The documentation at study group meetings also revealed insights about the dynamics within the group, such as relationships among early career teachers and established teachers, and between the teachers and the principal.

At the beginning of the study group meetings, the teachers described the children as different from themselves. They discussed the important values and practices they had been taught in their own homes as children. In contrast, the children's home environments were described as lacking essential training in social skills and moral values. The teachers seemed to make special efforts to disassociate themselves from the children culturally and socially. Toward the end of the first year, the teachers and the principal began to describe the relationship between their own experiential backgrounds and those of the children. For example, the principal related her own background experience to the situation of the children in the following statement: "I was raised...by my grandmother who did not have an education; who did not know how to help me with my homework.... So, if...teachers at school didn't give it to me, I wasn't going to get it at home." She continued by noting that some of the students at Wheatley School are in a similar situation, and teachers must provide the skills students need in the classroom rather than shifting blame to the family. This change in the conversation during study group meetings supports the potential influence of the internal model for teacher development on the habits of mind of the participants.

The dialogue during study group meetings progressed from a focus on daily challenges and defending their own practices to seeking insights from the research literature, sharing suggestions for instructional strategies, collaborating to develop new approaches, and expressing appreciation for time to dialogue and plan together. At times, these changes were uncomfortable for some teachers who experienced difficulty in letting go of some of their biased perceptions of the children's potential for successful academic performance.

The quantitative data from students' scores on the Stanford Achievement Test indicate that the internal model for teacher development may have contributed to teachers' ability to improve reading for the second- and third-grade students who were performing above and below the 25th percentile. What other factors may have contributed to this change is unknown; however, it is evident that the second- and third-grade students' performance at Wheatley School is not typical for the district averages. Thus, the recently instituted class-size reduction that occurred across the district in the primary grades would not account for this significant improvement at Wheatley School.

In summary, the findings from this study suggest that the conversations among the teachers at the study group meetings changed to being more positive about the children, making linkages between themselves and the culture the children bring to school, increasing enthusiasm for sharing their own strategies and engaging in public reflection, and collaborating in developing new instructional approaches. The principal assumed the role of facilitator, which indicates that the internal model has potential for fostering a self-sustaining learning community. Improvement in the children's performance on district-mandated standardized tests is one indication that the teachers' participation in the internal model has potential for supporting positive learning outcomes.

## Insights, Issues, and Questions for Reflection

In this research study, as in many others, we encountered challenges and perplexing situations from which we acquired new insights and raised important questions about how to do this work. We believe it is important to summarize here what we learned about in working with the central administration of a large urban school district on an applied research study, about establishing credibility and building rapport with teachers and principals, about the teachers with whom we worked, and about the complex context of the urban school in which we conducted this inquiry. We believe these findings are important because the preparation of classroom teachers and other school personnel and the improvement in learning outcomes for all students in public schools require that universities and public schools work collaboratively.

Our initial collaboration with the school district was with a planning team consisting of central office personnel (the superintendent and three district-level administrators appointed by the superintendent) and university administrators (the dean of the school of education and two coprincipal investigators for the research project). This team developed a skeletal design for the research study. A research team worked out the details. Participating in the initial planning process with the central office administration as a team allowed us to develop an approach that we all agreed on, and to establish credibility and build rapport among the collaborators. In retrospect, we question whether we made the best use of our collaboration with the central office administration. What other conditions could we have agreed on to better facilitate our work? For example, could we have agreed to work towards stabilizing teacher and principal turnover in the participating school? How could we have involved the principal and teachers at the participating school in the planning process?

When initiating the study at the participating school, we gained new insight into the importance of establishing credibility and building rapport with the teachers and principal with whom we worked. Our interactions in the school helped us comprehend the complexity of establishing credibility and that this involves being recognized by the participants as understanding the lives of the children they teach, understanding the context and nature of the work in an urban school, and having an authentic interest in improving outcomes for the children in their classrooms. We learned how important listening is to building rapport. During study group meetings, there were times when it was difficult to refrain from responding to comments with which we adamantly disagreed. We learned that practice and training are necessary for facilitators to understand when and how to respond during study group meetings in order to facilitate communication, planning, and better understanding of the teaching and teaming process for urban children in a low performing school.

We learned that teachers in the participating school were sensitive about their work, about what they know and what they have yet to learn, and about the performance of the children they teach. Their attitudes and feelings were expressed in various ways. Sometimes they expressed affection and caring, and other times the same teachers distanced themselves from the children and expressed frustration, resentment, and resistance to change. We learned to be sensitive in how we interpret and respond to the attitudes and feelings the teachers expressed. In retrospect, we wonder if we understood well enough at the outset of this study the conflicting feelings teachers expressed about their work, the children they teach, and the teaming outcomes that are so publicly displayed. We wonder how we might design better training for the facilitators that would provide greater insight into how to encourage, support, and facilitate shared learning. We would like to better understand how to make use of the new insights we acquired to promote a more powerful self-sustaining learning community.

Finally, we learned the reality of multiple and competing demands on urban teachers' and administrators' time. We learned that the daily work in the low performing school we studied can be intense, frustrating, and exhausting. We, as researchers, developed a respect and consideration for the commitment and energy expended by the teachers and administrators in the participating school. We were concerned about putting new demands on their time. We were careful about how we scheduled and used time in the school. We questioned whether we had understood the school well enough during the research-planning process, how we might have acquired a better understanding of the school, and whether our collaboration with the school district was inclusive enough. We were concerned about the short-term and long-term impact of our efforts in the participating school and tried to ensure that this concern was balanced with what our efforts might contribute to the knowledge base for professional development in urban schools. At the end of our project the teachers and administrators at the school and at the central office were pleased with our contribution to their understanding of ways to support teachers in improving literacy for African American students.

## REFERENCES

Allen, E.E., & Lederman, L. (1998). Lessons learned: The teachers academy for mathematics and science. *Phi Delta Kappan*, *80*(2), 158, 160, 162–164.

Denzin, N.K., & Lincoln, Y.S. (1998). *Strategies of qualitative inquiry.* Thousand Oaks, CA: Sage.

Foster, M. (1997). *Black teachers on teaching.* New York: New Press.

Gilmore, P. (1985). "Gimme room": School resistance, attitudes, and access to literacy. *Journal of Education, 167*(1), 111–128.

Guskey, T.R. (2000). *Evaluating professional development.* Thousand Oaks, CA: Corwin Press.

Hausman, A.J., & Ruzek, S.B. (1995). Implementation of comprehensive school health education in elementary schools: Focus on teacher concerns. *Journal of School Health, 65*(3), 81–86.

Jerald, C.D. (2001). *Dispelling the myth revisited: Preliminary finds from a nationwide analysis of "high-flying" schools.* Washington, DC: The Education Trust. (ERIC Document Reproduction Service No. ED462485)

Johnson, J.F., Jr., & Asera, R. (1999). (Eds.). Hope for urban education: A study of nine high-performing, high-poverty, urban elementary schools. Washington, DC: US Department of Education. (ERIC Document Reproduction Service No. ED438362)

Joyce, B., & Showers, B. (1995). *Student achievement through staff development.* (2nd ed.). White Plains, NY: Longman.

Ladson-Billings, G. (1994). *The dreamkeepers: Successful teachers of African American children.* San Francisco: Jossey-Bass.

Lewison, M. (1999). Why do we find writing so hard? Using journals to inquire into our teaching. *The Reading Teacher, 52*(5), 522–526.

Lytle, S.L., & Fecho, R. (1991). Meeting strangers in familiar places: Teacher collaboration by cross visitation. *English Education, 23*(1), 5–28.

Michaels, S. (1981). "Sharing time": Children's narrative styles and differential access to literacy. *Language in Society, 10*, 423–442.

Moats, L.C. (1999). *Teaching reading is rocket science: What expert teachers of reading should know and be able to do.* Washington, DC: American Federation of Teachers. (ERIC Document Reproduction Service No. ED445323)

Murphy, D.S., Colvin, C., & Morey, A.I. (1990). Helping new teachers become thoughtful practitioners. *Educational Horizons, 68*(4), 182–186.

National Assessment of Educational Progress (NAEP). (2000). *Reading assessment.* Washington, DC: US Department of Education, Office of Educational Research and Improvement.

Schon, D.A. (1987). *Educating the reflective practitioner.* San Francisco: Jossey-Bass.

Smith, A.L. (1989–1990). Collaborative induction model to support first-year minority teachers. *Action in Teacher Education, 11*(4), 42–47.

Speck, M., & Knipe, C. (2001). *Why can't we get it right? Professional development in our schools.* Thousand Oaks, CA: Corwin Press.

Stanford Achievement Test, 9th edition. (1996). San Antonio, TX: Harcourt Brace Educational Measurement.

Villasenor, A., Jr., & Kepner, H.S., Jr. (1993). Arithmetic from a problem-solving perspective: An urban implementation. *Journal for Research in Mathematics Education, 24*(1), 62–69.

# CHAPTER 18

# Reading Linguistic Features: Middle School Students' Response to the African American Literary Tradition

*Wanda M. Brooks*

## African American Literary Tradition

Offering students authentic literature to read is often connected to pedagogical practices that emphasize in-depth discussions about books and the meanings students derive from them. Although commercial reading programs are becoming more pervasive in elementary schools, middle school classrooms are still obvious sites for instruction centered on reading and responding to literature. For a qualitative research study, I observed this type of literacy pedagogy in an urban middle school classroom over a 10-month period. This chapter will focus on one facet of the study, which involved investigating African American eighth graders' oral and written responses to linguistic features found in African American children's literature.

Embedded within African American children's books are many distinct literary traditions that derive, in part, from the unique histories of their authors. These traditions are a type of cultural resource that educators who desire to build bridges between the home and school lives of children of color welcome. Embracing cultural resources was the norm for the classroom described throughout this chapter. Through her selection of novels, the teacher, Regina Holmes, (all names of participants are pseudonyms) dedicated herself to taking advantage of the cultural backgrounds of her 28 students.

The purpose of my discussion throughout this chapter is twofold. First, I present partial findings from a textual analysis of a book titled *Scorpions* (Myers, 1988). In this analysis, some of the many diverse language vernaculars and patterns embedded in the book are identified. Second, using three reader response categories, I unpack the various ways in which the students responded to these linguistic features when reading.

*Scorpions* was selected for the research because it met certain criteria. It is "culturally conscious" fiction, as defined by Sims (1982, p. 49), and exemplary, as indicated by the author's popularity and numerous earned book awards. *Scorpions* was written by Walter Dean Myers, one of the most well-known African American authors of children's literature. Briefly, the coming-of-age story is about an African American adolescent named Jamal Hicks. Jamal's older brother, who is incarcerated, is a former member of a gang who refer to themselves as the Scorpions. Joining the gang is a temptation for Jamal, but after his best friend is almost murdered, he decides against this risky lifestyle. In selecting this novel for the research (as well as a variety of other books by African American authors), the teacher and I hoped that many of the adolescent issues, urban influences, and cultural experiences embedded in the storyline would deeply resonate with the study participants.

## African American Vernacular English

True to the African American literary tradition, the linguistic features in *Scorpions* convey an authentic portrayal of a poor African American family living in a contemporary, urban setting (Sims Bishop, 1990). African American Vernacular English (AAVE) is spoken by most of the author's African American characters throughout *Scorpions*. According to Smithermann (1985), depending on context, AAVE is a language vernacular spoken by a significant portion of African Americans. AAVE includes sophisticated grammatical patterns, distinct lexicon, such as adolescent slang and idiomatic expressions, as well as rhetorical styles such as *signifying*. Signifying is a fast-paced, expressive rhetorical pattern identified by irony, double meanings, metaphors, quick responses, and rhetorical stance. In *Scorpions*, these linguistic patterns are all present in the ways in which the characters communicate with each other.

In regard to grammar, the following three sentences demonstrate syntax prevalent in AAVE and spoken by various characters in *Scorpions*:

(1) "You didn't give out no homework yesterday," Jamal said. (p. 17)

(2) "You scared?" (p. 62)

(3) "What I want to talk to him for?" Jamal said. (p. 52)

There are also instances when the verb "to be" is spoken or omitted in characteristic AAVE pattern:

(1) "He gonna be a Scorpion too?" Angel pointed toward Tito. "How old is he, six?" "He be one if I say he be one," Jamal said. "How old you is?" Mack asked Angel. (p. 84)

(2) "You in the Scorpions?" Darnell asked. "Who you, the F.B.I.?" (p. 119)

Morphological endings such as *ing, ed,* and apostrophe *s* are also routinely deleted from words in AAVE:

(1) "He said I had a gun?" "Yep!" "He lyin'." (p. 119)

(2) "He too big." (p. 69)

(3) "He act like he was all broke up over Randy." (p. 87)

Myers's incorporation of the AAVE lexicon is partially illustrated through the use of slang. The slang is consistent with that coined by urban teenagers during the early 1980s when this book was published. Changes in lexicon provide subtle barriers between the Scorpion gang members and other characters in the story. For example, although Jamal does speak in AAVE, his usage of slang occurs less often than that of the gang members. Those affiliated with the gang communicate very differently. Most of their dialogue is infused with a type of slang that is relatively incomprehensible outside of an extended story context. Washington (1981) would consider the Scorpions' linguistic patterns to be consistent with many African American writers of the late 1960s and 1970s who

> felt a need to communicate with the black population in ways that could not be detected easily by hostile forces at work against them. This concept of course, was not new.... The black population, unlike some other minority groups, has no native language. It has, therefore, developed a refined language code that enables it to communicate with its members while maintaining secrecy from the dominant society...such a secret language code serves as a means of self defense. (p. 212)

In the following excerpt, a Scorpion illustrates Washington's concept of a refined language code. Here is the way in which the gang member communicates his thoughts to Jamal:

> Yeah, uh-huh, you looking around to see what's shaking and everything, but I'm going to tell you what's shaking. The Indian is the chief, baby. That's my say, but I'm going to give you a play, cause that's my way, dig? The man with the long bread needs some legs, dig? Now we got to rap about who running the show so the man don't get confused. (p. 143)

Indeed, the passage is almost impossible to make sense of if one does not belong to a particular community at a certain time period.

Idiomatic expressions (which, unlike slang, are less susceptible to changes over time) are also a part of the lexical variety included in the book (Smitherman,

1994). Jamal's mother, Ms. Hicks, is the only character who uses idiomatic expressions in her speech. She offers one idiomatic expression during a confrontation with Jamal about his whereabouts. When he tells his mother about his aimless walking around after his curfew, she counters with, "Just walking my foot! When you think I was born? Sometime this morning?" (p. 49).

Last, Myers skillfully places in the mouths of his young characters the rhetorical pattern of signifying. Lee (1993) contends that, "In many social settings within the African American community, the adolescent, in particular, who cannot signify and has no status and no style, is a kind of outsider who is incapable of participating in social conversation" (p. 11). The teenage characters in the book relied upon signifying on numerous occasions. In this type of rhetorical exchange, participants aim to verbally insult one another and, thereby, assert themselves as worthy of respect. The meanings behind the insults, however, are not literally interpreted. Rather, as is demonstrated by the talk between Dwayne and Jamal in the upcoming excerpt, it is the rhetorical challenge and the ability to embarrass a competitor verbally that counts:

> "Yo, Jamal, what kind of sneakers you wearin'?"
> "None of your business," Jamal said.
> "They look like Brand X sneakers to me," Dwayne said.
> "I think you got a Brand X face," Jamal said.
> "Hey Billy, I think he got them sneakers from the Salvation Army."
> "I got these sneakers from Bradley's," Jamal said.
> "They look like they come from the garbage can behind Bradley's," Dwayne said.... "If I put one of these sneakers upside your head, you won't worry about where they come from." (p. 21)

The use of "mama jokes" or what Lee identifies as "playing the dozens" (p. 12) is also artfully included by Myers. In one instance, the intensity and playfulness of two adolescent boys challenging each other in a verbal duel is revealed through a sexual insult figuratively aimed at Dwayne's mother:

> "Dwayne want to know if you going to wait for him outside," Billy said aloud.
> "Or you gonna run like a punk?" Dwayne asked.
> "I'm going to run over to your house and see your mama," Jamal said.
> (p. 75)

Although Dwayne and Jamal actually engage in a fight some time after the conversation occurs, signifying is not the primary precipitator.

# Responses to African American Vernacular English

During the reading of *Scorpions*, the study participants responded to all of the linguistic patterns embedded in AAVE, but of these, the analysis revealed that the most in-depth and thoughtful discussions were focused on the characters' usage of slang. Because the inclusion of this linguistic pattern in one's speech most often occurs during the adolescent years, peer groups are usually the focal points for creating and speaking slang (Smitherman, 1994). As such, when the study participants responded to the language contained in the texts, their peer-group positioning appeared to become salient. It is through the students' affiliations with their friends that their interpretations and responses to the slang were filtered in the discussions of the text. As adolescents who are keenly aware of language usage and its connection to social popularity, the slang embedded in the texts seemed to be at the forefront of the students' thinking.

Fish's (1980) theoretical notion of "interpretive communities" is a theory that supports the findings presented here. According to Fish, interpretive communities are "made up of those who share interpretive strategies not for reading (in the conventional sense) but for writing texts, for constituting their properties and assigning their intentions" (p. 71). Because the students in the study were about the same age and had traveled together as a class-cohort for three years, they shared various levels of spoken and unspoken understandings as only a peer-group can. The participants' ways of relying on their adolescent peer group to construct meaning existed with regard to the ways in which they interpreted the novel, in general, and responded to the linguistic patterns in the book, in particular. Fish's (1980) notion of "interpretive communities" was relied upon during the analysis because of the students' shared levels of understanding in regard to their making sense of the language usage. Their interpretations went beyond their ethnic affiliations to the other interpretive communities of which they are a part; the most dominant of these being their peer group.

## Categories of Responses

For the analysis, the students' unique responses to this linguistic feature were categorized in one of three ways: translations of example, contemporary translations, and contextual translations.

### Translations of Example

This category describes the ways in which the children interpreted and explained the slang words in the book by giving examples of the meanings. An illustration of translating abilities occurred one day after the participants read the second chapter. In this part, the main character, Jamal, begins thinking about his older brother's friendship with Mack, a gang member. It was obvious to Jamal that Mack often influenced Randy in a negative way, so Jamal wondered why his brother would maintain an allegiance to such a person. Specifically, the students read from the following excerpt:

> Jamal didn't like Mack. Mack was different from anyone Jamal had ever met. He had a strange way of talking, running his words together so that is was hard to understand him.... But more than anything it was the fights that Mack got into. The summer before Randy had got into trouble, Mack had been in juvenile home for breaking a man's arm with a baseball bat. The man had stepped on his shoes. Mama didn't know that but Jamal did. "He my ace," Randy used to say. "You get in a fight or something and you need an ace, man." (Myers, 1988, p. 13)

In a discussion with Regina, the students' understanding of the word *ace* compelled them to define and also describe an occasion when they relied on an "ace." For instance, according to Viviana, "The only time I needed an ace man is when I was about to fight three big girls, so my sister came" (Viviana, spoken response). Here, Viviana defined the term *ace* by providing an example in which she needed someone's support, just as Randy depends on his "ace" in the story. Another participant, who I call Mark, envisioned counting on an ace, "when you are in jail so they can try to get you out" (Mark, spoken response). Still using examples to define the word, Lisa then stated that, "I don't have a ace because I don't need one, I fight on my own" (Lisa, spoken response). After listening to comments from her friends in the class, Heather chimed in with an unexpected translation by jokingly adding, "Yeah, I need an ace only when I'm playing Spades" (Heather, spoken response). During the discussion, Heather's comments were met with laughter by some of the others, who then quickly began talking about the familiar card game, Spades.

In their discussion of the excerpt, the students translated a slang word by providing an example of the word's meaning. Belonging to similar interpretive communities (Fish, 1980), the students shared an understanding of *ace* that seemed consistent. Even when Heather jokingly referred to another type of "ace," the students, who often play the card game Spades during their free time, instantly interpreted this meaning as well. Their reading of the word *ace* brought forth knowledge from the two different interpretive communities in which they belonged. Even though the participants are members of numerous interpretive communities, in large part AAVE is the primary mode of communication in these existing simultaneously in school, within their peer group, and within their families and community. Their shared levels of knowledge spanned across multiple settings, which explains how the children easily moved from one understanding of *ace* to another. African American students' shared understanding of linguistic features is consistent with the findings from a research study conducted by Lee (1993). In Lee's research, African American high school students utilized their familiarity with signifying (figurative and ironic language patterns present in AAVE) to interpret the contradictory, metaphoric, ironic, and proverbial language present in two African American fiction novels.

This type of straightforward understanding of the book's language did not always occur, however. Sometimes the children found themselves defining a slang word with another but more contemporary one, perhaps because *Scorpions* was published prior to 1988, and many of the words are no longer prevalent. This finding is illustrated through the second response category, contemporary translations.

## Contemporary Translations

In the following dialogue, Regina has asked the students to make sense of a conversation between Jamal and Indian (one of the Scorpion gang members) because a considerable amount of slang is incorporated throughout their talk. In this dialogue, Jamal's and Indian's speech also include grammatical patterns characteristic of AAVE. To figure out how the students constructed meaning with the passage, Regina first asked them to judge the authenticity of the conversation between Jamal and Indian and to then interpret the language into their own words:

(1) Regina:  Does the conversation between Jamal and Indian sound realistic? Is it something that would occur between a gang member and somebody else?

(2) Marcus: Yeah.

(3) Mark:  Yeah.

(4) Regina:  Well, what are they speaking, what kind of language?

(5) Mark:  Slang.

(6) Regina:  Now, if the average person was sitting down reading this or listening to the conversation, what words might confuse them?

(7) Mark:  When he said, "dig me."

(8) Regina:  And what does that expression mean?

(9) Tariq:  Do you understand me?

(10) Regina:  Right, and what about this, "I'm going to give you a play." What does that mean?

(11) Tramira:  I got you.

(12) Marcus:  I'm going to hook you up.

(13) Regina:  Well, hook you up or give you a what?

(14) Cedric:  A chance!

In this exchange, the students readily identified the characters' speech in the book as slang (line 5). Although there were grammatical patterns characteristic of AAVE in the dialogue between Jamal and Indian, this particular lexical pattern acted as a marker. In a later conversation, the students also referred to the characters' speech in *Scorpions* as "improper grammar," but it was not evident whether they were actually referring to grammatical patterns instead of lexicon. For the most part, slang words indicated to the participants the times when AAVE was included in the dialogue. Although AAVE is a very involved and linguistically complex communication system (i.e., distinct grammatical patterns and pronunciation, lexicon, metaphors, imagery, and idioms), the students in the study predominately associated AAVE with one type of linguistic feature.

In the latter part of the previous discussion, when asked to define the expression, "I'm going to give you a play," the students' initial responses illustrated how they preferred not to translate these words into standard English (lines 11, 12). Thus, contemporary expressions such as "I got you" and "I'm going to hook you up" were both offered as definitions by the students.

Due to her affiliation in at least one of the students' interpretive communities, Regina was familiar with these expressions and carefully scaffolded the contemporary lexicon into Standard English (line 13). The idea that slang in texts, once it is not contemporary, hinders meaning was not substantiated in the research.

## Contextual Translations

Despite the fact that the students only moderately considered the implications of recognizing AAVE, they did possess an awareness of it and noticed when it was not present in the books they read. The category of contextual translations, then, represents the contextual ways students understood slang. For example, when asked by Regina why the African American characters in another book did not speak with AAVE, Kevin responded with a seemingly derogatory but quite popular and neutral expression among their peer group, "They're not ghetto" (Kevin, spoken response), and Tariq countered with, "They didn't talk like that back in those days" (Tariq, spoken response). Indeed, some of the participants did associate AAVE with certain groups of people or distinct time periods. The discussion below demonstrates how one student relied on AAVE to figure out the setting of Scorpions during the first chapter:

(1) Regina:   What clues tell you about the setting?

(2) Heather: It's in their house.

(3) Regina:   But, do they live in the country or city?

(4) Bennie:   Neither, the projects!

(5) Regina:   How do you know that?

(6) Kiona:    Because of the way they talk.

(7) Regina:   What about the way they talk makes you say that?

(8) Tramira: They talk ghetto and they don't speak proper English.

(9) Regina:   Since they don't speak Standard English you assume they live where?

(10) Tramira: In the projects. (Group, spoken responses)

Throughout informal and formal discussions, many of those in the class shared the same type of association as Kiona above (line 6). Not speaking "proper English" and talking "ghetto," as Tramira mentioned (line 8), were both characteristics of living in the "projects." According to Tramira, in another discussion, *projects* were low-income housing developments lived in by African Americans and Latinos. Notwithstanding that association, a negative connotation was not linked to speaking a certain way. "Talking ghetto" was a familiar way of communicating, and "living in the projects" was a common lifestyle for the participants. To distance oneself from these ways of speaking and living meant not belonging on multiple levels. Everyone around them, even their teacher and myself, "talked ghetto" at one time or another. And, as members of the community in which they resided, study participants probably knew someone who lived in the projects, even if they did not live there. Despite the fact that the students opted not to immediately connect "talking ghetto" (actually AAVE) to something flawed or negative, they often discussed times in which saying certain words were inappropriate depending on the context.

Tramira's distinction above indicates the way in which her understanding and incorporation of slang in her speech was often contextually based. Her interpretation of the expression "talking ghetto" had been filtered through her lived experiences. The children's responses to the words in the books were often rooted in their own "interpretive communities."

Throughout the research, the participants' interpretations of slang, whether connected to "living in the projects" or "talking ghetto," extended beyond literal translations. Their interpretations were associated with feelings that ranged from affinity to disgust and, as such, linked to feelings of reading engagement.

## Implications and Conclusions

Of the diverse language vernaculars and patterns incorporated in the books read for this research, the students primarily responded to AAVE and, more specifically, slang. Although AAVE is a very involved and linguistically complex communication system with distinct syntax, morphology, and semantics, it was predominately associated with just one linguistic pattern. Because slang is context dependent, Smitherman suggests that usage of it relies, "on knowledge of the rules of [AAVE] grammar and pronunciation" (1985, p. 5). In other words, slang terminology acted as a lexical marker to indicate to the participants the times when AAVE was embedded in the text.

In conclusion, because there are numerous linguistic features from the African American literary tradition contained in novels such as *Scorpions*, it is important to consider how students might (for various reasons) find some features more salient than others. Future researchers must carefully consider the degree to which certain features, or an emphasis on certain features, such as language patterns, in a text influence reading engagement or meaning construction.

There are two significant implications of these findings. First, educators should not minimize the importance of students' resonance with AAVE when they hope to raise the reading engagement or comprehension of African American students, as well as all students of color, who often speak with various language vernaculars. Because language patterns influence the overall message of any text, teachers who focus on the nuanced aspects of meaning construction might benefit from taking into account the importance of selecting books, such as *Scorpions*, with diverse linguistic features.

Second, many books from the African American literary tradition include various linguistic features. In *Scorpions*, AAVE's grammatical patterns, adolescent slang, and signifying clearly marked the characters' speech. These vernaculars and speech patterns might prove to be excellent vehicles for the teaching of both reading and writing. There are many more questions left to be asked and answered such as, Does the use of adolescent slang in *Scorpions* help children to understand the text as compared to other types of linguistic variations? And, because other features from the African American literary tradition, such as language patterns, can be identified, can they be used to enhance reading instruction for African American students?

# REFERENCES

Fish, S. (1980). *Is there a text in this class? The authority of interpretive communities.* Cambridge, MA: Harvard University Press.

Lee, C.D. (1993). *Signifying as a scaffold for literary interpretation: The Pedagogical implications of an African American discourse genre.* Urbana, IL: National Council of Teachers of English.

Sims, R. (1982). *Shadow and substance: Afro American experience in contemporary children's fiction.* Urbana, IL: National Council of Teachers of English.

Sims Bishop, R. (1990). Walk tall in the world: African American literature for today's children. *Journal of Negro Education, 59*(4), 556–565.

Smitherman, G. (1985). "What go round come round": King in perspective. In C.K. Brooks (Ed.), *Tapping potential: English and language arts for the Black learner* (pp. 41–61). Urbana, IL: Black Caucus, National Council of Teachers of English.

Smitherman, G. (1994). *Black talk: Words and phrases from the hood to the amen corner.* Boston: Houghton Mifflin.

Washington, E.M. (1981). Black interpretation, Black American literature, and grey audiences. *Communication Education, 30*(3), 209–216.

# LITERATURE CITED

Myers, W.D. (1988). *Scorpions.* New York: Scholastic.

# CHAPTER 19

# A Culturally Based Cognitive Apprenticeship: Teaching African American High School Students Skills in Literary Interpretation

*Carol D. Lee*

Among the critical problems facing the teaching of literature at the secondary level are the debates over a literary canon for instruction and how to teach the complex strategies involved in interpreting rich literature. These two issues meet at a critical interface in urban U.S. high schools with predominantly African American student populations living in poverty.

Some researchers have observed that reading comprehension strategies are not adequately taught in language arts classrooms (Dole, Duffy, Roehler, & Pearson, 1991; Durkin,1979). This research claims that teachers tend to follow teacher guides in basal readers or literature anthologies that do not explicitly teach comprehension strategies. Critics have also claimed that teachers present worksheets focusing on specific comprehension skills in isolation. In other instances, researchers have noted that teachers often dominate classroom discussion, telling students "correct" interpretations of works of literature (Hillocks, 1989; Nystrand & Gamoran, 1989). The paucity of substantive discussion in literature classrooms has been found to be particularly acute in language arts or literature classes in schools serving disfavored ethnic and racial groups living in poverty (Marshall, 1990; Means & Knapp, 1991). This article describes a research intervention in two urban U.S. high schools that sought to address the problems described in ways that are culturally responsive and intellectually challenging.

This article addresses these problems by offering a theoretical argument for the efficacy of a culturally based cognitive apprenticeship based on the implica-

From *Reading Research Quarterly* (1995), *30*, 608–630. Copyright © 1995 by the International Reading Association.

tions of an empirical study by Lee (1993).[1] This study seeks to address the critical problems stated above by investigating the following: (a) some benefits of using ethnically diverse literature with ethnically diverse students, and (b) how to make explicit in instruction some of the important comprehension strategies needed to interpret complex fiction independently. The study reports the results of a process by which skills in making literary interpretations of complex inferences in selected works of African American fiction were taught to four classes of African American students in an underachieving urban high school. The process models the principles for a cognitive apprenticeship outlined by Collins, Brown, and Newman (1989) and Collins, Brown, and Holum (1991).

## Related Background Research

It is important to understand this study in the context of prior research on reading comprehension and language variation. There is a well-accepted and wide body of research which posits that reading comprehension strategies can be explicitly taught (Fitzgerald & Spiegel, 1983; Hansen & Pearson, 1983; Palincsar & Brown, 1984; Pearson & Dole, 1987). As evident in the earlier citations, a major obstacle, however, has not been so much the conceptualization of reading as a cognitive activity, but rather in the implementation or lack thereof of teaching strategies that are consistent with the research on reading comprehension strategies and constructivist principles of learning and teaching (Spiro, 1980). As stated earlier, this problem has been most acute in schools serving poor and ethnically and linguistically diverse students.

There are, however, several areas of conflict within the research community over the range of reading strategies that should be emphasized, particularly at the secondary level, and over the organization of a literature curriculum that follows from a particular set of assumptions about appropriate strategies (see Smagorinsky & Smith, 1992, for an extensive review of relevant literature). Smagorinsky and Smith (1992) have labeled this conflict one of general versus task-specific and community-specific strategies. General reading strategies would include the following, among others: posing questions, summarizing, text reinspection, predicting, and flexible allocation of reading time and resources. General strategies also include metacognitive strategies such as monitoring one's comprehension while reading and understanding characteristics of one's self as a reader in conjunction with the nature of the reading task in order to use strategies flexibly (see Garner, 1987, for a full review). Task-specific strategies, on the other hand, include, for example, use of reading strategies that are specific to certain kinds of problems in literary texts. These include strategies for identifying and understanding irony, point of view, and satire, for example (Booth, 1974,

1983; Smith, 1989). Rabinowitz (1987) has described an elaborate set of strategies that he argues more expert readers bring to the interpretation of fiction. Graves (1994) and Van den Broek (1994) demonstrate that expert readers in the process of constructing interpretations of fiction use what de Beaugrande (1987) calls "schemas for literary communication." These include a wide array of prior knowledge of genre, rhetorical and literary techniques, and knowledge of the author and of the social world of the text. When reading a story, such expert readers, they argue, posit very early on a hypothetical macrostructure informed by their prior knowledge to direct, test, and filter future data from their reading of the story. De Beaugrande (1987) concludes, "despite inevitable differences in personal experiences and specific responses, people agree on some major literary issues: what passages are salient,...[and] what problems and solutions are worth considering..." (p. 94).

The study described in this article proceeds from the assumptions that (a) reading comprehension strategies can be explicitly taught, (b) there is a powerful set of strategies specific to certain problems in the interpretation of fiction, and (c) these task-specific strategies can productively support traditionally underachieving students to construct not only basic comprehension of the plot, but also insightful interpretations of complex works of fiction. The teaching strategies employed in this study are aimed at helping culturally diverse, underachieving adolescents construct from culturally relevant models a set of task-specific reading strategies applicable to reading problems in complex fiction. In addition, the teaching strategies included routines that required the daily use of general reading strategies such as text reinspection and self-monitoring of understanding.

The problem of reading comprehension is complicated not only by the need for both general and task-specific comprehension strategies, but also by the influences of cultural background. A series of studies has demonstrated that perspective taking and cultural background can distort or support comprehension (Kintsch & Greene, 1978; Malik, 1990; Reynolds, Taylor, Steffensen, Shirey, & Anderson, 1982; Steffensen, Joag-Dev, & Anderson, 1979). When texts contain scripts (Schank & Abelson, 1977) for culturally specific events and social interactions where inferences must be constructed, readers tend to draw on their prior social knowledge to build interpretations. Thus general reading strategies, task-specific strategies for interpreting literature, and prior social and cultural knowledge combine in crucial ways to support problem solving in this complex domain of interpreting literary texts. Very little research, however, has been conducted on the implications of these findings for instruction, especially for ethnically and linguistically diverse students.

The influence of cultural background knowledge on reading comprehension is particularly problematic for students whose home language or language variety differs markedly from the mainstream standard dialect that is taught in most schools in the United States and that is reflected often in the canon of literary texts taught in most secondary schools (Applebee, 1989). Studies have shown that when the language variety of the student is one that is devalued by the larger society, effective transitions to school and the level of support available for learning to read and write are affected (Cazden, 1988; Delpit, 1988, 1990; Heath, 1983; Michaels, 1986). Sociolinguistic research during the 1970s showed that students' participation in instructional discourse was severely impeded when teachers did not take into account the language variation of their students (see Cazden, John, & Hymes, 1972). The devaluation in school contexts of African American English, particularly in its vernacular varieties, has been historically problematic (Smitherman, 1977). Again, during the 1970s, curriculum in early reading developed for African American children was often based on assumptions of cultural deprivation reflected in the uses of African American English vernacular (or what was then referred to as Black English Vernacular or BEV). So-called dialect readers were developed because it was argued that Black children had difficulty learning to read basal readers in standard English.

In stark contrast to prevailing theories of language deprivation, during that same decade another line of sociolinguistic research documented the richness and complexity of African American English and related discourse forms (Abrahams, 1970; Labov, 1972; Smitherman, 1977). However, in the decades since, insufficient empirical work or intervention research has been conducted to apply the findings from the sociolinguistic research on language variations and their impact on learning to read and write. This study has attempted to build on those findings of the 1970s by using as a foundation for reading instruction models of African American discourse and literary texts in which African American English is a dominant mode of narration.

## Theoretical Argument

An instructional model was developed that would draw upon the linguistic strengths that African American adolescents in many instances bring from their homes and community experiences. *Signifying*, a form of discourse in the African American community, is full of irony, double entendre, satire, and metaphorical language. Participation in this form of discourse is highly prized in many circles within the Black community. Signifying, as a form of talk, has persisted for many generations, across geographical regions within the United States, and even across class boundaries (although there are differences influenced by each of these variables). Inherent in signifying and what Smitherman

(1994) calls the African American verbal tradition is an attitude that language use that is valued should be creative and figurative. Many African American adolescents routinely participate in signifying speech events in which they must immediately interpret accurately the double entendre and ironies of each turn of talk. At the same time, a tradition of African American writers—of fiction, drama, and poetry—makes use of BEV, signifying, and other oral rhetorical figures characteristic of the African American verbal tradition (Gates, 1988; Jones, 1991; Paznik, 1976; Smitherman, 1977). However, these writers do not merely replicate what they hear in the community, but rather reshape these devices and oral patterns to fulfill literary functions within the texts.

Because of these connections between language use in the community and language use in a tradition of literary texts, I believe there is an important intellectual link that can be scaffolded in instruction. In addition, I argue that the strategies these adolescents employ to process turns of talk within signifying dialogues are similar to those used by expert readers to identify and process passages in literary texts that are ironic and that are intended by the author to be interpreted figuratively rather than literally. The problem is that this knowledge for the African American adolescent is often tacit, and because the knowledge is tacit and has been applied only to community oral interactions, its applicability to other related problems of interpretation is limited. The goal of the instructional model on which this study is based was to organize a learning environment in which an academically underachieving set of African American adolescents would study samples of extended signifying dialogue as a kind of metalinguistic activity. They would through questioning begin to articulate the strategies they used to come to interpretations of turns of talk within signifying dialogues and then apply those same strategies—which they themselves had now articulated—to the interpretation of a set of rich literary texts. Texts of fiction were chosen in which BEV and signifying were used to communicate themes, symbols, and ironies, that is, to fulfill literary functions. The goal of the model was to support the development of a set of both general and task-specific reading strategies that these students could then independently apply to other works of fiction that were not necessarily within the canon of African American literature. That is, the goal was to help them become better readers and to develop a taste, if you will, for literature in which the manipulation of language for aesthetic effect was valued in its own right.

Because the students' knowledge of strategies was tacit and because the problems the students would meet in the literary texts were complex, it was important to devise an instructional model that would make this thinking visible to the students. The model of a cognitive apprenticeship as outlined by Collins and colleagues (Collins, Brown, & Holum, 1989; Collins et al., 1991) proved a useful framework through which to understand the dynamics of the model and its potential applicability to other groups of diverse students.

In this article I will first describe the purposes and structure of cognitive apprenticeship as outlined by Collins and his colleagues. I will then discuss the cultural implications of the cognitive apprenticeship model as it relates to the teaching of literature. The study will then be presented. Finally, the discussion section will demonstrate how the instructional intervention fulfills the objectives of a cognitive apprenticeship based on a cultural foundation.

## Cognitive Apprenticeship

Collins and his colleagues distinguish between traditional apprenticeships, as in trades like tailoring or carpentry, and what they call cognitive apprenticeships, which they argue can most efficiently occur in school settings. The major distinction they make is that "in traditional apprenticeship, the process of carrying out a task to be learned is usually easily observable" (1991, p. 9). In contrast, in a cognitive apprenticeship, the goal is to make visible and explicit complex thinking strategies that experts use in particular domains. Such complex thinking strategies are mental, that is, they occur inside the mind and are therefore not easily observed by the novice. Appropriating the model of a cognitive apprenticeship challenges teachers of literature to study not only expertise among literary critics, but also to study themselves as readers. In devising the present study, I knew it was naive to assume that simply presenting African American students with texts of African American fiction would automatically mean they would know how to go about interpreting the texts beyond a literal recall of the plot. While underlining and making margin notes in the texts, I asked myself what rules I was appropriating in assigning significance to a passage and what knowledge base I drew upon in order to interpret such passages. This process of reflection about myself as a critical reader proved useful in addressing the dilemma of how to make explicit and observable mental and internal comprehension strategies for interpreting complex fiction.

## Cognitive Apprenticeship, Culture, and Literature

Cognitive apprenticeships attempt to help students conceptualize the intellectual problem in its wholeness, to situate the intellectual problem in real world contexts and applications, and to regulate their own strategy use over the course of the problem-solving activity. An example of using this framework for teaching reading comprehension is the reciprocal teaching model of Palincsar and Brown (1984). The studies reported for the reciprocal teaching model generally involve elementary school students learning to read expository texts about science and social studies concepts. This study extends the cognitive apprentice model to secondary school students and to the teaching of literature.

Collins and his colleagues offer a framework for designing learning environments that promote cognitive apprenticing. In terms of content, this framework involves domain knowledge, heuristic strategies, control strategies, and learning strategies. Collins and his colleagues offer examples of domain knowledge in reading as vocabulary, syntax, and phonics rules. In reading literature, however, particularly at the secondary level, domain knowledge is much more complex than the decoding examples offered. Reading and interpreting complex literature involves at least two domains: knowledge of the social world represented in the texts as well as the customs, values, motivation, and personality traits of typical and atypical characters; and knowledge of the rules of significance operating within particular literary genres and particular literary traditions. Social customs, values, and personality traits are not simply broadly human. They are specific also to particular cultures. Within multiethnic societies such as the United States, social customs and values bear relationships both to the national culture as well as the specific ethnic cultures. These customs and values are also the products of particular historical moments. Thus culture, ethnicity, and historical place are variables influencing the knowledge base implicit in the act of interpreting literature.

Rules of significance operating within particular literary genres include, for example, strategies for understanding how to detect satire and irony as well as rules for coherence when confronted with passages that do not on the surface appear to have any relation to one another. In addition, as literature develops within and responds to either specific or multiple literary traditions, principles that influence text structure, imagery, rhetoric, and theme may be culturally influenced. For example, Morrison (1984) addresses the question of what makes a work of fiction Black. Drawing upon African American cultural norms,[2] Morrison asserts that the following attributes, among others, characterize some Black fiction:

1. circularity of time,

2. veneration of ancestors and the presence of ancestors and/or elders as a force in the lives of characters,

3. an oral quality to the language of the text that draws upon African American speech norms,

4. the presence of a symbolic chorus to comment on the actions of characters, and

5. an expectation that the reader participate actively in the going-ons of the story. (p. 343)

Morrison says authors in this tradition make a "deliberate effort...to get a visceral, emotional response as well as an intellectual response" (p. 343). An analogy may be drawn between the aesthetics of Black fiction as described by Morrison and the sermon in many Black church traditions (especially Pentacostal and Evangelical Baptist denominations) in which the speech act requires community coparticipation among the preacher, the audience, and the choir as chorus. Thus expertise in the interpretation of literature is complex and may be culturally influenced. It is no accident, for example, that even within the European American– and European-dominated western literary canon,[3] expert literary critics often specialize in both a particular genre as well as a particular historical time period—such as that of the English Romantic poets—in order to develop a sufficient body of domain-specific knowledge to serve as the foundation for their interpretations.

In addition to domain knowledge, Collins and his colleagues (1991) include heuristic strategies as a necessary teaching focus in designing environments that support cognitive apprenticing. They define heuristic strategies as "effective techniques and approaches for accomplishing tasks that might be regarded as tricks of the trade" (p. 42). Examples of heuristic strategies in the interpretation of literature may include approaches such as Booth's (1974) strategies for recognizing that a passage or text is ironic, Smith's (1987) steps for reconstructing the intended meaning of an ironic passage or text, and Rabinowitz's (1987) rules for significance in fiction. It is important to note that these strategies are genre specific and not simply generic reading comprehension strategies. Neither are they simplistic algorithms leading to a predefined interpretation. Complex and subtle interpretations of necessity involve a fluid interplay among conscious use of such strategies as well as the application of social constructs and the implications of aesthetic traditions.

One of the core tenets of cognitive apprenticing is providing students with a conceptual representation of the task in its wholeness. Collins et al. (1991) say that "the challenge is to situate the abstract tasks of the school curriculum in contexts that make sense to students" (p. 9). To consider the conceptual representation of the task of interpreting complex inferences in fiction involves not only a recognition of the relevance of social knowledge, knowledge of strategies for interpreting specific genres, and knowledge of an aesthetic tradition; it also invokes certain habits of mind, certain attitudes toward language, and the incorporation of one's point of view as relevant to the task of interpretation. Csikszentmihalyi (1990), Goodnow (1990), and Spiro (1980) acknowledge that there are affective variables which influence the quality of thought students bring to the task of learning broadly and reading specifically. Collins and his colleagues recognize the importance of considering attitudes in planning cognitive apprenticeship environments by outlining necessary social characteristics of the environment that will foster student involvement.

# The Study

## Objectives

This study investigates the implications of *signifying*, a form of social discourse in the African American community, as a scaffold for teaching skills in literary interpretation. This investigation is related to the larger question of the efficacy of culturally sensitive instruction. The study is aimed at providing insights into the following questions:

1. Do prior social knowledge and knowledge of signifying affect the range of skills in reading and interpreting fiction achieved by African American adolescent novice readers?

2. Using their prior social knowledge and skill in signifying, how do students construct generalizations about African American "speakerly" (Gates, 1988) texts based on an analysis of the figurative language of such texts?

3. How do teachers support this scaffolding process?

4. What are the effects of instruction?

The hypotheses of this research claim that students' prior social knowledge of themes, values, and social conventions on which the texts are based and their skill in signifying may be productively drawn upon to teach skills in literary analysis.

## Signifying Defined

*Signifying* as a form of talk in the Black community may involve ritual insult and almost always involves the use of figurative language. It may be used to inform, persuade, or criticize. Mitchell-Kernan (1981) has made an extensive analysis of the variety of categories of signifying talk within the Black community. Signifying as ritual insult may involve what has traditionally been called "the Dozens": "Yo mama so dumb she thought a quarterback was a refund." Other forms of ritual insult include a form of verbal dueling called "sounding": One person says, "You so poor the roaches and rats each lunch out," and the other responds, "You so poor the rats and roaches take you out to lunch." Criticizing by sarcastically emulating the words of another is called "marking." Signifying almost always includes double entendre and a play on meanings. Language is to be interpreted figuratively, not literally. Although some argue that men are more likely to participate in signifying talk than women (Labov, 1972), there is no question that the difference is one of degree (Goodwin, 1990; Mitchell-Kernan, 1981). In addition to gender, there are also developmental differences. What little research has been conducted in this area suggests that older children and adolescents produce more complex and elaborated signifying talk. Because the ability to participate in such verbal play is often highly prized in adolescence, it was expected that the high school students in the study would be highly proficient in this arena. This proved to be the case (Lee, 1993).

Although popular views of signifying focus almost solely on signifying as ritual insult, signifying as verbal play is also very prevalent in the African American English speech community, particularly in its vernacular varieties. In order to avoid stereotyping and to access the richness of figurative language that characterizes signifying, I chose samples of signifying that included forms other than ritual insult. For example, Mitchell-Kernan (1981) cites a conversation between two sisters in which one sister has tried to conceal the fact that she is pregnant from the other sister.

Rochelle: Girl, you sure do need to join the Metrecal for lunch bunch.

Grace:    (noncommittally) Yeah, I guess I am putting on a little weight.

Rochelle: Now look here girl, we both standing here soaking wet and you still trying to tell me it ain't raining. (p. 323)

This conversation represents an example of signifying whose purpose is to instruct and inform rather than merely to insult and criticize. Rochelle admonishes her sister for not telling her about the pregnancy. The tenor of Rochelle's comment, however, does not have the sharp, cutting, critical wit of the Dozens or sounding examples. The figurative language in Rochelle's final response may be interpreted as either or both of the following: (a) both sisters really know what's going on (i.e., Grace is pregnant) or (b) Rochelle is informing Grace that she too is pregnant. The closing line is proverbial and symbolic and clearly invokes a playful attitude toward language.

## Data Source

Six classes from two urban high schools in a large midwestern U.S. school district participated in the study. The student body was entirely African American. Data on school achievement were made available through a school report card mandated by the state. The following data are from the year before the study took place. The two schools had graduation rates of 39.8% and 50.9%, respectively. Low-income rates were 34% and 26.4%, respectively. On the district-mandated standardized test of reading achievement, in the first school 85.7% and in the second school 84.7% of the 11th-grade students who took the exam scored at or below the 50th national percentile rank. More startling, in the first school, only 63% of the 11th graders even took the exam. Student standardized test scores in reading placed *all but 8.25%* of the students who participated in the study below the 50th percentile rank nationally. Four classes were involved in the instructional intervention and two classes maintained their normal course of study. All students were high school seniors. The senior English curriculum focused on world literature. The researcher taught two of the experimental classes; two teachers from the district each taught an experimental class; two others each taught a control group.

## Methods

This research involves both quantitative analysis of student achievement as well as qualitative analysis of instructional discourse within both whole- and small-group work. Before and again after instruction, students were given a story they had not read before and eight short-answer questions. The stories were excerpted from *The Bluest Eye* (Morrison, 1970). The questions ranged in difficulty from literal to complex inferences (Hillocks, 1980). Two readers independently rated the exams. Statistical analysis of pre- to posttest gain on essay exams subjected to Rasch scaling (Wright & Masters, 1982) are reported comparing experimental and control or no-treatment groups. Interrater percentages of agreement are available on both pre- and posttests (Lee, 1993). In addition, correlations between tests of prior knowledge of signifying and of relevant social knowledge with pre- to posttest change scores by treatment group are also reported.

Instructional discourse within both whole- and small-group work is analyzed in order to trace changes in students' understanding of signifying from a tool of popular culture to its use as a literary tool within selected texts of African American fiction labeled "speakerly" texts by Gates (1988). The analysis of instructional discourse also documents shifts from relative uninvolvement by students and dependence on the teacher to more sophisticated interpretations of complex inferential questions about the texts and greater independence from the teacher. The analysis of discourse also documents the distinctions between experimental classes and control or no-treatment classes.[4]

## Instruction

At the beginning of the instructional unit, students were given three dialogues of extended signifying taken from Mitchell-Kernan (1981). Students were asked in whole and small groups to interpret what each speaker in each turn of talk actually intended, since in signifying—and in these dialogues in particular—the words never meant what they seemed to mean. The interpretation came relatively easily to the students. The more challenging issue that they addressed was how they knew what they thought they knew about the text. From this discussion, the students generated a set of criteria that signaled to them that the words meant more than they seemed to mean on the surface. The students were then able to articulate the strategies they used to construct what that inferred meaning was. As expected, those clues and strategies were comparable to those identified by Booth (1974) and Smith (1987) as those used by expert readers to recognize and construct interpretations of irony in literature. The strategies extrapolated by the students fall under the rubric of rules of signification (an ironic twist of terminology), or rules for determining that a literary passage is important, as defined by Rabinowitz (1987).

Those strategies were then applied to the process of constructing answers to a plethora of intense, difficult inferential questions about a short story "My Man Bovanne" (Bambara, 1972), and each of two novels. "My Man Bovanne" is the story of an older Black woman who attends a political social gathering at the invitation of her adult children. She befriends a socially outcast blind man named Bovanne by dancing close with him on the dance floor and is criticized by her children for what they consider lower class ways of interacting. Examples of questions posed from the very beginning with "My Man Bovanne" are the following:

1. In terms of this story, what do you think the author means when the narrator says, "Blind people got a hummin' jones if you notice. Which is understandable completely once you been around one and notice what no eyes will force you into to see people" (p. 33).

2. How might the two hums she describes on page 33 be similar: the "hummin' jones of blind people" and the "hummin'" of "fat-chest ladies and old gents gruntin'" in church?

3. What does the ending of the story say to you about what Miss Hazel [the narrator] sees as the nature of beauty and what commitment to one's people means?

These questions are complex and difficult. There are no simple right or wrong answers, but a range of responses is supportable by both close textual analysis and critical thinking about social experiences and issues in the Black community.

After reading "My Man Bovanne," the students read *Their Eyes Were Watching God* (Hurston, 1937/1990) and then *The Color Purple* (Walker, 1982). Students also regularly wrote answers to questions that required inferencing, paying attention to salient details, interpreting figurative language, and drawing on evidence from disparate parts of the text, as well as their personal experiences of the social world embodied in the texts. They were constantly admonished that the teacher would not believe anything they said and that they would have to back up with evidence any claims that they made. The instructional unit was characterized by the following: (a) small-group discussions; (b) some whole- and small-group discussions focusing on student-generated questions; (c) the articulation of a set of criteria by which students would deem a passage worthy of additional investigation; (d) reading about, talking about, and thinking about signifying; (e) focus on the talk in the text—either by characters or the narrator—which is assumed to convey generalizations necessary to the construction and evaluation of themes, symbols, and significant relationships (such talk in the works in question is characterized as figurative language [metaphoric or proverbial talk]); (f) emphasis in whole- and small-group discussion on students justifying interpretations through reference to both the text and real world knowledge; and (g) emphasis on elaborating support for points of view by both much talk and much writing. Both observations and discussions with teachers of the control classes indicate that none of these strategies could be said to characterize instruction in the control classes. In addition, students often commented and complained that they were not accustomed to thinking this much in school.

It is noteworthy also that, in the beginning, some students did not feel this form of talk, namely signifying, was appropriate for a focus in school since signifying may include forms of ritual insult. When they began reading Hurston's speakerly text in *Their Eyes Were Watching God*, some students claimed they could not read the so-called "dialect" and saw no relationships between the speech of the characters and their own speech. Both of these attitudes changed over the course of the instructional experience.

## Results

Although the results below are discussed in more detail in Lee (1993), I include a brief synopsis of the achievement of these students to demonstrate the successes of this project. The experimental group achieved a gain from pre- to posttest over the control group by a broad ratio of 2.28 to 1. *T* tests indicate that the gain was statistically significant. (See Table 19.1 for the mean gain from

**TABLE 19.1 T Test—Significance of Change Score by Treatment (Independent Samples)**

| Group | N | Mean | SD | SE |
|---|---|---|---|---|
| Experimental | 52 | 1.5279 | 1.23 | .171 |
| Control | 25 | .6736 | 1.036 | .207 |

| T value | DF | 2 tail probability |
|---|---|---|
| 3.00 | 75 | .004 |

Pooled variance estimate

pre- to post-test for the experimental and control groups.) The T value indicates that a difference in gain of that magnitude statistically speaking would not occur by chance. This level of gain indicates increased independent mastery of problem-solving strategies.

(See Table 19.2 and Table 19.3 for correlations among the four measurement instruments for only those students who completed all four measures.) For both the experimental and control groups, achievement on prior knowledge (Experimental: $R = .42$, $p = .006$; Control: $R = .47$, $p = .02$) and signifying (Experimental: $R = .35$, $p = .014$; Control: $R = .63$, $p = .002$) correlated with achievement on the posttest. This may be a useful indicator that these cultural variables, prior knowledge and signifying, did bear some relationship to achievement in reading.

Both groups achieved gains from the pre- to posttest. For both the experimental and control groups, students who scored lowest on the pretest made the greatest change scores. These relationships are reflected in the correlations between pretest and change (Experimental: $R = -.61$, $p = .000$; Control: $R = -.63$, $p = .002$).

However, the achievement from pre- to posttest for the experimental group more than doubled that of the control group. Therefore, the correlation of posttest and change was significant for the experimental group only ($R = .33$, $p = .026$). In addition, students in the experimental treatment with the lowest prior knowledge appear to have achieved the greatest increase in positive change ($R = -.31$, $p = .034$).

Analyses of transcripts demonstrate a qualitative transformation of knowledge about signifying from an intuited informal social usage to a formal concept with psychological, structural, and symbolic functions within a literary context (see Lee, 1993).

**TABLE 19.2 Correlation Matrix—Prior Knowledge and Signifying Predicting Pre- and Posttests—Experimental (N = 34)**

| | Signifying | Pretest | Posttest | Change |
|---|---|---|---|---|
| Prior knowledge | .3632 | .6432 | .4276 | −.3174 |
| | $p = .017^*$ | $p = .000^*$ | $p = .006^*$ | $p = .034^*$ |
| Signifying | | .2920 | .3579 | .0267 |
| | | $p = .047^*$ | $p = .014^*$ | $p = .440$ |
| Pretest | | | .5394 | −.6113 |
| | | | $p = .000^*$ | $p = .000^*$ |
| Posttest | | | | .3367 |
| | | | | $p = .026^*$ |

*Statistically significant at $p > .05$.

**TABLE 19.3 Correlation Matrix—Prior Knowledge and Signifying Predicting Pre- and Posttest—Control (N = 19)**

| | Signifying | Pretest | Posttest | Change |
|---|---|---|---|---|
| Prior knowledge | .3365 | .3320 | .4761 | .0731 |
| | $p = .079$ | $p = .089$ | $p = .020^*$ | $p = .383$ |
| Signifying | | .3103 | .6359 | .2339 |
| | | $p = .098$ | $p = .002^*$ | $p = .168$ |
| Pretest | | | .5462 | −.6339 |
| | | | $p = .008^*$ | $p = .002^*$ |
| Posttest | | | | .3016 |
| | | | | $p = .105^*$ |

*Statistically significant at $p > .05$.

# Discussion

It is not possible to disentangle the effect of specific variables in the experimental treatment that account for the change from pre- to posttest. However, it can be argued that the cluster of instructional variables that distinguish the experimental treatment from the experiences of the control or no-treatment group can

**TABLE 19.4** Instructional Variables Characterizing the Experimental and Control Treatments

| Variable | Experimental | Control |
|---|---|---|
| 1. Organization of instruction | Small group work | Lecture and recitation |
| 2. Locus of control | Sequenced phasing of control from teacher to students | Teacher dominated |
| 3. Text selection | African American fiction | Euro-American and Western European texts |
| 4. Cultural foundations | Drawing upon students' knowledge of signifying and their prior social knowledge | Little evidence in transcripts of students' prior social or linguistic knowledge being allied to analysis of the texts |
| 5. Objectives | Emphasis on complex inferential questions | Focus on literal analysis and recall |

reasonably account for the progress of the experimental group. (See Table 19.4 for a summary of the differences in the cluster of instructional variables that characterize the two groups.)

There are many instructional implications of this experimental intervention (Lee, 1993). However, this article focuses on the instruction as an example of a cognitive apprenticeship based on a cultural foundation. D'Andrade (1984) defines "culture as consisting of learned systems of meaning, communicated by means of natural language and other symbol systems, having representational, directive, and affective functions, and capable of creating cultural entities and particular senses of reality" (p. 116). He goes on to say that "analytically, cultural meaning systems can be treated as a very large diversified pool of knowledge, or partially shared clusters of norms, or as intersubjectively shared, symbolically created realities" (p. 116). In this sense, culture provides a matrix through which meaning is created and negotiated. Natural language is among the most powerful mediators of knowledge, values, and thinking processes. Thus attention to characteristics of the language capabilities of ethnically and linguistically diverse students may yield significant information on which to base instruction.

Collins et al. (1991) posit that a cognitive apprenticeship should do the following:

1. Focus on complex or higher order thinking skills;

2. Make explicit and visible those heuristic strategies that experts use;

3. Model, coach, and scaffold novices to help them learn to monitor or self-regulate their use of those heuristics;

4. Through an evolving community of practitioners, develop those habits of mind that foster critical thinking.

The discussion of this instructional intervention will attempt to demonstrate how African American cultural norms for language use and the organization of instruction linked to support this cognitive apprenticeship.

## Representing the Essential Nature of the Task and Promoting Habits of Mind

In both the traditional apprenticeship as well as the cognitive apprenticeship models, it is argued that novices should experience the concept in its wholeness. Novice tailors, for example, will have experienced the entire process of constructing the clothing from start to finish so that when they are introduced to isolated chunks of the job, they have some sense of how a given isolated part fits into the whole process. As implied by Labov (1972) and Mitchell-Kernan (1981), African American students who are proficient in Black discourse forms may have either receptive or productive abilities, or both, along a continuum of expertise. Receptive abilities, for example, mean they can understand signifying. Productive abilities mean they can adeptly respond to turns of talk within signifying dialogues; they can respond with the kind of verbal one-upmanship required.

Many sociolinguists have noted the creative aspects of African American English (Gee, 1989; Heath, 1989; Labov, 1972; Mitchell-Kernan, 1981; Smitherman, 1977; Tannen, 1989). Members of the African American English speech community demonstrate the following attitudes toward language:[5]

1. the playful possibilities of language,

2. a love of double entendre,

3. the placement of value on the manipulation of language for its own artistic merit rather than simply as a tool of literal communication,

4. manipulation of the symbolic functions of language, and

5. the use of densely imagistic and figurative language to express complex ideas in a few words.

These same attitudes toward language are important prerequisites to the process of constructing interpretations of problems posed by literary texts. Although other groups demonstrate uses of figurative language routinely in social discourse (see Saville-Troike, 1989, for other examples), the uses of figurative language within signifying talk are specific and unique to the African American community. In a sense, the intuitive understandings that African American students have about signifying are analogous to the assumptions about language that the school task requires. Anecdotal examples from the transcripts of both whole- and small-group class discussions provide evidence of how students manipulated and played with language as a part of classroom discourse, a characteristic that has been known to cause discipline problems in some classrooms (Gee, 1989; Kochman, 1972).

Proverbs are widely used and valued in the African American community. They are used both in popular culture, as in the title of the Dells' song "Still Water Runs Deep," and as a socializing tool in Black family life (Smitherman, 1977; Smitherman-Donaldson, Daniel, & Jeremiah, 1987). Smitherman (1977) notes,

> Many proverbs are quoted by mothers to their children and serve as child-rearing devices to teach rapidly and in no uncertain terms about life and giving. "A hard head make a soft behind," "If you make yo bed hard, you gon have to lie in it," and "God don't like ugly" are three such frequently used proverbs. (p. 95)

In the test of prior knowledge given before instruction, all students, both experimental and control, did exceedingly well on the section that asked them to summarize the meaning of traditional Black proverbs. Smitherman (1977, p. 95) cites Nigerian writer Chinua Achebe, who notes that "the art of conversation is regarded very highly, and proverbs are the palm-oil with which words are eaten." Smitherman (1977), Dillard (1977), Vass (1979), and Gates (1988), among others, argue that many of the essential characteristics of how many African Americans use language can be traced to West African roots. Proverbs are densely metaphoric and aphoristic and clearly involve a play on language. It is not uncommon for proverbs to be appropriated in signifying talk. Smitherman (1977) notes "The rapper sprinkles his or her talk with familiar Black proverbs and drives home the points with short, succinct statements which have the sound of wisdom and power" (p. 95).

African American norms for language use are also evident in the structures of traditional personal narratives in the Black community. Because it is not uncommon to find lines of signifying embedded in personal narratives or to find personal narratives coconstructed by two or more parties participating in sounding rounds (Labov, 1972),[6] it is not unreasonable to assume that schemata for personal narrative structures and for signifying are related and interact. Thus to activate one is to offer good possibilities for activating the other. Labov (1972) has done extensive research documenting some of the traditional ways in which some African American narrators may present or structure information about personal experiences. Many speakers of BEV narrate, Labov observes, by describing an external action to represent or serve as a sign of an internal state. The White middle class narrators, Labov observes, would interrupt their narratives to make specific comments about their feelings or to make explicit the point they were trying to make. Gee (1989) makes similar observations about aspects of African American narrative style. Gee comments that traditional African American narrative styles include a high use of imagery, concrete detail, parallelism in syntactic structure, shifts in points of view, and representation of an emotional state by showing actions that demonstrate it. These characteristics noted by Labov and Gee have clear and important parallels in the uses of language and the structuring of narrative in the quality of fiction that we attempt to teach students to read in secondary schools.

Paznik (1976) argues that there is an artistic dimension of Black English that reflects an attitude toward verbal behavior that speakers of the language commonly infuse in their talk. She classifies five major language devices used to effect the artistic qualities attributed to Black English:

1. the dramatic figure—the manipulation of language to engage the sympathies of another;
2. the indirection figure—use of double entendre and irony;
3. the orational figure—exaggerated language and heightened delivery;
4. the orchestrational figure—use of rhythm, meter, and repetition to achieve aesthetic effect; and
5. the imagistic figure—use of figurative language to create word pictures. (p. 56)

In one sense, the artistic qualities of Black English meet the criteria for what Gardner (1983) calls "linguistic intelligence," later defined by Smagorinsky (1991, p. 2) as "sensitivity to the sounds, rhythms, and meanings of words and to the different functions of language." In thinking about how knowledge about signifying may be represented in the mind, one can imagine schemata for signifying as a file drawer with many folders. These folders contain criteria for language that is rhythmic, sharp-witted, and highly figurative, criteria for strategies to recognize irony and satire within the social contexts in which signifying is routinely used, and other folders containing knowledge about when signifying is appropriate and about various categories of signifying talk. These schemata are interrelated and the appropriate context can stimulate or activate this nexus of related knowledge. I thus argue that to tap African American students' related nexus of schemata for signifying is to bring into the classroom arena a set of attitudes about language that are most appropriate for learning to interpret complex and subtle inferences in fiction. The challenge, up until now, has been to figure out how to map these attitudes about language to the tasks of classroom instruction.

The question then is what relationships can be observed between these attitudes about language inherent in African American English forms—including signifying, proverbial use, and narrative styles—and the demands of rich literary interpretation. One way of thinking about these relationships is that the cognitive strategies required for comprehension and interpretation of both are similar. Langer (1991) argues that a sociocognitive perspective on literacy should focus on

> the complex ways of thinking that are used in nonreading and nonwriting situations.... Attention to cultural ways of thinking associated with literacy allows literacy instruction to focus on how students think, as well as on the skills they use to read and write. (p. 12)

Resnick (1990) describes a "truly 'literary' reading [as one] which involves deliberate attention to language and expressive device." She goes on to say, "This aspect of literary reading distinguishes it from more popular forms of pleasurable literacy in which language is 'transparent,' unattended to in its own right, just a vehicle for conveying a story" (p. 180). The attitudes toward language characteristic of African American English use are couched in speech events that necessitate "complex ways of thinking" and "deliberate attention to language and expressive device."

An expert representation of the uses to which African American English can be put may be found in what Gates (1988) refers to as "speakerly" texts of African American fiction. In such fiction, not only do characters speak in the voices of the vernacular of this speech community, but also the texts employ speech forms such as proverbs and signifying for literary effect. (See Table 19.5 for list of parallel forms from the oral as well as the literate or textual tradition.)

As these oral forms are appropriated into the literary texts, the authors are not merely replicating the voices of this speech community. Rather, these oral

## TABLE 19.5 Samples of Parallel African American Oral and Literate Forms

| | Oral | Print |
|---|---|---|
| Proverbs | The blacker the berry, the sweeter the juice. | "Some of dese mornin's and it won't be long, you goin tuh wake up callin' me and Ah'll be gone." (Hurston, p. 97) |
| | Grits ain't groceries, eggs ain't poultry, and Mona Lisa was a man. | "...take a stand on high ground." (Hurston, p. 18) |
| Signifying forms | (1) You mama so skinny she could do the hula hoop in a cheerio. | (1) Tea Cake: "Evening Mis' Starks. Could yuh lemme have uh pound uh knuckle puddin'* til Saturday? Ah'm sho tuh pay yuh then." |
| | (2) "Now look here girl, we both standing here soaking wet and you still trying to tell me it ain't raining." (Mitchell-Kernan, p. 323) | Janie: "You needs 10 lbs, Mr. Tea Cake. Ah'll let yuh all Ah got and you needn't bother 'bout payin' it back." (Hurston, p. 83) |
| | (3) "Baby, you a real scholar, I can tell you want to learn. Now if you'll just cooperate a li'l bit, I'll show you what a good teacher I am. But first we got to get into my area of expertise." (Mitchell-Kernan, p. 324) | (2) After Old Mr. signifies on Shug Avery, Celie responds silently and in writing in her letter, "Next time he come I put a little Shug Avery pee in his glass. See how he like that." (Walker, p. 57) |

*An idiom for a beating.

forms are transformed to fulfill literary functions and to make possible multiple layers of meaning (see Table 19.6 for two examples).

Thus, what it means to interpret fiction in a "literary" way is similar in important ways to what it means to understand the subtleties of signifying and other forms of vernacular Black talk. To help students understand this connection is to provide them with two critical lessons: (1) it gives them a way of pulling together a mental representation of this complex cognitive task, and (2) it invokes a set of attitudes toward language and sensibilities to ambiguity that are required to participate in such an interpretive community.

The texts chosen for the instructional unit on which this intervention is based were chosen for four crucial reasons. The texts are "My Man Bovanne,"

## TABLE 19.6 Examples of Literary Functions of African American Oral Forms in Literary Contexts

Proverbial form from *Their Eyes Were Watching God* (Hurston, 1937/1990)

...take a stand on high ground. (p. 18)

Literary functions within the text

| Function | Significance |
|---|---|
| 1. Foreshadowing | Foreshadows Janie's attempts to find a place of safety from the hurricane. |
| 2. Symbolic | Symbolizes the competing world views of Janie and Nanny. |
| 3. Retrospectively ironic | Author comments ironically on the world view of Nanny; there was no symbolic "high ground" on which Janie could ultimately stand. |

Signifying form from *The Color Purple* (Walker, 1982)

After Old Mr. signifies on Shug Avery, Celie responds silently and in writing in her diary, "Next time he come I put a little Shug Avery pee in his glass. See how he like that." (p. 57)

Literary functions within the text

| Function | Significance |
|---|---|
| 1. Symbolic | Represents character transformation and stasis; Celie is empowered by her prior action, this thought, and the act of writing it. Just before she thinks this thought, Celie spit into Old Mr.'s glass of water before serving him. This also symbolizes the impotence of her public silence. |
| 2. Ironic | Shows a reversal of roles between Mr. and Celie. |
| 3. Foreshadowing | Foreshadows the partial reversal of roles between Mr. and Celie near end of book. Recognizing these symbolic and ironic significances will shape the reader's anticipation of and emotional reaction to the unraveling of the storyline. |

(Bambara, 1972), *Their Eyes Were Watching God* (Hurston, 1937/1990), and *The Color Purple* (Walker, 1982). First, as speakerly texts, major characters spoke in BEV and included key passages in which signifying was used. Second, the uses of signifying and proverbial talk were used by the authors as symbolic of internal states of the characters and communicated essential themes of the stories. The rich figurative language shared much with Black discourse styles as described by Mitchell-Kernan (1981), Smitherman (1977, 1994), and others, but also served literary functions within the texts (see Gates, 1988; Jones, 1991; Lee, 1993; Paznik, 1976; Smitherman, 1977, for specific illustrations of uses of the African American verbal tradition in literary texts). Third, these texts were selected because the students possessed social knowledge about African American life experiences that were valuable foundations to inform their interpretations. Fourth, the texts were complex and challenging works of literature, worthy of instruction in a demanding curriculum for high school seniors, if taught in a way that necessitated close textual analysis.

Selected chapters from *The Bluest Eye* (Morrison, 1970) were chosen for the pre- and posttests. Two chapters from the same novel were chosen to heighten the likelihood that the passages were of comparable difficulty.[7] In addition, while the features of BEV are less stark than in the readings in the instructional unit, structural complexities of the pre- and poststories are similar to those in the instructional unit. Most important, however, is that both chapters are difficult texts in their own right and would provide useful insight into how well these students could apply what they learned.

## Making Complex Strategies and Heuristics Explicit

There are additional benefits besides the attitudes toward language made accessible by tapping African American students' cultural schemata for signifying and its related language forms. The instructional intervention provided conditions under which students extrapolated from their understandings of signifying dialogues those strategies that they intuitively used to make the interpretations. The students did not state the strategies as generalizations. Rather, the explanations they offered were specific to the examples they were analyzing. The following example demonstrates how the teachers modeled for and coached students into linking the specific observations they made to generalizations that were more broadly applicable. In this transcript excerpt (Mitchell-Kernan, 1981), the students are analyzing the following signifying dialogue:

The husband in this conversation works on a city garbage truck.

Wife:     Where are you going?

Husband: I'm going to work.

Wife:     You're wearing a suit, tie and white shirt? You didn't tell me you got a promotion. (p. 321)

This dialogue is an example of signifying that is not ritual insult, but is an indirect, figurative, and humorous way of informing. The teacher has asked the students to interpret what the husband and wife each means and to articulate how they came to know their interpretations are appropriate.

| | |
|---|---|
| S: She had an ulterior motive so she could find out where he was going. | **The student has a clear and immediate understanding of below-the-surface meanings.** |
| T: Okay. So she was trying to find out where he was going. | |
| S: And he was trying to keep it away from her. | |
| T: How do you know that? | |
| S: Because he said he was going to work. | |
| T: So how did you know that? | |
| S: I knew it because they told us what kind of job he had and then you knew from the clothing he had on. | **Student articulates a strategy or reasoning process that is contextualized to this specific example.** |
| [intervening dialogue] | |
| T: So he does or says something that is out of character, right? | **Teacher provides or models the language of generalization, posing students' contextualized thinking strategies as a proposition applicable across similar cases.** |
| S: Yes. In other words, he's lying. | |
| T: Okay, so he is obviously lying. But the main thing is that he does and says something that is unusual or out of character. | |

A series of classroom discussions of this order helped produce a list of general strategies for signifying that a passage demands interpretation beyond a literal level. There are four clues to watch for in the text that signal the need to make inferences and three strategies for students to use after spotting such clues in the text (see Table 19.7).

Making expert heuristics explicit, modeling both their generation and their use, and coaching and scaffolding students into the strategic use of these heuristics are at the heart of cognitive apprenticeship. The structure of small-group work, the strategic intervention of the teacher, and the intellectual difficulty of the tasks undertaken provided the ripe conditions for this apprenticeship model. I do not suggest that this organization of instruction would necessarily improve students' ability to read Hamlet (which one of the control classes read). I do suggest, however, that the level of both social and linguistic prior knowledge which these students brought to the particular texts of fiction under study, when coupled with this form of strategic teaching, holds great promise for scaffolding students into sensitive and subtle readings of rich texts.

| |
|---|
| **TABLE 19.7 How an Author May Use Clues in a Text to Signal the Need for Inferencing, and How a Student Can Make Use of These Clues in Understanding the Text** |
| *Clues signaling the need to make inferences:* |
| 1. A character says or does something that seems unusual for what the reader has come to expect; a character makes a significant change in personality, attitude, or values. |
| 2. A comparison is made. Often the comparison will be in the form of metaphor or simile or some other form of figurative language. |
| 3. A statement or passage presents an apparent contradiction or oxymoron. |
| 4. Images, colors, textures, smells, etc., appear to bear some possible relationship to the theme of the novel, short story or chapter. |
| *Reading strategies that make use of these clues:* |
| 1. Mark such passages when you discover them in the text, using self-sticking notes if you do not own the book or underlining/highlighting if you do own it. |
| 2. Write down your reactions to such passages, either in a journal, on self-sticking notes near the passage, or in the margin. In these notes, attempt to interpret what the passage means. You may also write down questions you have about the passage. |
| 3. Keep such questions and tentative answers in mind while you continue to read. |

## Modeling, Coaching, and Self-Monitoring

In an apprenticeship model, the expert models the practice to be mastered. In a cognitive apprenticeship, the teacher models for the student, often verbally, the kind of thinking she or he uses to solve the problem. As the apprentice is engaged in practice, the expert or teacher coaches by commenting on the novice's performance by evaluating, encouraging, and making specific suggestions for improvement or efficiency. The following transcript from the second week of instruction shows how students were applying the strategies listed in Table 19.7 to the following excerpt from the opening of *Their Eyes Were Watching God* (Hurston, 1937/1990), which describes the protagonist Janie Starks's return home after many years.

> So the beginning of this was a woman and she had come back from burying the dead. Not the dead of sick and ailing with friends at the pillow and the feet. She had come back from the sodden and the bloated; the sudden dead, their eyes flung wide open in judgment.
>
> The people all saw her come because it was sundown. The sun was gone, but he had left his footprints in the sky. It was the time for sitting on porches beside the road. It was the time to hear things and talk. These sitters had been tongueless, earless, eyeless conveniences all day long. Mules and other

brutes had occupied their skins. But now the sun and the bossman were gone, so the skins felt powerful and human. They became lords of sounds and lesser things. They passed notions through their mouths. They sat in judgment. (pp. 1–2)

From *Their Eyes Were Watching God* by Zora Neale Hurston. Copyright © 1937/1990. Reprinted by arrangement with HarperCollins.

The strategies are being applied in a social context in an effort to understand the nuances of the figurative language that characterize the opening of the novel. The teacher both models for and coaches the students.

T: And I want to see if you can find some sentences in there that fit these clues that stand out. Because the character does something that's odd or there's a statement made that doesn't seem to make sense. Things are put together that don't seem to fit or unusual kinds of comparisons are made and when you find those things on the page underline them. I'll give you around 4 minutes to do that. Does everybody understand what you're doing?

**Modeling function. Teacher talks aloud about strategies for signaling that an interpretation beyond surface meaning is required.**

[intervening dialogue]

T: What did you underline?

Bob: She had come back from the sodden and bloated and sudden dead. Their eyes flew wide open in judgment.

T: All right, she had come back. Does everyone see where that is, the third paragraph? "She had come back from the sodden and bloated and sudden dead. Their eyes flown wide open in judgment." Why did you underline that?

**Coaching function. Focuses student's attention to analyze and reflect critically about his own thinking.**

Bob: Because it's unusual. Because no one can come back from the dead.

T: Does this idea of her coming back from the sodden and the bloated.... What does sodden mean?

**Coaching function. Because the passage underlined by Bob includes more detail than just someone coming back from the dead, the teacher focuses the student on additional descriptive language in the passage. The teacher realizes that the details of sodden**

| Allen: | Swollen up, I guess. | and bloated will relate to later parts of the novel, and if the students begin to think in the opening passage about the conditions Janie has left, they may more readily think about possible connections between the opening and closing of the novel. |
|---|---|---|
| T: | Sodden, swollen up, so that the idea that she's come back from something that's all wet and bloated up is unusual and it's one of the things, when you read, did it go through your mind to say, what is she talking about? | **Modeling function. Teacher models the strategy of questioning what is puzzling in the text.** |
| Students: | Um hum. | |
| T: | Let me show you my book based on...[pause]. I'm not sure if you can see this in terms of the idea of writing in books. That's one good thing that good readers do with books that they own. And if you could glance through my book, which I'm just walking around here showing you, you can see that it is full of underlines and question marks and circled words all the way through. | **Modeling function. Teacher models that she as an expert reader has engaged in the same important tactic as the students, i.e., underlining and otherwise marking the text.** |

As this recitation continues between the teacher and the students, one student brings up an example that allows the teacher again to draw upon a cultural norm.

| Mary: | Where it says women forget all the things they don't want to remember and remember all the things they don't want to forget. It's not contradictory, but they're talking about two different things. | **The student senses something significant about the passage she quotes, but is unable to explain in clear terms what makes that passage stand out for her.** |
|---|---|---|
| T: | That's interesting and one reason why that statement might have stood out for you is...the fact that certain words are repeated in the way they are sounds very much the way preachers talk, doesn't it? | **Modeling function. Teacher models her own thinking process and draws upon a cultural model to represent the emphatic function that parallel structure can serve. The cultural model refers to how African American preachers use parallel structures to emphasize a point.** |
| Students: | Uh huh. | |
| T: | And that's a reason for it to stand out, I think to you, or to us, really, as an audience... | |

As the unit of instruction progresses, students become more confident in offering unusual and beyond-surface-level interpretations of passages. In addition, students' comments become longer. Students begin to initiate interpretations and to direct the course of classroom discussions. There is a section in *Their Eyes Were Watching God* when the protagonist, Janie, uses the following parable to explain her philosophy of life:

> She had found a jewel down inside herself and she had wanted to walk where people could see her and gleam it around. But she had been set in the market-place to sell. Been set for still-bait. When God had made The Man, he made him out of stuff that sung all the time and glittered all over. Then after that some angels got jealous and chopped him into millions of pieces, but still he glittered and hummed. So they beat him down to nothing but sparks but each little spark had a shine and a song. So they covered each one over with mud. And the lonesomeness in the sparks made them hunt for one another, but the mud is deaf and dumb. Like all the other tumbling mud-balls, Janie had tried to show her shine. (pp. 85–86)

> From *Their Eyes Were Watching God* by Zora Neale Hurston. Copyright © 1937/1990. Reprinted by arrangement with HarperCollins.

The students in the following transcript were addressing the difficult question of the significance or meaning of the title of the novel, using the above quote as a source of data. The following transcript excerpt is from the fourth week of instruction.

Pauline: Remember in our last discussion we said that Janie was one of the sparks. How could she be a spark and a god? How could she give herself the spark? So she got to be the spark or the god and we got to find out who is watching God and why they are watching God. That's what I don't understand.

Pauline is responding to an idea introduced earlier by Frances that everybody in the story is a lord, but there is only one god. Pauline extends the interpretation offered by Frances. She also monitors her own understanding by articulating the questions which must be answered in order to further this line of inquiry and recognizes that she doesn't know the answers to these questions yet.

T: The question, it seems to me, is what I said. Is Zora Hurston in this book saying that Janie is a god or is she saying that Janie has god-like qualities or the qualities that the god that is described in this book would want people to live by?

The teacher comments as both a coach offering advice on the performance of Pauline as well as a participant in a meaningful literary discussion with her students. These dual roles of coach and participant help to apprentice the student into a community of discourse.

| | | |
|---|---|---|
| Frances: | I don't think she is a god. I think she has god-like qualities. It doesn't say that she gave herself this spark. It says that God gave them the spark. God gave man the spark. Remember when I first started off saying that Janie was god and around her was the lords and they were watching her? | **Frances responds with close textual analysis.** |
| T: | Let's look back at the last two pages of the book and then I'm going to turn the question over to you. | **Scaffolding function. Teacher is sensitive about when to directly support the students and when to give them room for independent or semi-independent practice.** |

As participants in this complex problem-solving activity, students needed to learn to monitor their own understandings and to control their own strategy use by knowing how to pose questions to themselves. This was evident in Pauline's questions in the previous transcript selection. In terms of scaffolding, by the time the students were ready to read the second novel, *The Color Purple* (Walker, 1982), the teacher was ready to release more control to the students in directing the course of class discussions.

| | | |
|---|---|---|
| T: | Let me say, before I run out of time, a couple of things about *The Color Purple*.... I have been thinking about how we are going to approach *The Color Purple*. We will be going through *The Color Purple* in less time than it took us to go through *Their Eyes Were Watching God*. We will basically have 9 days. So what I thought was instead of my giving questions to you, I have questions, but part of what made me think about it was Charles. Charles came to see me sixth period and raised a very interesting question. It is really something that I've wanted to do all along, but we haven't taken the time to do it. It is something that all good readers do and that is while they are reading, they ask questions. What was your question, Charles? Could you share with the rest of the class? | **The teacher acknowledges the leadership role of Charles in initiating his questions, indicating his readiness and perhaps that of the class to assume responsibility for directing class discussions. The teacher also continues to model strategies for carrying out this task, namely reiterating that good readers ask questions.** |

| Charles: | Why every time it's for Mister, it is a Mister blank instead of Mister's name? That is his name, Mister. In the movie, they called him Mister. He never told her his name? She used Harpo's and Jake's name. But that is what she called him, Mister. | **As an indication that Charles is being apprenticed into a community of learners, a community of readers, he initiated this question not at the teacher's request or during the formal class period. Charles came to the teacher's room earlier in the day, during his lunch period, because he had this burning question that he wanted to discuss.** |
|---|---|---|

This approach of modeling, coaching, and scaffolding differs from more liberal views of reader response theory in literature classes where the valued norm is for students to control and direct discussions all along the way (Eeds & Wells, 1989). Delpit (1988) and Reyes (1991), among others, have suggested that teachers need to make explicit their expectations in order to empower students who may be academically at risk in part because of cultural and language differences between school curricula and home and community experiences. I argue that the cognitive apprenticeship model, especially when organized around culturally responsive propositions, bridges the gap between explicit teaching and the application independently of critical thinking strategies in specific subject matter content. Many arguments made for including elements of the cultural experiences, knowledge, and history of disfavored ethnic groups into the strategies for teaching and content of school curricula have focused on issues of equity and self-esteem. Although these reasons are laudable and important in their own right, this research attempts to link the incorporation of culturally specific content with a cognitive apprenticeship model of instruction in order to foster the development of critical thinking in reading. The most basic proposition of this article is not simply to embrace and build upon the strengths of African American English and African American literature, *but more broadly to reconceptualize cultural variables and critical thinking as linked, teachable, and empowering.*

Much of the students' analysis took place in small-group discussions. The teacher's role was to move from group to group listening carefully to the level of discussion, ascertaining whether students were generally participating and on focus. Most importantly, she needed to ascertain whether the interpretations they were putting forward were an easy way out or simply on the wrong track, and intercede in the group conversation only when these conditions were evident. There were two common threads in the teacher's role as coach. One was to challenge students routinely to prove any proposition they put forward with evidence from either the text or real-world social norms and conditions. The second was to play devil's advocate by offering contradicting evidence to propositions offered by the students that either could be extended further or might relate to another important problem in the text. Even on the last day of instruction, the teacher continued to challenge students' thinking.

The topic of the last day of discussion was why Alice Walker called the book *The Color Purple*. Although the statistical results of gains from pre- to posttest described earlier provide strong evidence that the students across the four experimental classes had been able to apply their newly acquired strategies to a short story they had not read or discussed before, the quantitative measures do not tell the whole story. More dramatic evidence of how these strategies had been appropriated may be seen through the final class discussions. An analysis of that last day's discussion demonstrates that the students had appropriated the goals of the instructional unit: (a) to begin to think about the act of interpreting fiction as expert readers do, (b) to develop a taste for tackling the language of literary texts, and (c) to support their responses to complex problems of interpretation with close textual analysis and by drawing on their knowledge of the social world of the texts. Their prior knowledge of signifying had been a bridge over which the students had traversed to aesthetic territory of great promise. During the last day's discussion, the students dominated talk in the classrooms. For lines of talk in the transcript that are four or more lines in length, the teacher produces only 24% of the talk while the students produce 76%. As with any community of inquiry, they challenge one another for the floor and feel deeply about their interpretations as evidenced by several references to other students' stealing their ideas before they had a chance to articulate them. They also draw on ideas initiated by one another. Responses from four students in one class are offered to demonstrate the quality of thinking achieved by some:

Pat: The reason that I feel that the book is called *The Color Purple* is because the color purple represents, in this book, sadness and also I think the purple represents Celie's life because the purple represents sadness to Celie. Therefore her whole life, she never had happiness until the end. When they said that God represented the pain and everything, even the little things, the purple represents sadness like I said and her life. By her life being so bad and she not having the right people to influence her. She didn't lead the life that she wanted to lead, that she felt would be good, I guess. I can't get my thoughts together, but all in all, that is why I think they named it *The Color Purple*. Through the whole book it is sadness and pain and that is all she had in her whole life, pain and sadness. Like when her sister was taken away and when she found out that her father wasn't her father, all this different stuff that happened to her.

Joe: Like Pat said, like in the beginning [purple] was like a gloomy color as well as a happy color so at the end it represented the life that she wanted to lead, like having her own house and stuff and having the people around her that she wanted. The purple represented happy times at that time.

Diane:    I said that *The Color Purple* was Celie's life and how she behaved all
          through the whole book. I came to this conclusion from what Shug had
          said about it pisses god off when you walk through the color purple in a
          field and don't notice it. On the next page Celie says that her eyes were
          opened and Sofia went through the color purple too. I think that the
          color purple was just like a depression or trying period and she went
          through that when she was in jail and she was working for Ms. Millie;
          and she transformed into someone else, when Celie came out of her
          shell, when she signified on Mr.; and I think that the red, they always put
          red and purple together, I think that would represent a transformation
          from being in a depression and coming into something new.

Charles:  I think, plus all that they stole from me [referring to prior comments
          made by others in the class], that the frog had something to do with
          it too because a frog is ugly when it is green, but if it's a purple frog it
          is beautiful and everything. When he gave her that frog it represented
          her life. She was treated like a step girl, like dirt and everything. She
          was like an eggplant, purple didn't mean much to her then. But then
          when she met Shug, she began to blossom like the flowers in that
          field and finally at the end she came out and just sat.

Besides the uniqueness of their interpretations, what is of special interest is
how the students argue through the images of the text. They initiate interpretations about the color purple, the eggplant image of how Sofia looked after being
beaten in jail, the frog image that Mr. gives Celie at the end, the flowers that go
unnoticed, all central images in *The Color Purple*. In a sense, one might speculate
that the attention to imagery and figurative language to which the students attend
in their participation in signifying talk in their community experiences has now
expanded to include attention to literary images in fiction. Although the quality
of response was not equal across all four classes, the analyses of pre- to posttest
change indicates that the students in most need made the greatest gains.

About a month after the instructional unit was over, one of the classes I
taught sent me a folder with letters of thanks from the students. Each letter confirmed that the students had never been asked in school to think this hard. One
student remarked that participating in this instructional unit was more difficult
than taking the Scholastic Aptitude Test. On the front of the folder was written in
huge colored letters "PROVE IT!" When the principal of the school saw the
folder (before it was sent to my home), she asked whether "PROVE IT!" was
some kind of code word. When I thought about it later, the motif of "PROVE
IT!" set in motion an epistemic habit of mind that loomed perhaps as the
overarching lesson learned by these students. Insisting that students consistently articulate how they knew something was true imposed a kind of conscious
regulation of their strategy use as well as an ongoing monitoring of their level
of understanding. Monitoring understanding and a conscious and strategic use
of heuristics are crucial components of any cognitive apprenticing.

# Discussion

During the 1970s, there was much sociolinguistic research that validated the richness of traditional African American manipulation of the English language. This research tradition also provided evidence of how cultural differences in interaction styles impeded the levels and quality of participation in classroom discourse dominated by the recitation mode. Although that body of research clearly laid the foundation for this current study, little work has been done since then investigating the positive cognitive consequences of linking the social languages of home, school, and literature. Since then, the argument for culturally responsive pedagogy has been well articulated (Irvine, 1990; King, 1990; Ladson-Billings, 1992; Shujaa, 1994). Although there is great fervor over the insights of Vygotsky and Bahktin into the social contexts under which learning occurs and the layers of meaning implicit in diglossic social languages, little work has been done to relate these propositions to disfavored ethnic and racial groups. In terms of the implications of African American English, Ball (1992) and Mahiri (1991) are two notable exceptions. Writers in the speakerly tradition (Gates, 1988) both emulate and creatively extend the linguistic traditions of the communities out of which they come. It is possible that somewhere in the interface of community language practices and the expert extensions of those community language practices lies an untapped whirlpool out of which culturally sensitive cognitive apprenticeships can be designed.

Although this study offers a beginning, many questions still need to be engaged. How individual students appropriate the reading strategies, how such appropriation is supported through small group interactions, and how students apply their evolving mastery of these strategies to texts that are culturally less familiar are important issues for future investigations. In addition, the model needs replication in larger settings in order to look at the implications for the overall organization of an English language arts curriculum and how teachers internalize and apply the principles underlying this model. I am currently engaged in several projects that consider these issues. However, equally crucial are two central questions raised concerning this study. One is whether this model helps students to engage literary texts whose themes are more distant from their contemporary experiences. The second is the applicability of the model to other populations of novice readers. Although research is under way to consider the first question, further discussion of the second is needed.

The interface between signifying as a pattern of discourse in the African American English speech community and the appropriation of such patterns of discourse by African American writers is an example of an interaction between oral and print media that is not unique to the African American community.

Distinct patterns of discourse among varieties of English speakers have been well documented in the sociolinguistic literature (Galindo, 1993; Gumperz & Hymes, 1986; Saville-Troike, 1989; Tannen, 1989). It is not uncommon for patterns of discourse and routine speech events to require participants to comprehend irony, satire, double entendre, and shifts in point of view, and in general to pay attention to the subtleties of language play. There are also traditions within American literature wherein authors cast their ears to the nuances of language play within specific speech communities and manipulate the patterns they hear to act as tropes through which layers of meanings, not explicitly stated, are communicated. The carefully crafted code switching from English to Spanish in the short stories of Sandra Cisneros (1991), the interplay of southern voices in *The Adventures of Huckleberry Finn* (Twain, 1988), and the presence of a Jewish verbal tradition in the work of Chaim Potok (1967) are all examples from other verbal traditions of this aesthetic territory where oral and literate rhetorical patterns meet.

The instructional framework I advocate rests on the assumption that the following strategies may provide a powerful conceptual model for what it means to read rich literature in a literary way: (a) structure a learning environment for students in which through active investigations they can unearth and articulate otherwise tacit strategies that they use to construct inferred meanings in oral speech events; (b) apply those strategies to literary texts in which the patterns of discourse studied in the oral context are appropriated for literary effect; and (c) sequence future series of texts within units of instruction so that the first texts are ones for which students initially have greater social and linguistic prior knowledge while they learn to master task-specific reading strategies and the second texts are ones for which students now have greater mastery of task-specific reading strategies and less social and linguistic prior knowledge. This set of assumptions about instruction has far-reaching implications for the content of English language arts readings in the secondary curricula. Traditional assumptions about chronological sequences within a national tradition (i.e., American literature, British literature) and about a set canon, often dominated by a White European male literary tradition, are challenged by the instructional framework I have described. This challenge is further supported by the claim of some that the goal of the literature curriculum, particularly at the secondary level, should be to apprentice novice readers into becoming lifelong readers of complex literature across a variety of historical, national, and ethnic traditions, as opposed to the goal of assuring that significant numbers of students at least read a prescribed set of canonical readings before they leave high school (Scholes, 1985; Smagorinsky & Gevinson, 1989).

The central problem that the cognitive apprenticeship framework seeks to address is how to make public and visible to novice learners those powerful problem-solving strategies and heuristics that more expert readers practice flex-ibly and use strategically. I believe a strong case can be made for the argument that, even within a highly literate society such as the United States, the uses of cognitive strategies to understand communication in oral contexts are likely to be more embedded, more automaticized, and ultimately more sophisticated for more people than their use of cognitive strategies to understand communication in print, especially highly specialized genres such as those within the domain of complex literature. If this is the case, then attention to reasoning in oral contexts, with special sensitivity to the significance of language variations within a na-tion state, may offer meaningful sources for conceptual modeling of reading strategies. This framework is controversial in large part because of the very strong set of attitudes that educational and work institutions as well as vested in-terest groups have about the relative status of one language or language variety over another (Saville-Troike, 1989; Gee, 1990). Such controversy is particularly problematic considering that the most pervasive symbol system through which thinking is mediated is language. However, current conditions convince me that a radical reordering of our vision of literacy instruction is needed. For the first time in history, teachers are charged to apprentice the vast majority of U.S. citi-zenry into very high levels of print literacy (Kaestle, Damon-Moore, Stedman, Tinsley, & Trollinger, 1991; Resnick & Resnick, 1988) while the most pervasive medium of communication is visual (television, movies, videos, etc.). We need both continued theoretical discussions and empirical research in the social con-texts of schools and communities that include the voices of minority scholars (Delpit, 1988) in order to deepen our understanding of the issues involved and the possibilities for opening up the world of rich literature to a majority of our students.

### Notes

1. Lee (1993) gives a full presentation of the study, including complete statistical analyses and a full description of the classroom intervention. This present article extends the initial study by offering a new theoretical framework for analyzing the data and additional illustrations of classroom discourse not found in the original report.

2. I acknowledge that African American culture is not monolithic. There are clearly differences in the manifestation of that culture influenced by class and gender, for example. However, I assert that these differences exist along a continuum and that there is a body of research which argues convincingly that African American culture exists and is distinct. The research upon which this present study is based draws on elements of African American culture evidenced in African American English.

3. In one sense, it is logical and appropriate that the western literary canon be dominated by European literature. My reference, however, is to that body of

literature which dominates the canon taught in American schools under the subject headings of American literature, British literature, and world literature. This body of literature is dominated by Euro-American and European authors (Applebee, 1989), even though there has been an increase in the representation of authors who are women and people of color (Stotsky, 1993).

4. For a more detailed discussion of these issues in the study, see Lee (1993).

5. I have consciously identified these attributes with speakers of African American English, particularly in its vernacular varieties, as opposed to members of the African American community, in order to acknowledge that not all African Americans speak African American English (Labov, 1972). The complexity of this matter of identity by language use may be demonstrated by Smitherman's (1994) observations of National Assessment of Educational Progress writing samples from 1969 to 1988/89. Smitherman found that although BEV syntax decreased, use of features of African American discourse continued.

6. Sounding is a category of signifying that involves ritual insult.

7. See Lee (1993) for details on the statistical measures on which comparability of pre- and postmeasures were made.

## REFERENCES

Abrahams, R.D. (1970). *Deep down in the jungle: Negro narrative folklore from the streets of Philadelphia.* Chicago: Aldine.

Applebee, A.N. (1989). *A study of book-length works taught in high school English courses* (Report Series 1.2). Albany, NY: Center for the Learning and Teaching of Literature.

Ball, A. (1992). Cultural preference and the expository writing of African-American adolescents. *Written Communication,* 9(4), 501–532.

Bambara, T.C. (1972). My man Bovanne. In T.C. Bambara, *Gorilla, my love* (pp. 1–10). New York: Random House.

Booth, W.C. (1983). *The rhetoric of fiction* (2nd ed.). Chicago: University of Chicago Press. (Originally published 1961)

Cazden, C. (1988). *Classroom discourse: The language of teaching and learning.* Portsmouth, NH: Heinemann.

Cazden, C., John, V.P., & Hymes, D. (Eds.). (1972). *Functions of language in the class-room.* New York: Teachers College Press. (Reprinted by Waveland Press, 1985)

Cisneros, S. (1991). *Woman hollering creek and other stories.* New York: Random House.

Collins, A., Brown, J., & Newman, S. (1989). Cognitive apprenticeship: Teaching the craft of reading, writing and mathematics. In L. Resnick (Ed.), *Knowing, learning, and instruction: Essays in honor of Robert Glaser* (pp. 453–494). Hillsdale, NJ: Erlbaum.

Collins, A., Brown, J.S., & Holum, A. (1991, Winter). Cognitive apprenticeship: Making thinking visible. *American Educator,* 6–91.

Csikszentmihalyi, M. (1990). Literacy and intrinsic motivation. *Daedalus, 119*(2), 115–140.

D'Andrade, R.G. (1984). Cultural meaning systems. In R.A. Shweder & R.A. LeVine (Eds.), *Cultural theory: Essays on mind, self and emotion* (pp. 88–119). New York: Cambridge University Press.

De Beaugrande, R. (1987). Schemas for literary communication. In L. Halasz (Ed.), *Literary discourse: Aspects of cognitive and social psychological approaches* (pp. 49–99). New York: Walter de Gruyter.

Delpit, L. (1988). The silenced dialogue: Power and pedagogy in educating other people's children. *Harvard Educational Review, 56*(3), 280–298.

Delpit, L. (1990). Language diversity and learning. In S. Hynds & D.L. Rubin (Eds.), *Perspectives on talk and learning* (pp. 247–266). Urbana, IL: National Council of Teachers of English.

Dillard, J.L. (1977). *Lexicon of Black English.* New York: Seabury Press.

Dole, J.A., Duffy, G.G., Roehler, L.R., & Pearson, P.D. (1991, Summer). Moving from the old to the new: Research on reading comprehension instruction. *Review of Educational Research, 61*(2), 239–264.

Durkin, D. (1978/1979). What classroom observations reveal about reading comprehension instruction. *Reading Research Quarterly, 14,* 481–533.

Eeds, M., & Wells, D. (1989, February). Grand conversations: An exploration of meaning construction in literature study groups. *Research in the Teaching of English, 23*(1), 4–29.

Fitzgerald, J., & Spiegel, D. (1983). Enhancing children's reading comprehension through instruction in narrative structure. *Journal of Reading Behavior, 15*(2), 2–17.

Galindo, D.L. (1993). Bilingualism and language variation among Chicanos in the Southwest. In A.W. Glowka & D.M. Lance (Eds.), *Language variation in North American English: Research and teaching* (pp. 199–218). New York: Modern Language Association.

Gardner, H. (1983). *Frames of mind: The theory of multiple intelligences.* New York: Basic Books.

Garner, R. (1987). *Metacognition and reading comprehension.* Norwood, NJ: Ablex.

Gates, H.L. (1988). *The signifying monkey: A theory of Afro-American literary criticism.* New York: Oxford University Press.

Gee, J.P. (1989). The narrativization of experience in the oral style. *Journal of Education, 171*(1), 75–96.

Gee, J.P. (1990). *Social linguistics and literacies: Ideology in discourses.* New York: Falmer Press.

Goodnow, J. (1990). The socialization of cognition: What's involved? In J.W. Stigler, R. Shweder, & Q.G. Herdt (Eds.), *Cultural psychology: Essays on comparative human development* (pp. 259–286). New York: Cambridge University Press.

Goodwin, M.H. (1990). *He-said-she-said: Talk as social organization among Black children.* Bloomington: Indiana University Press.

Graves, B. (1994, April). *Reasoning strategies in literary reading as a function of the communicative context.* Paper presented at the annual meeting of the American Educational Research Association, New Orleans, LA.

Gumperz, J., & Hymes, D. (1986). *Directions in sociolinguistics: The ethnography of communication.* New York: Basil Blackwell.

Hansen, J., & Pearson, P. (1983). An instructional study: Improving inferential comprehension of good and poor fourth-grade readers. *Journal of Educational Psychology, 75,* 821–829.

Heath, S. (1983). *Ways with words: Language, life, and work in communities and classrooms.* Cambridge, UK: Cambridge University Press.

Heath, S. (1989). Oral and literate traditions among Black Americans living in poverty. *American Psychologist, 44*(2), 367–373.

Hillocks, G. (1980). Toward a hierarchy of skills in the comprehension of literature. *English Journal, 69*(3), 54–59.

Hillocks, G. (1989). Literary texts in class-rooms. In P. Jackson & S. Haroutunian-Gordon (Eds.), *From Socrates to software: The teacher as text and the text as teacher* (88th yearbook of the National Society for the Study of Education, pp. 135–158). Chicago: University of Chicago Press.

Hurston, Z.N. (1990). *Their eyes were watching God.* New York: Harper and Row. (Original work published 1937)

Irvine, J. (1990). *Black students and school failure.* New York: Praeger.

Jones, G. (1991). *Liberating voices: Oral tradition in African American literature.* New York: Penguin.

Kaestle, C., Damon-Moore, H., Stedman, L.C., Tinsley, K., & Trollinger, W.V. (1991). *Literacy in the United States: Readers and reading since 1880.* New Haven, CT: Yale University Press.

King, J. (Ed.). (1990). In search of African liberation pedagogy: Multiple contexts of education and struggle [Special issue]. *Journal of Education, 172*(2).

Kintsch, W., & Greene, E. (1978). The role of culture-specific schemata in the comprehension and recall of stories. *Discourse Processes, 1,* 1–13.

Kochman, T. (Ed.). (1972). *Rappin' and stylin' out: Communication in urban Black America.* Urbana, IL: University of Illinois Press.

Labov, W. (1972). *Language in the inner city: Studies in the Black English Vernacular.* Philadelphia: University of Pennsylvania Press.

Ladson-Billings, G. (1992). Liberatory consequences of literacy: A case of culturally relevant instruction for African American students. *Journal of Negro Education, 61*(3), 378–391.

Langer, J. (1991). Literacy and schooling: A sociocognitive perspective. In E.H. Hiebert (Ed.), *Literacy for a diverse society: Perspectives, practices and policies* (pp. 9–27). New York: Teachers College, Columbia University.

Lee, C. (1993). *Signifying as a scaffold for literary interpretation: The pedagogical implications of an African American discourse genre* (Research Report Series). Urbana, IL: National Council of Teachers of English.

Mahiri, J. (1991, Summer). Discourse in sports: Language and literacy features of preadolescent African American males in a youth basketball program. *Journal of Negro Education, 60*(3), 276–290.

Malik, A. (1990). A psycholinguistic analysis of the reading behavior of EFL-proficient readers using culturally familiar and culturally nonfamiliar expository texts. *American Educational Research Journal, 27*(1), 205–223.

Marshall, J., Klages, M., & Fehlman, R. (1990). *Discussions of literature in lower-track classrooms* (Report Series Number 2.19). Albany, NY: National Research Center on Literature Teaching and Learning, State University of New York. (ERIC Document Reproduction Service No. ED333432)

Means, B., & Knapp, M.S. (Eds.). (1991). *Teaching advanced skills to educationally disadvantaged students.* (Data Analysis Support Center, Task 4 Final Report E338722). Washington, DC: U.S. Department of Education.

Michaels, S. (1986). Narrative presentations: An oral preparation for literacy with first graders: In J. Cook-Gumperz (Ed.), *The social construction of literacy* (pp. 94–116). Cambridge, UK: Cambridge University Press.

Mitchell-Kernan, C. (1981). Signifying, loud-talking and marking. In A. Dundes (Ed.), *Mother wit from the laughing barrel* (pp. 310–328). Englewood Cliffs, NJ: Prentice Hall.

Morrison, T. (1970). *The bluest eye; a novel.* New York: Holt, Rinehart & Winston.

Morrison, T. (1984). Rootedness: The ancestor as foundation. In M. Evans (Ed.), *Black women writers (1950–1980): A crit-*

*ical evaluation* (pp. 339–345). New York: Doubleday.

Nystrand, M., & Gamoran, A. (1989, April). *Instructional discourse, student engagement, and literature achievement.* Paper presented at the annual meeting of the American Educational Research Association, Boston.

Palincsar, A.S., & Brown, A.L. (1984). Reciprocal teaching of comprehension-fostering and monitoring activities. *Cognition and Instruction, 1*(2), 117–175.

Paznik, J. (1976). *The artistic dimension of Black English: A disclosure model and its implications for curriculum and instruction.* Unpublished doctoral dissertation, Columbia University Teachers College, New York.

Pearson, P., & Dole, J. (1987). Explicit comprehension instruction: A review of research and a new conceptualization of instruction. *Elementary School Journal, 88*(2), 151–165.

Potok, C. (1967). *The chosen; a novel.* New York: Simon & Schuster.

Rabinowitz, P. (1987). *Before reading: Narrative conventions and the politics of interpretation.* Ithaca, NY: Cornell University Press.

Resnick, D.P., & Resnick, L. (1988). The nature of literacy: A historical exploration. In E.R. Kintgen, B.M. Kroll, & M. Rose (Eds.), *Perspectives on literacy* (pp. 190–204). Carbondale, IL: Southern Illinois University Press.

Resnick, L. (1990, Spring). Literacy in school and out. *Daedalus, 119*(2), 169–185.

Reyes, M.L. (1991). A process approach to literacy instruction for Spanish-speaking students: In search of a best fit. In E.H. Hiebert (Ed.), *Literacy for a diverse society: Perspectives, practices and policies* (pp. 157–171). New York: Teachers College Press.

Reynolds, R., Taylor, M., Steffensen, M., Shirey, L., & Anderson, R. (1982). Cultural schemata and reading comprehension. *Reading Research Quarterly, 17*(3), 353–366.

Saville-Troike, M. (1989). *The ethnography of communication: An introduction.* New York: Blackwell.

Schank, R.C., & Abelson, R.P. (1977). *Scripts, plans, goals, and understanding: An inquiry into human knowledge structures.* Hillsdale, NJ: Erlbaum.

Scholes, R. (1985). *Textual power: Literary theory and the teaching of English.* New Haven, CT: Yale University Press.

Shujaa, M.J. (Ed.). (1994). *Too much schooling, too little education: A paradox of Black life in White societies.* Trenton, NJ: Africa World Press.

Smagorinsky, P. (1991). *Expressions: Multiple intelligences in the English class.* Urbana, IL: National Council of Teachers of English.

Smagorinsky, P., & Gevinson, S. (1989). *Fostering the reader's response: Rethinking the literature curriculum, grades 7–12.* Palo Alto, CA: Dale Seymour.

Smagorinsky, P., & Smith, M. (1992). The nature of knowledge in composition and literary understanding: The question of specificity. *Review of Educational Research, 62*(3), 279–306.

Smith, M. (1987). *Reading and teaching irony in poetry: Giving short people a reason to live.* Unpublished doctoral dissertation, University of Chicago, IL.

Smith, M. (1989). Teaching the interpretation of irony in poetry. *Research in the Teaching of English, 23*(3), 254–272.

Smitherman, G. (1977). *Talkin and testifyin: The language of Black America.* Boston: Houghton Mifflin.

Smitherman, G. (1994). The blacker the berry, the sweeter the juice: African American student writers and the National Assessment of Educational Progress. In A.H. Dyson & C. Genishi (Eds.), *The need for story: Cultural di-*

versity in classroom and community (pp. 80–101). Urbana, IL: National Council of Teachers of English.

Smitherman-Donaldson, G., Daniel, J., & Jeremiah, M. (1987). "Makin a way outa no way": The proverb tradition in the Black experience. *Journal of Black Studies*, *17*(4), 482–508.

Spiro, R. (1980). Constructive processes in prose comprehension and recall. In R. Spiro, B. Bruce, & W. Brewer (Eds.), *Theoretical issues in reading comprehension* (pp. 245–278). Hillsdale, NJ: Erlbaum.

Steffensen, M., Joag-Dev, C., & Anderson, R. (1979). A cross-cultural perspective on reading comprehension. *Reading Research Quarterly*, *15*(1), 10–29.

Stotsky, S. (1993). Antidote to controversy? Responses to Carolyn Henly. Secular Puritanism? *English Journal*, *82*(3), 20–21.

Tannen, D. (1989). *Talking voices: Repetition, dialogue and imagery in conversational discourse.* New York: Cambridge University Press.

Twain, M. (1988). *The adventures of Huckleberry Finn.* Berkeley, CA: University of California Press.

Van den Broek, P. (1994). *Comprehension of narrative texts: The role of causal inferences.* Paper presented at the annual meeting of the American Educational Research Association, New Orleans, LA.

Vass, W.K. (1979). *The Bantu speaking heritage of the United States.* Los Angeles: Center for Afro-American Studies, University of California.

Walker, A. (1982). *The color purple: A novel.* New York: Simon & Schuster.

Wright, B., & Masters, G. (1982). *Rating scale analysis.* Chicago: MESA Press.

# Assessment Issues

ong before the call of U.S. President George W. Bush, former U.S. Secretary of Education Rod Paige, and others in the administration when the No Child Left Behind Act of 2001 was enacted, and even before former President Bill Clinton's Goals 2000 initiative, African American educators and researchers were vitally concerned about the sociological impact of testing on children of color. Part IV represents the extent to which educators have gained knowledge, developed insight, and exhibited sensitivity to the issues surrounding assessment practices on African American children.

Only two articles were selected for Part IV, not because of a lack of materials from which to select for inclusion, but because the editors felt that these two selections, taken in the full context of this book, were more than adequate to demonstrate the point that, while progress has been made on the topic of assessing children of color fairly and accurately, there are many miles to go before the final goals in this area are reached. Further, only the surface has been scratched in reducing the tendency to blame the children for the shortcomings of the instruments used to evaluate their academic performance in school.

Noted psychologist and historian Asa Hilliard (2002) offers one of the best statements of the issues surrounding the need for improving the assessment practices for children of color:

> It cannot be denied that African American children are not achieving at optimal levels in the schools of the nation. Neither can it be said that there is a need for African American children to learn languages and content other than that which many have already learned up to now. The real problem we are forced to confront is this: Can we be explicit about how professional practice can be made to perform the normal and expected functions of facilitating the natural healthy learning processes of children? In particular, how can the assessment process be purified so as to operate in the service of African American children rather than against them? (p. 91)

Further, Hilliard (1995) suggests that we are faced with a rampant, unbridled ethnocentrism among the designers of standardized tests and assessment procedures for use with diverse cultural groups in the United States.

To remedy this problem, Hilliard and others (Aaron & Powell, 1982; Irvine, 1991; Simpson & Erickson, 1983) have suggested two solutions: (1) a systematic cultural-linguistic review of all testing and assessment devices that are used with African American children, and (2) teaching teachers so that their total orientation toward language and cultural linguistic principles represents the best that we know about the subject.

Taylor and Lee (1995) observe that, based on over two decades of study, it is a well-documented fact that incongruencies between the communicative behavior or language of the test givers and the test takers can result in test bias (Seymore & Miller-Jones, 1981; Taylor & Payne, 1983; Vaughn-Cooke, 1983). Taylor and Lee further suggest that, over the past 30 years, several significant court decisions— *Larry P. v. Riles, 1972; Dianna v. State Board of Education, 1970; Mattie T. v. Holladay, 1977,* and ultimately the Education of All Handicapped Children Act of 1975 (and subsequent amends)—have all upheld the notion that tests and other assessment procedures should not be linguistically or culturally discriminatory.

The primary question for our consideration on the topic of assessment, as related to children of color then, is, If there is a history of awareness of the limitations of our assessment procedures as relates to these children, and if our national concern is to adequately prepare our children to become contributing members of the larger society, why do procedures still exist that are inadequate to describe what our children know and how they know it? Additionally, what can and should be done to overcome these obvious shortcomings in our assessment procedures?

The two chapters in this section are offered with the hope of providing clarity and direction for future educational assessment discussions of fair practices. Chapter 20 is an update of an article written more than 20 years ago by Mary Eleanor Rhodes Hoover, founder and former president of the National Association of Black Reading and Language Educators (NABRLE), and her colleagues. Revisiting the initial discussion of bias in reading tests for Black language speakers, Hoover and her coauthors point to current practices in assessment that still exist to the detriment of today's children of color.

Chapter 21, a position statement of the California Speech and Hearing Association Task Force on the Assessment of the African American Child, presents a lucid and thoughtful approach to the issue and offers practical guidelines and suggestions for educators seeking to implement fair assessment procedures.

Finally, the editors of this book sincerely hope that the education community in general and our esteemed colleagues in the reading profession in particular will read these articles with an open mind and consider what might be done to ensure that our assessment practices match our overall goals for education so that no child will be penalized on any assessment measure for any reason.

## REFERENCES

Aaron, R., & Powell, G. (1982). Feedback practices as a function of teacher and pupil race during reading group instruction. *Journal of Negro Education, 51*(1), 50–59.

Dianna v. State Board of Education, C.A. 70 RFT (N.D. Cal., Feb. 3, 1970).

Education of All Handicapped Children Act of 1975, Public L. No. 94-142, 89 Stat. 773.

Hilliard, A.G. (Ed.). (1995). *Testing African American students.* Chicago: Third World Press.

Hilliard, A.G. (2002). Language, culture, and the assessment of African American children. In L.D. Delpit & J.K. Dowdy (Eds.), *The skin that we speak: Thoughts on language and culture in the classroom* (pp. 87–106). New York: New Press.

Irvine, J.J. (1991). *Black students and school failure: Policies, practices, and prescriptions.* New York: Praeger.

Larry P. v. Riles, Civil Action No. 0-71-2270, 343 F. Supp. 1306 (N.D. Cal., 1972).

Mattie T. v. Holladay, 552 F. Supp. 72 (N.M. Miss., 1977).

No Child Left Behind Act of 2001, Public L. No. 107-110, 115 Stat. 1428 (2002).

Seymore, H., & Miller-Jones, D. (1981). Language and cognitive assessment of Black children. In N. Lass (Ed.), *Speech and language: Advances in basic research and practice* (Vol. 6, pp. 203–263). New York: Academic Press.

Simpson, A.W., & Erickson, M.T. (1983). Teachers' verbal and nonverbal communication patterns as a function of teacher race, student gender, and student race. *American Educational Research Journal, 20,* 183–198.

Taylor, O., & Lee, D. (1995). Standardized tests and African American children: Communication and language issues. In A.G. Hilliard (Ed.), *Testing African American students* (pp. 37–50). Chicago: Third World Press.

Taylor, O., & Payne, K. (1983). Culturally valid testing: A proactive approach. *Topics in Language Disorders, 3*(3), 8–20.

Vaughn-Cooke, F.B. (1983) Improving language assessment in minority children. *American Speech and Hearing Association, 25*(9), 29–34.

CHAPTER 20

# Bias in Reading, Achievement, and Admission Tests for Black and Other Bidialectal Students: A Sociolinguistic, Cultural, and Political Perspective

*Mary Eleanor Rhodes Hoover,*
*Robert L. Politzer, and Orlando Taylor*

When we get through with a fellow, he can take my test, your test, anybody's test.
—Gertrude Wilks, Founder, Nairobi (CA) Schools (cited in Hoover, 1992)

As Wilks states, Black students, if taught, can pass most tests. It is a form of double jeopardy, however, to miseducate Black students—for example, 43% of Black fourth graders read below level (Barton, 2001)—and then test them on the very material they are not taught, using biased formats.

This dubious use of tests has a historical basis. Most of the earliest tests were used to sort people. They were developed with support from corporate foundations in the 1920s. Based on the early U.S. Army Alpha Test, used to assign soldiers to different tasks, the tests were intelligence quotient (I.Q.) tests used to select individuals having certain skills, values, and moralities (Hoover, 1998; Lemann, 2000). The same type of sorting goes on with testing today.

The competency of African American students needs to be measured by a variety of tests, and the tests that are given should be examined for cultural, linguistic, political, format, genre, class, and administrative bias (Hoover, 1998). The principles illustrated by this discussion are applicable to test bias against other socioeconomic, cultural, and ethnic groups and in other test genres such as language and speech. Some examples of these biases follow. (Many of the test items were selected from old editions of tests that are not specifically cited in order not to single out any one publisher for what are rather universal examples of bias in tests.)

Adapted from Hoover, M.R., Politzer, R.L., & Taylor, O. (1987, April),
*The Negro Educational Review, 38*(2/3), 81–98.

# Linguistic Bias: Specific Types of Language-Related Bias in Tests

In general, differences in language and culture might result in several types of bias in tests. Specifically, lexical-cultural, syntactic, and phonological bias will be addressed.

## Lexical-Cultural Bias

Students may fail an item in a test because they (a) are unfamiliar with a word because of class or geographical difference, (b) have a different orientation to or interpretation of the item, or (c) possess information that is so similar to what the item requires as to prove confusing. In each of these cases, students may respond incorrectly to an item—not because they can't read, or because they are emotionally disturbed, or perceptually handicapped—but because they have a different lexicon from that of the examiner. Examples of these categories are as follows:

- unfamiliarity—"Point to the picture of the toboggan" (a person from South Florida may not know what a toboggan looks like apart from unfamiliarity with the word);

- different interpretation—"Is this a picture of a house?" (if a picture of a high-rise housing project building is shown, an inner-city testee might say "yes," while the test might presume "no" since the stereotyped storybook house is a single, detached unit);

- similar information—"Are trains the only things that run on tracks?" (some urban dwellers may say "no" since subways and els also run on tracks, while the test may presume "yes").

Bias is also reflected in the word choices of the comprehension and vocabulary sections of most of the tests, and middle class values are assumed. In a vocabulary subtest, students are asked to respond to the following:

If a person does something against the law, he is an

ambassador

official

offender

officer

The answer not only could be "offender," but also "officer" for working-class children who may have witnessed or otherwise experienced incidents of brutality or graft and corruption involving police in their neighborhoods.

On a vocabulary subtest, students are asked to select the best synonym for *inequality*. Of the responses (absence, foreign, difference, similarity, and poor), all except *absence* and *similarity* could be "correct" in cultures in which students are aware that *difference*, *poor*, and *foreign* are associated with inequality.

Many items used in the selected tests are archaic, uncommon, and class-tied, representing "superstandard" English (Fasold, 1972), that is, an elaborated, stylized style rather than a simple, standard English style. For example, in one test, the sentence "only the person to whom you make it out" is used and the phrase "however, in and of itself" is used in another item. Labov (1972) has demonstrated that such constructions often carry less information than non-standard forms. The words are often relevant to no group, constituting almost a "new genre for English" (Fillmore, 1982, p. 25); they are particularly inappropriate for working-class children. For example, the word *chandelier* is used in one primary school vocabulary subtest and is an example of a superstandard vocabulary item, particularly familiar to middle and upper classes. (We are not endorsing here, however, that children should not acquire a wide vocabulary. What we are endorsing is the distribution of items across classes and cultures.) Several studies (Adler, 1979; Williams, 1974) have demonstrated that mainstream Whites do poorly on tests geared to the vocabulary and cultures of Blacks and Appalachians. (If joint exposure is not possible, students should at least be exposed to the most generally used terms in the society at large rather than super-standard English.)

The I.Q. test, also a type of language test in its verbal items, is often culturally and economically biased (Cummins, 1984). A typical example is as follows: Children are shown a picture of a man dressed in a suit and carrying a briefcase. They are asked, "Where is the man going?" The "correct" answer is "to work." White children will say, "He's going to work." Black and other working-class children, whose fathers may wear a suit only on formal occasions, will invariably answer "to church," thereby lowering their I.Q. by many critical points. Both answers are correct, however.

A final type of vocabulary bias is seen in the reading methodology featured. All the tests selected for our discussion are geared to the student who has been taught with a sight-whole language (Chall, 1996/1967) approach to reading. All the selections in the primary tests contain words selected on the same basis as words used in the whole language textbooks—nonpatterned literature excerpts. Obviously, children taught with one of the phonic-linguistic approaches—for example, Open Court (Foorman, Francis, Beeler, Winikates, &

Fletcher, 1997), Programmed Reading (Hoover, Dabney, & Lewis, 1990), Direct Instruction (Jones, 1995)—could be disadvantaged in that the reading method they have been exposed to uses words selected on the basis of spelling pattern "regularity" or decodable text. That bias is particularly severe for students in the first two grades. By the third grade, the student taught by a phonic-linguistic approach has been exposed to most English spelling patterns and, therefore, is more likely to compete successfully with the student taught by a sight approach. This bias is particularly insidious because there is some evidence that a phonic-linguistic or systematic phonics approach is one of the more successful approaches to teaching beginning reading skills to Black and other predominantly bidialectal speakers (McPhail, this volume; Hoover, this volume; Hoover et al., 1990).

Bias in style preference is related to lexical bias. It is evidenced in the middle class style of most items in the selected tests. Hymes (1972) elaborated a concept of language that includes not only the code (i.e., the phonology and syntax) mentioned in previous sections, but also the form and the topic of the message. African American communities are known to have distinct forms of styles of the "message." Mitchell-Kernan (1971) and Smitherman (2000) have described a variety of speech events in the Black community from "sounding" to "rapping." Johnston (1984) has described how these speech events affect the testing process for Black children; most of these speech events affect the testing process for Black children. Most of these speech events contain a heightened use of metaphor (Ortony, Turner, & Larson-Shapiro, 1985). One test item asks a child to pick the "right answer" in the following selection:

Father said: Once there was a land where boys and girls never grew up. They were always growing. What was father telling?

The truth

A lie

A story

The "right" answer could be any of them. Metaphorically, it could be "the truth" if the growth were mental and not physical. It could be "a lie" because the word *lie* in Black speech can also mean a joke or a story, and it could also be "a story." Other examples follow:

The hummingbird has a long slender bill. It thrusts this bill into flowers to get nectar and insects. When _____ (hopping, resting, flying, flowers, walking), it beats its wings so rapidly that they sound like the _____ (hum, scratch, grit, size, crash) of a tiny motor.

*Hum* or *crash* might be suitable responses for metaphorically sensitive children. On the same test, another item is ambiguous:

> In ordinary _____ (textbooks, thinking, feelings, materials, conversation), the qualities of the speaker's voice give important clues to his thoughts and feelings. But when you read someone else's written work, you must study the _____ (dictionary, letters, text, syllables, spelling) carefully so that you can interpret the _____ (enthusiastic, common, listeners, writer's, association) thoughts and feelings.

The answer to the last blank could be *enthusiastic* as well as *writer's* (that one should withhold enthusiasm in the absence of any specific justification for it is probably a culture-based judgment). The following example is also ambiguous:

> Speed was necessary, and Fred had tried to find a short cut through the forest. Now he knew that his _____ (purchase, safe, time, decision, speed) had not been a good one. He was _____ ( lost, large, asleep, torn, last), more time than he could have saved would not be _____ (saved, locked, spent, clocked, sent) trying to get his bearing.

The answer to the second blank in the above paragraph could be *torn, asleep,* or *lost.*

Though there are many categories of test bias, most seem to think that the major problem is lexical. For example, the Educational Testing Service (1998) includes inappropriate terminology, stereotyping, underlying assumptions, ethnocentrism, tone, and inflammatory material in its biased categories—all items embedded in the lexicon. Other scholars recognize a generic racial bias (Jencks & Phillips, 1998). Political, format, genre, and administrative bias, along with problems of validity and trickery are also not widely recognized.

## Syntactic Bias

Items worded in unnecessarily complex syntax, such as negative questions, "Which of the following is not," distractors such as "All of the above" and "None of the above," and incomplete question stems (Rubin, 1989) may constitute sociolinguistic bias.

Schonemann (1987) also asserts that Black students have problems with negatives. Yet the high-stakes Praxis Test (Educational Testing Service, 1999), which will lower the number of Black teachers, has numerous negative items in its sample booklet such as *except, least, not,* and *none.* Of the 10 examples given, there are three selections with negatives and three with graphs and charts, a nonBlack preference format. We should also try to include a fair amount of Black preference questions. Rosner (2001) of the Princeton Review Foundation, differentiates between White preference questions, that is, questions that Whites answer correctly, and Black preference questions, that is, questions that Blacks answer correctly.

On one of the tests, the directions state, "None of the following are true except...." This kind of wording is probably confusing for anybody regardless of ethnic or social background. The problem is that the one response that is correct is described by a negation ("except") of a negation ("None"). But for speakers of various speech varieties—especially Blacks—the double negation (or negation of a negation) is simply an emphatic negative. "None of the following is true except" is likely to be interpreted as "very definitely all of the following are false."

An oral comprehension subtest in which students are asked a series of questions about a poem uses the negative formation "neither you nor I." This formation would be superstandard (Fasold, 1972) to most children; awkward to many White nonstandard speakers, who form negatives differently; and foreign to many Blacks, who use a variety of negative formations still further from the superstandard norms. In addition, the form of the poem is culturally alien to many working-class children. Black poetry, by contrast, is rather concerned with stylistic devices such as sounding, shouting, and teaching (Smitherman, 2000).

## Phonological Bias

Many reading tests discriminate directly against Black and other predominantly bilingual or bidialectal speakers by asking them to distinguish among items that are homophones in their speech. The validity of this type of item is questionable; for example, Melmed (1970) has demonstrated that Black students have additional homophones in their speech that speakers of mainstream dialect do not have, but that this aspect of Black phonology does not interfere with the students' comprehension. As Shuy (1969) has stated,

> Urban disadvantaged Negroes [sic] should not find it difficult to discover that /jes/ is realized in print as *just*. Their grapheme rule would be "st" - /s/ in final position. This is certainly no more unreasonable than other double grapheme relations as single sounds, such as "th"- /θ/ in *thin* or "mb" - /m/ in *thumb*. That is, the decoding process of reading is already imbued with such rules. (p. 122)

Since phonology need not interfere with comprehension, it does not seem valid to have students discriminate between very similar words out of context as some indication of "reading" proficiency. This is particularly true when tests use certain words deliberately as distractors, words that in the speech variety of specific regional or cultural groups are homophones of the correct choice (e.g., *poe* and *poor* as items when the instructions are "Circle the word that means 'not rich.'")

A problem is created by the use of this type of item. First, the teacher is led to assume that the phonology of the Black student is incorrect. In typical achievement tests, approximately 33% of the items can be "dialect prejudiced" (Hutchinson, 1972). The teacher must assume, when given the results of such a test, that the Black child has an incorrect phonological system.

Many of the tests have subtests designed to measure pupils' knowledge of sound-letter relationships or skill in decoding. Students are asked to identify the dictated word from among several words. The following are possible homophones for bidialectal speakers (Black speakers, southern speakers, Appalachian speakers, Latino speakers), which, if used in tests, may result in biased test items.

Possible Homophones: *held, helm*

Rule: Consonant clusters reduced when both members of the cluster are voiced or voiceless.

Groups Disadvantaged: Southerners, Blacks

☐ held
☐ help
☐ head
☐ helm

Possible Homophones: *this, these*

Rule: Lack of contrast between the two /i/ phonemes; devoicing of final consonants.

Group Disadvantaged: Latinos

☐ his
☐ those
☐ this
☐ these

Possible Homophones: *tap, tab*

Rule: At the end of syllable, voiced stops "b," "d," and "g" are pronounced as voiceless stops "p," "t," and "k."

Group Disadvantaged: Blacks, Latinos

☐ tag
☐ tape
☐ tap
☐ tab

Possible Homophones: *tag, tack*

Rule: Same as rule for *tap* above.

Groups Disadvantaged: Blacks, Latinos

☐ tack
☐ talk
☐ tag
☐ take

Possible Homophones: *fur, for*

Rule: Loss of phonemic contrast before "r."

Groups Disadvantaged: Southerners, Blacks

☐ fur
☐ fare
☐ for
☐ fair

Rules and examples are included in Bartley and Politzer (1972), Baugh (2000), Hoover (1992), Rickford and Rickford (2000), Smitherman (2000), and Williams and Wolfram (1977).

Another example of phonological bias is found in the scoring of oral reading tests. In administering these tests, such as the oral assessments in the Ekwall/Shanker Reading Inventory (1993), no directions are given to the teacher in terms of scoring the tests for reading errors and not for speech errors. A reading teacher thus has no guidance on whether to score a student who pronounces "ask" as "axed" or "with" as "wif'"—both dialect-influenced patterns—as correct—if the student comprehends the paragraph—or incorrect. Cunningham (1976/1977) asserts that teachers grade dialect errors more negatively than traditional errors.

# Political Bias

Tests, as has been stated, are often used to identify individuals having the values, morality, and skills deemed appropriate for certain occupations. Other tests, including reading tests, are used for the same sorting purposes. To the extent that the sorting disproportionately places one group at a disadvantage to another, we can call it a form of political bias.

A form of this political bias can be seen in the use of tests for placement of students in reading groups. This placement often amounts to a tracking system in which low income children are effectively typed as *low* or *slow readers* for life. As Rist (1971) has demonstrated, children are often labeled *slow* in kindergarten, and they remain fixed in that category indefinitely. Because the teachers use the scores as a self-fulfilling prophecy, the students may never be taught adequately. Denied basic reading skills, these children become functional illiterates, adults unable to pass employment or college entrance tests, and thus are channeled into the ranks of the unemployed, of which members of minority groups make up a disproportionate percentage.

Another example is the use of tests for the disadvantage of one group and the advantage of others. Many states have literacy tests that penalize the student by issuing him or her a certificate rather than a diploma. Here you have an educational enterprise involving several groups: teachers, administrators, and students. The school fails in one of its endeavors to teach the students literacy skills. Of the groups involved in the failure, one group is singled out for penalty. Not the teachers who failed to teach in spite of the voluminous research demonstrating how simple it is to teach reading. Not the administrators who failed to administer a successful school program (and again we have voluminous research showing that a principal who knows something about instruction is a basic characteristic of schools that work) (Edmonds, this volume; McPhail, this volume; Weber, 1971). No, the group singled out to suffer for the failure of schools to educate Blacks is the group that had the least responsibility for the situation—the students.

Another example of political bias is seen in an item from the Law School Admissions Test (LSAT) (White, 1984). The item reflects a deficiency perspective related to the myth (Hoover, this volume) that parents are the cause of their children's educational problems rather than the proven reasons, for instance, lack of enforcement of the characteristics of schools that work (Edmonds, this volume; Hoover, this volume). The LSAT writers thus take a political position in the "great debate" over the cause of minority school failure—the parents or the school system.

> It is often true that children who perform poorly when they begin school have had few toys and no books to add the development of their minds. The parents of these unfortunate youngsters are remiss in failing to provide their children with these tools of development and, therefore, for causing their lack of preparedness for school. (White, 1984)

The author's argument is logically based on which of the following assumptions:

    I. Children supplied with toys and books excel in school.

    II. Parents should know the value of toys and books.

    III. Parents have the means to provide their children with toys and books.

        A. I only

        B. I and II only

        C. I and III only

        D. II and III only

        E. I, II, and III

"D" is the correct answer.

The following true story provides another example of political bias:

> Ten educators, including one of this book's authors, were brought into the Educational Testing Service (ETS) at Princeton, New Jersey, in 1991. Having spent seven years producing a series of nonbiased tests at the Stanford Center for Research in Teaching (Hoover, Politzer, Brown, et al., 1996), Hoover expected to be surrounded by others with testing experience. Instead, her nine coworkers were primarily classroom teachers.
>
> Because Hoover was so accustomed to being rejected on test-bias issues by colleagues—Black and White—because they feared opposing "standards" on issues of test bias, she was astonished when the entire group, in-

cluding the ETS representative, supported her assertions that the test was biased. It was biased because all the answers to the questions were based on the "whole-language" approach, only one methodology used in teaching students to read. The ETS representatives cited the International Reading Association as its authority on the whole-language hegemony in the test. (Whole language has not been demonstrated to be more effective in teaching reading than phonics or other methodologies [Delpit, 1995].)

The ad hoc group actually rewrote the test specifications so that some of the new questions had "decoding" answers, and that other aspects of reading acquisition, such as vocabulary, were given more emphasis. When the new test was distributed, to Hoover's dismay, she realized her first apprehensions were correct: None of the new questions and answers were on the exam. (Hoover, 1994)

## Genres

Bias is also present in the various test genres. For example, tests of comprehension are often more subject to bias than tests of vocabulary. The rationale for this difference is that comprehension measurements depend heavily on inference, which is much more culture bound and less objective a measurement than other components of reading, such as vocabulary (Carroll & Freedle, 1972). Students from a culture in which inference is often couched in proverbial usage and based on an African-oriented worldview, which Alleyne (1980) calls "inversion," may not be as familiar with European styles of inference as traditional students. African American students generally have higher scores on Vocabulary than on Comprehension subtests. Yet one of the newest tests, the Terra Nova Test, only assesses comprehension (not vocabulary) and is used as the major testing instrument in a number of districts.

## Format

Reading is the decoding of and the extraction of meaning from a written or printed message. Certain formats may have some diagnostic value, but they have no place in achievement testing. For example, the cloze format, used in many reading tests (e.g., the Florida Teacher Certification Examination Reading subtest) (Hoover, 1984) is a very efficient way of finding out whether the modes of communication are the same as those of the test maker; however, it may be difficult to determine to what extent performance on cloze tests indicates comprehension rather than test bias. Some researchers assert that the cloze-test format may be an unfair measure of the reading ability of a bidialectal speaker or a student with a field-dependent cognitive style (Stansfield & Hansen, 1983).

Formats found on the Stanford 9th Edition practice tests (Stanford Achievement Test, 1996), such as discrimination between sounds, compound words, endings, contractions, and same-word with multiple-meanings exercises, may again be interesting diagnostic tests, but are not what Carroll and Freedle (1972) call "pure" measures of comprehension.

## Ambiguity and Trickery

There is general ambiguity in many of the reading tests which would create a problem for most students, but particularly those students who are bilingual or bidialectal—that is, with different languages and dialects in their backgrounds—who understand standard English but perhaps not the superstandard English (Fasold, 1972) found on many tests. For example, in Florida's College Level Academic Skills Test (CLAST) (Florida Department of Education, 1983) word usage section, which is given to all sophomores who want to go on to the junior year, students must choose the best definition of an *outline* among the following: "essence," "major idea," "basic essentials," and "fundamental ingredient." All of the above could be correct.

In the sentence structure section of the same test, students are asked to select the correct answer or the best answer from among the following:

A. After falling down the steps, misplacing his mail, and failing his English test, John went to bed.

B. John decided to go to bed because he fell down the steps, misplaced his mail, and failed his English test.

"A" is allegedly the best answer, but both would appear correct to a student, however literate, who had learned standard English as a second language. Yet students will be penalized and not allowed to go to the junior year of college in Florida based on such ridiculous items as this.

## Validity

A final problem is that tests often are not valid; that is, they do not measure what is required on the job. Title VII of the Civil Rights Act of 1964, for example—prohibiting employment discrimination based on race, color, religion, sex, or national origin—requires that such a connection be established. In a study conducted by the Temple University Medical School in Philadelphia, it was found that minorities scoring below the median on an objective test in pathology were performing above the average on a clinical test in pathology designed by the same instructors (Hoover, 1998).

# Administrative Problems

One of the reasons that Rudolph Crew, New York City Schools' chancellor (Steinberg & Henriques, 2001), lost his job was because of gross errors on the CTB/McGraw-Hill Test. Nine thousand students were sent to summer schools because of this incorrectly scored reading test (Gewertz, 2002). More than 1,500 candidates for math teaching certificates from 17 states had their licensing tests rescored when the ETS admitted that 23 of the 50 questions on the January and June 2001 Praxis Test, a high-stakes test, had previously been published in an ETS study guide (FairTest, 2001). With errors such as these inherent in the administration of tests, test consumers should be careful about using only one assessment to place or diagnose students.

# To Test or Not To Test

Those of us who are accountable to our communities must insist on tests. Often the only means that parents have of assessing the performance of the school is the availability of achievement scores published annually in the newspaper. The Nairobi Day School's statement on testing appeared at the beginning of this article; the rationale for testing was as follows:

> Student test scores in the local District, which were published in the local papers twice a year, demonstrated the utter failure of the public school in educating the children in the community. Though Nairobi personnel were strongly opposed to excessive reliance on testing and were aware of the deleterious effects of tests on children of color, they were determined to prove that Black children could learn in a Black environment. Balanced, sensitive use of standardized and other tests was the only way to prove this. (Hoover, 1992, p. 208)

A second important rationale for testing is the placement of children within a particular curriculum and reading series. Some schools have adopted simple end-of-book tests in their reading series as the major means of assessment for placement. Some of the state criterion-referenced tests are also based on skills that are actually taught.

Most achievement and diagnostic tests are not designed to perform either assessment or placement functions. They do not do an adequate job of assessment for accountability because of bias in form and content, but they also do not do an adequate job of placement either because the diagnostic results are often not tied to a specific prescription or reading series.

# The Search for a Culturally Fair Test

Locating appropriate teaching materials for Black and miseducated students has been stated to be the goal of many urban school districts, yet there appears to be no such interest in appropriate assessment instruments to measure the achievement. For example, many have accepted the 30 years of research by Chall (1996/1967), Foorman et al. (1997), and others, revealing that African American and other bilingual or bidialectal children perform better when taught a "balanced approach to reading" with both phonics and literature utilized. Yet, oddly enough, there is no concomitant interest in finding the least biased test to measure the reading achievement. Incredibly, on occasion the lack of interest approximates purposeful misassessment: The Technical Manual for the Florida Teacher Certification Examination (as cited in Hoover, 1984) states: "A high rate of failure, particularly for Black students, possibly will result" from the test.

We must force our districts to not only adopt proven approaches to reading, but also to adopt a fair test. What are the elements of such a test?

If new, unbiased reading tests are to be constructed (Cazden & Dickinson, 1980), validity should be the first consideration. Reading is the decoding of and the extraction of meaning from a written or printed message. Tests of discrimination between sounds, and other real or presumed component skills of reading, such as endings discrimination, use of contractions, and same word with multiple meanings, may have some diagnostic value; but, they have no place in achievement testing. Diagnostic tests or tests of component skills should be made as linguistically fair as possible according to suggestions made previously (e.g., elimination of items that are found to be discriminatory). Achievement testing could then focus on the testing of reading rather than component skills.

Vocabulary, which has been estimated to constitute a major component of comprehension (Davis, 1968), also provides a relatively unbiased assessment of reading comprehension (Hoover, 1984). Though vocabulary items can be reflective of certain classes and geographical areas, they are less subject to the ambiguity, lack of validity, and trickery that is often characteristic of multiple choice "comprehension" items subject to the ambiguity, lack of validity, and trickery that is often characteristic of multiple choice "comprehension" items.

There are methods of testing pupils' comprehension of a written message that have relatively high face validity. Some of these methods have been employed in foreign language testing for some time, but they seem equally valid in testing reading comprehension in the native tongue. Among these methods are (a) carrying out of an instruction that has been given in written form, (b) judging whether statements are true or false according to a short paragraph that the examinee has just read, and (c) writing a short paraphrase of written material. We should also try to include a fair amount of Black preference questions in an unbiased test. Most tests consist of White preference questions, as asserted by Rosner (2001) of the Princeton Review Foundation. Rosner concludes that test makers do not select Black preference questions (questions that Blacks answer correctly) for the SAT, and recommends tests that are made up of questions with the smallest gaps between White and Black preference.

Freedle (2003) has also discovered questions on the SAT that Blacks succeed in answering; for instance, they tend to perform better on "hard" questions rather than "easy" ones because easy questions use a common vocabulary that ethnic and cultural groups will interpret differently, as we described in the Genres section in this chapter.

## What Do We Do While We're Waiting to Create a Fair Test?

We must test, as we have stated, for accountability (to the community) purposes. Until the time that we produce a fair test, however, we must locate those tests that are relatively fair. One example is the Gates-MacGinitie Reading Test (MacGinitie & MacGinitie, 1989), which uses two simple formats, one in Vocabulary and one in Comprehension. It is probably as close to fairness as you can get in a group multiple-choice test.

Another unbiased assessment, the Nairobi Method, now called the One-Two-Three Method (Hoover et al., 1989; Hoover & Politzer, 1982), is the use of simple-recall, multiple-choice questions following the oral reading of a short paragraph containing most of the spelling patterns of English as a decoding assessment. Comprehension is tested by a series of questions based on simple recall rather than the culture-bound inference formats. The students then write a short composition using information from the orally read paragraph.

Testing all aspects of students' language proficiency is also an unbiased assessment. Black students, predominantly bidialectal, should be tested not only in standard English but also in Ebonics. In a battery of tests developed at Stanford University (Hoover, Politzer, et al., 1996) and administered to several hundred students, students' proficiency in Ebonics and in standard Ebonics (Taylor, 1971) were measured in three dimensions—discrimination, repetition, and production—thus proving that the students have proficiency in some variety of English, an important fact in the improvement of teacher attitudes, which remain low (Bowie & Bond, 1994; Cecil, 1988; Hoover, McNair-Knox, Lewis, & Politzer, 1996). Interestingly enough, those students who were bidialectal—that is proficient in both language varieties—also tested higher on standardized reading tests (Hoover, 1998).

The point here is not that there should be no standards. Students must be literate and tested for their literacy in order to cope with our highly technological society. Where tests are used to penalize one group and not all participants in the educational act, where there is no attempt to balance test items between Black-preference and White-preference questions, and where there is no attempt to avoid items that discriminate against certain groups, however, bias exists, and it should be eliminated.

In conclusion, we must do what is fair. School administrators, who purchase the tests, must consult test advocates. If administrators rejected biased tests and aggressively insisted on the development of a fair test, bringing in test bias experts, we would not have the biased state of affairs that we have. For example, an official in Atlanta, Georgia, Mayor Andrew Young's office called in a host of experts, including one of the authors of this article (Hoover), to evaluate an entrance exam that was given to prospective city police officers. The evaluators found that the test was extremely biased against minority officers and recommended a multitude of changes before the test could be considered fair. The changes would have been so expensive that the test writer withdrew his contract. New tests were written but were, unfortunately, eliminated with the ouster of the official who brought in the test-bias consultants (Hoover, 1998; Wiley, 1990).

The authors of the Florida Teacher Certification Examination (as cited in Hoover, 1984) stated in their manual, again: "A high rate of failure, particularly for Black students...possibly will result." A nondeficiency approach, however, is seen in Cole and Scribner's (1974) research: In measuring the abilities of the Vai people in Liberia, the authors found the Vai to be deficient on one of their tests. They decided to alter the instrument until they could produce a culturally appropriate one—which was done.

Black students are certainly capable of performing. Wilson (1992) has discovered that African African American children up to the age of 2 years are in advance of all other children. Schools have existed across the country for decades in which Black students achieve at grade level (Hoover, this volume; Ichinaga, this volume). Given these facts, it is impossible that there be any genetic or cultural reasons for Blacks to have low test scores. Given these facts, the creation and mandation of fair tests is a priority, as well as the mandation of schools that work. As Hilliard (1992) states,

> We have a mistaken notion that we should "concentrate on testing school children rather than on teaching them; on blaming and embarrassing school children for low test scores instead of teaching and nourishing them; on

decapitating...teachers professionally by holding them up to public ridicule and scorn...because of their test scores rather than encouraging them and teaching them how to teach children." (p. 35)

## REFERENCES

Adler, S. (1979). *Poverty children and their language: Implications for teaching and testing.* New York: Grune and Stratton.

Alleyne, M.C. (1980). *Comparative Afro-American: An historical comparative study of English-based Afro-American dialects of the New World.* Ann Arbor, MI: Karoma.

Bartley, D., & Politzer, R. (1972). *Practice-centered teacher training: Standard English for speakers of nonstandard dialects.* Philadelphia: Center for Curriculum Development.

Barton, P.E. (2001, March). *Raising achievement and reducing gaps; Reporting progress toward goals for academic achievement: On the NAEP report.* Washington, DC: National Education Goals Panel.

Baugh, J. (2000). *Beyond Ebonics: Linguistic pride and racial prejudice.* New York: Oxford University Press.

Bowie, R.L., & Bond, C.L. (1994). Influencing future teachers' attitudes toward Black English: Are we making a difference? *Journal of Teacher Education, 45*(2), 112–118.

Carroll, J.B., & Freedle, R.O. (Eds.). (1972). *Language comprehension and the acquisition of knowledge.* New York: Winston.

Cazden, C.B., & Dickinson, D. (1980). Language in education: Standardization versus cultural pluralism. In C. Ferguson & S. Heath (Eds.), *Language in the U.S.A.* (pp. 446–468). New York: Cambridge University Press.

Cecil, N.L. (1988). Black dialect and academic success: A study of teacher expectations. *Reading Improvement, 25*(1), 34–38.

Chall, J.S. (1996). *Learning to read: The great debate.* New York: McGraw-Hill. (Original work published 1967)

Cole, M., & Scribner S. (1974). *Culture and thought.* New York: John Wiley.

Cummins, J. (1984). *Bilingualism and special education: Issues in assessment and pedagogy.* Clevedon, UK: Multilingual Matters.

Cunningham, P.M. (1976/1977). Teachers' correction responses to Black-dialect miscues which are nonmeaning changing. *Reading Research Quarterly, 12,* 637–653.

Davis, F. (1968). Research in comprehension in reading. *Reading Research Quarterly, 3,* 507–545.

Delpit, L.D. (1995). *Other people's children.* New York: New Press.

Educational Testing Service. (1998). *Overview: ETS fairness review.* Princeton, NJ: Author.

Educational Testing Service. (1999). *Praxis II test preparation workshop.* Princeton, NJ: Author.

Ekwall, E., & Shanker, J. (1993). *Ekwall-Shanker reading inventory* (3rd ed.). Boston: Allyn & Bacon.

FairTest, National Center for Fair and Open Testing. (2001). Teacher test scoring flunks. *Examiner.* Retrieved February 9, 2004, from http://www.fairtest.org/examarts/Fall%2001/Teacher%20Test%20Scoring%20Flunks.html

Fasold, R. (1972). *Sloppy speech in standard English.* Paper presented at the Fourth Triennial Conference on Symbolic Processes, Washington, DC.

Fillmore, C. (1982). *Ideal readers and real readers.* In D. Tannen (Ed.), *Georgetown University roundtable on language and linguistics: Analyzing discourse: Text and talk* (pp. 248–270). Washington, DC: Georgetown University Press.

Florida Department of Education. (1983). *College Level Academic Skills Test (CLAST).* Tallahassee: Author.

Foorman, B.R., Francis, D.J., Beeler, T., Winikates, D., & Fletcher, J.M. (1997). Early intervention for children with reading problems: Study designs and preliminary findings. *Learning Disabilities: A Multidisciplinary Journal, 8*(1), 63–71.

Freedle, R.O. (2003). Correcting the SATs ethnic and social class bias: A method for Reestimating SAT scores. *Harvard Educational Review, 73*(1), 1–43.

Gewertz, C. (2002, November 20). Test firm, NYC officials say scores were "overstated." *Education Week, 20*(41), p. 6.

Hilliard, A.G. (1992). *Testing African American students.* Morristown, NJ: Aaron.

Hoover, M.R. (1984). Teacher competency tests: The Florida teacher certification examination as genocide for Blacks. *Negro Educational Review, 35*(1), 70–77.

Hoover, M.R. (1992). The Nairobi Day School: An African American independent school, 1966–1984. *Journal of Negro Education, 61*(2), 201–210.

Hoover, M.R. (1994, December). Testimony on *The Bell Curve* on C-SPAN given at the Howard University symposium on The Bell Curve.

Hoover, M.R. (1998). Ebonics speakers and cultural, linguistic, and political test bias. In T. Perry & L.D. Delpit (Eds.), *The real Ebonics debate* (pp. 126–133). Boston: Beacon Press.

Hoover, M.R., Dabney, N., & Lewis, S. (Eds.). (1990). *Successful Black and minority schools.* San Francisco: Julian Richardson.

Hoover, M.R., Lewis, S., Daniel, D., Blackburn, R., Fowles, O., & Moloi, A. (1989). *The one-two-three method: A writing process for bidialectal students.* Edina, MN: Bellwether Press.

Hoover, M.R., McNair-Knox, F., Lewis, S.A.R., & Politzer, R.L. (1996). African American English attitude measures for teachers of bidialectal students. In R.L. Jones (Ed.), *Handbook of tests and measurements for Black populations* (Vol. 1, pp. 383–393). Hampton, VA: Cobb and Henry.

Hoover, M.R., & Politzer, R. (1982). A culturally appropriate composition assessment: The Nairobi method. In M. Whiteman (Ed.), *Variations in writing: Functional and linguistic-cultural differences.* Hillsdale, NJ: Erlbaum.

Hoover, M.R., Politzer, R.L., Brown, D., Lewis, S.A.R., Hicks, S., & McNair-Knox, F. (1996). African American English tests for students. In R.L. Jones (Ed.), Handbook of tests and measurements for Black populations (pp. 353–366). Hampton, VA: Cobb and Henry.

Hutchinson, A.O. (1972). Reading tests and nonstandard language. *The Reading Teacher, 25,* 430–437.

Hymes, D. (1972). Toward ethnographies of communication: The analysis of communicative events. In P. Giglioli (Ed.), *Language and social context.* Baltimore: Penguin Books.

Jencks, C., & Phillips, M. (1998). *The Black–White test score gap.* Washington, DC: Brookings Press.

Johnston, F. (1984). Prior knowledge and reading comprehension test items. *Reading Research Quarterly, 19,* 219–239.

Jones, J.M. (1995). *Educational philosophies: A primer for parents.* Milwaukee, WI: Press.

Labov, W. (1972). The logic of nonstandard English. *Language in the inner city.* Philadelphia: University of Pennsylvania Press.

Lemann, N. (2000). *The big test: The secret history of the American meritocracy.* New York: Farrar Straus and Giroux.

MacGinitie & MacGinitie (1989). Gates-MacGinitie Reading Tests. Chicago: Riverside Publishers.

Melmed, P.J. (1970). Black English phonology: The question of reading interference. Berkeley, CA: Language Behavior Research Laboratory. (ERIC Document Reproduction Service No. ED063613)

Mitchell-Kernan, C. (1971, February). *Language behavior in a Black urban community.* Berkeley, CA: Language Behavior Research Laboratory.

Ortony, A, Turner, T.J., & Larson-Shapiro, N. (1985). *Cultural and instructional influences on figurative language comprehension by inner-city children.* Cambridge, MA: Bolt, Beranek and Newman.

Rickford, J.R., & Rickford, R.J. (2000). *Spoken soul: The story of Black English.* New York: Wiley.

Rist, R. (1971). Student social class and teacher expectations. In *Challenging the myths: The schools, the Blacks and the poor* (pp. 76–110). Cambridge, MA: Harvard Educational Review.

Rosner, J. (2001). Disparate outcomes by design: University admissions tests. *La Raza Law Journal, 12*(2), 377–386.

Rubin, D. (1989). *Sociolinguistic test item review.* Montgomery, AL: Center for Business and Economic Development, Auburn University. (ERIC Document Reproduction Service No. ED321525)

Schonemann, J. (1987). An experimental, exploratory study of causes of bias in test items. *Journal of Educational Measurements, 24*(2), 97–118.

Shuy, R.W. (1969). A linguistic background for developing beginning reading materials for Black children. In J.C. Baratz & R.W. Shuy (Eds.), *Teaching Black children to read* (pp. 117–137). Washington, DC: Center for Applied Linguistics.

Smitherman, G. (2000). *Talkin' that talk: Language, culture and education in African America.* New York: Routledge.

Stanford Achievement Test (9th ed.). (1996). San Antonio, TX: Harcourt College.

Stansfield, C., & Hansen, J. (1983). Field dependence–independence as a variable in second language cloze test performance. *TESOL Quarterly, 17*(1), 29–38.

Steinberg, J., & Henriques, D. (2001, May 21). When a test fails the schools, careers and reputations suffer. *The New York Times*, pp. A1, A10.

Taylor, O. (1971). Response to social dialects and the field of speech. In R. Shuy (Ed.), *Sociolinguistic theory: Materials and practice* (pp. 13–20). Washington, DC: Center for Applied Linguistics.

Weber, G. (1971). *Inner-city children can be taught to read.* Washington, DC: Council for Basic Education.

White, D.M. (1984). *The effects of coaching, defective questions, and cultural bias on the validity of the Law School Admission Test.* Berkeley, CA: National Conference of Black Lawyers.

Wiley, E. (1989, May 25). Biased textbooks and exams: Cultivating illiterate minority population. *Black Issues in Higher Education.*

Williams, R.L. (1974). Scientific racism and IQ: The silent mugging of the Black community. *Psychology Today, 7*, 32–41.

Williams, R.L., & Wolfram, W. (1977). *Social dialects: Differences vs. disorders.* Rockville, MD: American Speech and Hearing Association.

Wilson, A.N. (1992). *Awakening the natural genius of Black children.* New York: Afrikan World Infosystems.

# CHAPTER 21

# Practice Guidelines for the Assessment of the African American Child

*California Speech-Language-Hearing Association Task Force on the Assessment of the African American Child*

## Background

*Larry P. v. Riles* (1979) is a case that was filed against the state of California by African American parents who argued that the administration of culturally biased standardized intelligence tests resulted in the disproportionate identification of African American children as mentally retarded and inappropriate placement in special education classes for the educable mentally retarded.

The California Department of Education (CDE) is obligated to prohibit the administration of I.Q. tests that have not been validated for the purpose of identifying African American children as mentally retarded or which have not been reviewed for evidence of racial and cultural bias by the Federal Court of Appeals.

Although the original ruling applies to the use of standardized I.Q. tests with African American children, many standardized speech and language tests also fall under the Larry P. mandate because they directly or indirectly purport to measure I.Q. and their construct validity is partially or fully determined through correlations with other I.Q. tests.

There are numerous issues that need to be taken into account when evaluating the speech and language performance of African American children on standardized tests that are primarily normed on children from differing racial and ethnic backgrounds. These differences can lead to various forms of test bias during the testing process including (a) situational, (b) format, (c) value, and (d) linguistic. Test bias is most likely to occur when using tests or other assessment procedures that have been primarily normed on or developed for use with non–African American child populations. Test bias can also occur when testing African American English (AAE) child speakers with tests that are based on

Reprinted from California Speech-Language-Hearing Association (2003). Retrieved July 1, 2004, from http://www.csha.org/Positionpapers/LarryP.pdf

theories and models of standard American English (SAE) grammar, phonology, or language development.

# Practice Guidelines

Step 1: Review tests for possible test bias influences.

    (a) Determine whether the test was primarily standardized on African American children and/or AAE child speakers.

    (b) Look for information on the performance of African American/AAE child sub-groups within the standardization sample.

    (c) Examine test items, picture stimuli, test administration procedures, and/or instructions that appear to contain possible bias.

Step 2: Review tests for compliance with Larry P.

    (a) Important questions to ask:

    Is the test standardized and does it purport to measure intelligence (cognition, mental ability, or aptitude)?

    Are the test results reported in the form of I.Q. or mental age?

    Does the evidence of the construct validity of the test rely on correlations with I.Q. tests?

    (b) How to answer questions:

    Review the test manual for a description of its purpose.

    Determine whether the test generates I.Q. or mental age equivalents.

    Look at the test manual for information on how content/construct validity was established.

    Look at other sources of test validity (e.g., are correlations established between the test and standardized I.Q. assessment tools?)

Step 3: Use alternative assessment procedures when standardized tests are determined to be invalid or inappropriate:

    (a) Parent and teacher report.

    (b) Observations of peer interactions.

    (c) Language sample.

    (d) Criterion-referenced testing procedures.

    (e) Dynamic assessment procedures.

Step 4: If standardized tests are used:

    (a)  Reword test instructions

    (b)  Increase the number of practice items

    (c)  Continue to test beyond the ceiling

    (d)  Record a child's entire response

    (e)  Use alternative scoring

Step 5: When examining and analyzing data:

    (a)  Look for evidence of dialect markers that can't be confused with normal developmental or disorder influences

    (b)  Look for evidence of dialect use patterns that do not represent normal patterns of AAE or SAE dialect use

    (c)  Focus on the more universal aspects of language development for identifying patterns of possible disorder

    (d)  Look at case history information for evidence of obvious medical or health risk concerns

Step 6: Report findings from testing in a least biased fashion:

    (a)  Provide a comprehensive overview of the child's language strength and weaknesses.

    (b)  Include information from the case history on the child's overall developmental and health history.

    (c)  Report any test modifications made during the assessment process.

    (d)  Avoid reporting normative test scores.

    (e)  When using standardized tests, include a cautionary statement concerning the reliability and/or validity of test results.

    (f)  Identify linguistic productions possibly related to dialect influences.

    (g)  Describe possible language differences using nondeficit terminology.

## Common Problems of Currently Available Standardized Tests

At present, there are several standardized speech and language assessment tools that violate the *Larry P.* court ruling or that contain some form of test bias that make them inappropriate for use with some African American children. Some common problems of these tests are as follows:

(a) There are no tests, to date, that have been primarily standardized on African American or AAE child speakers. For most tests, African American children make up only a small percentage of the tests' standardization sample (e.g., 12–15% of the sample). This means that tests continue to be primarily standardized on children from other cultural backgrounds.

(b) Few tests provide important demographic information on the characteristics of their African American sample (e.g., family income, parental education, dialect status). This makes it difficult to evaluate whether the African American children participating in the sample match the backgrounds of African American test takers.

(c) Most tests contain some form of cultural, linguistic, or format bias.

(d) Although few tests are explicitly described as tests of cognitive or intellectual ability, test developers often allude to the relationship between cognition and language. In some cases, developers consider their test to serve as an indirect measure of cognition.

(e) Many of the speech and language tests currently available in the field of speech-language pathology have construct and/or other forms of validity established through correlations with other standardized tests.

## Important CDE/IDEA Regulations and Guidelines

In addition to being familiar with the CDE's restrictions against the use of standardized tests in light of *Larry P.*, Speech Language Pathologists (SLPs) need to also be aware of current CDE and Individuals With Disabilities Education Act (IDEA) regulations pertaining to the assessment of children from diverse backgrounds. Specifically, CDE guidelines assert the following:

(a) Whenever "standardized tests are considered to be invalid for the specific pupil, the expected language performance level shall be determined by alternative means" (CDE, 1989, p. 69). Alternative means of assessment should be used whenever there is a professional concern about the validity of a test [5 CCR 3030(c)(B)(4), 5 CCR 3030(j)(2) (B)].

(b) Nondiscriminatory techniques, methods, and materials should be used for ethnic and culturally diverse children [5 CCR 3022, Education Code (EC) 56320 (a)].

(c) Assessment personnel must be competent and appropriately trained to administer and interpret test results and, when necessary, be knowledgeable of and sensitive to the cultural and ethnic backgrounds of students [5 CCR 3023; EC 56320(b) (3), 56322; 56324].

(d) When an assessment has been completed, a written report must be developed that addresses any effects of environmental, cultural, or economic disadvantages, where appropriate [EC 56327].

(e) When appropriate, the Individualized Education Plan (IEP) should contain linguistically appropriate goals, objectives, programs, and services [5 CCR 3001(s); EC 56345].

The potential problems of using standardized tests and recommendations for increased use of other forms of assessment are also addressed by federal regulations under IDEA (1999, 34 C.F.R. Part 300). A review of these regulations reveals that IDEA regulations

(1) mandate that no single criteria be used for making eligibility determinations [Section 300.532(f)];

(2) emphasize the importance of using multiple sources for determining a child's eligibility for special education services (e.g., information provided by the parent, teacher, and information obtained from classroom-based assessments and observations) [Sections 300.532(b), 300.533 (a)(1)(i, ii, iii); 300.535(a)(1)];

(3) state that tests and other evaluation materials used to assess any child must be (a) selected and administered so as not to be discriminatory on a racial or cultural basis, (b) be administered in a child's native language, (c) measure the extent to which a child demonstrates a true disability rather than a child's level of language proficiency in English [Sections 300.532(a)(1)(i), 300. 532(a)(1)( ii), and 300.532(a)(2)];

(4) specify that any standardized tests given to a child be validated for the specific purpose for which they are used, and administered by personnel who are trained and knowledgeable. In addition, evaluation procedures must include those tailored to assess specific areas of educational need and not merely to provide a single general intelligence quotient. Finally, when tests are given under nonstandardized conditions, a description of how the test administration varied must be included in the final evaluation report [Sections 300.532(c)(1) (i, ii,) 300.532(2), 300.532(2)(d)]; and

(5) stress that no child is eligible for special education services if the determinate factor for eligibility is lack of instruction in reading, math, or limited English proficiency [Section 300.534(b)(1)(i, ii)].

## Closing and Summary

In summary, it is the responsibility of speech, language, and hearing professionals to ensure that African American children are appropriately evaluated in light of the current CDE *Larry P.* mandate and IDEA regulations. California Speech-Language-Hearing Association (CSHA) members are encouraged to familiarize themselves with issues related to the *Larry P.* ruling and the assessment of African American children and all children from diverse cultural and language backgrounds including the history of *Larry P.* and the intelligence testing of minority children, cognitive referencing and implications for testing African American children, relevant CDE and IDEA guidelines regarding the assessment of children from diverse backgrounds, sources of test bias and the most appropriate methods for minimizing test bias, alternative assessment and report writing, and best practices for distinguishing difference from disorder.

### *Note*

The California Speech-Language-Hearing Association Task Force on the Assessment of the African American Child is made up of the following members: Toya Wyatt, Geri Brown, Marsha Brown, Marsha Dabney, Pamela Wiley, and Gloria Weddington.

### REFERENCES

California Department of Education. (1989). *Larry P. task force report: Policy and alternative assessment guideline recommendations.* Sacramento, CA: Author, Special education division.

Individuals with Disabilities Act (1999), 34 C.F.R. § 300.532 et seq.

Larry P. v. Riles 495 F. Supp. 926 (ND Cal.1979)

# Epilogue

*Mary Eleanor Rhodes Hoover*

The editors of this publication have five recommendations on the teaching of African American students. Our first recommendation is that we must mandate the use of successful materials wherever we are because we know that African American students can learn to read at high levels if taught. Those of us in the National Association of Black Reading and Language Educators (NABRLE) and other organizations of African Americans and people of color have been saying this for 40 years through our book *Successful Black and Minority Schools* (Hoover, Dabney, & Lewis, 1990), through our annual presentations at the International Reading Association (since 1972), through presentations at the College Language Association, and through other forums over the years.

The record is clear: There is a more than 30-year track record for the successful teaching of reading to Black students, from Chall's *Learning to Read: The Great Debate* in 1967 (revised 1996) to Weber in 1971; to Hoover in 1978 (and 1990) (see chapter 5 of this volume); to Edmonds in 1985 (see chapter 3 of this volume); to McPhail in 1983 (see chapter 7 of this volume); and to Foorman, Francis, Beeler, Winikates, and Fletcher in 1997.

Our second recommendation is that all methodologies for the teaching of reading should be respected in the future, including phonics-inclusive and cultural approaches. This book gives examples of decoding approaches, literature approaches, and cultural approaches. From the 1980s to the present, the literature methods have been highly published, but very little regarding cultural and almost nothing on decoding methods has been published. We must be sure that this kind of exclusion, perhaps caused by the unfortunate and untrue association in the media between conservatism and phonics, and by Thomas Kuhn's (1970) belief that it is very difficult to change a field from one paradigm to another, does not continue through the 21st century. Though phonics/decoding/decodable text and multicultural methods are far from being the entire answer to the teaching of reading, they certainly are an important component. Investigations of all methodologies deserve balanced attention and study.

The terror that the exclusion of a particular method can cause is demonstrated by two episodes in my experience.

I was a recent graduate of Howard University's English Department and Chicago Teachers College, where I took the education courses required to teach in Chicago in 1959. A student eager to make a contribution to literacy for African Americans and other children of color, I quickly absorbed the unresearched teaching approaches offered at the teachers college. (Chicago, of course, was the home of the "progressive education movement," originated by Dewey but propagated by his less-than-objective followers.)

Leaving Chicago to return to my hometown in Florida in the early 1960s, I arrived at my first first-grade teaching assignment, filled with enthusiasm. Despite all my vigor and hope, it took all of about two months for me to become so depressed that I was about to resign. It seemed that no matter how hard I tried, my students weren't learning.

I decided to visit the classroom of Mrs. Hussein, who taught in a nearby classroom. When I walked in the room, I noticed that the students quickly slipped something in their desks. "What are they hiding?" I asked Mrs. Hussein. Her reply has remained with me to this day. "They're phonics books," she said. "But you have to keep it a secret because if the state knew I was using them, I'd be fired. We are being forced to use a look-say approach that simply doesn't work."

Not long after, I bought a set of those same books that Mrs. Hussein was using and soon realized that I could also be effective in teaching students to read. That was almost 40 years ago, but as I travel around the United States lecturing and conducting workshops for teachers, I see just how little progress we've made in three decades.

For example, a few years ago I gave a speech to a group of English teachers in San Diego, California. After I finished speaking about the need to combine phonics with literature, history, and anything else you're teaching, four very scared teachers came up to me and said, "What you said is wonderful, and we wish we could use it, but our supervisor said that if he finds anything even smacking of phonics in our classrooms, he will write us up."

We talk a great deal about a balanced approach to reading methodology— but we really don't endorse this. We need true balance between literature, decoding, and culture, and all the other aspects of the reading process: phonemic awareness, phonics, fluency, vocabulary, and comprehension (National Institute of Child Health and Human Development, 2000). Sharroky Hollie (2001; see also chapter 15 of this volume) of the Los Angeles Public School District works with a school that combines three approaches: a phonic reading method, a literature reading method, and an African American language curriculum. We must acknowledge these models, as well as the other ones discussed in this book.

Our third recommendation is that educators must be much more cautious about research. Many fads and panaceas are offered as solutions to African American student failure. Kramer (1991) states that research appears to be so arbitrary and capricious that any solution is given as much weight as any another.

For example, one writer advocates squeezing the skulls of students in order to help them learn to read (Ludlow, 1988). Another writer glorifies discipline at the expense of achievement, as seen in the beatification of Joe Clark, a high school principal who did improve discipline in his school but accomplished very little academically (Williams, 1983). Other fads include increased funding for schools (Kozol, 1991); school-based management (Shear, 1994); exclusive reliance on whole language methodology (Pogrow, 1997); belief in the lack of genetic ability (Herrnstein & Murray, 1994); belief that to African Americans, academics is "acting White" (Fordham & Ogbu, 1986), and that Black culture is a barrier to achievement (McWhorter, 2000; Ogbu, 2003).

Solutions to complex problems are almost never one-answer panaceas, however. The point is that some of these ideas, in conjunction with researched efforts, might work; in isolation, very few one-answer solutions work.

Another problem with research is seen in the way it often is interpreted to fit the needs of a particular paradigm or philosophy more than to benefit children. Kuhn (1970) has stated that it takes a considerable amount of time for a paradigm or philosophy to change within a field. Research opposed to the current paradigm is often ignored or distorted. For example, many authors strongly advocate the theories of Freire (1973), which were successful in teaching peasants in Brazil, Chile, and Mozambique. Freire conducted what we might call ethnographies of literacy, for instance, searching the culture of the people for their most relevant words, themes, and idioms, and he labeled these words *generative.*

Most scholars ignore the fact, however, that the method also includes a decoding/phonics focus. The "generative words" Freire used in teaching were not only generative in the sense of generating ideas and interest, they were generative phonetically. An example of a generative word in Brazil would be *favela*, generative philosophically because it means a hut or a small house occupied by most Brazilian peasants. The same word, *favela*, is a generative word not only because of relevance, it is also generative phonetically in that the student learns other patterns from it; for example, each syllable generates four other syllables: *Fa* generates *fe, fi, fo,* and *fu. Ve* generates *va, vi, vo,* and *vu. La* generates *le, li, lo, lu* (Freire, 1970/2000). The first syllable in Malcolm, *mal,* a syllable that conforms to the simple vowel spelling pattern, one of the most regular spelling patterns in English, would, in turn, generate regular syllables in English: *Mal* would generate *Mel, mill, moll,* and *mull.* The 2000 edition of *Cultural Action for Freedom* actually omits the appendix on phonics that was included in the 1970 edition.

In addition to faulty interpretation of research, educational researchers are often so career-oriented that they are more concerned about their lifelong hypotheses than they are about achievement for students. For example, Ken Johnson, an early researcher in African American language, visited the

Ravenswood City School District in California where reading scores were above grade level following the adoption of a phonic–linguistic approach to reading ("Civil Rights Leader," 1970). When Johnson was informed of this feat, he stated that such an increase was impossible because it is in opposition to his "hypothesis," which was that Black children's phonology was so different from "standard" phonology that they could not learn to read with a decoding reading method. He was willing to write off the literacy success of 5,000 children in the district because it opposed his hypothesis.

Another example of disingenuous reporting of research is seen in Bond and Dykstra's (1967) research, which clearly revealed the superiority of phonic-linguistic reading approaches as compared to other methods. Dykstra (1977) had to defend these findings by stating,

> Many of my colleagues in the field of reading have made and continue to make misleading and inaccurate statements concerning the major conclusions of the first-grade studies.... The popular view among professionals...is that the first-grade studies found the teacher to be the most important variable in beginning reading instruction...we came to no such conclusion. (p. 11)

And the following testimony of Emily Washington (cited in Wiley, 2003) reveals another study fraught with problems, yet seized upon by the media as a blame-the-victim explanation for African American lack of achievement.

> I began teaching at Frank W. Ballou High School in September 1973 and remained there until the mid-1980s. Ethnographic research conducted by Fordham and Ogbu (1986) reportedly found that many bright students attending Ballou did not live up to their academic potential for fear of being accused of "acting White." When this study was conducted, 99.9 % of Ballou's students were Black. The only "White" individuals in the school were teachers who were in the minority. The students who were the subjects of the research were in my humanistic studies class and were, in fact, among the brightest and best performing students who were recruited to enroll in Ballou's science–math program, an accelerated academic program begun in the mid-1970s; hence, their classes were more rigorous than regular classes.
>
> I lived less than three blocks from Ballou and was, therefore, very much a part of the community. At no time during my tenure at Ballou, particularly during the time of the study, did I ever hear reference made to students "acting White." Many of the students in question were revered by their peers; they were looked up to and frequently referred to as "smart." They were often school leaders and contest winners, and they participated in numerous cultural visits to theaters and museums as a part of their studies. Moreover, they traveled to Europe and national points of interest as a result of their studies in the humanities program. (p. 1)

Students who were subjects of the study attended universities such as Yale, Princeton, Massachusetts Institute of Technology, Howard, and a host of historically Black colleges.

A fourth recommendation concerns the role of minority reading researchers and authors. Though African American students constitute a disproportionate percentage of the remedial reading population in our public schools, this book by notable African American educators and researchers is the first one on the topic to be published by the International Reading Association. We are pleased about its publication and hope it is the beginning of a long process of inclusion.

Our last recommendation is that we must work toward the creation of unbiased tests. New unbiased tests can be constructed using vocabulary items that are less open to trickery than multiple choice comprehension items, and using items that instruct the children to carry out instructions and paraphrase.

In conclusion, as Ronald Edmonds states (this volume), "We can, whenever and wherever we choose, successfully teach all children whose schooling is of interest to us;... We already know more than we need to do that."

## REFERENCES

Bond, G.L., & Dykstra, R. (1967). The co-operative research program in first-grade reading instruction, *Reading Research Quarterly, 2,* 5–142.

Chall, J.S. (1996). *Learning to read: The great debate* (3rd ed.). Ft. Worth, TX: Harcourt College. (Original work published 1967)

Civil rights leader eyes success of phonics at Ravenswood. (1970, December 3). *The Palo Alto Times,* p. 2.

Dykstra, R. (1977, November). What the 27 studies said. *Reading Informer,* pp. 11–12, 24.

Fordham, S., & Ogbu, J. (1986). Black student school success: Coping with the burden of acting White. *The Urban Review, 18,* 176–206.

Foorman, B.R., Francis, D.J., Beeler, T., Winikates, D., & Fletcher, J.M. (1997). Early intervention for children with reading problems: Study designs and preliminary findings. *Learning Disabilities: A Multidisciplinary Journal, 8*(1), 63–71.

Freire, P. (1973). *Education for critical consciousness.* New York: Seabury Press.

Freire, P. (2000). *Cultural action for freedom.* Cambridge, MA: The Harvard Educational Review Monograph Series, No. 1. (Original work published 1970)

Herrnstein, R.J., & Murray, C. (1994). *The bell curve: Intelligence and class structure in American life.* New York: Free Press.

Hollie, S. (2001, March). Acknowledging the language of African American Students: Instructional strategies. *English Journal, 90*(4), 54–59.

Hoover, M.R., Dabney, N., & Lewis, S. (Eds.). (1990). *Successful Black and minority schools: Classic models* (Rev. ed.). San Francisco: Julian Richardson.

Kozol, J. (1991). *Savage inequalities: Children in America's schools.* New York: Crown.

Kramer, R. (1991). *Ed school follies: The miseducation of America's teachers.* New York: The Free Press.

Kuhn, T. (1970). *The structure of scientific revolutions* (2nd ed.). Chicago: University of Chicago Press.

Ludlow, L. (1988, March 16). Unorthodox "cure" for kids spawns lawsuits, outrage. *San Francisco Examiner*, p. A20.

McWhorter, J. (2000). *Losing the race: Self-sabotage in Black America.* New York: The Free Press.

National Institute of Child Health and Human Development. (2000). *Report of the National Reading Panel. Teaching children to read: An evidence-based assessment of the scientific research literature on reading and its implications for reading instruction* (NIH Publication No. 00-4769). Washington, DC: U.S. Government Printing Office.

Ogbu, J. (2003). *Black American students in an affluent suburb.* Mahwah, NJ: Erlbaum.

Pogrow, S. (1997, November 12). The tyranny and folly of ideological progressivism, *Education Week*, pp. 34–36.

Shear, M.D. (1994, August 24). School-based management gets graded: Student achievement a question, says GAO. *The Washington Post*, p. D5.

Weber, G.O. (1971). *Inner-city children can be taught to read.* Washington, DC: Council for Basic Education.

Wiley, E., III. (2003, July 16). School choice is actually a bad choice for Black children, critics argue. *BET.com.* Retrieved February 23, 2004, from http://www.bet.com/articles/0%2C%2Cc1gb68 72-7675%2C00.html

Williams, L. (1983, September 17). Tough principal tames a rough Jersey school. *The New York Times*, p. 11.

# Author Index

Note: Page numbers followed by *f* indicate figures; those followed by *t* indicate tables; those followed by *n* indicate notes.

## A

Aaron, R., 306
Abelson, R.P., 266
Abrahams, R.D., 267
Adger, C.T., 189
Adler, S., 181
Aiello, J.R., 205
Akbar, N., 222
Alexander, L., 107–108
Allen, E.E., 236, 237
Allen, J.B., 147–148
Allington, R.L., 96
Altwerger, B., 148
Amidon, E.J., 62
Anderson, J.D., 43, 177
Anderson, L.M., 211
Anderson, R., 266
Applebee, A.N., 267
Aronson, E., 139
Asante, M., 73
Aschenbrenner, J., 205, 206
Ascher, C., 150
Asera, R., 239
Atwell, N., 150
Au, K.H., 97, 154
August, G.J., 223

## B

Bacon, M., 206
Ball, A., 296
Bambara, T.C., 275, 285
Banikowski, A.K., 140, 142, 144
Banks, J.A., 99, 100
Baratz, J.C., 92 *n.* 1
Barclay, A., 210
Barlow, W., 2
Barnard, D.P., 89

Barnes, B.L., 107
Barrentine, S.J., 138
Barrett, R., 202
Barry, A., 148
Barry, H., 206
Barton, P.E., 3, 66
Battle, E.S., 213
Bauer, E., 204
Baxter, J.C., 204
Beattie, M., 213
Beeler, T., 44, 67, 71, 333
Bekerie, A., 11
Bell, Y.R., 100
ben-Jochannan, Y., 26
Bennett, L., Jr., 3, 9, 15, 66
Bennink, C.D., 221–222
Berdan, R., 169
Berlin, I., 12, 21
Berman, J.J., 202
Bernal, M., 11
Berry, J.W., 201
Bettelheim, B., 108
Billingsley, A., 92 *n.* 1
Birnback, S., 210
Bishop, R.S., 110
Black, H., 203
Blackman, S., 214, 215
Bloom, B.S., 222
Blythe, T., 116
Bond, G.L., 67, 90, 336
Botel, M., 90
Botkin, B.A., 43
Bradby, M., 105–106
Brady, S., 1
Bridgeman, B., 220
Brody, G., 205
Bromley, K., 140
Brookover, W.B., 50

BROOKS, C., 194, 198
BROWN, A.L., 265, 270
BROWN, J.S., 265, 268–269, 271, 280
BROWN, S., 2
BROWNE, A., 107
BRUNER, J.S., 207
BRYSON, J.A., 204
BUEHL, D., 140
BULGREN, J., 142
BULLOCK, H.A., 13
BUNTING, E., 98
BURKE, C.V., 152
BURNES, K., 221
BURNS, M.S., 127
BUSSE, T., 211, 217
BUTTRAM, J., 220

## C

CALKINS, L.M., 148
CAMBOURNE, B., 148
CAMPBELL, E.Q., 47, 54
CANNON, J., 72
CARLSON, J.S., 210–211
CARLSON, R., 205
CARPENTER, G.C., 206
CARRINGTON, J.F., 11
CATTS, H.W., 175, 176
CAZDEN, C.B., 148, 155, 167, 267
CENTER FOR THE STUDY OF SOCIAL POLICY, 67
CHALL, J.S., 44, 71, 72, 89, 149, 333
CHANCE, J., 203
CHEPP, T., 210, 217
CHEW, C.R., 150
CHILD, I., 206
CHOMSKY, N., 174
CHRISTIAN, D., 189
CHURCHWARD, A., 11, 25, 30
CISNEROS, S., 297
CLARK, D.H., 208
CLARK, T.R., 100
CLARKE, J.H., 2
CLARKSTON, J., 161
CLIFTON, L., 166
COCHRAN, J.A., 141
COHEN, J., 220, 221
COHEN, M., 86, 89

COHEN, P., 181
COHEN, R., 201, 217
COHEN, S.A., 86
COHEN, Y., 201
COLE, L.T., 176
COLE, M., 155
COLE, S., 221
COLE-HENDERSON, B., 18
COLEMAN, J.S., 47, 54, 92 *n.* 1
COLLINS, A., 265, 268–269, 271, 280
COLVIN, C., 235
CONNALLY, P.R., 204
COOP, R.H., 217
CORNELIUS, J., 43, 72
CORNET, J., 30
COSBY, B., 97, 101, 101*f*–103*f*
COX, P.W., 219
CRAIG, H.K., 177, 178
CRAIG, M.T., 144
CSIKSZENTMIHALYI, M., 272
CULLINAN, B.E., 148, 155
CUNEN, J., 72
CUNNINGHAM, P.M., 168
CURETON, G.O., 60, 74
CUSUMANO, D.R., 210
CUTTING, J., 173

## D

DABNEY, N., 18, 44, 45, 67, 71, 72, 87, 88, 90, 333
DAMON-MOORE, H., 298
D'ANDRADE, R.G., 279
DANIEL, J., 8, 73, 281
DARLING-HAMMOND, L., 20, 151, 155
DATES, J.L., 2
DAVIDSON, K.S., 220
DAY, H., 204
DE BEAUGRANDE, R., 266
DE LA PAZ, S., 142
DEBLINGER, J., 220
DEGRAMONT, S., 28
DELPIT, L.D., 44, 70, 73, 149, 150, 193, 267, 293, 298
DENMARK, F., 217
DENZIN, N.K., 241
DEREN, M., 29

# Subject Index

Note: Page numbers followed by *f* indicate figures; those followed by *t* indicate tables; those followed by *n* indicate notes.

practice guidelines regarding, 327–328; recommendations regarding, 337

ASTRONOMY, 31

AT-RISK LEARNERS: disagreements regarding, 148–151; learning principles of, 151–156; new trends affecting, 147–148; overview of, 147; teachers of, 149–150, 156. *See also* African American learners; middle school learners

ATTITUDES: about home environment, 55; about standard English learners, 189, 191, 193; in effective urban schools, 48, 51; of teachers at below-grade-level schools, 68–69

AUDITORY LEARNERS, 139

AUTHORITARIANISM, 215

AVARIS, 35

## B

BALLANA, 27–28

BANTU, 30

BASIC SKILLS INSTRUCTION: and Black learning style, 61–62; in effective urban schools, 17–19, 51, 57; pros and cons of, 150–151; recommendations for, 55–56

BEHAVIORAL VERVE, 207

BELIEF SYSTEMS, 214–215

*THE BELL CURVE: INTELLIGENCE AND CLASS STRUCTURE IN AMERICAN LIFE* (HERRNSTEIN & MURRAY), 1

BENNETT-KEW SCHOOL, 80–83

BEST PRACTICE, 15–19. *See also* pedagogy

BIAS. *See* assessment bias

BIDIALECTAL LANGUAGE, 88, 177, 178

BILINGUAL DICTIONARIES, 166

BLACK ENGLISH VERNACULAR (BEV), 88

BLACK FICTION, 270–271

BLACK LEARNING STYLE: and action approach, 61–64; and assessment, 60, 63–64; and basic skills, 61–62; and comprehension skills, 63; and computer-assisted instruction, 63–64; controversy regarding, 162; definition of, 59; and discussion, 63; importance of time and day to, 60–61; versus

motivation, 59; and phonics method, 60. *See also* learning styles

BLACK NATIONALISTIC ALTERNATIVE, 215

BLAME, 68–69, 336–337

BLENDING SKILLS, 61–62

*BLUE-BACKED SPELLER* (WEBSTER), 106, 108

*THE BLUEST EYE* (MORRISON), 274, 286

BOOKS: importance of, 107–110; new trends regarding, 148; selection of, 97. *See also* multicultural literature

BOUSSAC, P.H., 27

BOZOS, 28

BRODEUR, G., 27

BUDGE, E.A.W., 29

BUSH ADMINISTRATION, 305

## C

CALIFORNIA DEPARTMENT OF EDUCATION, 326

CATEGORIZATION STYLE, 211–212

CENSORSHIP, 111–112

CENTER FOR THE STUDY OF SOCIAL POLICY, 67

CERTIFICATES, HIGH SCHOOL, 315–316

CGI. *See* Cognitively Guided Instruction (CGI)

*CHANGES IN SCHOOL CHARACTERISTICS COINCIDENT WITH CHANGES IN STUDENT ACHIEVEMENT* (BROOKOVER & LEZOTTE), 50–53

CHARACTER EDUCATION, 100–101

CHICK SCHOOL, 72–73

*CHILDHOOD AND COSMOS* (ERNY), 35

CHILD-ORIENTED TEACHERS, 223

CHOICE, 148

CHORAL RESPONSE, 62

CHRISTIANITY, 34

CHURCH TRADITIONS, 271

CIRCLE-SEAT-CENTER STRATEGY, 139

CLARK, S.P., 13

CLAS. *See* Culture and Language Academy of Success Elementary School (CLAS)

CLAST. *See* College Level Academic Skills Test (CLAST)

CLINK AND CLUNK STRATEGY, 138

CLINTON ADMINISTRATION, 305

CLOSED BELIEF SYSTEM, 214

CODE APPROACH, 44

CODE-SWITCHES, 166, 178

COGNITIVE APPRENTICESHIP: central problem with, 297–298; direct teaching of heuristics in, 286–287, 288*t*; environment to promote, 270; modeling in, 288–295; and multicultural literature, 269–271; overview of, 269; theoretical argument for, 267–269. *See also* apprenticeship

COGNITIVE FLEXIBILITY, 215

COGNITIVE STYLE: definition of, 208; and field articulation, 209–210; overview of, 207–208; versus perceptual style, 219–222; and schooling process, 216–219, 222–224; socializing influences on, 205–207

COGNITIVELY GUIDED INSTRUCTION (CGI), 236

COGNITIVE-STYLE MAPPING, 60

COLLECTIVE RESPONSIBILITY, 206

COLLEGE ADMISSIONS, 13–14

COLLEGE LANGUAGE ASSOCIATION, 333

COLLEGE LEVEL ACADEMIC SKILLS TEST (CLAST), 318

*THE COLOR PURPLE* (WALKER), 276, 285–286, 285*t*, 292–295

COMMUNITY, OF LEARNERS, 155

COMPENSATORY EDUCATION, 52–53

COMPREHENSION SKILLS: assessment of, 320–321; and Black learning style, 63; Dual-Text Reading Initiative for, 116–126; middle school instructional strategies for, 137–145; middle school learners' struggles with, 136–137

COMPUTER-ASSISTED INSTRUCTION, 63–64

CONCEPTUAL STYLE, 210–212

CONCEPTUAL TEMPO, 212

CONSCIENTIZATION, 7

CONTEMPORARY REALISTIC FICTION, 98

CONTEMPORARY TRANSLATIONS, 259–260

CONTEXTUAL TRANSLATIONS, 260–262

CONTINUED APATHY, 215

CONTRASTIVE ANALYSIS, 196

COOPERATIVE LEARNING, 139–140, 154

COUNTER-CULTURE ALTERNATIVES, 215

CPS LEARNING SYSTEMS (EINSTRUCTION), 126

CREOLIST VIEW, 192

CREW, R., 319

CRITICAL THINKING, 154

CROSS-VISITATION PROJECT, 238

CTB/MCGRAW-HILL TEST, 319

CULTURAL MEDIATION, 16

CULTURAL PLURALISM, 66

CULTURAL STYLES, 196–197

CULTURE: and at-risk learners, 154–155; as blame for below-grade-level schools, 68; cognition's relationship to, 207–208; definition of, 201; overview of, 161–162, 201–203; and reading methodology, 72; in sociolinguistic model, 13; unity of, 25, 28–30, 31

CULTURE AND LANGUAGE ACADEMY OF SUCCESS ELEMENTARY SCHOOL (CLAS), 195–198

CURRICULUM, AT BENNETT-KEW SCHOOL, 81

# D

*THE DAY I SAW MY FATHER CRY* (COSBY), 101

DEEP STRUCTURE, 30

"DEFICIT" VIEWS, 85, 92 *n.* 1, 192, 193

DETROIT, MICHIGAN, 53–55

DEWEY, J., 43

DIAGNOSTIC TESTS, 319, 320

DIALECT: and assessment bias, 313–315; definition of, 177; selection of, 165; study of, 166–167

"DIFFERENCE" VIEWS, 85, 92 *n.* 1

DIPLOMAS, 315–316

DIRECT INSTRUCTION: and African American English, 178–181; in effective urban schools, 51; of heuristics, 286–287, 288*t*

DIRECTED READING ACTIVITY (DRA), 141

DISCIPLINE, 335

DISCUSSION, 63, 154

DISTRICT 2, MANHATTAN, NEW YORK, 79–80

DIVERSITY, OF AFRICAN AMERICAN LEARNERS, 156–157, 298 *n.* 2

DJENNE, 29

DOMAIN KNOWLEDGE, 270

DOUGLASS, F., 15

DRA. *See* Directed Reading Activity (DRA)

DRAMATIC FIGURES, 282

DRAW A PICTURE STRATEGY, 144

accomplishing, 10; and teaching to tests, 20

LIBRARIES, 112

LIFELONG LEARNING, 152–153

LINGUISTIC BIAS, 309–315

LITERACY: Africans' tradition of, 11–13; Africans' view of, 12; Freirean perspective of, 10; origin of, 11; proper versus improper, 9–10; role of, 9–10; as source of power and hope, 110–112; threat of, 111–112. *See also specific types*

LITERACY RATES, 3, 66

LITERARY TRADITION, 253–254

LITTLE BILL SERIES (COSBY), 100–103

LOS ANGELES UNIFIED SCHOOL DISTRICT, 190, 194–198, 334

*THE LOTUS SEED* (GARLAND), 113

LUXOR, 33

# M

MALCOLM X, 14–15

MAMA JOKES, 256

MANN, H., 43

MARTINE, D.H., 157

MASPERO, G., 27

MASSEY, GERALD, 24, 41

MEMPHITE THEOLOGY, 40

METACOGNITION, 117

METHODS. *See* pedagogy

MICHIGAN DEPARTMENT OF EDUCATION, 50–51

MICHIGAN EDUCATIONAL ASSESSMENT PROGRAM (MEAP), 52

MIDDLE EAST, 30

MIDDLE SCHOOL LEARNERS: comprehension strategies for, 137–145; comprehension struggles of, 136–137; teachers of, 136, 137. *See also* African American learners; at-risk learners

*THE MIS-EDUCATION OF THE NEGRO* (WOODSON), 3

MONITORING. *See* assessment

*MORE THAN ANYTHING ELSE* (BRADBY), 105–106

MORPHOLOGICAL COMPONENT, OF LANGUAGE, 175

MOTHER–CHILD RELATIONSHIP, 206–207

MOTIVATION: in at-grade-level schools, 72–74; versus Black learning style, 59; as blame for below-grade-level schools, 68; evidence of, in Egyptian history, 73

MT. KILAMANJARO, 26

MUHAMMAD, E., 14

MULTICULTURAL LITERATURE: African American themes in, 100; and at-risk learners, 155; benefits of, 97–99, 253; and cognitive apprenticeship, 269–271; evaluation and selection of, 99; for standard English learners, 195–196; strategies for use of, 297. *See also* books; *specific texts*

MUT, 34

"MY MAN BOVANNE" (BAMBARA), 275, 284–286

MYERS, W.D., 110–111

# N

NABRLE. *See* National Association of Black Reading and Language Arts Educators (NABRLE)

NAIROBI DAY SCHOOL, 72–73, 319

NARRATIVES: of Black versus White students, 167–168; importance of, 107–110

NATION OF ISLAM, 14

NATIONAL ASSESSMENT OF EDUCATIONAL PROGRESS (NAEP), 239, 299n.5

NATIONAL ASSOCIATION OF BLACK READING AND LANGUAGE ARTS EDUCATORS (NABRLE), 2, 84–85

NATIONAL COUNCIL OF TEACHERS OF ENGLISH (NCTE), 194

NATIONAL INSTITUTE OF CHILD HEALTH AND HUMAN DEVELOPMENT, 71–72, 334

NATIONAL INSTITUTE OF EDUCATION (NIE), 57

NATURE, OBSERVATION OF, 38–39

NELSON READING TEST, 130–131

NIE. *See* National Institute of Education (NIE)

NILE RIVER, 25–28, 30, 31

NO CHILD LEFT BEHIND LEGISLATION, 194, 305

NONVERBAL COMMUNICATION, 174

NUBIA, 27–28

## O

OAKLAND, CALIFORNIA, 105, 166
OAKLAND UNIFIED SCHOOL DISTRICT, 166
OBSERVATIONS, OF NATURE, 38–39
OCEAN HILL–BROWNSVILLE SCHOOL, 91
ONE-TWO-THREE METHOD, 321
OPEN BELIEF SYSTEM, 214–215
OPENBOOK LITERACY SYSTEM, 125–126
OPINIONS, 140–141
ORAL COMPREHENSION, 313
ORAL LANGUAGE: acquisition of, 173–175,
    184–185; components of, 175–176;
    direct instruction in, 178–181; new
    trends regarding, 148
ORAL READING TESTS, 315
ORAL TRADITION, 11–12, 100
ORATIONAL FIGURES, 282
ORCHESTRATIONAL FIGURES, 282
ORDER STRATEGY, 142
ORGANIZATIONAL SKILLS, 141–142
ORGANIZATIONAL STRUCTURE, 18–19
ORPHIC TEMPLE, 33
OSIRIS, 33
OUTLINES, 141–142

## P

THE PAGEANT OF CIVILIZATION (BRODEUR), 27
PARAPHRASING, 138–139
PARENTS: of at-risk learners, 152;
    involvement of, 52, 88
PARTNER PREDICTION STRATEGY, 140
PEDAGOGY, 38–40; in effective urban
    schools, 17–19; ineffective methods of,
    2–3; recommendations for, 19. See also
    best practice; reading methodologies
PERCEPTUAL STYLE, 209–210, 219–222
PERSONALITY STYLE, 212–216
PHILOSOPHIES, 73
PHONICS METHOD: and at-risk learners, 153;
    and Black learning style, 60; history of,
    43; importance of, 89–90; in on-grade-
    level schools, 71–72; recommendations
    for, 333
PHONOLOGICAL BIAS, 313–315
PHONOLOGICAL COMPONENT, OF LANGUAGE,
    175

PIECE OF ACTION, SEEKING OF, 215
PIMA INDIAN LANGUAGE, 165
PLATO LEARNING SYSTEMS, 126
PLAYING THE DOZENS, 256, 272–273
POETRY, 313
POLITICS: and assessment bias, 315–317;
    definition of, 47; and power of literacy,
    112
POVERTY, 69, 147
POWER: literacy as source of, 110–112; in
    process-oriented classrooms, 149
PRACTICE. See best practice
PRAGMATIC COMPONENT, OF LANGUAGE, 176
PREDICTIONS, 140
PREJUDICE, 1, 68–70
PRESCHOOL INSTRUCTION, 178–180
PRESERVICE TEACHER EDUCATION, 91
PRINCIPALS: in effective urban schools,
    51–52; ethnic background of, 91; role in
    study group meetings, 244
PRIOR KNOWLEDGE, 140–141, 197
PRISONS, 112
PROBLEM SOLVING, 154
PROFESSIONAL DEVELOPMENT: in at-grade-
    level schools, 74; overview of, 233; past
    research studies of, 234–239; rationale
    for studying, 239; for teachers of at-risk
    learners; and teaching of standard
    English learners, 198
PROGRESSIVE EDUCATION, 43–44
PROPER LITERACY, 9–10, 21
PROVERBS, 39, 73, 284t
PTAHOTEP, 39
PUBLIC EDUCATION ASSOCIATION, 235
PYRAMIDS, 27, 31
PYTHAGORAS'S LODGE, 33

## Q

QUESTION–ANSWER RELATIONSHIP (QAR),
    142–143
QUESTIONS: for interactive read-alouds, 138;
    for journals, 144

## R

RAVENSWOOD CITY SCHOOL DISTRICT,
    CALIFORNIA, 72, 336

STANDARD ENGLISH LEARNERS (SELs):
  attitudes about, 189, 191, 193; current
  treatment of, 189–190; definition of,
  189. *See also* African American learners
STANDARDIZED TESTS. *See* assessment
STANFORD ACHIEVEMENT TEST, 318
STEREOTYPES, 98
STEWART, T., 12, 21
*STOLEN LEGACY* (JAMES), 33
STORIES. *See* narratives
*THE STRONG BROWN GOD* (DEGRAMONT), 29
STRUCTURED DIALOGUE APPROACH, 242–251
STUDENT CHOICE, 148
STUDY GROUP MEETINGS, 242–251
STUDY SKILLS STRATEGIES, 142–143
STYLISTIC APPROACH, 222–224
SUMMARIZING, 138–139
SUPPORT SERVICES, 50, 57
SURFACE STRUCTURE, 30
SUSPICIOUSNESS, 202
SWAHILI, 71
SYNTACTIC BIAS, 312–313
SYNTACTICAL COMPONENT, OF LANGUAGE,
  175–176

# T

TACTILE LEARNERS, 139
TALENTED TENTH, 13–14
TALKING GHETTO, 261–262
*TAPPING THE POTENTIAL* (NATIONAL COUNCIL
  OF TEACHERS OF ENGLISH), 194
TEACHER ACADEMIES, 237
TEACHER COLLABORATION PROGRAMS,
  237–238
TEACHER NETWORKS, 156
TEACHER QUALITY, 90
TEACHERS: of at-risk learners, 149–150, 156;
  and Ebonics corrections, 164–165,
  168–170; in effective urban schools, 48,
  51, 52; essential tasks of, 90–91; ethnic
  background of, 91; historical knowledge
  of, 15; and home environment, 157;
  importance of, 90; incentives for, 156; of
  middle school learners, 136, 137;
  response to African American English,
  179–181; role of, 149–150

TEACHING, FOR UNDERSTANDING, 116
TECHNOLOGY, 31–32, 63–64
TEMPLE AT LUXOR, 30, 34, 37
TEMPLE OF AMON, 37
TEMPLE OF DENDERA, 31
TEMPLE OF HORUS, 27
TEMPLE OF THE SUN, 40
TEMPLE UNIVERSITY MEDICAL SCHOOL, 318
TEST ANXIETY, 64
*THE TESTING OF NEGRO INTELLIGENCE*
  (SHUEY), 1
TESTS, TEACHING TO, 20
TEST-TAKING SKILLS, 64, 92
TEXTBOOKS, 148, 319
TEXT-TO-SELF CONNECTIONS, 96, 98
TEXT-TO-TEXT CONNECTIONS, 96
TEXT-TO-WORLD CONNECTIONS, 96–97
THEBES, 33
*THEIR EYES WERE WATCHING GOD*
  (HURSTON), 276, 285–286, 285*t*,
  288–291
THEMES, 109
THEORIES, 7–8. *See also specific theories*
THINK-ALOUD STRATEGY, 143–144
THINK-PAIR-SHARE/THINK-PAIR-SQUARE
  STRATEGY, 140
TIME, 75, 156
TITLE VII (CIVIL RIGHTS ACT), 318
TRACKING, 156, 315
TRADEBOOKS, 148
TRANSFORMATIONALIST VIEW, 192–193
TRANSLATIONS, OF EXAMPLE, 257–259
TRUST, 202
TURKISH, 71

# U

UNDERSTANDING, CHECKING FOR, 138–139
UNIVERSITIES, 33
URBAN SCHOOLS: at-grade-level reading at,
  70–75; characteristics of effective,
  17–19, 47–57; critique of Weber's study
  of, 84–92; nonessential characteristics
  of, 90–92; rationale for below-grade-
  level reading at, 67–70; school-level
  success factors of, 87–90
U.S. ARMY ALPHA TEST, 308

## V

VALIDITY, 318
VERBS, 254
VICTIMIZATION, 202
VINDICATIONISM, 70, 72
VIRTUES, 32–33
VISUAL LEARNERS, 139
VISUALS, 144–145
VOCABULARY: assessment of, 309–311, 320; instruction in, 197
VOODOO RELIGION, 28–29

## W

WASET, 33
WASHINGTON, B.T., 105–106, 107, 109–110

WECHSLER INTELLIGENCE SCALE FOR CHILDREN (WISC), 209, 220
WESTERN LITERATURE, 298–299 *n.* 3
WHEELER, R., 72
WHITE CHAPEL, 37
WHOLE LANGUAGE, 44
WHOLE-WORD METHOD, 43
*THE WIZARD OF EARTHSEA* (LE GUIN), 109
WORKBOOKS, 153
WORKSHOPS, 236–237
WRITING: definition of, 10; new trends regarding, 148; rule application to, 170; skills instruction in, 128–129
WRITING SYSTEMS, 11–12